MASS
IMMIGRATION
AND THE
NATIONAL
INTEREST

LABOR AND HUMAN RESOURCES SERIES

MASS IMMIGRATION AND THE NATIONAL INTEREST

POLICY DIRECTIONS FOR THE NEW CENTURY

THIRD EDITION

VERNON M. BRIGGS, JR.

M.E.Sharpe
Armonk, New York
London, England

Library of Congress Cataloging-in-Publication Data

Briggs, Vernon M.
    Mass immigration and the national interest : policy directions for the new century /
Vernon M. Briggs, Jr.—3rd ed.
        p. cm.
    Includes bibliographical references and index.
    ISBN 0-7656-0933-9 (cloth: alk. paper) ISBN 0-7656-0934-7 (pbk.: alk. paper)
        1. United States—Emigration and immigration—Government policy—History.
    2. Alien labor—United States—History. 3. Labor market—United States—History.
    I. Title.

    JV6483.B75 2003
    325.73—dc21

                                                                                    2003042761

Printed in the United States of America

The paper used in this publication meets the minimum requirements of
American National Standard for Information Sciences
Permanence of Paper for Printed Library Materials,
ANSI Z 39.48-1984.

∞

BM (c)   10   9   8   7   6   5   4   3   2   1
BM (p)   10   9   8   7   6   5   4   3   2   1

It is both a right and a responsibility of a democratic society to manage immigration so that it serves the national interest.

U.S. Commission on Immigration Reform (1994)

Contents

_____ List of Tables and Figures

Tables

Figures

Acknowledgments

As was the case with the two earlier editions (in 1992 and 1996), I have greatly benefitted in the preparation of this edition from access to several research institutions and the assistance of a number of persons. I have been fortunate to have been able to use the staff services and relevant materials of the Catherwood Library at the New York State School of Labor and Industrial Relations at Cornell University in Ithaca, New York; the Franklin D. Roosevelt Presidential Library at Hyde Park, New York; and the Center for Immigration Studies in Washington, DC. Several officials at the U.S. Census Bureau in Suitland, Maryland, have also been very helpful to me with respect to specific data interpretation questions. I am, of course, solely responsible for the meanings given to such information.

I am also deeply appreciative of the professional work done by Sandra Frey, Thomas Mendez, and Cheryl Noble. Over the past many months they faithfully and competently prepared the numerous drafts that led to the final manuscript. Words alone cannot express the indebtedness I feel.

V.M.B.

MASS IMMIGRATION

AND THE

NATIONAL INTEREST

1

Introduction: The Revival
of Mass Immigration

The United States is entering the twenty-first century as it did the twentieth century: in the throes of a period of mass immigration. Between these century markers, however, immigration had fallen dramatically for much of the time. Indeed, at mid-century it had declined to such a low level as to have become virtually insignificant in scale and almost irrelevant in importance. In 1965, the foreign-born population accounted for only 4.4 percent of the population—the lowest percentage in all of U.S. history. When the twentieth century began, the equivalent rate was 13.6 percent and rising; as the twenty-first century begins, it is 11.1 percent and rising.

The post-1965 return of mass immigration as a distinguishing feature of American life has been the product of public policy changes that had inadvertent consequences. It was entirely accidental. No national leader—president or legislator from either major political party—sought its resurrection. In fact, all of the key legislators responsible for its revival promised the public at the time that it would not happen if the nation agreed to their procedural reforms. But it has, and, once under way, few political leaders have been willing to address the consequences except in broad platitudes.

By the late 1980s, an international team of social science scholars assembled by Oxford Analytica and commissioned by three large U.S. corporations (American Express, Sun Oil, and Bristol-Myers) identified the reawakening of this sleeping policy giant from out of the nation's distant past. They observed that "America's biggest import is people."[1] Their report concluded with the powerful observation that "at a time when attention is directed to the general decline in American exceptionalism, American immigration continues to flow at a rate unknown elsewhere in the world."[2] Since these words were written, the magnitude of immigration has soared to even higher plateaus. During the decade of the 1990s, the foreign-born population grew from 19.7 million persons to 31.1 million persons—or by 57 percent.[3] Even this high number is recognized as underestimating the actual scale of what is transpiring, due to the acknowledged statistical undercount of millions of illegal immigrants who have not been officially recorded.

The long-term effects of mass immigration on U.S. population growth are even more startling. During the decade of the 1980s, immigration accounted for 37 percent of the growth in population; for the 1990s, it was 47 percent. As for the twenty-first century, two demographic studies of the projected influence of prevailing immigration trends on population growth have been made—one by the U.S. Bureau of the Census and the other by the National Research Council (NRC) of the National Academy of Sciences. Using both of their "intermediate projections" of the effects of immigration (i.e., an annual entry of 820,000 immigrants through to the year 2050, which is the closest of their estimates to the annual level that is actually occurring), they projected that the 1995 population of the United States of 263 million persons will increase to 387 million persons (NRC)[4] or 394 million persons (Census Bureau)[5] by 2050. Of this aggregate growth of from 124 to 131 million people (depending which projection is used), both studies agree that two-thirds of the total growth, or approximately 80 million people, will be the consequence of the arrival of the immigrants themselves and of their future children who will be born in this country. In the summary words of the NRC study, "immigration, then, will obviously play the dominant role in our future population growth."[6]

As the new millennium begins, there is no reason to expect that these growth trends will lessen unless specific public policy measures are enacted to reverse course. Immigration stands out among the multitude of change-creating forces buffeting the U.S. economy, its population, and its labor force: Immigration alone is a purely policy-driven occurrence. But, as will be documented, policymakers are reluctant to confront the reality that immigration has both benefits and costs. While extolling the benefits—often for political advantages—there has been a reluctance to confront the societal costs—for fear of adverse political reaction by special interest groups and ideologues. Sound public policy, however, rests on the necessity that both concerns be taken into account if national interests—and not special interests—are to be served.

The efficacy of any public policy initiative—immigration policy in this instance—cannot be judged in the abstract. Its relevance and usefulness depend on its congruency with existing economic and social circumstances. Because the revival of mass immigration was not planned or even sought as a policy objective, it would have been a pure coincidence if its subsequent effects turned out to be consistent with the changing national needs over this time period. The country has not been so fortunate. The post-1965 era has been one of unprecedented transformation of both its economy and its workforce. The pervasive and rapid introduction of new forms of technology, along with the advent of globalization trade pressures, has radically altered the nature of the demand for labor and its derivative job requirements. Those workers with skills and educational abilities have generally prospered; those without such human capital attributes have tended to flounder. Likewise, the United States has simultaneously experienced unparalleled demographic and social changes that have dramatically affected the size and composition (i.e., the racial, ethnic, and gender makeup) of its labor supply. Mass immigration has affected both the demand and the supply of labor in these dynamic times—but not symmetrically.

Despite what many theoreticians assert and most want to assume, the entry of foreign-born persons into the U.S. population and labor force is not entirely a market-driven phenomenon. It is a regulated process. Immigrants are not admitted simply because they want to come or because they are sought by someone. To the contrary, each person who enters must meet a criterion specified by some element of the nation's immigration laws (or illegally in violation of the terms of such laws). Specifically, the policy components are the laws that pertain to legal immigrants, illegal immigrants, refugees, asylees, and foreign workers who are temporarily permitted to work in the United States. Collectively, their presence constitutes the mass immigration phenomenon of the current era.

As for the concept "mass immigration" itself, the term implies that the chief characteristic of prevailing public policy is the quantitative size of the annual inflow of foreign-born persons into the nation's population and labor force. Implicit in its usage also is the fact that there is a general disregard for the human capital characteristics of those who enter—especially as it relates to concerns over incongruity with evolving economic trends and social changes.

But, regardless of the reasons for specifically admitting or indifferently permitting such entries, all immigrants must support themselves by their own work or that of others. Hence, there are always economic consequences associated with their presence, whether intended or not. As the scale of immigration has become larger, it follows that its economic effects on the labor market have likewise increased.

As public policy determines the scale and nature of the immigrant inflow, it is these policies—not the foreign-born persons themselves—that raise the question of congruence of mass immigration with the national interest. The foreign-born entrants themselves are only responding to the opportunities afforded by prevailing public policy.

To be sure, the post-1965 occurrence of mass immigration is not without precedents. As is well known, the phenomenon has been a significant characteristic of the nation's past. The nation's political structure that has postulated such ideals as freedom, equality under the law, and a toleration of diversity has long appealed to persons from all corners of the globe. Thus, as the immigration history of the nation clearly shows, there has never been any problem in attracting would-be immigrants when the nation thought it needed them. But historical and economic circumstances change. What is both necessary and positive in its effects at one time may not be so at another time. Too much of modern economic analysis is ahistorical in its quest to interpret labor market happenings. But, with respect to immigration, an appreciation of historical circumstance is key to understanding the policies that govern the scale and shape the composition of the immigrant flows at any given time. For immigration policy is not made; it emerges. Thus, while the basic questions pertaining to the state of the nation's immigration policy remain the same—How many immigrants should be admitted? What criteria should be used to choose who is admitted? How should the policy be enforced? What are the anticipated effects and unanticipated outcomes?—the answers will often be different.

Mass immigration is, after all, an integral part of the matrix of forces that is transforming the U.S. labor market. The issue for study is not whether immigrants themselves are good or bad, but, rather, whether mass immigration itself is consistent with the national interest as the nation enters the third millennium. Is there a different role that immigration policy should play? If so, what is it?

As the twentieth century ended, the Brookings Institution examined all of the major federal statutes (i.e., public policies) enacted over the preceding fifty years (i.e., from 1944 to 1999) and ranked them in terms of their perceived effectiveness. "Controlling immigration" was ranked forty-ninth out of the fifty policy issues that were identified.[7] In this regard, immigration was classified as being one of the "government's greatest failures" over this time span.[8] Given its importance, it follows that immigration reform should be high on the agenda for policymakers as the new century commences.

2

Immigration Policy:
A Determinant of
Economic Phenomena

There are two ways to study the economic effects of immigration on the population and labor force of the United States. One is to study immigration as a determinant of what is happening; the other is to analyze the consequences of immigration after the fact. In principle, the two approaches should come to the same conclusions. But in a social science such as economics, it is not possible to do the clinical research in a controlled laboratory environment. It is often impossible to identify and to isolate all of the key variables that influence an actual outcome. Other factors may be identifiable but are not measurable. Some key variables may be quantifiable but the poor quality of the available data limits their usefulness for analytical purpose. Furthermore, the study of economics is about people and the human condition, which means its relevant teachings often change as circumstances change. Economics is a time-sensitive field. The particular experiences with which it deals and purports to analyze are often nonrepetitive in terms of historical similarity. What policy research finds to be good at one time can be bad at another. Hence, there is no certainty that the different approaches used to study a complex subject like immigration will produce complementary conclusions at any one time or over time. On those occasions when they do, the confluence adds confidence to the findings of both approaches. If they differ, it is imperative to know why.

Measuring Consequences: The Standard Approach

The more commonly used methodological approach is to the study the consequences of a particular economic phenomenon. This methodology ignores the search for explanation amidst the complex forces of historical circumstances over time or the influences of societal institutions and practices at any given time. It is an ex post approach that becomes feasible only *after* the particular events have occurred. By examining only consequences, the causes are ignored in favor of a focus on what the empirical data reflect about what seems to have happened. Outcomes are what matters. With this approach, research typically focuses on such issues as the effects of immigrants on wages, employment, unemployment, labor force participation, labor mobility, and the use of social services. The outcomes approach seeks only to measure quantitatively what it can while carefully avoiding any comment about how to interpret the causative factors.[1] Impact research quickly finds its way into policy debates. The research is picked up by special interest groups, if it is consistent with their predilections, and used to support their advocacy positions. If the findings are contrary to their goals, these studies are simply ignored by proponents while cited by opponents. It is not surprising, therefore, to find impact research done by different scholars or research done at different times by the same scholar to be used by both critics and supporters of prevailing immigration policy.

The strength of the study of consequences, however, depends primarily on the quality and the availability of the relevant data. When it comes to the study of immigration, the gross inadequacies of the existing data virtually always render this methodology vulnerable to skepticism about the strength of its findings. For no matter how elaborate the design of the econometric model is or how sophisticated the statistical techniques used to extract meaning are, the data cannot be tortured to confess to information that is not there. This does not mean that some researchers will not try. But to most scholars who work in the immigration field, attempts to draw conclusive findings from the use of available statistical sources can breed only a sense of humility, not confidence, about what insights can be safely drawn.

Data Limitations: An Ongoing Issue

Without diverting to a lengthy discussion of how severe the data limitations plaguing the study of immigration are, a few brief cautions are necessary.[2] The bulk of the available data on immigrants is collected for administrative purposes. It flows from the administration of the immigration statutes by the Immigration and Naturalization Service (INS) of the

U.S. Department of Justice (in the U.S. Department of Homeland Security [DHS] as of mid-2003). When a congressional committee sought in 1978 to study the mounting effects of immigration on the size and composition of the U.S. population, it initially sought to tap this data. To its chagrin, it soon concluded that "despite these long established data collection programs, immigration-related data are still deficient in scope, quality, and availability" and it concluded that "immigration statistics are particularly inadequate as tools for policy analysis."[3] In this same vein, the Panel on Immigration Statistics of the National Research Council, after conducting an exhaustive study of immigration statistics in 1985, found that: "Immigration for some reason is the Cinderella of the federal statistical system. In essence, a history of neglect has afflicted the record keeping concerning one of the most fundamental processes underlining the development of American society."[4]

Nonetheless, almost a decade later, the U.S. Commission on Immigration Reform echoed the same lament as it struggled to perform its assessment duties. In 1994, the commission said:

> Throughout the Commission's own inquiry, we have found it difficult to assess the effects of immigration policy and of immigration itself because of inadequacies in the data.[5]

Unfortunately, funding for improvements in data collection is never a popular issue when the INS budget is under consideration by Congress. Hence, the prospects for better data in the near future are slim.

The alternative to administrative data from the INS is data on the foreign-born population that are collected by the U.S. Bureau of the Census. Until the late 1980s, these data were available only every ten years when the Census Bureau conducted its mandated (by the U.S. Constitution) headcount of the total population. In performing this duty, the Census Bureau counts not only citizens but also permanent resident aliens and all citizens of any foreign country, regardless of their immigration status, who live in the United States at the time.[6] The census tabulation of the foreign-born component of the U.S. population, however, is restricted to only those persons who are asked to complete the long form of the census. The long form is given to about 17 percent of the nation's housing units. The long form is distributed on the basis of a variable-rate sample. This means that a larger proportion of the households living in small governmental (i.e., small towns and villages) units received the long form to complete than was the case for households living in large governmental units (i.e., large cities). The goal of this sampling procedure is to increase the reliability of data in small population areas while, admittedly, reducing somewhat the quality of the data collected in large population units. The foreign-born population, however, is not randomly distributed across the nation. Rather, it is highly concentrated in a few large governmental units (i.e., in the central cities of metropolitan areas of only a selected number of large states). In 2000, for example, 94.9 percent of the foreign-born population lived in metropolitan areas (opposed to 79.3 percent of the native-born population); 45.1 percent of the foreign-born population lived in central cities of metropolitan areas (opposed to 27.5 percent of the native-born population); and only 5.1 percent of the foreign-born population lived in nonmetropolitan areas (opposed to 20.7 percent of the native-born population).[7] This means that the methodology used by the Census Bureau virtually guarantees that the official measures of the foreign-born population that come from the decennial census are underreported. Furthermore, the actual published data on the foreign-born population are based on a 5 percent sample of the data that are collected from tabulating the data from the long forms. It is this information that comprises the public use data file that is used by most scholars who study the impact of immigration on U.S. society.

Until the 1980s, there were no regular interim measures between the decennial census counts of the yearly experiences of the foreign born as there are for other personal characteristics of population subgroups (e.g., age, gender, or race) of the population and labor force. During the 1980s, however, periodic supplemental sample studies were conducted by the Census Bureau of the aggregate foreign-born population as part of the monthly Current Population Survey (CPS). Referred to as a postcensual estimate, a special "add-on" question to the CPS sample for one particular month (March) was added to the survey. This attempt to obtain more up-to-date information, however, was done only on an irregular basis (about once every two years in the late 1980s), depending on the availability of funds by either INS or the Census Bureau. The CPS monthly sample is the best methodology yet devised for keeping abreast of changing population and labor force trends between the ten-year census counts, but it, too, is ill-suited for collecting data on the foreign born. The monthly CPS samples are taken from information provided by about 60,000 households in the entire nation that are selected from designated enumeration areas designed to reflect certain features of the nation's population distribution (e.g., the rural to urban population). The foreign-born population is *not* one of the selection criteria used to establish these areas. Once the areas are defined (they do not cover the entire United States), a random sample of households in each area is drawn for actual interviewing. But, as previously indicated, the foreign-born population is definitely not randomly distributed. Hence, the CPS is not an ideal source of information about the foreign-born population, yet it is all that is available between the ten-year census counts.

In recognition of the growing importance of immigration, the Census Bureau began in 1994 to collect labor market data on the foreign-born population on an annual basis as part of supplementary questions asked on the March CPS. To compensate for some of the aforementioned survey limitations of the CPS, the March sample size was increased each year by adding 2,500 housing units in which at least one family member is a Hispanic as identified in the CPS conducted during the previous November survey. Such a practice, of course, does nothing to increase the probability of including foreign-born persons who are not from Hispanic backgrounds.

Indicative of the measurement problem is the significant difference in the size of the foreign-born population as tabulated by the March 2000 CPS sample (i.e., 28.4 million persons or 10.4 percent of the total U.S. population) and the actual 2000 census population count taken one month later in April 2000 (i.e., 31.1 million persons, or 11.1 percent of the population).[8] The difference of 2.7 million foreign-born persons means that it is likely that all the research done in the 1990s using CPS data was significantly understated in its conclusions.

In addition to concerns over the adequacy of data-collection methods, there is also a significant statistical undercount of the foreign-born population in both data collection systems due to the sizable illegal immigrant population. These persons fear contact with governmental officials. The Census Bureau acknowledges that there is a general undercount problem with its decennial data.[9] For the 2000 census, for example, the acknowledged undercount was 1.2 percent of the population (or 3.3 million people). Those most likely to be missed are low-income working-aged males from minority groups as well as some proportion of the nation's illegal immigrant population in general.

In 2001, the Census Bureau issued the most detailed report yet conducted of the size of the nation's illegal immigrant population.[10] It stated that there were 8.7 million illegal immigrants in the country as of the year 2000 and that their ranks were swelling by about 500,000 illegal immigrants a year as the twenty-first century was beginning. The same study estimates that about 1 million of these illegal immigrants are uncounted in the official census calculations.

In short, whenever conclusions are reached that are based on the use of census data, they must always be understood to be substantial underestimates of the "real" dimensions of the foreign-born population. As a consequence, there is no way for the statistical analyses used in econometric studies that purport to assess the immigrant experience to be precise.

The Issue of Emigration

Another limitation on efforts to assess the net impact of immigration is the issue of emigration. There have been no official data on emigration published by the INS since 1957. The collection of such data was terminated because its reliability had been seriously questioned. Unlike most nations, the United States does not exercise any departure controls over citizens and permanent resident aliens who wish to leave the country. When such data were collected, their total effect had to be crudely estimated because when citizens and permanent resident aliens leave, they seldom formally give up their citizenship or residency rights. Some of those who leave for extended periods of time later decide to return. In other cases, people emigrate after they have finished their working years. Such retirees affect the population statistics of the United States if they emigrate, but they do not affect the labor force statistics since they have already quit working, and, for purposes of labor market analysis, it no longer makes any difference whether retirees reside within or without the United States. Consequently, there is no reliable way to know how to measure emigration or to interpret its labor market consequences.

As will be discussed, emigration was believed to be relatively high during the periods of mass immigration in the nineteenth and early twentieth centuries. Since the number of immigrant men (especially single men) greatly exceeded the number of immigrant women in that era, it is believed that a significant number of these men emigrated back to their families after earning a target amount of money in the United States. In contrast, there is reason to believe that the mass immigration that began in the mid-1960s and continues to the present time has evidenced less emigration because the number of women, children, and adult parents accompanying these immigrants greatly exceeds that of those earlier periods. Indeed, since 1980, more family immigrants are coming to the United States for permanent settlement than ever before (see Chapter 10). Hence, their subsequent emigration is less likely.

One long-term study of emigration that covered the years from 1900 to 1980 estimated that about one-third of all immigrants who entered the United States over this period subsequently left.[11] Due to budget cuts in 1981, the data series used in that study, which would be needed to continue its estimates beyond 1980, are no longer collected. Nevertheless, the INS, as late as 1998, was still saying that "for every 100 immigrants admitted, roughly 30 returned home," even though there is little basis for such a guess and the agency was simultaneously lamenting the absence of any solid data.[12] Although there is ample reason to believe that the post-1980 emigration rate is lower than that of the pre-1980 era, there is absolutely no way to know for certain. All that can be said is that there is some degree of annual emigration that is not taken into account in any of the published immigration-related data series.

For its annual estimate of the size of the U.S. population, however, the U.S. Census Bureau must use some measure of annual emigration if its population estimate is to have any degree of credibility. In the late 1990s, the bureau used an annual emigration figure of 220,000 foreign-born persons who returned to their homelands plus 48,000 native-born persons (e.g., those who decide to retire in another country or who may marry someone from another country and choose to move to that country).[13] Data from United Nation's sources report that Mexico, the United Kingdom, and Germany, in that order, are the primary destinations of those persons who emigrated from the United States.[14]

The lack of reliable emigration data is but another example of the huge data gap that plagues attempts to adequately assess the impact of immigration with precision.

An Alternative Approach: Studying the Determinants of Economic Phenomena

William Baumol, a former president of the American Economic Association, has decried the chronic imbalance in economics research on critical issues that rely on only ex post data manipulation while largely ignoring the efforts "to derive an understanding from the explicit study of institutions and history."[15] There is an alternative approach to focusing only on measuring the consequences of particular economic actions. It is to examine what Baumol has called "the substance of economic phenomena."[16] This approach does not deny the merits of quantifying, but it forces attention on understanding what actually causes a particular economic occurrence. In certain circumstances—the study of immigration being one—explaining the determinants may be more useful than merely measuring consequences. By focusing on understanding the causes of these economic phenomena, it is possible to anticipate how events and public policy interventions affect subsequent consequences. If the focus is only on measuring consequences, one obtains findings without substantive indications of what led to those outcomes or what changes might produce alternative results. The limitations of such analyses are succinctly conveyed in the candid comments by George Borjas after he completed his comprehensive examination in 1990 of the ex post impacts of recent immigrants on the U.S. economy. He concluded by stating, "I do not know what our immigration policy should be."[17]

Treating immigration policy as a determinant also provides the useful point of making it clear that there are choices for society that flow from choosing different policy alternatives. Immigration policy can be tailored to serve the national interest if policymakers are disposed to do so. Understanding how the "fourth wave" of mass immigration came into being and what maintains its momentum is crucial to any attempt to assess its compatibility with the emerging national interest. Therefore, this study will pursue this less traveled road: It will examine immigration policy as being an economic determinant.

The Paramount Role of Public Policy

With regard to immigration, the phenomenon that has spawned and perpetuated the fourth wave of immigration is easy to identify. It is the relevant public policy measures exercised by the federal government. In the modern era of sovereign nation states, each with their established geographical borders, immigration has become a discretionary act of national governments. Foreign-born persons can enter the territory of another for permanent settlement or temporarily to work or to visit only if they are legally admitted. Otherwise, their entry is illegal and can occur only if there is governmental indifference to those who enter surreptitiously or who violate the terms of properly issued visas by not leaving when their visas expire. Public policy determines how many foreign-born persons are admitted and under what circumstances. Thus, the relevant economic phenomena to study are the component parts of the nation's overall immigration policy. This is not to say that all forms of public policy represent economic phenomena. Rather, it is to argue that immigration is a special case whereby public policy itself is the catalyst for determining what actually transpires. Immigration policy does not reflect what is happening; it causes the phenomena. It is the institutional arrangement that actually sets the level and shapes the character of subsequent economic consequences. The immigration policy that exists at any given time is, of course, significantly influenced by the historical context out of which it has been formulated.

Although many types of public policy are complex, few are as difficult to comprehend as immigration policy. Indeed, immigration policy is often compared only to the internal revenue codes in terms of the intricacies of its multiple provisions. At its core, of course, are the statutory provisions set forth by Congress. These legislative enactments often are intended to serve multiple purposes. The product at any given time is influenced by both the historical circumstances that generate the need to enact the legislation and by the consensus-building response imposed by a political forum functioning in a free society. Once passed, the actual implementation of these statutes is affected by the institutional capacities and practices of the federal agency in the executive branch of government that is charged exclusively with its administration. Since 1940, it has been the Immigration and Naturalization Service (INS) of the U.S. Department of Justice. But in 2003, the process of shifting the INS into the newly created U.S. Department of Homeland Security (DHS) began. It is expected to take several years to be totally completed. Once there, the INS will be split into two separate bureaus: the Bureau of Border Security and the Bureau of Immigration and Citizenship.

The INS (as will its subsequent equivalents) also plays the vital role of writing the actual rules, regulations, and guidelines that are required to implement the legislative language. Unfortunately, the dialogue associated with this administrative process is essentially carried on between lawyers for the INS and lawyers for the immigration bar (who are usually members of the influential American Immigration Lawyer's Association). This lawyer's association, of course, has a vested interest in expanding immigration levels as well as adding complexity to the administrative processes. Lastly, of course, there is the role of the judiciary, whose rulings are generally intended to resolve disputes over legal meanings and procedural applications. But, as will be seen, the courts can sometimes create new policies and cause unanticipated policy outcomes.

Just as public policy brought a cessation to mass immigration in the 1920s, it was public policy that revived mass immigration in the mid-1960s, and it is public policy that continues to drive the phenomenon as the nation enters the twenty-first century. It will be public policy that will determine how long the fourth wave continues and, in the meantime, what effects it exerts on the nation's economy, population, and labor force. For as Napoleon once said, "policy is destiny."

Unlike the major influences that are impinging on the size and composition of the contemporary U.S. labor force—such as the growing labor force participation of women or the declining labor force participation rates for men over the age of forty-five, or the demographic effects associated with the progressive movement of the baby boom generation within the nation's population age distribution, or the labor force implications of the differences in fertility rates between racial and ethnic groups—immigration is a policy-driven activity. It is no accident that the United States has stood alone over the past three decades among other advanced industrial nations in terms of the scale of its annual admission of immigrants for permanent settlement. Immigration is the one element of a nation's labor supply that is a direct consequence of governmental choice; it is not a necessary and inevitable state of affairs. Indeed, most other major industrialized nations have conscientiously chosen not to follow this path at this stage of their economic development.[18]

The Advantage of the Policy Approach

As will be revealed in later chapters, a commonality of conclusions emerged in the 1990s between those who study immigration policy as a manifestation of economic phenomena and those who only measure economic consequences as to the effects of the fourth wave of immigration on the U.S. economy.[19] The congruence is comforting because it lends strength to the credibility of the research findings by both camps even though the methodological approaches are vastly different. It means that those who saw in advance where specific immigration policies were leading have found their views confirmed by those who waited to assess what happened later.

There is, however, a fundamental advantage that the public policy approach has that the outcomes approach does not. Namely, the way that immigration data are produced by the Census Bureau is in aggregate form. All persons who are foreign born are lumped together. No distinction is made among the various entry possibilities: legal, illegal, refugee, asylee, nonimmigrant who is specifically permitted to work, or nonimmigrant on a visitor or tourist visa who is not supposed to work while in the United States. With regard to the labor market, however, there are significant differences in the human capital characteristics between those who enter via each route.[20] Accordingly, different local labor markets and different labor force segments of the native-born population may be affected in ways that are totally ignored by relying on only the aggregate foreign-born classification. In aggregate data, the positive benefits of certain policies can be canceled out by the negative effects of other policies. Under such circumstances, the aggregation of data on the foreign-born produces an average picture of a conjectural reality that does not actually exist. Accordingly, one could easily conclude that no policy changes are needed, when, in fact, considerable gains could be achieved from expanding one policy component and contracting another. The public policy approach, therefore, has the clear advantage of being able to generate recommendations as to what immigration policy should be if it is to serve the national interest under conditions of ongoing change. Given the economic environment entering the twenty-first century, it is essential that all components of immigration policy be in step with the broader transformation processes that are restructuring the nation's labor market. Studies that rely exclusively on aggregate data cannot identify which elements of immigration policy should be expanded, reduced, repealed, or left alone. By focusing on the role of public policy, the differential components individually become the object of attention.

In the process of examining how each of these components contributes to the overall immigration flow, policy-oriented research also produces data. It is, however, far less systematic. Such studies produce particularistic data about specific immigrant groupings—such as refugees or illegal immigrants—or about effects of the presence of immigrants in certain industries, occupations, and geographic areas. Given the concentrated geographic nature of immigration, however, specific studies are more likely to provide insight into the nature of the immigration phenomenon than are data collected and analyzed about the foreign born as a collective whole.

The Perplexing Issue of Immigration Policy and the Study of Economics

Of all the multiple issues that fall within the domain of the study of economics, none evinces less agreement among economists than the issue of immigration. As a consequence, most economists have purposely chosen to neglect the topic. Indeed, Henry Simons, a pioneer advocate at the University of Chicago of the benefits of free market economics, has frankly written that "as regards immigration policy, the less said the better."[21] He explained:

> Wholly free immigration, however, is neither attainable nor desirable. To insist that a free trade program is logically or practically incomplete without free migration is either disingenuous or stupid. Free trade may and should raise living standards everywhere. . . . Free immigration would level standards, perhaps without raising them anywhere.[22]

Milton Friedman, the most well-known member of the "Chicago School" of economics, seems to have taken Simons's advice—to say as little as possible about immigration—to heart. Friedman is known to share Simons's views with regard to the necessity of governments in free societies having restrictive immigration policies.[23] But in his best-known books, he either totally ignores the role of government to set immigration policy in free market economies or he only briefly acknowledges the immigration experience of the United States, with no mention of government's paramount role in this area. It is startling in *Capitalism and Freedom,* where Friedman specifically states what he sees to be the role of government in a free society, that there is absolutely no mention of immigration policy.[24] Likewise, in *Free to Choose,* references are made only to the positive adjustment experiences of a few immigrants at the turn of the twentieth century.[25] Many of the benefits to U.S. workers in general and black workers in particular that Freidman attributes to capitalism in the time periods examined by these books occurred only because of the restrictive immigration policies that were in continuous effect in the United States from the mid-1920s through to the mid-1960s.

But there is hardly a word about the entire subject of immigration in these heralded books on free market economics. Likewise, the praise in *Free to Choose* that is heaped on Margaret Thatcher for the free market policies she championed as prime minister of Great Britain during the 1980s does not mention the highly restrictive immigration policy that she helped to put in place during her tenure and that is the most restrictive immigration policy among all European Union members.[26] It was her actions that, as will be discussed in the next chapter, led Britain, in 1981, to abandon the citizenship principle of *jus soli* (i.e., "the right of soil"), which had been in place for over 700 years and which is still in effect in the United States. No longer does British citizenship occur merely from the fact that a person is born on British soil.

Another former member of the economics faculty at the University of Chicago, Melvin Reder, has observed that "free immigration would cause rapid equalization of per capita income across countries accomplished mainly by leveling downward the income of the more affluent . . . [and] I resist this proposal."[27] Indeed, Reder, a specialist in labor economics, was the author of one of the most perceptive articles yet to be written on the topic of immigration policy and its labor market effects. Writing in 1963, just before the events that would trigger the beginning of the fourth wave of mass immigration commenced, Reder warned: "In short, a greater flow of immigration will injure labor market competitors with immigrants; these are, predominately, Negroes, Puerto Ricans, unskilled immigrants presently able to enter the country, and native rural-urban migrants (Negro and White)."[28] He also noted that employment and income opportunities of such "secondary earners" as "married women, youth, and aged persons" would be adversely affected by substantial increases in immigration.[29] As a consequence, mass immigration "would slow the approach toward distributional equality within the United States."[30] He observed that substantial progress had been made toward improving the income position of the poor both in the United States and in the other "Western democracies" as the result of the "deliberate state action" to restrict immigration "during the past 25 years to 50 years" (i.e., in the years before the fourth wave of mass immigration to the United States began).[31] Reder further notes that the national benefits that occurred over the years when immigration was restricted probably contributed to international inequality in income distribution. Nevertheless, he concluded with the following powerful observation about the importance of U.S. immigration policy:

> Consequently, our immigration policy inevitably reflects a kind of national selfishness of which the major beneficiaries are the least fortunate among us. We could not *completely* abandon this policy, even if we so desired.[32]

Likewise, on the same day it was announced that Gary Becker—also a member of the Chicago economics faculty—had won the 1992 Nobel Memorial Prize in Economics, he published a commentary in the *Wall Street Journal* that explained why restrictive immigration policies were essential for the contemporary U.S. experience and for the other industrialized democracies. He contrasted the economic setting of the mass immigration experience of the United States at the beginning of the twentieth century with the economic setting at the end of that century and concluded:

> But the world is now a very different place. Because of the expanded welfare state, immigration is no longer a practical policy. These days open immigration would merely induce people in poorer countries to emigrate to the United States and other developed countries to collect generous transfer payments.[33]

Given these views by the paragons of free market economies, it is not surprising that the role of immigration as a potential influence on the supply of labor of the United States is one of the least-examined features of contemporary economic analysis. The leading advocates of the free market paradigm of labor market operations have essentially agreed to say as little as possible on the subject. This posture clearly reflects a normative judgment on their part that such equilibrating adjustments are not in the national interest despite the alleged benefits that this model usually propounds for those who adopt its noninterventionist principles. In other words, immigration is a time-sensitive topic. Its merits depend on past historical events as well as present circumstances—not theoretical dogma. As Joseph Schumpeter, a renowned scholar of the history of economic analysis, has stated, unless the examination of a particular economic issue "presents a minimum of historical aspects, no amount of correctness, originality, rigor, or elegance will prevent a sense of lacking direction and meaning" to what is being examined.[34] Such is certainly the case with the study of immigration—no matter whether one adheres to the free market approach or any other paradigm to assess policy relevance. No economic policy can be judged in the abstract. Its merits depend entirely on the *prevailing* economic and historical circumstances. Immigration policy cannot be immune from meeting this commonsense standard of judgment.

Other voices in economics have taken a polar opposite view. The *Wall Street Journal,* for instance, has editorialized for the total elimination of border restrictions on those persons from other lands who wish to live and work in the United States. In a famous 1989 editorial attacking federal legislation to curb illegal immigration, it stated: "If Washington still wants to do something about immigration, we propose a five word Constitutional Amendment: 'There shall be open borders.'"[35]

In the same camp was the late Julian Simon (not to be confused with the aforementioned Henry Simons). While not calling for the entire abandonment of immigration restraints, Simon advocated "greatly increased immigration" above and beyond the already high levels legislatively in place for the 1990s.[36] Simon did not bother with any theoretical paradigms to rationalize his views. He did not seek to understand the historical development of immigration in terms of any differential role it might play at different stages of a nation's economic development or to delve into any of the institutional intricacies associated with public policy development that have resurrected and perpetuated mass immigration. He started with his conclusion that, whatever the immigration level is at present, it is insufficient. There should be more. He did not include refugees or asylees as immigrants in most of his statistical data used to justify his conclusions, and he totally ignored the substantial labor market presence of nonimmigrant foreign workers legally permitted to work in this country. Nor was there any recognition of the sizable undercount of illegal immigrants in the data he used. For these reasons, all of his data greatly underestimated what was already happening. There was no concern in his work for any adjustment difficulties that citizen workers might be experiencing under present conditions or any worry about what distributive effects would occur if he had his way and even higher levels of immigration occurred. As he once said, "it is important to focus on the long-run situation rather than the little blips" that may occur in the short run.[37] Virtually every economic benefit one can imagine is foreseen if only more immigrants are admitted. Simon claimed that the rate of technological advance would be spurred, business would be able to hire more workers, retirees of the baby boom era would have more workers to support them, tax revenues would rise, the nation would be more competitive, the image of the United States would be enhanced, and more people would be able to enjoy the "blessings of life in the United States." In essence, mass immigration is described as having only benefits, and if he saw any costs, he did not detail them.

Stephen Moore, who, like Simon, favors a libertarian approach to economic policymaking, asserts that mass immigration has been a positive influence at earlier times in U.S. history, so it is logical that it must be beneficial now and for the future.[38] He argues that immigrants create jobs and are an engine for economic growth; that immigrants are reviving inner city economies through the addition of new entrepreneurial skills; and that the economy should have no problem absorbing high levels of immigration on a sustained basis.

There are also economists who argue for enlarged immigration in a more reasonable way. One is John K. Galbraith, who envisions it as part of a broader strategy to reduce poverty in the world.[39] He does not contend that mass immigration is a panacea for solving the dilemma of the extensive variations on the standards of living that separate the advanced and the less economically developed nations of the world. But he does believe that immigration should be a vital factor in any global strategy to reduce income inequality in the world. Jagdish N. Bhagwati shares Galbraith's concern for the use of immigration policy for humanitarian concerns to help underdeveloped countries. But he also believes that the United States will confront a general shortage of labor in the early twenty-first century, which large-scale immigration could help to prevent.[40] Bhagwati's proposals are not very specific, and it is not clear how the entry of large numbers of unskilled workers from less-developed nations would remedy what appears to be a growing surplus of poorly prepared citizen workers already in industrialized nations such as the United States.

The aforementioned perspectives are not meant to be a definitive review of all of the views pertaining to the role of immigration in a free market economy. They are, however, intended to be representative of the range of perspectives on this vital, yet contentious, policy issue. It is hoped that what follows will contribute to the ongoing discourse.

3

Citizenship and Naturalization

Before proceeding with a discussion of immigration policy, it is necessary to examine the related issues of citizenship and naturalization. On whom does a nation state bestow membership and under what circumstances? To, and on, whom are rights and benefits provided as well as responsibilities and obligations imposed? Under what circumstances can citizenship be acquired by a foreign-born person?

William Brubaker has observed that "states [i.e., nations] are free in international law to define the circle of their citizens as they see fit."[1] As a consequence, the practices of nations vary widely due to differences in historical experiences, specific interests, cultural influences, and political ideologies. As with all elements of man-made laws, these policies evolve. They are subject to reconsideration and to changes over time.

In the case of the United States, both citizenship and naturalization have, in the past, been subjects of extensive controversy. The revival of mass immigration has caused renewed interest and debate over both issues. Consequently, they require mention before turning to the principal subject of immigration itself.

Methods of Acquiring Citizenship

Although there are variations, there are four means by which nations grant citizenship and define their members. These are: by descent, by naturalization, by registration, and by birth. Combinations of these four methods are common. The United States uses all four. They are not mutually exclusive categories.

Worldwide, the most common practice is to grant citizenship on the basis of descent. Appendix A shows which of thirty-eight major nations rely on this principle to convey citizenship. It is a principle whose roots go back to the time of ancient Greece, where political power, for the first time, was separated from kinship structures (i.e., clans) and vested in public bodies of free citizens. This legal concept is also known as *jus sanguinis* (i.e., the "right of blood"). Allegiance is assumed to go to the country of origin of a child's parents, regardless of where the child may be born. As is also indicated in Appendix A, there are differences between nations over which parent's descent is relevant. Most nations that use this principle permit the transfer to occur via either parent; some only by the father's nationality, and some only by the mother's nationality.

Virtually all countries have a means by which they can grant citizenship to persons who are citizens of another nation (i.e., the foreign born). It is called naturalization. The conditions for naturalization vary widely. Among the considerations used are the fulfillment of a specific period of residency in the country before application can be made, a basic knowledge of the language of the new nation and its structure of government, good moral character, and an oath of allegiance to the new nation to which one wishes to become a naturalized citizen.

In the case of the United States, the current residency requirement is five years, except for those who come as spouses of U.S. citizens, for whom it is three years. Children of immigrants who themselves are foreign born can gain citizenship by derivation at the time that their parents naturalize. They need only to be registered. Until such time as an immigrant chooses to naturalize, the individual is considered to be a permanent resident alien (popularly called a "green carder" in reference to the color of the original cards when first issued in 1940—but cards issued in the 1990s were pinkish blue; a hologram was added in 2000). There is, however, no obligation for any permanent resident alien to ever become a naturalized citizen of the United States. Most never do.

In some countries, naturalized citizens must renounce their former citizenship. In others, they can retain it. The United States, for instance, permits dual citizenship but it does not recognize any citizenship rights of other countries that conflict with the obligations of U.S. citizenship. Under U.S. law, therefore, there are no special benefits that accrue to anyone as a result of dual citizenship. Although there is no data collected on the number of U.S. citizens who are also citizens of another nation, the number is believed to be "large" because "90 percent of all immigrants [to the United States] come from multiple citizenship-allowing countries."[2] Thus, the perceived growth of dual citizenship in the United States has raised questions of divided loyalties and concerns that it has weakened assimilation pressures on new immigrants.

In some instances, citizenship is by acquired registration. Some members of the British Commonwealth, for instance, permit citizens of one Commonwealth nation to become citizens of their country by merely registering. The United States allows the attorney general, at his or her discretion, to allow foreign aliens to register on an individual person basis for legal permanent resident status even if they have previously entered the country illegally. To do so, however, they must have lived in the United States continuously since January 1, 1972, be of good moral character, and be generally admissible as immigrants under existing immigration law.[3] If they wish to become citizens, they must subsequently go through the regular naturalization procedures. As will be discussed in Chapters 10 and 12, the United States initiated a practice in 1986 that designated certain groups of people who had previously entered the country illegally or who overstayed their temporary legal admission to come forth and register during a designated time period. Those who did so and who met all other criteria for legal admission were given permanent resident status or, in some cases, citizenship itself. Generally, these group actions were referred to as "amnesties." Such actions were granted on seven different occasions between 1986 and 2000 to over 6 million persons. In most sessions of Congress since 1986, there have been efforts made to pass some form of amnesty for some designated group even though the collective effect is to undermine the integrity of the entire immigration system. The frequency of amnesties fosters the belief that, if persons illegally enter the country or overstay temporary admission, their status will eventually be legalized, so why not come (or overstay)?

Finally, there is the category of citizenship gained by birth. As mentioned previously, the legal term used to describe this method of bestowing citizenship is *jus soli* (i.e., the "right of soil"). Under its provisions, citizenship is granted to virtually all persons born on the "soil" of a particular country regardless of the nationality of the parents. This is the concept used most often in the United States. There are some exceptions. The United States does not give citizenship to the children born in the United States of foreign diplomats or other persons performing official governmental duties for their native countries, as such actions could be seen as forcing dual allegiances on such persons.

As indicated in Appendix A, *jus soli* is used by far fewer countries than is the principle of *jus sanguinis*. *Jus soli* is most common in the nations of the New World (i.e., the Western Hemisphere)—all of which have been significantly affected over the past 500 years by the immigrant experience.

Because of the importance of *jus soli* to a discussion of U.S. immigration policy, its legal evolution as a characteristic of U.S. institutional practices deserves elaboration.

The Institutionalization of *Jus Soli* Citizenship

One of the enduring legacies of the fact that the United States became an independent nation, after 169 years of being a British colony, has been the lasting imprint of Anglo law on U.S. law. The legal principle of *jus soli* dates back to the thirteenth century in England. Under English law, anyone born on English soil was English and, therefore, a subject of the king and his rule. The principle held sway in Britain until 1981, when, as part of an effort to curtail immigration, the practice was terminated. Since then, one parent must be a citizen or legal resident of the United Kingdom before a child born in Britain can be considered to be a British citizen.

The principle of *jus soli*, however, was in effect throughout the British colonial era in North America. After gaining its independence from Great Britain, and with the subsequent ratification of its Constitution in 1788, the United States was at once confronted with the citizenship issue. As with much of its law at the time, the United States continued to follow the principle of *jus soli* in the form of its common law. But there was a big problem. Slavery was still legal in all states south of the Mason-Dixon line (i.e., the boundary between the states of Pennsylvania and Maryland). While *jus soli* provided citizenship for all free white persons in the country, its application to slaves was contested. Moreover, the importation of slaves continued in South Carolina and Georgia, where it was still legal by state laws and was constitutionally protected until slave trading from abroad was terminated in 1808 by federal statute (to be discussed in the next chapter).

The states of the South said blacks were not citizens, regardless of whether they were born in the country. The states of the North said blacks born in the country were citizens, but they were at a loss to explain how a person could be a citizen whose rights and liberties were protected by the Constitution and still be a slave. As about 95 percent of the black population lived in the South at the time, the reality of the situation was that citizenship was essentially restricted only to free white persons.

The ongoing issue of citizenship for blacks came to a head in the famous *Dred Scott* v. *Sandford* decision by the U.S. Supreme Court in 1857. Scott was a slave who belonged to an Army surgeon stationed in Missouri, a state where slavery was legal. In 1834, Scott was taken by his master to the free state of Illinois and later to the free territory of Wisconsin before being brought back to Missouri. Scott later sued for his freedom on the grounds that he had been taken to a territory where slavery was prohibited. His cause was joined by opponents to slavery as part of their efforts to establish the principle that a slave is automatically free when he or she enters a free state or territory. Eventually, the case made it to the Supreme Court.

Six of the nine members of the Court (including Chief Justice Roger Taney, who wrote the decision) ruled that Scott's status was determined by the state in which he resided (i.e., Missouri), so he was still a slave. This ruling was sufficient to settle the case at hand, but Taney took the occasion to go further. Supported by two other justices, he also ruled that Scott had no right to even bring the case because no black person could be a citizen of the United States. Furthermore, with five other members in agreement, the decision went on to say that Congress has no power to prevent slave owners from taking slaves into any of the territories of the United States that had yet to become states, because to do so would mean depriving citizens of their property without due process of law. Slavery, therefore, was legal in the states of the North and as far west as the Oregon Territory. Taney wrongly believed that the Court's decision would finally settle the issue of black citizenship and cause sectional conflict over the contentious issue to subside. Instead, the decision itself became one more incendiary force leading to the Civil War a few years later.

The *Dred Scott* ruling meant that there could be no degrees of citizenship. Blacks had no constitutional rights. As a consequence, when the Civil War ended in 1865 with the defeat of the South, the issue of black citizenship became an immediate concern of Congress. The Civil Rights Act of 1866 was quickly passed, which legislatively extended citizenship rights to blacks by virtue of birth in the country. But there was still fear by the victorious Northerners in Congress that the South could not be trusted to remain loyal to the Union. Fearing that the ultimate return of white Southerners to Congress might lead to a repeal of the legislation, Congress in 1866 also initiated the process of amending the U.S. Constitution to make it difficult for any group in the future to attempt to deprive or deny blacks of their citizenship rights. These efforts culminated in the ratification of the Fourteenth Amendment to the Constitution in 1868. It incorporated the key provisions of the Civil Rights Act of 1866 whereby "all persons born or naturalized in the United States and subject to the jurisdiction thereof, are citizens of the United States and of the States wherein they reside."[4] The principle of *jus soli*, therefore, became and remains the constitutional law of the United States.

Jus Soli Citizenship and Illegal Immigration

At the time of its adoption, the Fourteenth Amendment was viewed as a form of civil rights protection. Except for its mention of naturalized citizens, the broader implications of the amendment to future immigration policy were not foreseen. The language of the Fourteenth Amendment has been applied to include not only the children of native-born and naturalized citizens, but also the children born to nonimmigrant aliens (who are legally in the country for only temporary periods) as well as those born to illegal immigrants (who are not supposed to be in the country at all).

It was not until the issue of illegal immigration exploded on the national scene in the 1970s that concern over the nation's unambiguous citizenship provisions began to be questioned. As the scale of illegal immigration soared (see Chapter 10), the policy of automatically granting citizenship at birth surfaced as a component among the array of proposals suggested to combat illegal entry.

It is contended that, whereas legal immigrants and refugees enter the United States with the consent of the people of the country, they and their progeny are entitled to become citizens. But illegal immigrants do not enter with consent, so their children should not automatically be citizens even if they are born in the United States.

Those who wished to change the *jus soli* policy rallied in the 1990s around the voice of then governor of California, Pete Wilson. Noting that many—perhaps the majority—of the illegal immigrants coming into California are poor, Wilson pointed out that the children born of illegal immigrants often need medical, welfare, education, and housing services that the public sector in California is obligated by law to provide. In 1993, therefore, Wilson proposed to amend the U.S. Constitution to deny citizenship to children born in the United States to illegal immigrants. In announcing his proposal, Wilson said: "Two-thirds of all babies born in Los Angeles County public hospitals are born to illegal immigrant parents. It's time to amend the Constitution so that citizenship belongs only to the children of legal residents of the United States, not to every child whose mother can make it [to]an American hospital."[5] Subsequent support for his position was manifested by five separate bills that were introduced in the 103rd Congress (in session from 1993 to 1994) to begin the process of repealing the relevant section of the Fourteenth Amendment.[6] None, however, were seriously considered.

In the next Congress, however, a bill calling for such a repeal made it to the stage of having a formal congressional hearing on the proposal.[7] A spokesman for the Clinton administration testified against the proposal by saying that it would create "a permanent caste of aliens generation after generation born in America but never to be citizens."[8] No further action was taken. The initiative then shifted to the Republican party's platform for the presidential campaign in 1996. It called for the passage of an amendment to the Constitution to withhold U.S. citizenship from children of illegal immigrants born in the country, but their candidate was defeated in the election.

Often, critics of automatic citizenship for such children contend that the Fourteenth Amendment was never intended to confer blanket rights to children of adult illegal immigrants who are not supposed to be in the country. They claim that the language of the amendment applies only to persons "subject to the jurisdiction" of the United States. Citing the words of the author of the Fourteenth Amendment, Senator Lyman Trumbell (R–Ill.), the word "jurisdiction" was meant to refer to the person's "complete" allegiance.[9] Hence, Trumbell felt it would be wrong to automatically extend citizenship to children of American Indians as well as those of foreign diplomats, who, respectively, owe their allegiances to either a tribe or foreign nation regardless of their birth in the United States. Indeed, the U.S. Supreme Court subsequently ruled in 1884 that the Fourteenth Amendment did not apply to the children of American Indians for that very reason.[10] Subsequently, in 1887, the Dawes–Severalty Act did grant citizenship to American Indians who renounced their tribal allegiances. In 1924, however, the Burke Act granted U.S. citizenship to all Indians regardless of any tribal loyalties they may retain.

Reaction to mass abuse of the nation's immigration laws, however, is not the only reason for questioning the continuation of the *jus soli* policy. Brubaker claims that the assignment of citizenship at birth is a form of attribution by a particular society to individuals, which, he feels, is a fundamental contradiction of "the central claim of liberal political theory: the idea that political membership ought to be founded on individual consent."[11] Brubaker, however, answers his own concern by simply noting that a nation "is not and cannot be a voluntary association."[12] If citizenship were voluntary, individuals could escape certain societal duties such as military service or loyalty. Regardless of whether nations actually choose to impose such membership obligations, without them there would be adults and, perhaps, many children with no citizenship living in a country. All nations regard their citizens as being bound to them. Citizenship means that, while citizens have an incontestable right to enter and reside in a particular nation, all others do not. Allowing citizenship to be voluntary would make the practice of controlling immigration difficult, if not impossible, for any nation to regulate.

Only in a world of zero immigration would voluntary citizenship be feasible. But, even then, it would not, as noted earlier, be as acceptable to any modern state that provides rights and imposes duties on its members.

Citizenship Rights of Children Born out of Wedlock
Outside the United States

With U.S. military troops stationed in over 100 countries as the twenty-first century begins, and with millions of U.S. citizens traveling abroad each year for business, leisure, and educational purposes, there are numerous instances in which children are born abroad but outside of wedlock with adult foreign nationals who are not U.S. citizens. The citizenship claims of these children was the subject of extensive legal debate in the 1990s. Under U.S. naturalization law, the rights of the child differ, depending on whether the mother or the father is a U.S. citizen. If the mother is a U.S. citizen, the child is a U.S. citizen at birth. On the other hand, if the father is a U.S. citizen, the child is a U.S. citizen at birth only if the father acknowledges paternity and agrees to support the child until he or she is eighteen years old; otherwise, the child has no citizenship claims to the United States. In two separate decisions in 1998 and 2001, the U.S. Supreme Court affirmed this differential treatment.[13]

The legal distinction obviously sets a higher standard for fathers than for mothers. As such, it is viewed by some as a form of gender discrimination and has drawn the wrath of some women's organizations who have sought to purge U.S. laws of such features. Although the legal reasons for the difference are complex, it rests on the fact that the identity of the mother of a child is revealed at birth (and can be easily affirmed by genetic testing). But the identity of the father is not always so simple. By the time of birth, the father may be geographically far away and/or his identity may be unknown when later in life the issue of U.S. citizenship arises.[14] As citizenship is regarded as being an attribute of a country's sovereignty, a foreign-born child should have a substantial tie with the United States as a condition of citizenship. If the mother is a U.S. citizen, the relationship exists from her experience of giving birth. For fathers who are citizens, it is necessary that a relationship—such as a commitment of financial support—be established to manifest the tie.

The Issue of Naturalization

Precisely because of the phenomenon of immigration, nations that permit immigration require a procedure whereby citizens of foreign countries can legally change their citizenship to their new country of residence. As mentioned earlier, this process is called naturalization, and the participants are known as naturalized citizens. Although naturalization is usually considered to be a relatively benign aspect of U.S. immigration policy, it, too, has had its moments of controversy. Indeed, as the number of persons seeking naturalization soared in the 1990s, its provisions also returned to the limelight of public scrutiny.

Unlike the subject of immigration (which is not mentioned in the U.S. Constitution), naturalization is specifically cited. The Congress of the United States is explicitly given the power "to establish a uniform rule for naturalization."[15] Accordingly, the first Congress adopted legislation in 1790 indicating how foreign-born persons who immigrate into the United States could gain citizenship. A uniform requirement was imposed that specified a two-year period of residency before a foreign-born person was eligible for naturalization. This action was later modified by the Naturalization Act of 1798. It required the clerks in state courts to report information on those persons whom they naturalized to the U.S. Secretary of State. It also required all aliens living in the United States, as well as those who subsequently arrive, to register with the state courts, and that regular reports by these courts be forwarded to the U.S. Department of State. It also raised the residency requirement to fourteen years before an alien could be eligible for naturalization.

After only four years, however, the Naturalization Act of 1802 revamped the entire existing law. It established a five-year residency period as well as the requirements of being of good moral character, expressing allegiance to the U.S. Constitution, and having witnesses. There were no major changes in U.S. naturalization law until 1906.

The reason was the race issue, or, more specifically, the issue of black citizenship. If blacks born in the country could not be citizens, then, it follows, foreign-born blacks could not become naturalized citizens. Foreign-born blacks were essentially—if not exclusively—entering the country as involuntary immigrants (i.e., as slaves). Although slave importation was legal until 1808, most states—even in the South—had banned the practice before that year (the exceptions being South Carolina and Georgia). But as long as slavery was legal, the practice of illegally importing African slaves continued in the South until ended by the Civil War. The aforementioned *Dred Scott* case, however, removed any uncertainty about whether any blacks—native born or foreign born—could be citizens. The answer was no.

Following the Civil War, when the legislative and constitutional changes were made that guaranteed citizenship to native-born blacks, the Naturalization Act of 1870 extended the existing naturalization laws to include aliens of African nativity and persons of African descent. But that did not end the issue of racial discrimination in naturalization law.

By the 1870s, immigration from Asia had reached significant proportions. The initial immigrants from Asia during the mid-nineteenth century were the Chinese, who were later followed by Japanese immigrants near the end of that century and, for a brief period in the early twentieth century, by Koreans. The Burlingame Treaty, signed by the governments of China and the United States in 1868, guaranteed the right of Chinese immigrants to enter the United States under the same terms as all other immigrants. However, the treaty restricted the rights of Chinese immigrants to become naturalized citizens. There was a subsequent surge in Chinese immigration—specifically in California but also in other western states. A negative social reaction ensued (see Chapters 5 and 6) that led to the enactment of a series of anti-Chinese laws at the state level and that culminated in the passage of the Chinese Exclusion Act of 1882 at the national level. This legislation not only restricted all immigration from China, but it also barred all foreign-born Chinese from being naturalized for citizenship.

In 1922, the U.S. Supreme Court ruled that previous congressional enactments had restricted eligibility for naturalization to "free white persons" and to "persons of African descent." Until Congress said otherwise, foreign-born persons of other races (i.e., Asians) were banned from naturalization.[16] It was not until 1952 that the Immigration and Nationality Act would stipulate that all races are eligible for naturalization, which, in effect, eliminated race itself as a barrier to immigration.

Returning to the evolution of naturalization law, there was continual concern that there was a lack of uniformity in the application of naturalization by the various state courts that administered the federal law. The issue came to a head during the "third wave" of mass immigration (see Chapter 7), which was in progress at the turn of the twentieth century. The federal agency responsible for immigration at the time, the Bureau of Immigration in the existing U.S. Department of Commerce and Labor, reported in 1904 that "naturalization frauds are [being] perpetrated . . . to an extent that is appalling."[17] The lack of "federal supervision" was cited as the explanation for this deterioration of conditions. It was also believed at the time that the citizens of the country were demanding that "higher naturalization standards be imposed."[18] It was alleged that large blocs of immigrants were being naturalized just before election days and they were being manipulated for political purposes. Furthermore, there was mounting concern in the country that many of the immigrants were illiterate, not only in English, but also in their native tongues, and, accordingly, they would be difficult to assimilate.[19]

In response to these concerns, the Naturalization Act of 1906 combined into a single federal agency the regulatory responsibility for both the immigration and naturalization functions. The power to actually grant or deny naturalization remained, however, vested in the state courts. But uniform application fees, standards, and forms were specified, with copies required to be filed with the Bureau of Immigration and Naturalization. The legislation also made knowledge of the English language a requirement for naturalization.

In the 1930s, naturalization once again became a subject of major controversy. With the mass unemployment associated with the economic depression of that decade, a number of municipal and state agencies acted to restrict public employment opportunities to citizens only. A number of these agencies also sought to exclude noncitizens from public relief rolls. In the wake of their efforts, there was a flurry of charges of naturalization fraud by aliens seeking public jobs and eligibility for relief benefits. Extensive changes in the procedures for verification of compliance requirements were enacted by the Nationality Act of 1940. They were intended to overcome the shortcomings revealed in the 1930s, but the major impetus for the changes arose from concerns over national defense. With the mounting belief that the United States would eventually become involved in World War II, the fear of entry of saboteurs and spies as well as concerns over the loyalty of some of those permanent resident aliens in the United States (especially those who were still citizens of Japan, Germany, and Italy) caused naturalization documentation to come under exceptionally close scrutiny. Indeed, it was during this era that the nation's naturalization laws were enforced more diligently than at any period either before or since that time.[20]

With immigration during the war years at historically low levels, naturalization became the central focus of public policy attention concerning immigration matters. This was because there were limitations imposed on what types of jobs noncitizens could seek, specific occupations that only citizens could hold, and pressures to facilitate the naturalization of noncitizens serving in the military. For these reasons, naturalization rates rose significantly during the war years. By 1946, over two-thirds of the eligible permanent alien population had elected to become naturalized citizens. Following the end of the war, however, the naturalization rates began to decline significantly.

In the early 1950s, the topic of naturalization became embroiled once more with national security concerns. Cold War politics, associated with fears of the spread of communism, took hold of the national consciousness. The Internal Security Act of 1950 barred the naturalization of anyone who had been a member of a totalitarian organization in the preceding ten years; required that citizens be able to read, write, and speak English; and prohibited naturalization if there is a deportation order outstanding against the individual. As there was an increase in immigration in the 1950s (associated largely with the admission of postwar refugees) over the very low levels that had existed during the 1930s and 1940s, the number of naturalizations did increase (but at levels well below those experienced during the actual war years).

It was not until the return of mass immigration after passage of the Immigration Act of 1965, that naturalization levels began once more to rise. But, in terms of percentages, only little more than one-third of immigrants granted permanent resident alien status were following through to become naturalized citizens as the twenty-first century commenced.

Signs of Changes in the Propensity to Naturalize

It is a general principle of citizenship laws in free societies that no government should coerce or entice immigrants to naturalize. Naturalization, therefore, involves a bilateral relationship of consensuality between the government of the nation that has received the immigrants and the immigrants themselves. Once one has attained U.S. citizenship, it is hard to lose. It cannot be revoked unless one has lied about answers to questions during his or her naturalization proceedings. The only other way is to renounce one's citizenship.

Over the years, the differences between being a U.S. citizen and being a permanent resident alien have steadily diminished. All human rights are equally protected. Only in the area of political rights do three significant differences in treatment occur. Permanent resident aliens are not permitted to vote even though they are subject to the same taxes appropriate to citizens, and they may not serve on juries. Citizens may travel outside the country for indefinite periods while permanent resident aliens may leave for periods not to exceed six months. With regard to the labor market, both groups have equal access to virtually all job opportunities in the private sector (except where private contractors are performing certain national defense research work for the federal government), and, in most circumstances, both are entitled to equal coverage by all prevailing labor standard protections. Discrimination against the hiring of permanent resident aliens in the private sector has been prohibited since 1986, with the only caveat being that, if a private employer finds citizens and permanent resident aliens to be *equally* qualified for available job openings, the employer may *always* give hiring preference to the citizen applicants. In the public sector, the federal government does not allow noncitizens to be employed in many federal agencies (although they may be employed by the U.S. Postal Service). State governments may also exclude noncitizens from serving in certain public jobs, and many have chosen to do so (e.g., teaching in public schools, being a police officer, or serving in certain public safety capacities). The dramatic growth in the foreign-born population in the 1990s has led many states to reduce, but not to eliminate, these exclusions.[21] Also, under existing immigration law, citizens have a higher priority and may sponsor more of their adult family members as legal immigrants than may permanent resident aliens.

As mass immigration resumed in the post-1965 years, the federal government was content for many years to pursue a policy of benign neglect with respect to naturalization. But several other policy developments have led to a surge in naturalization applications. In the early 1990s, naturalization levels were averaging over 300,000 approvals a year (almost 100 percent higher than the average levels of the 1970s). By the end of the decade, however, the annual number had almost tripled (i.e., in 2000 there were 888,788 naturalizations).

There are multiple causes for the acceleration of naturalization requests. First, there have been the dramatic increases in the number of eligible persons due to the aforementioned seven amnesty programs since 1986 for over

6 million former illegal immigrants and persons who overstayed various temporary admission programs. After fulfilling their residency requirements, many have become naturalized citizens. Their numbers have been added to the growing number of eligible legal immigrants and refugees admitted over the past two decades who have also chosen to naturalize after meeting their residency requirement.

The second factor causing naturalizations to surge was the result of an INS-implemented administrative policy in 1993 to replace all of the existing "green cards" and to reissue a new card. The cost of a replacement card was set at seventy dollars, and it is valid for ten years, after which it will have to be replaced again and a new fee paid. As the one-time fee charged for naturalization at the time was ninety-five dollars, many persons elected to pay this fee and become a naturalized citizen instead.

A third prompting force has been the derivative effect of the nation's efforts to reform its welfare systems. In 1996, the federal government adopted the Personal Responsibility and Work Opportunity Act and the Illegal Immigration Reform and Immigrant Responsibility Act. Both laws greatly restricted public benefits for noncitizens, to only medical emergency funds. As a disproportionate share of the nation's poor are recent immigrants and refugees, some resident aliens have felt it better to become naturalized citizens to ensure their continued eligibility for food stamps, temporary assistance for needy families, Medicaid, and supplemental security income. Many high immigrant impact states took similar restrictive actions that added to these pressures to naturalize.

Fourth, in 1995, the INS initiated a program called "Citizenship USA" to promote naturalization by streamlining procedures and using various community-based nonprofit organizations to process applicants. As 1996 was a presidential election year, the intentions of the program were roundly criticized by Republicans who charged that the Clinton administration was using the program to attract more Hispanic voters—especially in California. After the election, there were revelations of numerous cases whereby persons ineligible for citizenship had been wrongly naturalized. Some prosecutions did occur, but the actual magnitude of wrongdoing is indeterminable. Similar charges were made after the 2000 presidential election concerning expedited citizenship procedures used in Florida.

Lastly, the terrorist attacks on the United States on September 11, 2001, triggered a sudden surge in naturalization applications.[22] There was a 61 percent increase in applications in October and November 2001 over the same months the previous year. It is speculated that the crisis, with its focus on national unity, triggered a recognition of what citizenship really means among many permanent resident aliens.

In addition to these general factors, it is also the case that there are significant differences in the naturalization rates of the various component groups that comprise the nation's resident alien population. Immigrants who are young adults when they arrive, immigrants who come from distant parts of the world (such as Asia and Africa), or immigrants who are in professional occupations, as well as persons who are refugees (e.g., from countries of the former Soviet Union) are far more likely to naturalize than are older immigrants, immigrants from nearby nations (e.g., Mexico), or nonrefugees and immigrants who are unskilled and poorly educated.

Concluding Observations

Although citizenship and naturalization issues have been contentious public policy issues in the nation's past, they faded from the spotlight of public attention for many years only to resurface with the return of mass immigration to the American experience since 1965. To its credit, the United States has pursued a policy of inclusiveness over the years with regard to its adherence to *jus soli* principles and easy naturalization procedures for those who immigrate and wish to become U.S. citizens.

On the other hand, the mass abuse of the nation's immigration laws by illegal immigrants does raise a legitimate concern that current citizenship law may be too inclusive. Certainly, there has been no consent extended by the American polity that children born to parents of illegal immigrants, who should not be in the country to begin with, ought to be automatically granted U.S. citizenship with all of the rights, benefits, and entitlements that accrue to that status. The best way to deal with this issue, of course, is through strengthened prevention of illegal immigration. This could be accomplished by enhanced border management, the rigorous enforcement of workplace laws forbidding illegal immigrants from being employed in this country, and swift deportation of all illegal immigrants found in the country. But, to date, politicians have been unwilling to devote the financial resources or to adopt the types of policies necessary to make the nation's immigration laws enforceable.[23] Under these conditions, it would seem that the only remaining alternative is to modify the existing *jus soli* principles, as the United Kingdom has done, to require that at least one parent must be a U.S. citizen before automatic citizenship at birth is granted. Such a change, of course, would require a change in the Constitution. If, however, the child and his or her parents still remain in the country illegally, it would seem necessary to create a statutory right that would permit eventual naturalization to U.S. citizenship of such persons born in the United States. Such provisions would be available only to those children who actually have lived in the United States for a long period of time. The precedent for such a policy already exists and was discussed earlier: It is citizenship by means of registration. The prevailing law would have to be only modified to cover the situation of children who, say, reach their eighteenth birthday and who have spent most or all of their years residing in the United States.

As for naturalization, U.S. policy ought to be to promote naturalization. The decision definitely should not be coerced. But with almost 20 million permanent resident aliens in the country as the new millennium begins, and many having been in that status for years, it would be in the national interest to encourage naturalization in order to ease the assimilation process. Too many urban areas, where immigrants cluster, now have significant numbers of persons who cannot vote or serve on juries and cannot hold certain public jobs. As long as they remain in a noncitizen status, there is a tendency to maintain allegiance to their native country and to resist becoming assimilated. The situation tends to fracture the social harmony of many cities by strengthening ethnic identities, which tends to foster conflict between ethnic segments of the urban population. All that is being suggested is that public policy should move away from its essentially neutral stance to become more proactive in stressing the benefits of naturalization and, where possible, to facilitate the procedural processes to its achievement. For as the Chair of the U.S. Commission on Immigration Reform, Barbara Jordan, said in 1995, "naturalization is the most visible manifestation of Americanization."[24]

The promotion of naturalization of eligible persons does not mean, however, that there should be any less attention given to strict compliance with the actual naturalization requirements. For, as Jordan has also said, while expediting the processing of naturalization requests, the "INS must maintain rigorous standards in processing applications" to screen out those ineligible for such status.[25] Given the widespread fraud that was associated with many of the amnesty programs, the naturalization procedures provide an opportunity to deny citizenship to those many persons who lied about their original eligibility for such programs. It is an opportunity to regain credibility for the earlier abuse that marred that extension of goodwill by the nation's immigration policymakers.

4

Prelude to Mass Immigration

The Treaty of Paris in 1783 granted the thirteen colonies the independence they sought from England. The treaty not only ended the war, but it also ceded all British land claims south of the Great Lakes. Thus, the original landmass of the new nation was extended from the Atlantic Seaboard (except for Florida) west to the Mississippi River.

During the war years, the thirteen colonies had been linked by the Articles of Confederation that were adopted by the Continental Congress in 1777 (but not accepted by all until 1781). It was not until July 1788, however, that the U.S. Constitution was actually ratified and the United States formally became a nation. As of that date, it existed as a political entity, but it remained to be seen whether it could establish and maintain its economic viability.

Before discussing the subsequent role that mass immigration played in the human settlement and economic development of this new country, it is necessary to address two subjects. The first pertains to the colonial heritage that shaped the nation's population and labor force at its historical starting point. The second relates to the issue of "involuntary immigration" of those groups who did not of their own volition seek to be included in the building of the new country, but who were.

The Colonial Roots

Although the Dutch, French, and Spanish had laid claims to land areas and established earlier settlements, it was the English who, beginning in 1607, were the first Europeans to colonize successfully the part of the New World that formally became the United States in 1788.[1] The English claim to sovereignty over much of North America was based on the explorations in 1497 and 1498 of John Cabot, who had been employed by King Henry VII to conduct these expeditions. Initially, England was too preoccupied with wars on the European continent and domestic religious conflicts associated with the Reformation to undertake colonization. By the 1570s, however, the idea did gain limited acceptance, and in the mid-1580s, a colony was established on Roanoke Island in what is now North Carolina. It failed, and the fate of the original colonists is a mystery to this day. By the late sixteenth and early seventeenth centuries, England was in the process of urbanizing its population. In the wake of this urbanization, there developed a popular perception of a growing surplus of labor and mounting fears of overpopulation. These beliefs, in turn, sparked a political consensus favoring the creation of colonies along the Atlantic Coast region in the New World claimed by England.[2] It was with the full support of the English Crown, and with the firm expectation that English society would financially benefit from the consequences, that the settlement process recommenced.

The legal theory under which English colonization proceeded was one that held that all of the land belonged to the Crown. Specific grants of land were made by the Crown to individual proprietors or to commercial companies to establish their separate colonies. When these entities received their royal charters, they acquired the right to govern their respective colonies. These entities, in turn, could transfer land titles to the actual settlers. The English settlers of the colonial era were English citizens when they embarked, and they believed they were still English citizens when they arrived in the colonies.

Indeed, the founding colonies had no central governmental organ of expression. They were tied to each other during this era only by the distant English Crown. Thus, the colonial white settlers from England were not seeking to enter a foreign nation, nor did they believe they were abandoning their original citizenship. They believed that they were entitled to exactly the same rights and privileges as their fellow countrymen who remained behind. Thus, unlike those who would immigrate to the United States after it became a nation in 1788, the English colonists did not consider themselves to be immigrants. Hence, they should be distinguished from those persons from other countries who were absorbed (the Dutch and the Swedes who had also tried to establish their own colonies in parts of the same land area) during the settlement process and those who had, in fact, immigrated from elsewhere (the French, German, Swiss, and Scotch–Irish from Northern Ireland) prior to 1788.

As for the colonists themselves, they came to settle for myriad reasons. For some, it was the opportunity to escape religious persecution. Others, especially those in the Chesapeake colonies, came initially as servants to richer settler families; still others came as free men who paid their own passage and who were enticed by the opportunity to own land and to develop it for themselves and their families. It was also the case that some came in lieu of imprisonment in England for being in debt or having committed crimes.

Most of the colonists of the seventeenth century who actually came from Europe (as opposed to those born in the colonies) came from urban backgrounds. Most were unskilled workers, although there were some skilled artisans as well. Most had urban work experiences. Gradually, over the ensuing years, the labor supply process became institutionalized by the creation of the indentured servant system. These participants, before boarding ships, agreed to be contractually bound to work for a set period of time for someone in one of the colonies in return for payment of their transportation costs.

When, in the eighteenth century, the Industrial Revolution began in England, the economic forces of its labor market changed. There was a perceived need for workers to fill the jobs in the factories that the industrialization process had spawned. Hence, in England, political pressures developed to reduce the outflow. The only exception was for convicted felons, who continued to be sent to the colonies, where they, too, were usually sold into indentured servitude. Convicts were not welcomed in the New England colonies, but in the Middle Atlantic and Southern colonies, the settlements were generally glad to receive anyone they could. In this new environment, a new source of labor supply for the colonies had to be found. It came in the form of redemptioners. These were usually poor peasants from Northern Ireland (i.e., the Scotch–Irish), Germany, and Switzerland who were mostly Protestant in their religious beliefs. Redemptioners signed repayment contracts after they arrived in the colonies. Hence, local demand and supply forces for labor determined their actual length of subsequent servitude. In total, it is estimated that from one-half to two-thirds of the white immigrants to the English colonies came originally under one of these forms of bonded labor.[3]

Throughout the colonial period, the population grew rapidly. Most people lived close to the ocean or along navigable rivers. By 1776, when the Revolutionary War began, Philadelphia, was the second-largest city in the British Empire with a population of 40,000. The growth of cities led to an increased demand for a variety of workers in various trades—tailors, shoemakers, coach makers, shipbuilders, silversmiths, and glass makers. Wages were much higher in the colonies (ranging from 30 to 200 percent higher) than in England and the other source countries for workers in similar occupations. This situation further encouraged free skilled workers to emigrate from their homelands. But in all of the colonies, most workers had close ties to agriculture. The relative ease by which free workers could acquire land meant that many skilled workers as well as semiskilled and unskilled workers who completed their indentures (or those who simply wandered away before their bondage period was up) could become independent farmers. In every colony, therefore, agriculture was, by far, the dominant industry of the economy, and farming was the predominant occupation of the labor force.

The rapid population growth of the colonial era was also spawned by very high birth rates. With abundant land and shortages of labor, there was a strong inducement for raising large families. Thus, the first census of the new nation in 1790 recorded a population of 3.9 million people—with 94.9 percent of the population living in rural areas. The first data on the nation's labor force (which measured persons "engaged in work, self employment or unpaid family work over the age of 10") set its size in 1800 at 1.9 million workers, of whom 1.4 million were free workers and 500,000 were slaves (to be discussed in the next section). Of the free workers, 74 percent were employed in agriculture.[4] Indicative of the pre-industrial stage of the economy was the fact that 90 percent of the free labor force in 1800 were *not* employees.[5] They were self-employed as farmers, tradesmen, and mechanics. It was from this baseline that the free labor force of the United States was to be built.

The Exceptions to Voluntary Immigration

To be sure, not all of the people who populated the country during this critical period of nation building had voluntarily affiliated. Three groups in particular require special mention. Two were of consequence during the colonial era and continued to be so after the United States was established in 1788. They were the Indians and the black population. The third group, those of Mexican heritage, subsequently became of consequence during the nation's first century of existence, but for the sake of convenience will be discussed in this section.

The Indian Heritage Population

The most obvious of those who did not immigrate, of course, were the native people whom Christopher Columbus had earlier misnamed "los Indios," or the Indians. The word was subsequently applied to all of the indigenous inhabitants of the Americas. In the sixteenth century, when the Europeans first arrived in the portion of the landmass of North America that would later become the United States, it is estimated that somewhat less than 1 million Indians inhabited the entire area. The North American Indians had not developed the structured and highly organized civilizations of some of the Indian tribes of Central and South America. Some of the North American tribes were nomadic, but most were settled in particular regions where they lived communally off the land and wildlife. From the initial contact with the Spanish explorers and missionaries in what would later become the American Southwest to the extended subsequent encounters in later years with the explorers, trappers, traders, and settlers from England, Spain, France, Holland, Sweden, and elsewhere, the Indian population began to decline. The combination of the introduction of diseases for which the Indians had no immunities; the introduction of alcohol, for which they had little tolerance; and the consequences of numerous violent conflicts that ensued from the clash of cultures exacted an enormous human toll on the Indian population.

From the Indians, the colonists learned how to grow indigenous vegetables like corn and how to use plants with medicinal and narcotic properties like tobacco. Although there were numerous good faith efforts by early colonists to establish friendly relations and to convert some Indians to Christianity, "it proved impossible for the two races to live peacefully side-by-side."[6] There was no concept of private ownership of land in the Indian culture, whereas the principle was fundamental to the culture of the colonists. Consequently, as the white settlers cut down forests and expanded their land under cultivation, they reduced the area in which the Indians could hunt and fish. When Indian chieftains permitted settlers to use their hunting grounds, they soon found that the land was being cleared, fenced, and treated as the settlers' private property. Thus, when the settlers were interested only in hunting and trapping, good relations usually existed, but "whenever the whites developed agriculture, conflicts developed quickly."[7] When fighting erupted, the tactics used by the Indians seemed to be incredibly cruel to the whites, and they soon reciprocated in kind. Although colonial British officials often sought to protect the Indians from unfair treatment, the colonists typically feared the Indians and pressed for their removal.

Of those Indians who survived, most were subsequently relocated—sometimes voluntarily but often forcibly—away from the eastern lands. Initially, they moved to areas west of the Allegheny and Appalachian Mountains or north to Canada. Later, it was to areas west of the Mississippi River. The twin processes of population decline and physical displacement of the Indians began during the colonial era, but they accelerated after the country became independent and began the process of acquiring the land west of the Mississippi in the nineteenth century.

When the former thirteen colonies became a unified nation in 1788, it is estimated that there were only about 76,000 Indians living along the Atlantic Seaboard in the same geographical area.[8] Other Indian tribes, however, soon found themselves under the aegis of the United States as the nation expanded its landmass and consolidated its political boundaries.

In the East, the United States seized parts of west Florida in 1810 and 1813 and purchased the remainder of Florida from Spain under the terms of the Adams–Onis Treaty of 1819. Florida, while under Spanish rule, had been a haven for runaway slaves from Southern plantations, and it had also been a base for hostile attacks by the Seminole Indians on plantations in Georgia. With the acquisition of this new land, of course, came the Seminoles. As white settlers flooded into Florida, a protracted war with the Seminoles broke out, lasting from 1835 to 1842. The upshot was that most of the surviving Seminoles were forcibly moved out of the area and resettled in the governmentally designated "Indian Territory" of the West (later to become Oklahoma). Those who escaped this fate fled into the vast swamp region of the Florida Everglades.

The treatment of the Seminoles was in concurrence with the federal government's general policy that was enunciated in the 1820s. Namely, the only solution to the Indian issue in the East was to physically remove most of them to land west of the Mississippi and Missouri Rivers. The relocations were supposed to be voluntary, with the federal government assuming the financial costs and giving the relocated Indians a year's supplies. In fact, force was used to accomplish this feat. The Indians in the Southeast (i.e., the Cherokees, Chickasaws, Choctaws, and the Seminoles) resisted efforts to take their lands, but, after President Andrew Jackson took office in 1829, they received no protection from the federal government as local authorities denied Indians legal rights and allowed their lands to be taken over by settlers and plantation owners.[9] Thus, by 1840, most of the eastern tribes had been deprived of their lands and were confined to reservations or moved west. The treatment of the Indians remains a national blemish, but it is not possible to blame particular individuals or groups for what transpired in this formative period of nation building. As the historian Henry Bamford Parkes has written, "it was the mass of the American people who insisted that the Indians had no right to keep their lands."[10]

The larger concentrations of Indians were west of the Mississippi River even before they were joined by the exiled Indians from the East. These western Indians were involuntarily incorporated into the nation as the result of the series of land acquisitions that occurred during the first half of the nineteenth century. These include the Louisiana Purchase of 1803 from France; negotiated border agreements in 1818 and 1846 with Britain, formally making the 49° parallel the northwestern boundary with Canada; and a war with Mexico from 1846 to 1848. Unfortunately for everyone involved, as the settlement process expanded into these regions, fighting with the Indians usually ensued. Treaties that supposedly had guaranteed certain western land areas to the Indians "for as long as they wished to occupy them" were often unilaterally abrogated.

By the 1880s, the Indian population of the entire United States had declined to about 200,000 persons. The vast majority were confined to desolate rural reservations—mostly in the West.[11] Thus, the surviving Indians were forcibly subsumed into the nation's population but largely left out of the development of its industrial labor force during these critical years of economic development.

The African Heritage Population

The clearest exception to the voluntary immigration phenomenon to be subsequently discussed was, of course, the imported black population. Those who entered in bondage from Africa (as opposed to their descendants who were later born in the English colonies or in the United States) were involuntarily immigrants. Blacks originally arrived in the Virginia colonies in 1619 aboard a Dutch slave ship. Because slavery did not exist at that time in the English colonies, these black immigrants were initially treated the same as most white settlers. They became indentured servants who eventually earned their freedom. Sometime between 1640 and 1660, for reasons that are still unknown, these practices ceased, and the policy of treating blacks as permanent slaves began and continued for more than two centuries.

Slavery grew slowly in the South until the 1690s, when the rise of the Southern plantation system caused the demand for slaves to increase sharply. The flow of slaves became enormous. By 1710, it had reduced the supply of white indentured servants in the South to negligible numbers.[12] The legacy of this largely regional labor supply policy was that the white indentured servants from Europe, and their lineal successors—the European immigrants—became the backbone of the workforce of the North and Midwest but not of the South.

It is ironic that the only provision in the U.S. Constitution that had anything tangentially to say about immigration pertained to the importation of slaves. It was the product of compromise language whose inclusion was essential to the effort to unify the former colonies into a single nation after the Revolutionary War. Both Georgia and South Carolina had threatened to withdraw from the union before it could be established if the importation of slaves was banned. The compromise was that the Constitution would permit slaves to continue to be brought into the new nation for twenty years—or until 1808—after which time Congress would have to decide the issue. Subsequently, in December 1806, President Thomas Jefferson recommended to Congress that the importation of slaves be prohibited as of January 1, 1808 (i.e., the earliest possible date). Congress responded in late 1807 by passing such a ban.

This legislation, however, did not actually end slave trading, nor did it have any immediate impact on the institution of slavery. In fact, the demand for slaves increased markedly in the years after 1808. During the 1820s, cotton became "king," and the modern cotton industry of the South began to develop.[13] The number of slaves in the labor force grew from 893,602 slaves in 1800 to 3,953,760 slaves on the eve of the Civil War in 1860. Much of the growth was the result of the natural reproduction of the slave population. Some of the growth—about 40,000 slaves—was the result of the slaves being included with the land in the Louisiana Purchase of 1803. Another 60,000 slaves were acquired by the annexation of Texas in 1845. But the continual import of slaves was also a factor in the continuing growth of the South's slave population. Obviously, no data exist as to how many slaves were imported after the practice became illegal in 1808, but it is estimated that the number was at least 279,000 slaves—and probably more.[14]

In short, slave trading flourished despite the ban on the practice. The agencies given responsibility for enforcing the importation ban (first the Department of the Treasury, then the U.S. Navy, and later the Department of the Interior) all had multiple duties to perform, and the funds appropriated by Congress for patrol of the long sea border of the southeastern United States were grossly inadequate. Nationwide, there was general public apathy about the importance of addressing the slave trade issue, because it was seen as regional in nature.[15] As a consequence, slave trading did not end until slavery itself was abolished. This process began when President Abraham Lincoln, in 1862, issued the Proclamation of Emancipation, which freed the slaves as of January 1, 1863, in those states that had seceded from the Union; it was completed after the war, with the ratification of the Thirteenth Amendment to the Constitution in 1865, which forbade the practice of slavery everywhere in the nation.

The effect of slavery on the composition of the labor force was, of course, primarily felt in the South. In 1800, 28 percent of the nation's labor force was made up of slaves, but 96 percent of the slave population was in the South. By 1860, the slave population accounted for 21 percent of the nation's labor force, with 97 percent of the slave population being in the South. Some of the slaves worked in towns and cities of the South, but most were tied to rural plantations. These slaves worked in a variety of occupations, as most plantations sought to be self-sufficient, but primarily the slave population worked in agriculture, which remained overwhelmingly the employment base of the entire southern economy.[16]

Unfortunately, with the end of the Civil War, the resurgence of mass immigration to the North and West precluded any opportunity for the newly freed black population of the South to leave the region, even if they had been inclined to do so. Most remained in the rural South and became tenant farmers. As late as 1910, over 90 percent of the black population still lived in the South.

It was not until mass immigration was sharply reduced during World War I and restricted in the immediate years following its ending that the black population could begin its exodus from the South. Thus, throughout the nineteenth century and the first decade or so of the twentieth century, blacks were essentially isolated from the nation's rapid industrialization—with its new array of occupations—which was occurring in the North and West. Throughout this transitional era of economic development, blacks remained concentrated in the poverty-stricken South and tied to its agriculturally dominated employment structure.

The Mexican Heritage Population

Another group acquired under terms of duress was the portion of the Mexican population, in 1848, who had lived in what is today the southwestern United States. This vast land area, first explored by Spaniards in the early sixteenth century, had originally been claimed by Spain. But in 1821, there was a revolt against almost three centuries of Spanish rule, and Mexico became an independent nation. During both the Spanish and Mexican eras of domination, extensive efforts were made to subjugate the regional Indians, to establish missions and trading centers across the land, and to link these separate outposts over time.[17] These plans were frustrated by violent opposition from the two most intractable Indian tribes in all of the Americas: the Apaches and the Comanches. As the result of their unrelenting attacks, the remnants of the Spanish settlement efforts that were acquired by Mexico consisted mostly of isolated outposts. The largest of these surviving communities in 1848 were located in what is today northeastern New Mexico (in the Taos–Santa Fe area). There were smaller settlements where the cities of Los Angeles and San Francisco in California are presently situated and in scattered parts of what is now Texas.

As a consequence of the terms of the Treaty of Guadalupe Hidalgo in 1848, which ended the war with Mexico, the United States acquired this vast land area. It extended from Texas west to California, setting most of the southern border of the country. It also reached as far north as parts of present-day Colorado and Wyoming. The newly acquired territory represented a land mass about the size of present-day India (i.e., over 1 million square miles of land). The remainder of this border was set a few years later with the Gadsden Purchase of 1853, which acquired 45,000 square miles of land from Mexico, comprising what is today most of the southern parts of the states of Arizona and New Mexico.

The war had been fought over land as a part of the "manifest destiny" philosophy of the federal government of that time. It was not fought over people, but they were included in the political settlement.[18] By far, the largest group of people acquired in this new territory was the Indians. It is estimated that they numbered about 250,000 persons, and, as Carey McWilliams has written, they were "the real masters of the Southwest in 1848."[19] In addition, there were also about 75,000 persons of Mexican and/or Spanish heritage (with the vast majority concentrated in the Taos–Santa Fe area), who were in nominal political control of the region.[20] Nonetheless, the land having been annexed by conquest, the terms of the Treaty of Guadalupe Hidalgo specified that all former citizens of Mexico in the ceded lands be given one year to leave the territory. Only about 2,000 persons chose to do so. A few thousand others subsequently took advantage of the formal naturalization procedures to become U.S. citizens. The remainder became U.S. citizens "by default."[21]

Many of the Spanish-speaking people in 1848 in this region were mestizos (i.e., they were descendants of a new race that was a mixture of the Indians of the region and the Caucasian Spanish explorers). Unlike the later colonists from England who mostly came to settle in the East, most of the original Spanish *conquistadores* did not bring their families. They came for personal glory, to gain wealth, and to spread Christianity, after which accomplishments most returned to Spain. Consequently, the *conquistadores* did transplant their language, religion, and many other institutional practices to the people of the region, but they "did so largely through the instrumentality of other groups."[22] In the land area later to be taken over by the United States, the Spanish *conquistadores* mixed mostly with the women of the four branches of the sedentary Pueblo Indian tribe (i.e., the Pueblo, Zuni, Hopi, and Pima). It was their descendants who primarily represented the portion of the Mexican population who were incorporated into the United States in 1848.

Due largely to the continuing resistance of the nomadic Apaches and Comanches of the region, there was relatively little new settlement or economic development of the region outside of California from 1848 to the mid-1880s.[23] In the late nineteenth century, however, these tribes were finally subdued by the U.S. military, and economic activity gradually spread. Some people of Mexican ancestry became involved in railroad building and mining development in the Southwest. But, for the most part, the Mexican heritage population continued to survive off the land as a small and geographically isolated segment of the U.S. labor market. It was not until the early twentieth century when economic development of the Southwest began in earnest that immigration caused their numbers to become significant.[24] The vast preponderance of the nation's Mexican heritage population today are, therefore, descendants of immigrants to the United States in the twentieth century.

5

Creating a Nonagricultural Labor Force: The "First Wave" of Mass Immigration

Throughout its first 133 years as an independent nation (1788–1921), there were no annual limits on the aggregate number of immigrants who could enter the United States. It was the period when the combination of a political and military revolution (from Britain), land purchases (from France, Spain, Mexico, and Russia), boundary negotiations (with Britain), war (with Mexico and Spain), and unilateral annexation (of the Hawaiian Islands) established all of the land boundaries that presently constitute the United States. But setting the political jurisdiction was easier than enforcing the boundaries as barriers to entry. Throughout most of this critical period of nation building, the vastness of the land area relative to the actual population of adult citizens meant that there was little that could be done to keep unwanted people out. For most of the period, there was little inclination on the part of public policymakers even to try. It was a time of industrial growth and economic development as well as geographical expansion that was characterized by frequent shortages of all categories of labor—unskilled, semiskilled, and skilled; illiterate and educated; English speaking and non–English speaking.

When the nineteenth century began, over 90 percent of the U.S. population of 5.3 million people lived on the Atlantic slope of the Appalachian highlands, with two-thirds of the population living within fifty miles of the Atlantic tidewater. But the movement west was in progress. The westward movement was further spurred by the Louisiana Purchase in 1803 from France, which added 1 million square miles of land that reached from the mouth of

Table 5.1

Foreign-Born Population and Its Percentage of Total Population, 1790–1860

Year	Total foreign-born population (millions)	Foreign born as percentage of total population
1790	0.5	12.8
1800	0.6	11.3
1810	0.8	11.1
1820	1.0	10.4
1830	1.2	9.3
1840	1.4	8.2
1850	2.2	9.7
1860	4.1	13.2

Sources: 1790–1840: Elizabeth W. Gilboy and Edgar M. Hoover, "Population and Immigration," in *American Economic History* (New York: McGraw Hill Book Company, 1961), Table 6, p. 267; 1850 and 1860: U.S. Bureau of the Census, "Historical Census Statistics on the Foreign-Born Population of the United States," *Population Division Working Paper No. 29* (Washington DC: U.S. Department of Commerce, February, 1999), Table 2.

the Mississippi River to the south, westward to the Rocky Mountains, and north to Canada.

The abundance of "free land" available for settlement throughout most of the nineteenth century also meant that it was difficult to keep significant portions of the native-born population from moving westward. The pioneering of the new areas was chiefly the task of the native-born farmers. Land, in this era, was often equated with opportunity. Indeed, it was the need for an urban, nonagricultural workforce that created the labor demand that set the "first wave" of mass immigration into motion.

The Early Years of the New Nation

From the end of the Revolutionary War until 1820, there was relatively little immigration. Although data are scant, it is estimated that about 250,000 persons immigrated over this period. Most were from the same sources as during the colonial period—England, Northern Ireland (i.e., the Scotch–Irish), and the area of continental Europe that would later become Germany. During this initial phase of nation building, the number of immigrants slowly increased in absolute terms; but, in relative terms, the percentage of the population that was foreign born actually declined from 1790 through to 1840 (see Table 5.1).

Throughout these early years, the nation's economy continued to be dominated by agriculture. Aside from providing most of the jobs, the native-born farm population also provided most of the workers for both the farm and nonfarm sectors until about 1850. In New England, the newly emerging textile industry initially relied on children and women as its source of labor, many of whom originally came from farm families. The lure of available land often made it hard for employers to attract and retain many of the region's native-born young men for factory work.

Although the proportion of the nation's workforce employed in farming increased slightly from 1800 to 1810, it declined thereafter from about 80 percent in 1810 to about 55 percent in 1850.[1] The seeds of industrial diversification and of urbanization were beginning to sprout. New jobs were created in manufacturing, trade, construction, and in various services. Initially, these developments were highly localized and largely restricted to the Northeast and the Midwest. In the contract, the percentage of the labor force employed in agriculture in the South actually increased over the first half of the nineteenth century (from 82 percent in 1800 to 84 percent in 1850).

It was against this economic backdrop that the phenomenon of mass immigration had its beginnings. The historian Marcus Hansen has written that the very word "immigrant" itself dates from 1817. Although the piecemeal process had been going on for over 200 years, the new arrivals during the seventeenth and eighteenth centuries were known as "emigrants" to the English colonies. The emphasis was on the fact that those who came to the colonies had "migrated *out* of something." By 1817, however, the newcomers were being called "immigrants" because they were "migrating *into* something"—that being the new nation that had come into being.[2] It is a subtle but significant shift in wording and it provides support for Stanley Lebergott's contention that, in the nineteenth century, it was the "pull" force of the emerging U.S. economy that overshadowed the "push" factors in workers' homelands and triggered the process of mass immigration.[3]

In 1818, Congress made a crucial decision that would have lasting consequences on how the future immigrant experience would unravel. In that year Congress refused to respond to a petition from the New York Irish Emigrant Society for a sizable land grant of the public lands in Illinois to establish an Irish immigrant community.[4] Other Irish and German immigrant groups had been considering making similar requests to create culturally homogeneous communities. But Congress refused to permit such settlements when it accepted a special committee report that said "it would be undesirable to concentrate alien people geographically."[5] If permitted, the precedent would have been set for the creation of "a patchwork nation of foreign settlements." Hansen asserts that "no decision in the history of American immigration policy possesses more profound significance."[6] For, unlike the fate that be-fell the late Soviet Union in contemporary times, the United States did not try to become a "nation of nations." Ethnic enclaves of immigrants would periodically develop, but the land had to be purchased by individuals and open market competition would determine the results. Such enclaves could not be maintained over time by keeping others out. There would be no spe-cial privileges given to specific immigrant groups to encourage them to come or to stay.

Beginning in earnest in the late 1830s and continuing into the early twen-tieth century, immigration became the nation's major human resource devel-opment policy. The pace of this inflow was almost continual, but the tide of the influx was punctuated by three distinct spurts of mass immigration. Each of these early waves deserves separate mention.

The First Wave of Mass Immigration

The nation's initial experience with mass immigration began in the 1830s. The flow became significant in the 1840s, and it continued to be so until the mid-1850s, after which, the domestic tension associated with the forthcom-ing Civil War led to its rapid diminishment (see Table 5.2).

In order to grasp the significance of the onset of the "first wave" of mass immigration, it is necessary to reflect on only three points. First, the cumula-tive number of immigrants—voluntary and involuntary—from 1607 to the early 1830s had been no more than 1 million people. Second, over this entire time span, while the United States was a British colony and then an indepen-dent nation, it was seldom that more than 20,000 immigrants arrived in any one year. Third, the vast preponderance of those who came prior to the early 1830s had come from two places: the British Isles and Africa. Suddenly, there was a surge of new immigrants to the United States, and they were from ethnic and religious backgrounds that were significantly different from those of the immigrants who had come previously. Their collective arrival was not viewed as a benign development. Immigration quickly became the subject of extensive domestic controversy.

From the mid-1830s until the mid-1850s, about 5 million immigrants ar-rived. As shown in Table 5.1, the percentage of the population that was for-eign born, which had been declining for the first fifty years of the nation's history, suddenly reversed course and began to rise during the 1840s.

Most of the immigrants in this period came from Germany, Ireland, and the French-speaking region of Eastern Canada. French Canadian emigration to the United States began in the wake of a failed rebellion against British rule in 1837, which was followed by a prolonged depression in the timber

Table 5.2

Immigration to the United States, 1820–1860

1821–1830	143,439		1841–1850	1,713,251
1821	9,127		1841	80,298
1822	6,911		1842	104,565
1823	6,354		1843	52,496
1824	7,912		1844	78,615
1825	10,199		1845	114,371
1826	10,837		1846	154,416
1827	18,875		1847	234,968
1828	27,382		1848	226,527
1829	22,520		1849	297,024
1830	23,322		1850	369,980
1831–1840	599,125		1851–1860	2,598,214
1831	22,633		1851	379,466
1832	60,482		1852	371,603
1833	58,640		1853	368,645
1834	65,365		1854	427,833
1835	45,374		1855	200,877
1836	76,242		1856	299,436
1837	79,340		1857	251,306
1838	38,914		1858	123,126
1839	68,069		1859	121,282
1840	84,066		1860	153,640

Source: U.S.Immigration and Naturalization Service.

industry in Eastern Canada in the 1840s. Irish immigration in the 1840s was prodded by a potato blight, following years of inadequate agricultural practices, that destroyed crop production. Famine and unemployment ensued. Thousands died, and many more lived at subsistence levels. Almost a quarter of a million persons chose to emigrate from Ireland to the United States. German immigration was a consequence of a wave of political unrest, attempted reforms, and violent reaction to these efforts in the late 1840s through the mid-1850s. In these turbulent times, more than a million Germans fled to the United States. Most of the Canadian, Irish, and German immigrants were unskilled. But there were also some skilled workers, mostly from England, who came during this time as well. Attracted by the prospect of higher real wages, these were craft workers "whose skills were being undermined by the industrial revolution in England but still in demand in the more backward American economy."[7]

As for the settlement process in the North and Midwest, pioneering was primarily the task of native-born farmers.[8] They tended to migrate westward from more developed to less developed regions of the nation. Most of the European immigrants of this era did not. They tended to settle in the easterly cities or other interior areas of the Great Lakes region. To the degree that these immigrants moved westward, it was a gradual process that usually followed a period of adaptation in the eastern cities. When they moved west, they tended to stay in the towns and the cities.

There were exceptions, of course, where immigrants did arrive in the East and go directly into farming (e.g., Germans in Pennsylvania as well as in territories that would later become Wisconsin and Minnesota). But Lebergott best stated the paradox as follows: "Somewhat surprisingly, the greatest beneficiary of the flow of immigrant labor was never agriculture, though farming was our primary industry for a century or more."[9] Rather, it was work in construction (especially of infrastructure such as building canals, roads, and railroads) in the 1820s and 1830s and then mining, services, and factory work in the 1840s and 1850s that attracted many new immigrants. The result, according to Lebergott, was that immigration generated a "supply of labor to a specific group of industries."[10] This pattern of occupational clustering of immigrant workers—rather than of industrial dispersal—has been an employment characteristic of all subsequent waves of mass immigration.

Immigrant workers were especially important to the cotton textile industry in southern New England. It was the first industry in the United States to become fully mechanized and was the nation's largest manufacturing industry at the time. As already noted, it initially recruited native-born children and women, but Irish immigrants soon displaced them in the late 1830s, only to be largely displaced themselves by French Canadians a few years later. Flour milling, meat packing, and other light manufacturing enterprises also began to develop. The growth in manufacturing enterprises necessitated a machine tool industry, which required iron foundries, which, in turn, required an expansion of mining activities. All of these growth sectors led to expanding demand for various local services. In each of these new employment sectors, immigrant labor played a prominent role.

It was also the case that the public sector was directly involved in the employment of immigrants. It is estimated that one-third of the nation's regular army in the early 1840s was composed of foreign-born persons, and they played a significant military role in the war with Mexico from 1846 to 1848.[11] The percentage of immigrants serving in the various state militias in the Northeast and Midwest at the time was believed to be even higher.

There was also another new group of immigrants, who, beginning in the late 1840s and accelerating throughout the 1850s, entered the United States along its new West Coast: the Chinese.[12] Although they made up only a small fraction of first wave immigrants, the numbers would become significant after the Civil War. But in this period, their importance stems from the fact that they represented an entirely new source of immigrants to the United States. A violent peasant rebellion broke out in seventeen provinces in southern China in 1850 and lasted until 1864. Known as the Taiping Rebellion, its leaders sought to combine politics with religion in what proved to be a vain effort to arouse the masses of impoverished persons to create a more equitable Chinese society. Over 20 million lives were lost and countless numbers were injured. Many sought to flee from the terror and disorder by emigrating to California. The territory of California had been formally acquired by the United States on February 2, 1848, from Mexico, and gold had been discovered there just nine days before. Consequently, its population and labor force needs expanded rapidly. By the end of 1849, California had a population of 90,000 people, and it was admitted to the union as a state in 1850.

The Chinese immigrants were overwhelmingly male. About 41,000 Chinese immigrants arrived during the decade of the 1850s, and most settled in California. Initially, many sought work as miners. Others gained employment in myriad unskilled jobs in service industries, domestic work, and small factories. Despite the fact that most of the Chinese immigrants were from agricultural backgrounds, few were employed in agriculture in California or elsewhere in the West. Accordingly, their occupational transition to the U.S. economy resembled the experiences of the European immigrants in the East.

The Occupational Backgrounds of First Wave Immigrants

With respect to the occupational experiences of the immigrants of the first wave *at the time of their arrival*, the data from official series are fragmentary and the job categories are vague. But Table 5.3 indicates that those who reported a previous occupation in their homeland were overwhelmingly in manual jobs that were largely unskilled—especially in the 1840s and 1850s when the inflow was the largest. It was into the unskilled ranks of the urban labor force that most entered after their arrival.

The Reaction to the First Wave of Mass Immigration

The reaction of the populace to the first wave of mass immigration was anything but benign. The urban labor market in the 1840s and 1850s was rapidly transformed. As labor historian Foster Rhea Dulles observed, immigrants "were available for all kinds of work, more often unskilled than skilled, at wages greatly reduced from anything which native artisans and mechanics considered essential for decent conditions."[13] Immigration, Dulles explained, was for the first time "providing a labor surplus which counteracted the cheap

54

Table 5.3

Percent Distribution of Immigrants by Major Occupation Group at Time of Arrival, Selected Years 1820–1860

Year	Total[a]	Professional	Commercial	Skilled	Farmers	Servants	Laborers	No occupation[b]
1820	10,311	1.0	9.0	10.6	8.5	1.3	3.2	66.3
1825	12,858	1.6	14.3	11.0	12.8	0.5	5.0	54.7
1830	24,837	0.5	5.7	7.0	5.7	0.1	2.9	78.0
1835	48,716	1.0	8.0	12.3	12.6	1.2	5.9	59.0
1840	92,207	0.5	5.8	11.7	20.0	0.2	10.5	51.3
1845	119,896	0.5	4.2	9.1	16.1	2.1	13.8	54.3
1848	229,483	0.2	1.5	10.8	13.8	1.9	20.1	51.7
1850	315,334	0.3	2.0	8.4	13.6	1.0	14.8	59.9
1855	230,476	0.3	6.4	7.6	15.1	1.1	18.5	51.0
1860	179,691	0.4	6.2	10.8	12.1	0.8	17.4	52.3

Source: U.S. Department of Labor.
[a]For 1820–1860 the data include returning citizens.
[b]Includes dependent women and children and other aliens without an occupation or who did not report an occupation.

land and the frontier drawing workers off from the eastern states."[14] In other words, mass immigration served to suppress wages, worsen working conditions, and reduce pressures to shorten work hours so that employers in the East no longer needed to use economic incentives to keep the native-born workers from moving west. An alternative source of labor had been found.

The adverse impact at the workplace was accompanied by deterioration in the living conditions of virtually all urban workers. Historians who have studied social unrest in U.S. cities have noted that the harsh living and working conditions during this period triggered "the greatest urban violence that America has ever experienced."[15] Over this time span, there were at least thirty-five major riots in the four principal cities of the Northeast: Baltimore (12), Philadelphia (11), New York (8), and Boston (4).[16] Anti-immigrant sentiments were frequently the explicit or implicit cause of these civil outbursts. Summarizing the actions of native-born workers at the time, Dulles concluded that "the workers themselves began to protest against immigration as creating a numerous poor and dependent population."[17]

Added to the concerns over economic and living conditions was the fact that the first wave immigrants were mostly from different ethnic and religious backgrounds than most of those in the country from its colonial and earlier years of development. The Irish, Germans, and French Canadian immigrants also brought their customs, languages, and religion (predominantly Roman Catholicism). In the Northeast, these differences contributed to a xenophobic response by the numerically dominant Anglo-Saxon and strongly Protestant citizens of the region. Initially it took the form of verbal and journalistic assaults, but sometimes these led to physical attacks.

It was not long before all of these considerations spilled over into the political arena. Symptomatic of this happening was the emergence of the "Know Nothing Movement" in the late 1840s. A clandestine organization called the Order of the Star Spangled Banner had been founded in 1849. When members were asked about the organization, they used the password, "I know nothing about it" (hence, the unofficial name of the movement). The rise of this organization was a manifestation of nativist sentiment against non–Anglo-Saxon and Catholic immigrants.

This short-lived political movement reached its zenith in the mid-1850s when it went public and formed the Native American Party (which, of course, had nothing to do with Indians). Nonetheless, it "attracted considerable support," as witnessed by the fact that, in 1854, their party elected six state governors and seventy-five members of the U.S. Congress.[18] In 1856, the party actually fielded a candidate for the presidency, who was a former president of the United States, Millard Fillmore of New York. He carried only one state—Maryland, which, ironically, had been the one colony originally founded by Catholic settlers but was by now firmly under the control of Protestant influences. Only the mounting national concern over slavery— which split the party—was able to quell its growing influence. Nonetheless, the disdain for xenophobia should not be used to mask the fact that unregulated mass immigration was exacting a human toll on the economic well-being of most urban workers and, in the process, it was suppressing the early union-organizing efforts that began during these same years.[19]

In the meantime, on the West Coast, the new Californians experienced a similar negative reaction to the arrival of the Chinese workers. The Chinese were perceived as being persons who would work under the worst circumstances, for the lowest pay, yet seldom complain. Consequently, a host of anti-Chinese laws was quickly enacted by the State of California in response to citizen demands. A state tax was placed on all Chinese miners in 1852, a head tax on Chinese immigrants was imposed in 1855, and a reconfirming resolution to enforce these statutes was adopted in 1862. All of these laws were subsequently struck down by both the California Supreme Court and the U.S. Supreme Court, but, nonetheless, they served as a statement of popular ill will.

6

Expanding the Urban Labor Force: The "Second Wave" of Mass Immigration

The Civil War, which lasted from 1861 to 1865, brought economic ruin to the agrarian economy of the South, but it served to accelerate business development in the Northeast and Midwest. Government contracts for immense quantities of munitions, clothing, tents, wagons, and food supplies to support the war effort were an immediate stimulus. Major physical improvements in the nation's transportation system were also made. As labor was scarce—due in large part to the military conscription of soldiers—the higher production levels could be met only through greatly increased uses of machinery. Thus, the industrial boom hastened the introduction of mass production techniques that displaced the extensive use of hand labor. Under such circumstances, large corporations had significant advantages over small-scale enterprises. New factories were built in the Northeast and Midwest, and mining grew rapidly in the Midwest and West. In the decades following the war, these structural changes became continuing trends.

Agriculture in the West also received a similar boost as hundreds of thousands of pioneers moved westward and brought new land under cultivation. The Homestead Act of 1862, which provided that a citizen or resident alien who had declared an intention to become a citizen could obtain the title to 160 acres of public land for a nominal fee after he had lived on the plot for five years, was a major prod to settlement. As was the case with industrial employers, the general scarcity of labor also led to a rapid spurt in the spread of labor-saving machinery in agriculture. In addition, the Morrill Land Grant

57

Act of 1862 set the stage for the promotion of agricultural development in the decades after the war through its support for the creation of public colleges that conducted training and research for scientific advancement in agricultural production.

It was also in 1862 that Congress passed the long-sought legislation for the construction of a transcontinental railroad. The earlier political controversy over the precise route to be taken that had held back this project was no longer an obstacle, as the South had withdrawn from the Union. The alternative Southern route, for the time being, ceased to be an option. Hence, the Union Pacific Railroad was commissioned to build westward from Nebraska, while the Central Pacific Railroad was contracted to build eastward from mid-California. Each company was provided generous grants of public land and loans from the federal government for each mile of track they laid. Most of the actual construction did not begin until after the war ended in 1865, but then the pace of work moved rapidly. The two lines met in Utah in May 1869.

It should also be noted that in 1861, the Morrill Tariff Act raised the *ad valorem* duty on imports to 47 percent—the highest rate in U.S. history up until that time. The immediate impetus for the new schedule of tariffs was to raise revenue to support the war effort, but they also served to protect expanding business enterprises from foreign competition. When the war ended, Northern industrialists who now held power over Congress kept the high tariffs in effect even though the government no longer needed the revenue they provided. Against this backdrop of economic change, labor shortages during the war years spawned renewed interest in immigration. The enticement was magnified soon after the war with the expansive pressures of industrial growth and diversification.

The Scale and Nature of the Second Wave Immigration

From 1861 to 1890, over 10 million immigrants entered the United States (see Table 6.1). Reflecting this surge, the percentage of the population that was foreign born rose to 14.8 percent in 1890—the highest percentage in U.S. history to date (see Table 6.2). The preponderance of the immigration, however, occurred from the mid-1860s (after the war was over) through to the mid-1880s (when the economy slipped into the worst recession period it had yet experienced). The major population and labor force growth of the nation during this era occurred in the north central states of the Midwest (those adjoining the Great Lakes). Their expansion was more than twice the concurrent growth in the Northeast and almost twice that of the South.[1] Collectively, the mass immigration of this time span constitutes the "second wave."

Table 6.1

Immigration to the United States, 1861–1890

1861–1870	2,314,824		1881–1890	5,246,613
1861	91,918		1881	669,431
1862	91,985		1882	788,992
1863	176,282		1883	603,322
1864	193,418		1884	518,592
1865	248,120		1885	395,346
1866	318,568		1886	334,203
1867	315,722		1887	490,109
1868	138,840		1888	546,889
1869	352,768		1889	444,427
1870	387,203		1890	455,302
1871–1880	2,812,191			
1871	321,350			
1872	404,806			
1873	459,803			
1874	313,339			
1875	227,498			
1876	169,986			
1877	141,857			
1878	138,469			
1879	177,826			
1880	457,257			

Source: U.S. Immigration and Naturalization Service.

Table 6.2

Foreign-Born Population and Percent of Population Foreign Born, 1860–1890

Year	Total foreign-born population (millions)	Percent of population foreign born
1860	4.1	13.2
1870	5.6	14.4
1880	6.7	13.3
1890	9.2	14.8

Source: Bureau of the Census, "Historical Census Statistics on the Foreign Born Population of the United States, 1850-1990," Population Division, Working Paper No. 29, (Washington, DC: U.S. Department of Commerce, February 1999), Table 1.

The immigrants of the second wave came largely from the United Kingdom, Canada, eastern Germany, and Austria, and there was also a significant infusion of persons from Scandinavia. The Swedish, Danish, and Norwegian immigrants were fleeing from their homelands due to a combination of factors that included religious persecution, compulsory military service, and stagnant economies. Collectively, there was a common cultural, linguistic, and institutional heritage among most of these immigrants. So much so, in fact, that historian Marcus Hansen has described this human inflow as being "the most homogeneous of all the immigrations to America."[2]

During this time period, the nation's largest employment sector remained agriculture, though its proportion of the nation's total labor force remained virtually constant at about 50 percent. The general employment pattern for most second wave immigrants continued to be one whereby they were employed disproportionately in nonagricultural industries—especially in manufacturing, mining, and service work. Only 10 percent of the nation's agricultural workers in 1870 were foreign born.[3] The Scandinavians (and some Germans) were the exception to the immigrant employment experience in that they tended to pursue agricultural work after entry into rural areas of the upper Midwest. As most of the immigrants were unskilled, they could easily have become the mainstay of the agricultural labor force. But they did not. Instead, most became the backbone of the urban labor force of the expanding industries of the Northeast and the north central states.[4]

There was, however, a significant exception to the general ethnic uniformity of the second wave. It was the renewal of Chinese immigration following the Civil War. Over 5,000 Chinese workers were recruited by the Central Pacific Railroad to help construct the western portion of the aforementioned transcontinental railroad. These workers were joined by thousands more workers from their homeland who sought unskilled jobs in mining, service industries, and small-scale manufacturing. By 1870, Chinese workers were the largest single component of the foreign-born workforce in California. By the mid-1870s, adult Chinese males comprised about one-third of the adult male population of the state. Gradually, Chinese immigrants became dispersed into the local labor markets elsewhere in the West—especially after the completion of the transcontinental railroad in 1869.

But regardless of their country of origin, it was a dramatic increase in the demand for unskilled workers that was the immediate cause of the resumption of mass immigration. There was no need for educated or trained workers, nor was it necessary for workers to be literate in either English or even their native tongue. What was required was large numbers of manual workers, and this is what mass immigration again provided. In every decade through the 1880s (indeed, this pattern continued to 1930), the largest category of immigrants reporting an occupation on entry was that of unskilled "laborers" (see Table 6.3).[5]

Table 6.3

Percent Distribution of Immigrants by Major Occupation Group at Time of Arrival, Selected Years 1860–1890

Year	Total	Professional	Commercial	Skilled	Farmers	Servants	Laborers	Miscellaneous	No occupation[a]
1860	179,691	0.4	6.2	10.8	12.1	0.8	17.4	—	52.3
1865	287,399	0.6	4.4	12.7	7.0	3.2	15.7	0.1	56.2
1870	387,203	0.5	1.8	9.2	9.2	3.7	21.8	0.2	53.5
1875	227,498	1.1	2.2	14.9	7.2	4.7	20.6	2.5	46.9
1880	457,257	0.4	1.7	10.9	10.3	4.1	23.0	2.1	47.6
1885	395,346	0.5	1.7	10.1	7.0	5.1	21.0	1.0	53.6
1890	455,302	0.7	1.7	9.8	6.4	6.3	30.6	1.5	43.0

Source: U.S. Department of Labor.

[a]Includes dependent women and children and other aliens without an occupation or who did not report an occupation.

The Encouragement of Second Wave Immigration and the Subsequent Public Reaction

The worker shortage in the North during the Civil War was so severe that it prompted the passage of the first immigration statute in the nation's history. Business interests sought to find a way to increase the supply of urban male workers, but not of settlers who would bring their families and be tempted to move westward. In response, President Abraham Lincoln, in a message to Congress in December 1863, proposed a law to foster immigration. Early in 1864, the Act to Encourage Immigration was adopted. Due to its unique procedural aspects, it was more popularly called the Contract Labor Act. The law allowed private employers to recruit foreign workers and to pay their transportation expenses to the United States. The enlisted workers signed legally binding contracts whereby they agreed to pledge their wages for up to twelve months to the employer to repay their transportation costs. In addition, they were often induced to sign similar contracts for additional years of work to defray the costs of their maintenance during the initial year. In a real sense, the status of contract workers was quite similar to that of indentured servants of the colonial era. Under these conditions, it was very difficult for free labor to compete with them.

Under the law's terms, private employment agencies such as the American Emigrant Company entered into very lucrative business ventures. In return for recruiting immigrants in foreign countries, these companies were paid fees by both the employers for whom they contracted workers and the steamship lines that transported the recruits from Europe.

Domestic opposition to the Contract Labor Act from existing worker organizations arose at once. In some instances, the new immigrants were used in labor disputes as strikebreakers. When the war ended, the economy slipped into a serious recession that lasted from 1866 to 1868. Organized labor—especially the newly formed National Labor Union (NLU)—blamed the new immigration law for the unemployment and depressed wages.[6] Accordingly, the NLU sought repeal of the Contract Labor Act and was successful in doing so in 1868. Contract labor continued into the mid-1880s, however, as a private sector recruiting method because the practice itself was not banned.

One of the immigrant groups that was particularly affected by the use of contract labor was the Chinese. As mentioned earlier, the immediate impetus for expanded Chinese immigration in the mid-1860s came from their employment as contract laborers on the construction of the western portion of the transcontinental railroad. When this feat was accomplished in 1869, these workers had to look elsewhere for employment.

The completion of the railroad also meant that it was now possible for workers from the East to come west to California. These workers, as well as those white workers already in California, viewed the Chinese as people who would work for meager wages and would accept any conditions of work no matter how minimal or oppressive they might be. Indeed, the Chinese were despairingly referred to as "coolie labor" by white workers who felt deterred from competing with them.

The bitter reaction by white workers against the Chinese workers was due in part to the conditions used by Chinese recruiters to transport many of these workers to the United States, and by the degrading employment conditions imposed on them by local Chinese employers themselves. Many of the unskilled Chinese immigrants arrived in "ships as crowded and filthy" as those used during the earlier African slave trade era (indeed, some of the ships involved in the "coolie trade" were the same ones that had been used after 1808 to smuggle African slaves to the Southern states before the Civil War).[7] Such treatment reinforced the view of white workers in port cities that the Chinese immigrants were a subservient people. The view was enhanced by the fact that "many of the Chinese labor contracts were set by Chinese contractors and were enforced through the informal political systems within the Chinese community, usually unbeknown to American authorities."[8]

Under these circumstances, there was agitation for the restriction of further immigration from China. A number of laws were passed in California and later in other western states to restrict employment of Chinese workers in certain industries. There were anti-Chinese riots in several California cities in the 1870s. As a consequence and with strong support from the union movement, Chinese immigration became a national issue.

The largest labor organization in the 1870s was the Knights of Labor, which had been formed in 1869 and, by this time, had become a national organization. As with the earlier but now defunct NLU, the Knights were convinced that it was impossible for unskilled American workers to compete with unskilled "coolie" labor because most of these workers were obligated by contracts.[9] Indeed, many of these Chinese workers had been peasants who were literally kidnapped, or "Shanghaied," by Chinese labor brokers who recruited for these employer groups.[10] But, in addition, they also believed that Chinese workers simply could not be assimilated into American life.

Accordingly, the Knights began to agitate for the repeal of the Burlingame Treaty of 1868. This treaty formally recognized the right of Chinese citizens to immigrate into the United States on the same terms as people from Europe, although it denied them the prospect of becoming naturalized citizens. The primary intention of the treaty was to open the Chinese domestic market to American trade, as significant immigration from China was already occurring. Responding to the repeal pressures, Congress passed legislation to abrogate the treaty in 1879, but it was vetoed by President Rutherford B. Hayes. He did, however, appoint a commission to renegotiate the treaty, and in 1880, Congress adopted the negotiated changes in the treaty, which gave the United States the right to "regulate, limit or suspend" but not "entirely prohibit" the entry of Chinese immigrants.[11] The adoption of this amendment paved the way two years later for the passage of the Chinese Exclusion Act that was signed into law by President Chester A. Arthur in 1882. It "suspended" immigration of all persons from China for ten years. Subsequently, the Act was renewed every ten years until 1902, when it was made permanent. It was not repealed until 1943 (when China was an ally in World War II), and China was given a minimal annual quota of 105 immigrants a year that remained in effect until 1965.

The practice of excluding specific groups from eligibility to immigrate had begun in 1875 when persons who had been prostitutes or criminals were banned from entry, regardless of what country they came from. By 1882, the list had been expanded to include "lunatics," "idiots," and "paupers." But the Chinese Exclusion Act was of far greater importance than were these selective exclusions. Its passage represented the first significant step taken by Congress to restrict the level of immigration to the United States.

As for the broader issue of contract labor, it required the extensive political pressure of the Knights of Labor—as well as some independent craft unions—to finally ban the practice. To this end, Congress passed the Alien Contract Act in 1885. It prohibited any business enterprise in the United States from financially assisting or encouraging in any way the immigration of any foreign worker to the United States. Organized labor had become openly hostile to prevailing public policies that favored high tariffs to protect industrialists from foreign competition but permitted new immigrants to enter in virtually unlimited numbers to compete directly with citizen workers for jobs. The enactment of the Alien Contract Act (and its strengthening amendments in 1887 and 1888) is also significant because it was the first legislation to restrict immigration from Europe of workers who were capable of self-support. The only way that such a restriction was politically palatable was that organized labor was able to demonstrate that it needed special protection from a definable evil. In this case, the "evil" was the contention that contract labor was an artificial stimulant to immigration used by employers for the primary purpose of undermining the effectiveness of unions to organize workers and to improve their wages, hours, and working conditions.[12] Contract labor, in other words, was distorting the normal operations of the domestic labor market. Under the terms of this Act and its amendments, businesses that violated its provisions could be fined, and any foreign workers employed under such contracts could be deported. Despite this legislation, however, there continued to be violations of the law for many years afterward due to lax enforcement. Laws never enforce themselves.

Concluding Observations

During the period from 1861 to 1890, the process whereby the United States became a nation of employees took hold. Slavery came to an end, the pace of mechanization quickened, large enterprises began to rapidly displace smaller businesses, machines lessened the need for self-employed craftsmen, and local labor markets became increasingly influenced by national employment trends. In this context, the re-emergence of mass immigration affected the size and composition of the nation's labor supply and, once more, became a center-stage issue.

In his study of the movement of real wages during these years, Stanley Lebergott found that the ebbs and flows of immigration significantly and adversely affected the real wages of workers.[13] Subsequent studies by economic historians Timothy Hatton and Jeffrey Williamson confirmed these findings. They estimated that urban real wages would have been 14 percent higher in 1890, in the absence of the surge in immigration that occurred between 1870 and 1890.[14] These wage findings, plus the fact that the nation experienced frequent recessions during this time span (from 1866 to 1868, from 1873 to 1878, and from 1884 to 1886), indicate that the economy was demonstrating signs of having labor surpluses. It is not surprising, therefore, that the nation's fledgling labor movement fought so vigorously to defend working people from the immigration policies of these times.

Rapid Industrialization Expands the Demand for Labor: The "Third Wave" of Mass Immigration

The period lasting from roughly 1891 to the early 1920s witnessed the emergence on the world scene of the United States as a nation of economic importance and political significance. Domestically, the era was marked by the ascendancy of corporate domination of the business sector; manufacturing replaced agriculture as the largest employment sector; the steel industry, which had been a localized collection of independent firms, was regionally consolidated through mergers to become the nation's first truly large-scale manufacturing industry; the internal combustion engine was introduced and came into widespread use (which revolutionized the transportation industry and accelerated development of the petroleum industry); businesses and homes began to be electrified; and the assembly line method of mass production was introduced in the automobile industry. Internationally, the nation successfully went to war with Spain in 1898 and entered World War I in 1917 on the side of the victorious allied forces in Europe against Germany.

The economic accomplishments were facilitated in part by a prolonged period of pro-business legislation by the federal government that was itself dominated and influenced by corporate interests. Symptomatic of this relationship was the nation's tariff policies. Tariffs had been high since the Civil War years. But beginning with the McKinley Tariff Act of 1890, protectionism of American industrial interests simply ran wild as an instrument of public policymaking over the ensuing three decades. Not only were rates raised on existing imports to historic heights, but the list of covered products was greatly enlarged. Tariffs were briefly reduced after Woodrow Wilson was elected president in 1912, when, in 1913, the Underwood Tariff Act passed. But, with the outbreak of war in Europe in 1914, there was scant opportunity for foreign imports to make any inroads into the American economy. After the war, Republicans recaptured the White House in 1920 with the election of Warren Harding, and higher tariffs were quickly reinstated by emergency legislation in 1921 and formally by the Fordney–McCumber Act of 1922.

More indicative of the nature of the times was the spread of anticompetitive practices. As the scale of production increased, corporations began to replace proprietorships and partnerships as the preferred form of business organization. In the process, individual enterprises began to merge to form bigger enterprises so that "by the late 1890s combination became a positive rage."[1] As government initially showed little inclination to regulate business, the free competition that resulted meant there was virtually unrestricted economic opportunity. As a consequence, the business sector itself began to look for ways to control competition for its own self-interest. Mergers were a way to reduce the number of competitors, to restrict production, and to raise prices. The larger the size of enterprises, the more difficult it is for newcomers to enter their industries. The fewer businesses, the easier it is to avoid overproduction and any cutthroat price competition that might otherwise occur. The mergers led to the spread of price-fixing agreements, interlocking corporate directorates of supposed competitors, price maintenance agreements, and price discrimination tactics among the surviving enterprises. Free competition, therefore, did not lead to freer competition. Rather, it fostered oligopoly with all of its counter-competitive tendencies.

It is true that the federal government passed the Sherman Antitrust Act in 1890 as a response to earlier public outcries against mounting corporate concentrations of economic power. But there was no inclination on the part of any of the three presidential administrations of the 1890s to take the law seriously. Indeed, the first application of the law in 1895 was directed against union organizing activity even though there was no mention of the use of this legislation for such purposes when it was being debated or enacted.

In the labor market, however, competition was allowed to flourish with virtually no restrictions. Following the end of the depression era of 1893–97, the "third wave" of mass immigration commenced. The labor supply rapidly swelled. Immigration soared to record levels until the outbreak of World War I interrupted the process in 1914. Still, real wages increased—due mostly to productivity improvements—throughout most of the 1897–1920 period. They did so, however, at a very moderate rate of about one-half of 1 percent (0.5 percent) a year. But for workers and their families, the more important measure was family income. Wage levels were very low to begin with, and spells of unemployment frequently interrupted anticipated income streams. Thus, labor economists Harry Millis and Royal Montgomery found that "probably three-fourths of the adult male wage earners did not earn enough prior to the war to support standard families at a minimum level and many did not earn enough to maintain families at the poverty level."[2] Once the war broke out in Europe and immigration flows were reduced, there were slight improvements in real wages and family incomes between 1914 and 1920. But, as Millis and Montgomery cautioned, "the difference was only one of degree—and certainly not a great degree."[3] The fact remains that the majority of American families during these years lived in poverty, and many more lived just barely above its threshold. Most urban workers lived in miserable conditions in crowded slums, which lacked adequate sanitation and minimal public health services and where disease spread easily, fires were frequent, and general lawlessness prevailed.[4]

At the workplace, conditions were deplorable and often perilous. The standard workday in most enterprises regularly exceeded ten hours. In the steel industry, the practice was to employ two shifts; each worked twelve hours a day, seven days a week. Every two weeks the shifts switched; one shift had a day off while the other worked the infamous "24 hour shift." It was not until 1923 that this industry ended this practice by switching to three 8–hour shifts.[5] In addition to the long hours, there was little concern for the health or safety of workers. The introduction of mechanized work to both factories and farms dramatically increased the hazards of working. Every industry had its unique perils, which included cave-ins, explosions, lead poisons, moving vehicles, overhead cranes, and hand-coupling of railroad cars. The dangers were not just machine related. In 1906, Upton Sinclair shocked the nation with his account of the appalling lack of concern for worker welfare and consumer health by the meatpacking industry as a result of dangerous and unhygienic working conditions.[6] With the advent of the assembly line in the automobile industry in 1914 came an increase in the pace of factory work, which worsened workplace stress and increased accidents. Unhealthy and unsafe conditions were especially acute problems in the garment industry. It employed mostly women and children, many of whom were immigrants who worked in factories often located in tenements. In 1911, the nation was shocked when a fire at one of these sweatshops, the Triangle Shirtwaist Company, trapped and killed 148 female workers.

When World War I began in southeastern Europe in 1914, the U.S. economy was in another recession. As the fighting spread during the summer of that year, immigration from Europe rapidly declined. People could no longer leave. It was not until the spring of 1917 that the United States entered the war. The military draft was reintroduced and 4 million men were called to service.

The hard lessons of the past had taught the nation that wars cannot be fought unless there is government control of production and prices in the private sector. Hence, the easygoing ways of the unfettered free market that had reigned supreme had to be suspended. The War Industries Board was established by the federal government to coordinate the industrial activity needed for war production, to reduce civilian production, and to eliminate duplication and waste. The antitrust laws were shelved. Private businesses were asked to comply voluntarily with the directives of the board or be compelled to do so if they resisted. Disputes between labor and management were settled by mediation and arbitration, not by strikes.

Against this backdrop of government control and economic planning, production soared to heights that had never before been experienced or even imagined. Ironically, much of the actual military production was never used. By the time the economy had tooled up, the war came to an abrupt end on November 11, 1918, when Germany's leaders agreed to an armistice. With no plans in place on the home front for how to demobilize the economy, the readjustment process back to free market conditions became chaotic as shortages of consumer goods quickly fueled inflationary pressures. In response, there was widespread labor strife in 1919. Furthermore, there were signs that mass emigrations of people from the devastated regions of Europe to the United States were about to recommence. But this time, there was a new policy response. A hundred years of mass immigration—as manifested by three separate waves—was brought to an end.

The Scale and Nature of Third Wave Immigration

Shortly after the decade of the 1890s began, the economy slipped into the worst depression the nation had yet experienced. The annual levels of immigration dipped sharply (see Table 7.1). But when a recovery began in late 1897, immigration levels soon rose and the third wave of mass immigration was under way.

The third wave of immigration quickly reached historic heights. Over 8.7 million immigrants entered between 1901 and 1910, and record annual levels of immigrants continued until 1914. During the years 1905, 1906, 1907, 1910, 1913, and 1914, over 1 million immigrants entered the United States each year. It would not be until 1989 that there would be another year when over 1 million immigrants were legally admitted in a single year. The pace of mass immigration revived briefly after World War I, but, as will be discussed in the next chapter, the third wave of immigration came to an end in the early 1920s as the result of legislation.

To be sure, not all of these immigrants stayed permanently. It is crudely

Table 7.1

Immigration to the United States, 1891–1920

1891–1900	3,687,564		1911–1920	5,735,811
1891	560,319		1911	878,587
1892	579,663		1912	838,172
1893	439,730		1913	1,197,892
1894	285,631		1914	1,218,480
1895	258,536		1915	326,700
1896	343,267		1916	298,826
1897	230,832		1917	295,403
1898	229,229		1918	110,618
1899	311,715		1919	141,132
1900	448,572		1920	430,001
1901–1910	8,795,386			
1901	487,918			
1902	648,743			
1903	857,046			
1904	812,870			
1905	1,026,499			
1906	1,100,735			
1907	1,285,349			
1908	782,870			
1909	751,786			
1910	1,041,570			

Source: U.S. Immigration and Naturalization Service.

estimated that, throughout the late nineteenth and early twentieth centuries, the emigration rate was about 30 percent.[7] As the number of male immigrants exceeded the number of females by more than a 2 to 1 ratio over this time span, some immigrants simply carried through with their original intentions to return home to their relatives and families that they had left behind.[8] These immigrants were known as "birds of passage": They came for a while, only to later migrate back to their homelands. Others, who had originally intended to stay, left because they could not adjust to the new society or they became disenchanted with the harshness of American life—especially in the large cities. Some others were deported for criminal activities or other violations of existing laws, as immigration restrictions imposed in the 1890s were being seriously enforced for the first time.[9] Thus, the flow of immigrants over time was far greater than the stock of immigrants in the country at any given time. Table 7.2, for example, shows that, while the number of immigrants counted by the decennial census (the only data available for this period) rose considerably between 1890 and 1920, the percentage of the population who were foreign born actually declined over this interval. There

Table 7.2

Foreign-Born Population and Percent of Population Foreign Born, by Decade 1890–1920

Year	Foreign-born population (millions)	Percent of population foreign born
1890	9.2	14.8
1900	10.3	13.6
1910	13.5	14.7
1920	13.9	13.2

Source: U.S. Bureau of the Census, "Historical Census Statistics on the Foreign-Born Population of the United States, 1850–1990," Population Division, Working Paper No. 29 (Washington, DC: U.S. Department of Commerce, February, 1999), Table 1.

were, however, many more immigrants in the country and in the labor force than the ten-year data reveal. Many individuals emigrated back to their native lands between the times when the population was counted.

Aside from the escalation in the level of immigration, the third wave is also distinctly characterized by the shift in the lands of origin of the new entrants. The emerging trend had begun slowly in the 1880s, but the pattern quickly became discernable in the immediate decades that followed. Prior to 1890, 85 percent of all the immigrants since 1820 had come from western and northern European countries. In the early 1890s, the number of immigrants from these countries began to decline, while the number from eastern and southern European nations increased dramatically. In 1896, for the first time, immigration from eastern and southern European nations exceeded that from western and northern Europe, and the gap quickly widened. By 1910, 70 percent and 20 percent, respectively, of all the immigrants to the United States came from these two separate regions of Europe.[10]

The most numerous of the "new" immigrants came from Italy, followed in only slightly lower numbers by those from the mostly Slavic-speaking nations of Poland, Slovakia, Hungary, Serbia, Slovenia, Dalmatia, Croatia, Romania, Bulgaria, Russia, and the Ukraine. There were also other eastern and southern European immigrants from Austria and Greece. As for their religions, most were Catholics, Orthodox Christians, or Jews. Furthermore, unlike the previous waves of immigrants, third wave immigrants were overwhelmingly from rural areas where they had usually been peasant farmers. Some were from families that were only a generation away from centuries of serfdom. Most were illiterate in their own languages, not to mention in English as well. Typically, they had known only poverty-level living conditions, had no previous experiences with democracy, and knew government largely as an oppressive force. Most of these new European immigrants settled in the cities of the Northeast and the Great Lakes area of the Midwest.

Meanwhile, on the West Coast, a new source of immigrants was evolving: Japan. It was not until 1884 that the Japanese government permitted its citizens to emigrate and to work in foreign lands. It was that same year that the United States established diplomatic relations with Japan, and sugarcane growers (mostly U.S. citizens) on the Hawaiian Islands (an independent monarchy at the time) initiated efforts to recruit Japanese workers for their plantations. Americans had become numerous on the Islands since the 1830s, when waves of Protestant missionaries from New England arrived "to save souls" from contact with sailors from whaling ships and "to raise the moral level" of the inhabitants. The indigenous population, mostly people of Polynesian heritage, was soon virtually wiped out by diseases brought by these settlers, for which they had no immunities. In later years, descendants of these missionaries had established large agricultural enterprises that, by the 1870s, dominated the Islands' economy. After a series of disputes, a group of Americans led a coup d'etat in 1893 against the native government and assumed control of the Islands. They sought annexation by the United States, but President Grover Cleveland, who considered himself to be an anti-imperialist, refused to consider the idea, so the Hawaiian Islands became an independent republic. In 1896, the Hawaiian sugarcane growers entered into a cheap labor convention with Japan to bring a large number of workers to the Islands. Fearing the growing Japanese influence, however, the Hawaiian government, in March 1897, refused to grant entry to 1,174 Japanese who sought to immigrate. An international incident was triggered. Following diplomatic mediation by the U.S. government, the dispute was settled; in the aftermath, the United States annexed the Hawaiian Islands on August 12, 1898.[11] President William McKinley was in office by this time, and he had no trepidation about the pursuit of expansionary actions. In 1900, Hawaii was made a U.S. territory. At that time, 40 percent of its total population was Japanese.

In the wake of these political changes, thousands of Japanese workers began to migrate from Hawaii to the U.S. mainland in search of better employment opportunities.[12] The 1890 census had reported only 2,039 persons of Japanese heritage in the United States, but by 1900, the number had jumped to 24,326 such persons. Many more arrived over the next few years—both from Hawaii and from Japan itself. These Japanese immigrants had agricultural backgrounds that resembled the heritages of many of the European immigrants of the third wave. The Japanese, too, were typically illiterate in their own language, knew virtually no English, and had little experience with democracy. Unlike the European immigrants who typically entered the urban labor market, however, most of the Japanese immigrants sought employment in the agricultural and food-packing sectors of California and a few other western states.[13] Some sought laborer jobs on the railroads or in construction or mining. Unlike the earlier Chinese immigrants to the West Coast, the Japanese did not seek work in the manufacturing sector.[14] As will be discussed, Japanese immigration came to an abrupt halt in 1908 as the result of diplomatic agreement between the governments of Japan and the United States.

It was also in the 1890s and early 1900s that immigrants from Korea first appeared on the West Coast. They, too, had often followed the route of initially working in Hawaii as agricultural workers before migrating to the U.S. mainland. But Korean immigration came to a quick end in 1905 when Japan invaded Korea, made it a protectorate for the next forty years, and prohibited emigration.

The other Asian country that became a significant source of immigrants to the West Coast during these years was the Philippines. It had become a U.S. colony in 1898, after being ceded to the United States in the aftermath of the Spanish-American war of that same year. Given its special status, immigration from these islands began during this era, but it did not become significant until the 1920s. Philippino immigrants, who were mostly men, tended to concentrate their employment in the agricultural sector of the California economy.

In passing, it is of consequence to note that as the third wave of mass immigration from Europe and Asia was coming to an end, immigration from an entirely new source was just beginning to become significant. Starting in 1909 and continuing over the ensuing decade, 250,000 Mexicans immigrated to the United States as a consequence of a violent and prolonged civil war that erupted in Mexico. The extent of violence can be measured by the fact that 1 million people are estimated to have been killed in the fighting, out of a total Mexican population of about 15 million. Many more were injured or maimed. To escape, many fled north to the United States.

Most of the Mexican immigrants of this era were also from agricultural backgrounds, and it was in the agricultural sector of the American Southwest that most sought work. Their arrival occurred at precisely the same time that southwestern agriculture was expanding. Due to the completion of an extensive system of federal government–financed irrigation projects in California and South Texas, vast rural areas in both states were opened around 1910 and the following few years to the production of specialty crops (e.g., citrus fruits, grapes, and lettuce) by private interests. Other Mexicans found employment doing construction and maintenance work on the railroads that were spreading throughout the region. Some worked in mining. A significant number of this initial wave of Mexican immigrants settled in the Chicago area as well, where they sought unskilled jobs in the manufacturing (especially meat packing) and service sectors.

Thus, in summary, a disproportionate number of third wave immigrants came from agricultural backgrounds.[15] As shown in Table 7.3, the occupation of "farm laborers" *at time of arrival* was extremely high from 1905 until 1914. This background characteristic distinguishes the third wave of immigrants from the previous two waves of mass immigration. More important, however, is the fact that the two entry categories of "farm laborers" and "laborers," when combined, dominated by far the previous work experiences of third wave immigrants and documents the fact that the flow was primarily composed of unskilled workers. Nonetheless, most of the unskilled European immigrants sought employment in the urban economy of the United States after their arrival, whereas most of the Japanese, Korean, Philippino, and Mexican immigrants to the West continued to seek jobs in the agricultural sector after entry.

As for the broader industrial employment patterns during these years when industrial expansion and diversification became rampant, it was still the case that agriculture was the largest single employment sector of the economy until 1920. But whereas agricultural employment had held virtually constant at about 50 percent of total employment during the previous second wave of massive immigration (as discussed in Chapter 6), new employment patterns began to emerge in the 1880s that signaled that long-term structural adjustments in that industry were under way. These changes did not bode well for the native-born workers in the rural economy during the period when the third wave of immigration occurred. Namely, there was a rapid introduction of labor-saving agricultural technologies in the 1880s, and the years that followed led to a surge in output that caused rapidly falling prices for most farm goods. In the wake of these developments, employment in agriculture began to decline—first in relative terms and, later, in absolute terms. The 1890 census showed that less than half of the nation's labor force (43 percent) were employed in agriculture for the first time. By 1920, the percentage had fallen to 26 percent. It has continued to fall—with only scant exceptions—ever since.

By 1920, the expanding manufacturing sector had become the nation's major employment sector. During this critical period of industrial transition, the historic immigrant employment pattern continued: The vast majority of third wave immigrants did not work in agriculture. In 1900, only 13 percent of all agricultural workers were foreign born; by 1930, after the third wave had ended, the percentage was 11 percent.[16] It was during this period that the other goods-producing industries—manufacturing and mining in particular—emerged to dominate the industrial employment patterns of the economy. Between 1890 and 1920, manufacturing employment increased by about 150

Table 7.3

Percent Distribution of Immigrants by Major Occupation Group at Time of Arrival, Selected Years 1900–1920

	Fiscal year						
	1900	1905	1910	1914	1915	1920	
Professional, technical, and kindred workers	0.5	1.2	0.9	1.1	3.5	2.5	
Farmers and farm managers	1.2	1.8	1.1	1.2	2.0	2.8	
Managers, officials, and proprietors	1.6	2.7	1.4	1.8	3.3	2.2	
Clerical, sales, and kindred workers (except farm)	0.6	1.2	1.2	1.5	2.9	3.3	
Crafts, operatives, and kindred workers	12.2	15.5	11.7	12.3	14.0	13.0	
Private household workers	9.0	12.2	9.3	11.9	12.2	8.7	
Service workers (except private household)	1.0	0.6	0.9	1.6	3.7	4.3	
Farm laborers and supervisors	7.1	13.9	27.7	23.6	7.6	3.5	
Laborers (except farm and mine)	36.6	28.3	20.8	18.8	15.2	19.4	
No occupation[a]	30.1	22.6	25.0	26.3	35.8	40.3	
Total immigrants, in thousands (000)	449	1,026	1,042	1,218	327	430	

Source: Adapted from U.S. Department of Labor.
[a]Includes dependent women and children and other aliens without occupation or occupation not reported.

percent and mining employment by 168 percent. The corresponding occupations that increased the most in absolute terms were those of operatives and laborers. The need was for unskilled workers capable of doing manual work.

In this economic environment, the paucity of the human capital endowments of the third wave of immigrants was of no great consequence. The fact that they came from largely impoverished peasant family backgrounds, that they had few skills and little, if any, education, and that most were illiterate in their own language, to say nothing of their inability to speak or to understand English, was not a barrier to their finding employment in the growing goods-producing sector. In 1910, for example, immigrants accounted for over half of all operatives in mining and apparel work; over half of all laborers in steel manufacturing, bituminous coal mining, meat packing, and cotton textile milling; over half of all bakers; and about 80 percent of all tailors.[17] Likewise, their presence was disproportionately concentrated in the urban workforce—especially in the cities of the Northeast, the Great Lakes region of the Midwest, and the West Coast. In major cities such as Buffalo, Chicago, Detroit, Milwaukee, Minneapolis, New York, Portland (Oregon), and San Francisco, foreign-born men constituted over half of the male labor force throughout most of this period.[18] Indeed, it was the influence of mass immigration into these industries and urban centers that was largely determining the prevailing wage levels and working conditions. For the most part, the effect was to retard wage pressures and hamper efforts to enhance the workplace environment.[19] It is not surprising, therefore, that the nation's labor movement as well as various socialist political organizations during this time were actively crusading for immigration restrictions for these very reasons.[20]

Administrative Responsibility and Authority:
A Critical Digression

Before discussing the specific responses to the third wave of mass immigration, it is essential to address the more fundamental regulatory issue that occurred during these years; namely, the evolutionary process by which the federal government assumed the sole responsibility for the formulation and implementation of immigration policy. To the degree that the nation ever had an era of open borders, it was about to end. Circumstances were changing—as they always do—and so must public policy responses in a democratic society.

The initial effort to centralize control of immigration was a by-product of the aforementioned Act to Encourage Immigration of 1864 (see Chapter 6). To administer that legislation, a commissioner of immigration was appointed by the president, and he was stationed in the U.S. Department of State. An administrative office was opened in New York City. When this controversial legislation was repealed shortly afterward in 1868, however, these activities ceased.

But the initial retreat of the federal government from any regulatory role of immigration did not mean that the need for direct supervision went away. To the contrary, the subject became increasingly controversial in the states that were experiencing mass immigration. Various states, therefore, began to adopt immigration-related statutes themselves. As could be expected, conflicts and inconsistencies occurred, and a series of U.S. Supreme Court decisions ensued. In 1876, the Supreme Court declared the state immigration laws of California, Louisiana, and New York unconstitutional.[21] States could no longer regulate immigration or exclude certain groups of immigrants. The Court ruled that Congress was the more appropriate body to deal with the subject of immigration. Since then, state and local governments have been placed in the position of responding to the actions or inaction of the federal government in this vital policy area.

Accordingly, the federal government began to place piecemeal screening restrictions on immigration in the 1870s and 1880s (see Chapter 6). But in adopting such restrictive legislation, it was quickly apparent that ongoing enforcement procedures would also be required. Hence, the Immigration Act of 1882 introduced a semblance of control over immigration. The secretary of the treasury was assigned general supervisory authority and was empowered to create state boards (which were filled by appointees by the state governors) to examine would-be immigrants on their arrival to be sure they did not fall into one of the excludable groups established by Congress (see Chapter 6). A tax of fifty cents was charged to each immigrant who entered through a water port, and this money was used to cover these costs of enforcement. In 1887 (as an amendment to the Alien Contract Law of 1885), responsibility for immigration enforcement was formally specified in law to be the duty of the Department of the Treasury, but the actual enforcement of the federal laws was delegated to state officials.

In response to continuing complaints (especially from the labor movement) that the existing immigration laws were not being adequately enforced, Congress launched an investigation in 1888. The ensuing report confirmed these charges by finding numerous violations and circumventions. These problems were attributed to the fact that authority for immigration control was divided between federal and state government officials. As a direct consequence, the Immigration Act of 1891 was adopted, which ended state involvement in immigration matters. It created the Bureau of Immigration (BI) in the Department of the Treasury, and all duties previously performed by state agencies at seaports were transferred to the federal agency. What would become the largest and most famous of the immigrant-processing centers— Ellis Island, located in the harbor of New York City—was opened in 1891. Over two-thirds of all third wave immigrants entered through this single entry point. The legislation also provided for regulation of overland immigration from Canada and Mexico, and it created several more categories of exclusions pertaining to such issues as persons likely to become public charges, persons with contagious diseases, polygamists, and persons convicted of certain crimes. It also forbade the encouragement of immigration by advertisement and provided for the deportation of any alien who entered the country illegally. In 1892, the U.S. Supreme Court upheld the law with its exclusive preemption by the federal government of all matters pertaining to the formulation, implementation, and enforcement of immigration policy.[22]

In 1903, the BI was shifted to the newly established U.S. Department of Commerce and Labor. This administrative shift was implicit recognition by Congress that immigration is primarily a labor issue. Over the next few years, the commissioner of the BI expressed concern over the concentration of immigrants in New York and Pennsylvania and concluded that it would be better if they were more geographically dispersed. He also warned that illegal immigration across the Mexican border was becoming an increasingly serious issue.[23] In 1904, the BI assigned seventy-five inspectors to patrol the 1,945–mile southern border with Mexico on horseback. It was too meager of an effort to be much of a deterrent, but it was a beginning of preventive enforcement. Due to mounting concerns about fraud and carelessness by state courts, which still retained control over naturalization, the BI became the Bureau of Immigration and Naturalization (BIN) in 1906. The state courts still had the power to grant naturalization, but uniform national requirements over the process were established, and all records had to be submitted to the federal agency.

In March 1913, the BIN was shifted to the newly created U.S. Department of Labor, with its dual functions split into two separate bureaus, one for immigration and one for naturalization. This administrative change reiterated the belief by policymakers that immigration is a labor issue, and that immigration policy should recognize this reality.

Public Reaction and Policy Development

With the sanction of the Supreme Court in 1892 that the federal government has sole responsibility for the nation's immigration policy, efforts to influence that policy began at once. Immigration levels had been rising (see Table 7.2) and the largest wave of mass immigration the nation would experience was poised to start. There was still no ceiling on the annual level of immigration, and relatively few screening requirements were in place to cull would-be immigrants.

Various organizations began to press for an immigration policy that had both limits and accountability for its consequences. The American Federation of Labor (AFL), which had only recently been established in 1886, was "among the first organizations to urge such policies."[24] As its founding president (and the most influential labor leader in American history), Samuel Gompers, later said in his autobiography, "We immediately realized that immigration is, in its fundamental aspects, a labor problem."[25] At its 1896 annual convention, a resolution was introduced favoring a reduction in the level of immigration. Speaking in support, Gompers stated that "immigration is working a great injury to the people of our country."[26] But instead of adopting it, the convention authorized the creation of a committee on immigration to make future recommendations. Subsequently, the committee recommended that the AFL press for stricter enforcement of the existing exclusionary bans against the entry of criminals and paupers, punishment by imprisonment of employers who violate the Alien Contract Act by willingly paying the fines when they break the law by recruiting abroad for contract workers, and the imposition of a literacy test (in the applicant's native language) for immigrant admission to the United States.[27]

It was also in 1896 that Senator Henry Cabot Lodge (R-Mass.) proposed, and Congress passed, legislation to require a literacy test for all immigrants as a condition for admission. It was, however, vetoed by President Grover Cleveland. In 1897, the AFL at its next convention formally adopted a resolution favoring the enactment of a literacy test as a means to reduce the level of unskilled immigration.

In 1902, the Chinese Exclusion Act was renewed as it had been every ten years since its original passage in 1882. But this time, the ban was made permanent. It was in this context that the issue of restricting Japanese immigration surfaced at the national level. As discussed earlier, Japanese immigration to the West Coast (especially to California) had risen sharply during the 1890s, with much of it coming by way of migration from Hawaii, which was now a U.S. territory. As the number of Japanese immigrants increased, fears identical to those that had been raised earlier about the Chinese soon manifested themselves in California. The Japanese were also viewed as workers who would work for low wages and who would seldom complain about working conditions, no matter how oppressive they might be. They also were used as strikebreakers. In response, a grassroots coalition of workers in San Francisco pressed in 1902 to have a ban on Japanese immigration included in the legislation renewing the Chinese Exclusion Act. It did not happen, but the issue did not go away. At its convention in 1904, the AFL took action demanding that the Chinese Exclusion Act be amended to include would-be Japanese immigrants. In 1905, a bill was introduced in Congress to accomplish this objective, but it did not pass due to the stated opposition of President Theodore Roosevelt. Meanwhile, petitions to Congress arrived from the state legislatures of California, Nevada, Idaho, and Montana demanding a cessation of Japanese immigration.

The issue suddenly erupted on the national scene in 1906 when the San Francisco school board ordered all Japanese children to attend the segregated Oriental School located in Chinatown.[28] The decision prompted a formal protest from the government of Japan, which meant that President Roosevelt became involved. At the time, he was attempting to formulate a policy to expand U.S. commercial interests in the Far East. Roosevelt labeled the action of the school board as "wicked absurdity," which comforted the Japanese government but did not assuage attitudes in California. Softer tactics were required. The president invited the school board to Washington for direct discussions. At this meeting, he promised to end Japanese immigration in return for the rescinding of the ethnic classification policy by the school board. It agreed to do so. Legislation (although it never specifically mentioned the word "Japan") was quickly passed by Congress in 1907 to stop the labor migration of Japanese workers from Hawaii to the mainland.[29] Attention then shifted to how to stop immigration from Japan directly to the continental United States.

Secretary of State Elihu Root proposed that the government of Japan itself impose restrictions that forbade its citizens from immigrating to the United States. In return, the United States would agree not to enact any formal legislation to exclude Japanese citizens from emigrating to the United States. This face-saving understanding is referred to as the Gentlemen's Agreement. It was finalized through an exchange of diplomatic correspondences by the two governments in February 1908 and became effective at once.

Paralleling these developments—and with third wave immigration well under way—the AFL renewed its call for literary tests at its 1905 convention and did so at each successive convention until such legislation was finally enacted in 1917.[30] Congress took up the issue again in 1906. The bill required literacy in one's native language as a condition of entry, and proficiency in English as a condition for naturalization. Supporters of the bill were unable at the time to pass the literacy test for entry, but they did succeed in making proficiency in English a condition for naturalization (which it continues to be to this day).

Despite mounting public displeasure over the unregulated nature of ongoing mass immigration, politicians were hesitant to address the issue of immigration reform directly. The powerful Speaker of the House of Representatives, Joseph Cannon (R-Ill.), feared that the subject could split the Republican party. He had the complete power at the time to control what issues could come before the House. Cannon's aversion to the issue was shared by President Roosevelt. Not only did Roosevelt fear the divisive effects on his party, but he was also concerned that public debate could disrupt the aforementioned secret diplomatic negotiations in progress to restrict Japanese immigration. Hence, when the literacy test resurfaced in 1906, Roosevelt joined with others to block the move and he lent his support to an alternative congressional proposal that called for a careful investigation to be made into the entire subject of immigration. Most Republicans felt that this would be an effective way to bury the issue.

The Immigration Commission

Although there was widespread public support for establishing a formal immigration policy, there was also suspicion that politicians would not take such a study seriously. Aware of these reservations, Roosevelt suggested a variance from the normal investigative procedures used by Congress. He urged that the study be conducted by outside experts. A compromise was ultimately reached whereby the commission would be comprised of nine members: three from the House of Representatives, three from the Senate, and three outside experts appointed by the president. The plan received widespread endorsement. Accordingly, in February 1907, legislation was passed that created the U.S. Immigration Commission. Senator William Dillingham (R-Vt.) was chosen as its chairman.

During the time (more than three years) that the commission took to complete its work, the American public developed high expectations that a body of verifiable facts about the impact of immigration would be produced, which there would be little to debate and which would serve as a basis for reform legislation. Subsequent reviews of its work have strongly criticized the study's methodologies and its impartiality.[31] Nonetheless, the undertaking was one of the most ambitious social science research projects in the nation's history up to that time.

The Dillingham Commission issued its final report in 1911. It documented that there was a disproportionate concentration of immigrants in unskilled occupations, specific industries, and geographic localities. As a consequence, immigration was adversely influencing wage levels and working conditions in these sectors of the economy. The effect was to depress wages, to cause unemployment, to spread poverty, to breed overcrowded slums, and to make it difficult for workers to form unions.

Subsequent studies have confirmed the adverse economic effects of third wave immigration on the American labor market. Economists Timothy Hatton and Jeffrey Williamson, for example, have found that, in the absence of the large-scale immigration that occurred after 1890, the urban wage levels would have been 34 percent higher in 1910. They observed that "with an impact that big, no wonder the Immigration Commission produced a massive report in 1911 which supported quotas!"[32] Likewise, economists Millis and Montgomery wrote of this era that "labor markets were flooded, the labor supply was made more redundant, and wages were undermined."[33]

Had the Dillingham Commission limited its inquiry purely to the economic effects of mass immigration, it would have supplied sufficient evidence for the need to adopt significant reforms. Unfortunately, the commission also sought to link these adverse economic effects with negative sociological and anthropological attributes designed to distinguish the third wave immigrants from those of the two earlier waves of mass immigration. Using various pseudo-scientific theories pertaining to "superior" and "inferior" races, it concluded that the recent immigrants were "inferior" and possessed personal attributes that would make it very difficult for them to assimilate. The mixture of legitimate economic arguments with dubious ethnocentric arguments has plagued all efforts to discuss and to legislate immigration reforms ever since.

The Dillingham Commission concluded that the nation should restrict the level of immigration, and that a much slower rate of entry was preferable to the high rate it was experiencing. It also recommended that the nation should be more selective as to whom it encourages to immigrate and whom it discourages.

The Immigration Act of 1917

Following the release of the report, immediate efforts were made to enact its recommendations. In 1912, Congress again took up a bill requiring literacy tests for immigrants. The AFL strongly supported the proposal, as did various socialist labor organizations that had taken up the banner of reducing immigration. Socialists in Milwaukee, for instance, openly stated that their advocacy of the worldwide labor solidarity did not mean that they believed that workers in other nations had a right to come to Milwaukee to look for jobs.[34] But the legislation met strong opposition from business groups (such as the National Association of Manufacturers) and lobbyists for various steamship lines (who transported immigrants to the United States). Nevertheless, the bill finally passed Congress in 1912. But when it reached the desk of President William Howard Taft, he vetoed it. Thus, for the third time, Congress had passed legislation to impose a literacy test as a means of reducing the scale of immigration, only to have it vetoed by the sitting president.

In late 1914, similar legislation was again adopted by Congress, only to be vetoed in 1915 by President Woodrow Wilson. In 1917, legislation requiring a literacy test for all immigrants once more passed Congress. It was again vetoed by President Wilson, but this time, Congress voted to override the veto, and the Immigration Act of 1917 became law. Its passage marks the beginning of serious efforts to screen immigrants so as to reduce the entry of large numbers of unskilled and poorly educated job seekers. This legislation also created the "Asiatic Barred Zone," which banned immigration from most Asian countries. Japan was excluded because it was already covered by the Gentlemen's Agreement, and so was the Philippines, because it was a U.S. colony.

The Immigration Act of 1921

Following the end of the war, there were reports from U.S. consulates in Europe that millions of persons were planning to immigrate to the United States. As the actual numbers began to mount in 1920, it also became apparent that many immigrants were still coming from eastern and southern Europe and that the literacy test requirement was not having the expected impact. One reason, it turned out, was that it was possible to prepare people to take the test. In Italy, for example, special schools were established to teach peasants testing fundamentals. As these outcomes became apparent, support was renewed to restrict immigration based on the earlier findings of the Dillingham Commission. In late 1920, the House of Representatives passed a bill calling for a complete suspension of all immigration for one year. In response, the Senate adopted a bill calling for the imposition of an annual numerical ceiling on immigration and, for those who would be admitted, preference to be given to those of western and northern European ethnic backgrounds. The Senate bill was adopted at the end of the Congressional session. But President Wilson, who by this time was seriously ill and in his last days in office, gave the bill a pocket veto by refusing to sign it. When his successor, President Warren Harding, took office in March 1921, he indicated that he had no qualms about the need for such restrictive legislation. Hence, Congress quickly adopted a slightly revised version of the earlier Senate bill, and Harding signed the Immigration Act of 1921 into law on May 19, 1921.

This legislation imposed the first statutory ceiling on immigration in U.S. history (about 358,000 immigrants a year), and it contained ethnic quotas limiting the number of European immigrants from any nationality to be admitted in any year to no more than 3 percent of that European nationality who lived in the United States in 1910. Within this ceiling, about 55 percent of the available entry visas were for immigrants from northern and western Europe; about 45 percent were for immigrants from southern and eastern Europe. There were a few thousand visa slots available for countries in Africa and Asia not previously banned from entry. It is important to note for later discussion that this legislation did not apply to any countries in the Western Hemisphere. Entry from these nations was not limited except for the fact that any individual applicant was subject to any of the explicit excludable categories that applied to immigrants from all countries. The legislation was considered to be "temporary" until more carefully constructed legislation could be drafted and enacted at a later date.

Setting the nationality quotas for each eligible country quickly proved to be a daunting task. The assignment was given to a committee composed of the secretaries of state, commerce, and labor. The process was complicated by the fact that nine new nations had been created in Europe and Asiatic Turkey after World War I, and thirteen countries had their boundaries changed after the war.

The legislation expired on June 30, 1922, but was extended by joint resolution of Congress until 1924.

The Immigration Act of 1924

Despite the fact that immigration levels fell sharply after 1921, the political momentum for the establishment of a permanent and comprehensive immigration policy was unabated. The reform movement was sustained by a groundswell of popular support from virtually every quarter. Protestant church leaders feared that the influx of members of the Catholic, Jewish, and Orthodox faiths was undermining the Protestant character of the nation. Sociologists, anthropologists, economists, and social workers—whose research had lent credibility to the earlier findings of the Dillingham Commission report—reiterated their conclusions that uncontrolled immigration was creating insoluble assimilation problems.[35] Business leaders, for the first time, joined the chorus. Based on a controversial and protracted strike in the steel industry in 1919, they felt that immigrants were infiltrating the labor force with radicals and communists.[36] Extremist groups such as the Ku Klux Klan fanned the emotional flames with worries about allowing more Catholics and Jews into the nation. But it was the AFL that assumed the leadership in articulating the importance to American workers of bringing the days of virtually unlimited immigration to a halt.[37] One of the most articulate supporters of this position was A. Philip Randolph, who was editor of *The Messenger* magazine (which promoted trade unionism and socialism) at the time. Randolph, who was destined to become the nation's foremost black labor leader as well as an instrumental voice of the nation's civil rights movement in the 1960s, stated in 1924 that the country was suffering from "immigrant indigestion" and that he favored reducing immigration "to nothing."[38]

It was within this context that the Immigration Act of 1924 (popularly known as the National Origins Act) was passed and signed into law by President Calvin Coolidge. As enacted, it set the annual admission quota at 2 percent of the number of foreign-born persons of such nationality who resided in the country as of 1890. This translated into an overall ceiling of 164,667 immigrants (plus immediate relatives, who were defined as spouses and minor children) who could be admitted each year. The exact country ceilings were to be determined jointly by the secretaries of the departments of labor, commerce, and state. The legislation did not apply to immigrants from the Western Hemisphere. It took five years of painstaking effort to work out the exact methodologies for setting the country quotas. The use of the 1890 census data was strongly criticized as being blatantly discriminatory against those immigrants who had disproportionately entered after 1890 (i.e., those from eastern and southern Europe). The use of the 1910 census, on the other hand, was criticized as being equally as discriminatory against the nationalities that had dominated the first and second waves of immigrants, as well as those that were living in the country when it became independent (i.e., those persons largely from northern and western Europe). Thus, when the final version of the law went into effect in 1929, it represented an entirely different selection methodology than was originally enacted. Namely, it established an admissions quota system based on the national origins of both the native-born and the foreign-born populations as enumerated in the 1920 census. Each country had a specific quota, and that number represented the same proportion of the total ceiling (set, at the time, at 150,000 immigrants a year) as the proportion of the people who, by birth or descent, represented that nationality in the population as counted in the 1920 census. The only exception to the formula was that each nationality (except those specifically excluded) was assured a minimum quota of 100 immigrants, so the actual ceiling became 154,277 persons a year (plus immediate relatives) who could be admitted.

By including the native-born nationalities in the design of the selection system, the effect was to greatly favor immigrants from northern and western Europe. The calculations totally excluded the descendants of slaves, of Indians, and of most Asians. As a consequence, northern and western European countries received 82 percent of the total available quota slots each year, eastern and southern European countries received 14 percent, and the remainder of the Eastern Hemisphere nations received 4 percent of the quota slots. More specifically, Great Britain alone received 65,000 of the total slots available each year. Accurate statistics as to nationality were not available from the earlier censuses or from colonial records, so the list of names used to compile the actual country quotas was haphazard. The entire process was scientifically "indefensible."[39]

The Immigration Act of 1924 is also informally known as the Japanese Exclusion Act, due to a provision it contained that had the effect of banning all immigration from Japan. The Gentlemen's Agreement had reduced immigration from Japan but had not stopped it. Many noncitizens of Japanese ancestry continued to migrate to the mainland from the territory of Hawaii. During the 1923 congressional session, there was strong agitation from groups in California as well as from such diverse groups as the American Legion and the AFL for a total ban. The language used to accomplish this purpose was cleverly drawn so as not to mention Japan but yet apply specifically to Japan. The provision prohibited the immigration of all persons who were "ineligible for citizenship." Two years earlier, the U.S. Supreme Court had used this precise phrase to rule that persons of Japanese ancestry could not become citizens through naturalization.[40] The United States had unilaterally abrogated the Gentlemen's Agreement. When the law took effect, Japan declared a day of national mourning and humiliation.

Thus, the era of a relatively "open door" to immigration was over—at least for the time being.

Concluding Observations

When the industrialization process began in earnest in the United States during the latter decades of the nineteenth century, the technology asked little in the way of human resource preparation. Available jobs required mainly blood, sweat, and tears, and most workers—native born and foreign born—amply provided all three. The enormous supply of immigrants who came during this time generally lacked human capital attributes, and the same can be said of the native born. Nonetheless, they reasonably matched the prevailing demand for labor.

As one immigration scholar at that time wrote in 1913: "we may yearn for a more intelligent and better trained worker from the countries of Europe but it is questionable whether or not that type of man would have been so well fitted for the work America had to offer."[41] Thus, the supply of immigrant workers of that era may have been highly heterogeneous in their ethnic, racial, and religious characteristics, but the demand for labor was essentially homogeneous in what it required of those who came. Indeed, noted immigration historian Oscar Handlin observed of the third wave of immigrants, "it was the unique quality" of this era "that the people who moved entered the life of the United States at a status equal to that of the older residents."[42]

On the negative side of the equation, there was an alternative source of unskilled workers who could have been recruited to fill many of these new jobs. They were the millions of native-born workers living in the nation's vast rural areas, mostly in poverty. These persons were also lacking in human capital endowments, but, given the types of unskilled jobs that were being created, they were certainly as minimally qualified as were most of the immigrants who became the chosen alternative.

Most of these rural workers were whites, but the most obvious source of surplus labor was the black population still trapped in the South since being freed from slavery. The percentage of the black population living in the South in 1910 (92 percent) was essentially the same as it had been on the eve of the Civil War fifty years earlier in 1860. Indeed, the famed black educator of the era, Booker T. Washington, had made this issue the central theme of his famous speech at the Atlanta Exposition of 1895. He pleaded with the assembled industrialists not to look "to the incoming of those of foreign birth and strange tongue and habits."[43] Instead, he asked them to turn to native-born blacks "who shall stand with you with a devotion that no foreigner can approach" and by "interlacing our industrial, commercial, civil, and religious life with yours . . . [we] shall make the interests of both races one."[44] His words—while cheered at the time—were ignored. It remained until immigration was cut off during World War I before the blacks in particular and rural whites in general could migrate and compete for the new occupations being created in the urban North and West.

Reprieve: The Cessation
of Mass Immigration

The enactment of an immigration policy with both numerical limits and restrictive screening in 1924 put the labor force of the United States on a new
developmental course. Literally for the first time, the nation would have to
depend almost exclusively on its native-born population for its future economic welfare and competitiveness. For the next forty years, the percentage
of the population that was foreign born steadily declined (see Table 8.1),
until in 1965 it registered 4.4 percent—the lowest percentage in all of American history. Beginning in the 1930s, the size of the foreign-born population
also contracted—and significantly so—until the mid-1960s. Thus, this lengthy
reprieve from the mass immigration experience offers an opportunity to see
what the alternative effects of low immigration levels were.

The Short-Run Response to Immigration Limits

When the Immigration Act of 1924 brought an end to the mass immigration
from Europe, past experience would have suggested that the immediate concern would be how the demand for unskilled workers could be met. It turned
out to be a nonissue. The short-run effect of the new law was far less than
could have been anticipated with respect to reducing the annual level of immigration (see Table 8.2). Over 4.1 million immigrants were legally admitted to the United States during the 1920s, with 1.8 million admitted after
1924. The Immigration Act of 1924 did, however, dramatically reduce immigration from most of the eastern and southern European countries that had

Table 8.1

Foreign-Born Population and Percent of Population Foreign Born, by Decade 1920–1960 and for 1965

Year	Foreign-born population (millions)	Percent of population foreign born
1920	13,920	13.2
1930	14,204	11.6
1940	11,594	8.8
1950	10,347	6.9
1960	9,738	5.4
1965	8,549	4.4

Sources: (1) For 1920–1960: Bureau of the Census, "Historical Census Statistics on the Foreign Born Population of the United States, 1850–1990," Working Paper No. 29 (Washington, DC: U.S. Department of Commerce, February 1999), Table 1. (2) For 1965: Jeffrey S. Passel, "30 Years of Immigration and U.S. Population growth," Paper presented at the annual meeting of the Association for Public Policy Analysis and Management (Washington, DC, November 1995), unnumbered chart.

dominated the flow over the previous three decades. But, the law did not apply to the countries of the Western Hemisphere. As a consequence, immigration from Canada and Mexico soared during the 1920s.[1] Immigration from the Caribbean area also increased, as did the migration of U.S. citizens from the island of Puerto Rico (which had been acquired by the United States in 1898 from Spain as part of the treaty ending the Spanish-American War, and whose residents were granted U.S. citizenship by Congress in 1917).[2]

Over 900,000 Canadians immigrated to the United States in the 1920s. Most settled in U.S. communities near the U.S.–Canadian Border.[3] The urban economies of the Great Lakes states, with their large durable goods manufacturing sectors, were thriving during this decade.

Likewise, along the southern border, Mexican immigration, which had started in earnest during the years of its Civil War (1909–1917), continued into the 1920s. The country was still experiencing internal chaos, verging on anarchy in many regions, which continued to produce sporadic outbreaks of violence. Consequently, 459,000 Mexicans immigrated to the United States during the 1920s. The vast majority of these Mexicans settled in the four border states of the Southwest: California, Texas, New Mexico, and Arizona. Much of this region was still in its early stages of economic development. Indeed, Arizona and New Mexico had just become states of the Union in 1912. The demand for unskilled workers—especially in the Southwest's agricultural sector—was substantial. As mentioned in the previous chapter, the

Table 8.2

Immigration to the United States, 1921–1970

1921–30	4,107,209	1951–60	2,515,479
1921	805,228	1951	205,717
1922	309,556	1952	265,520
1923	522.919	1953	170,434
1924	706.896	1954	208,177
1925	294,314	1955	237,790
1926	304,488	1956	321,625
1927	335,175	1957	326,867
1928	307,255	1958	253,265
1929	279,678	1959	260,686
1930	241,700	1960	265,398
1931–40	528,431	1961–70	3,321,677
1931	97,139	1961	271,344
1932	35,576	1962	283,763
1933	23,068	1963	306,260
1934	29,470	1964	292,248
1935	34,956	1965	296,697
1936	36,329	1966	323,040
1937	50,244	1967	361,972
1938	67,895	1968	454,448
1939	82,998	1969	358,579
1940	70,756	1970	373,326
1941–50	1,035,039		
1941	51,776		
1942	28,781		
1943	23,725		
1944	28,551		
1945	38,119		
1946	108,721		
1947	147,292		
1948	170,570		
1949	188,317		
1950	249,187		

Source: U.S. Immigration and Naturalization Service.

need for agricultural workers was spurred by the completion of a massive system of federally financed irrigation projects that stretched from the lower Rio Grande Valley in Texas to the Imperial Valley of California.[4] Millions of acres of previously arid land were brought into production after 1910 and over the following two decades. As noted historian of the Southwest Carey McWilliams has written, "irrigation had more to do with the economic growth of the Southwest than any other factor."[5] The parallel expansion of railroads into these previously remote border areas during these years facilitated both the entry of Mexican workers and the exit of agricultural produce to markets across the country. Thus, "the economic development of the American Southwest coincided with the northward drift of Mexico's population."[6]

The entry of Mexican workers into the agricultural labor force of the Southwest provided growers with yet another cheap supply of hard-working labor that seemingly could be hired for a pittance. By Mexican standards, however, the U.S. wage rates seemed high. As a result, many agricultural employers came to believe that reliable Mexican workers could be hired for considerably less than non-Mexican workers. It is an industry perspective that has persisted ever since.

Agriculture in the Southwest did not suffer the severe contractive effects that other agricultural areas of the nation experienced during the 1920s. In part, this was due to the lower costs made possible by the use of cheap Mexican labor, but it also reflected the fact that the mix of agricultural products in the Southwest was (and still is) dominated by specialty produce. Such crops were less susceptible to the decline in general agricultural prices that occurred during the 1920s in other parts of the country.

By no means, of course, did all Mexican immigrants of this period seek agricultural employment, nor did they all remain in the Southwest. The urban areas of the Southwest as well as some cities of the Midwest (especially the Chicago area) also attracted a significant number of Mexican immigrants.[7]

The Emergence of the Illegal Immigration Issue

Another reason why there was no shortage of unskilled workers in the 1920s was that many foreign-born nationals, who were prohibited from entry, simply came anyhow. As mentioned earlier, from the time screening restrictions were imposed in the 1870s, there were countless numbers of supposedly excludable persons who still sought to enter. Usually they were successful.[8] The major obstacle to enforcing immigration laws stemmed from the existence of the extensive land borders with both Canada and Mexico. The United States had been able to secure some preventive assistance from the government of Canada but little from Mexico. Of particular concern was the frequent use of the Mexican border as the entry point of illegal immigrants from China. Over the years, the problem had worsened. With the passage of the quota laws in 1921 and 1924, the pressures to enter illegally were further exacerbated by the efforts of Europeans who could no longer enter in unlimited numbers. Responding to the pleas from immigration officials for more deterrent measures, Congress established the U.S. Border Patrol in 1924 as a uniformed enforcement agency in the U.S. Department of Labor to deter the entry of illegal immigrants and to deport those found illegally in the United

States. Congress provided funds to hire 450 persons to perform these duties. Nearly all who were originally appointed were chosen from a register of applicants for federal jobs as railway postal clerks, as there was no civil service register in existence at the time for their particular positions.[9]

During the decade of the 1920s, the number of apprehended aliens, deportations, and arrests of smugglers of illegal aliens soared. Despite these stepped-up efforts, many persons escaped detection and were successful in their illegal entry.

The Changing Domestic Economy of the 1920s

There was an even more consequential development under way that rendered moot any serious concern over the availability of a supply of unskilled workers. Namely, the earlier national trend toward urbanization of the population accelerated. During the 1920s, 6 million persons moved from the rural to the urban sector of the economy. It was the first decade in U.S. history in which the rural population sustained a net loss. The historian Arthur Link has called this internal movement "one of the most important changes in the American social fabric."[10] It was a harbinger of a trend that would continue over most of the remainder of the twentieth century. The rural out-migration was part of a long-term decline in the demand for agricultural workers due to the mechanization of much of the work. The reduction in the need for agricultural workers, in turn, led to a diminished need for other rural workers in local support industries. The pace of rural employment contraction was hastened by the collapse of most agricultural prices throughout the 1920s. The depression that was to hit the nation in the 1930s had already begun in these agricultural regions.[11]

The pull factor that attracted the rural workers was the sharp increase in real wages that occurred in these urban industrial centers in the 1920s.[12] In what has been described as "the largest decennial increase up to that time," the annual gain in nonagricultural real wages tripled over the decade.[13] During World War I, the capacity of the nation to produce had been greatly expanded by the requirements of the military. The extensive investments in research and development that had been made by many corporations during World War I began to produce results in the 1920s and enhanced production expansion still further. Moreover, much of the manufacturing sector of the economy was in the process of adopting assembly line production techniques—known also as continuous process technology. Although this major advancement in technology had been introduced in the automobile industry just prior to World War I, it was not until the 1920s that it was widely replicated in other mass production industries, such as home appliances, radios, and machinery manufacturing.[14] As a consequence, productivity in manufacturing rose by 40 percent during the 1920s.

Bearing these developments in mind, it is not surprising that, for urban America, the 1920s were known as "the prosperity decade." The significant increases in productivity and real wages generated an increase in the capacity to consume, which, in turn, led to enhanced employment opportunities. The labor force increased by 6 million workers with all of the increase in employment sustained in the nonfarm sector of the economy. The rapid decline in agricultural employment elevated manufacturing to the position as the nation's largest employment sector. It would retain this status for the next fifty years. Manufacturing employment had expanded in absolute terms during the military buildup phase associated with World War I. But, ironically, during the 1920s, the overall level of manufacturing employment remained virtually constant. The stability over this decade, however, masks the fact that the manufacturing sector was in the midst of considerable flux. Significant employment expansion occurred in the manufacturing of electrical appliances, electrical machinery, aviation equipment, and radios, while employment contracted in other manufacturing enterprises associated with the production of nonmotorized transportation and nonelectrical appliances. The major employment growth sectors of the 1920s were construction, wholesale trade, retail trade, finance, and government. The nation's economy was continuing to diversify in terms of the types of jobs it was creating. It was a period when numerous openings were created for entry-level employment opportunities. It was also a time of extremely unbalanced geographic growth in employment. While the rural economy was floundering almost everywhere, large urban centers in the North and West sustained significant growth and diversification.

As noted, the major source of new workers to respond to the growing needs of the urban economy was a native-born people who migrated from the nation's declining rural sector. By far, the majority of these workers were whites, but they also included a substantial number of blacks. As noted in the previous chapter, the percentage of the black population living in the South in 1910 (about 90 percent) was about the same as it had been on the eve of the Civil War in 1860. Moreover, in 1910, over two-thirds of the nation's black population of 9.8 million people lived in rural areas (almost exclusively in the South). During the decade 1910–1920, there was a net out-migration from the South of 454,000 blacks; during the 1920s, it jumped to 749,000 blacks.

One of the push factors was the collapse of the "cotton culture" of the rural South following the devastation of the cotton crop by the boll weevil in the 1920s. Planters were forced to diversify their crops, but the prices for these new crops generally remained depressed throughout the period. As a result, many blacks were forced to leave the South and seek jobs elsewhere.

It was also the case that, in the period from 1890 to 1920, the South had imposed on itself a comprehensive system of de jure racial segregation (i.e., "Jim Crow" laws), and it was the period when the Ku Klux Klan was reorganized. Life in the South for blacks was both demeaning and fearful.

With the magnetic lure of rising real wages in the nonagricultural industries of the Northeast, Midwest, and the West Coast, blacks in the South joined in the general migration of rural workers to these urban sectors. The significance of the black exodus lay not in its size (which was small compared to the parallel out-migration of rural whites), but rather in the fact that the departure of blacks from the South had finally begun. This trend would continue until the mid-1980s and 1990s when, as will be discussed later, the return of mass immigration to urban labor markets in the North and West since 1965 led to the retreat of many blacks back to the South.[15]

The Actual Cessation of Mass Immigration

It was not legislation alone, therefore, that finally brought an end to the nation's mass immigration experience. It was accomplished with the onset of the Great Depression in late 1929 and its continuance throughout the 1930s. With the collapse of employment, wages, and prices in all industrial sectors and geographic regions of the country, the urban attraction of opportunities for better jobs and higher income vanished. There was even a brief period of movement of people back to rural communities in the 1930s, where they could at least grow some food on which to survive. As shown in Table 8.2, immigration fell during the 1930s to its lowest levels in over a hundred years. In 1933, only 23,068 persons immigrated to the United States. Even the minimal quotas assigned to eastern and southern European countries were not met. It is believed that, in 1933, more people emigrated than immigrated. There were even attempts made by some state and local governments, burdened by high relief costs, to encourage and to pressure recent Mexican immigrants of the 1920s to return to their original homeland.[16] Mass unemployment had replaced mass immigration as the labor market crisis of the times. With a general labor surplus, there was no need for immigrant workers of any skill capability. Workers who formerly held skilled jobs took unskilled jobs, if they could be found, and unskilled workers were bumped into the ranks of the unemployed or out of the labor force.[17]

The Emergence of the Refugee Issue

Despite the significant reductions in the scale of immigration throughout the 1930s, immigration policy itself lost none of its controversial aura. It was in this decade that one of the most perplexing issues to confront immigration policymakers—then and now—first emerged. It pertained to the admission of refugees in the context of a legislative ceiling on overall immigration flows.

Prior to the Immigration Act of 1924, there was no need for the United States to be concerned about how it might respond to the needs of persecuted people who wished to flee their homelands. If they could physically get to the United States, they were generally admitted with few questions asked. But once an immigration ceiling was put into place with specific country quotas as well as specific prohibitions on entry from certain other countries, the era of automatic admissions ended. Indeed, the Immigration Act of 1924 contained no provisions for any exceptions to its terms.

In the 1930s, when the events in Asia and Europe that would culminate in World War II began, there were people in Japan, Germany, and Italy who feared the actions of their own governments, as well as others in neighboring nations who either sensed imminent danger or were already experiencing the effects of actual persecution. Many wished to immigrate to the United States— or to any country that would have them.

The United States, having just ended a century of mass immigration and being in the throes of the worst economic collapse it had ever experienced, was, understandably, preoccupied with its domestic priorities. Consequently, as one scholar wrote of this era, "the force of events are surging the pendulum of public opinion so far in the direction of anti-immigration that, unfortunately, we might say that for all practical purposes we have become opposed to immigration on a selective or any other basis."[18]

To be sure, there were many persons who fled their homelands in fear who were able to be admitted under the available quotas. About 250,000 such refugees from the Axis nations or Axis-occupied countries in Europe were admitted to the United States for permanent settlement from 1933 through to U.S. entry into the war in late 1941. This flow represented about one-half of all of the immigrants to the United States over this time span. Germany was the single largest source country (which had not happened since the 1880s). It alone accounted for 22 percent of the total immigrant flow during the 1930s, but, in all, the refugees came from twenty-one different nations.[19] About two-thirds of these refugees were Jews. More would have come but were prohibited from doing so by the restrictions of prevailing policy.

With regard to their characteristics, the European refugees who were admitted represented a sharp departure from the immigrants of the past. By and large, they were people who did not want to leave their countries under normal conditions but now felt they had no choice. They were not from the rural peasant classes as had been the case with most of the third wave of European immigrants. Instead, they were from the "middle and upper economic classes and included disproportionately large numbers of white-collar workers, professionals, businessmen, and manufacturers. Among the professional groups, the most numerous were physicians, scholars, and scientists."[20] It is not surprising, therefore, that the occupations cited by these immigrants of this period showed "professional, managers and administrators" to be the most dominant group—the highest percentage, in fact, in U.S. immigration history up until this time—while those citing "laborers" as their occupation were the least dominant group (see Table 8.3 and compare with Tables 6.3 and 7.3). Moreover, "most of the refugees were from the larger cities rather than rural villages and towns . . . and were comparatively well educated, many having attended or been graduated from universities, colleges, or professional or technical schools."[21]

In a real sense, the European refugees of this era were an aberration with respect to their human capital endowments, compared to those of either previous or subsequent immigrant flows. The refugees who were admitted in the 1930s and 1940s (and, as will be discussed, in the 1950s, too) came at a time when the overall immigration levels were low. This smallness of numbers magnifies the disproportionately high incidence of levels of human capital characteristics of the immigrants of these years over those who immigrated before or since. Consequently, econometric studies that neglect to note explicitly the unique historical circumstances of this period when they draw comparisons about the qualitative attributes between these immigrants flows and the post-1960s immigrant flows are distorting the picture of what public policy sought to accomplish.[22] One could mistakenly conclude that the prevailing "national origins" system of that era was responsible for the high human capital characteristics of the immigrant flows of these decades when, in fact, it had virtually nothing to do with these results in any causative sense. These refugees did not come to the United States because they planned to do so, but, rather, because they feared persecution. In every sense, most were "involuntary immigrants" from their homelands. Prevailing policy, if it did anything, served to restrict the number who came. It certainly did not encourage them to come.

The War Years: Eliminating Labor Surplus and Creating New Opportunities

As the world events that eventually led the United States into World War II unfolded, the country began to take preemptive steps. In mid-1940, President Franklin Roosevelt began rearming the nation. Various committees were established to plan for the possible conversions of domestic industries to military production and for the enlargement of the military services. In the latter months

Table 8.3

Percent Distribution of Immigrants by Major Occupation Group at Time of Arrival, Selected Years 1930–1965

	Fiscal year								
	1930	1933	1935	1940	1945	1946	1950	1955	1965
Professional, technical, and kindred workers	3.6	7.0	6.4	9.6	7.5	5.7	8.2	5.9	9.7
Farmers and farm managers	3.5	1.3	1.7	1.2	1.3	0.9	7.1	1.9	1.0
Managers, officials, and proprietors	1.9	3.0	3.9	10.5	3.8	3.3	2.6	2.2	2.4
Clerical, sales, and kindred workers (except farm)	6.0	2.6	2.9	6.2	9.7	7.7	6.7	7.6	10.0
Crafts, operatives, and kindred workers	13.4	7.9	7.7	8.1	11.8	8.1	16.6	14.4	10.7
Private household workers	12.0	2.4	4.1	4.1	3.9	2.3	3.6	5.0	3.3
Service workers (except private household)	2.8	4.0	4.0	1.3	2.7	2.0	2.0	2.7	3.6
Farm laborers and supervisors	5.7	0.6	1.2	0.4	0.6	0.2	1.6	2.3	1.0
Laborers (except farm and mine)	7.5	3.8	3.9	3.0	2.3	1.4	2.3	7.4	2.9
No occupation[a]	43.7	67.4	64.3	55.7	56.2	68.5	49.3	50.7	55.9
Total immigrants, in thousands (000)	242	23	35	71	38	109	249	238	297

Source: Adapted from U.S. Department of Labor.
[a]Includes dependent women and children and other aliens without occupation or occupation not reported.

of 1940, funds were appropriated by Congress to accumulate strategic resources, and the military draft was reintroduced. Most citizens sympathized with the victims of the aggression by Germany, Italy, and Japan. But it was not until after Japan attacked Pearl Harbor, Hawaii, on December 7, 1941, when the nation actually declared war with Japan and, four days later, with Italy and Germany, that the full-scale war mobilization of the economy commenced.

It was fortunate, in a way, that the massive increase in the demand for labor associated with rearmament occurred at a time when there was still a significant backlog of unemployed citizens from the lingering effects of the depression. In 1940, the unemployment rate for the year was 14.6 percent (or 8.1 million unemployed workers). Even a year later, in 1941, the unemployment rate for the year was 9.9 percent, with 5.5 million workers still unemployed. With unemployment this high, the transition to all-out war production was accomplished with far less strain than would have been the case if every needed worker and soldier had to be taken from the ranks of the employed civilian workforce. Nonetheless, labor shortages quickly developed for particular kinds of jobs and in particular geographic areas.

On the military front, about 18 million men between the ages of eighteen and thirty-five years old were screened for the military draft, and about 11.4 million were actually accepted during the war years. About 700,000 draftees were rejected because they were illiterate; another 600,000 were taken into the military but put into special training programs to achieve literacy before they could actually be trained for combat. Still another 700,000 servicemen were inducted but classified as being on the borderline of literacy (e.g., they could sign their names but they could not write a letter).[23]

Of those who were drafted or enlisted, about 60 percent were employed at the time they were inducted or, under normal circumstances, would have been employed in the civilian employment sector.[24] Not only did they have to be replaced, but, with the dramatic expansion of military production needed to support the war effort, additional sources of home front workers had to be found. President Roosevelt created the War Manpower Commission in April 1942, which, in conjunction with the U.S. Employment Service, was responsible for recruiting workers in areas of labor surplus, advising and aiding them in relocating in areas of labor shortages, and placing workers in the most highly skilled jobs for which they were qualified.

Despite the massive withdrawal of millions of men and thousands of women from the civilian labor force to enter the armed forces, the civilian labor force still expanded by over 5 million workers over the course of the war years. This remarkable feat was accomplished by tapping existing domestic reserves that, in the past, had been ignored, underutilized, or arbitrarily prevented from exercising or developing their employment potential.

The farm sector, which during the 1930s had briefly reversed its downward slide in employment of the 1920s and had grown over the decade, was an obvious source of underutilized human resources. During the war years of the 1940s, farm employment declined by over 1 million workers, while nonfarm civilian employment grew by over 6 million workers. The percentage of the population living in rural areas declined from 43.4 percent in 1940 to 40.4 percent in 1950. Speaking of the workings of the domestic labor market, one labor economist observed, "the vacuum created by the wartime demands was sufficient to reach into the most backward areas."[25] The rural South proved to be an especially fruitful source of workers, and blacks were especially responsive to the new employment opportunities. Indeed, during the decade of the 1940s, there was a net out-migration of 1.6 million blacks from the South to the urban areas of the North and the West Coast.

Special efforts were also made to encourage older workers to defer retirement, or to entice them back to employment on a full- or part-time basis. Likewise, national programs were initiated to assist handicapped workers to be prepared for jobs and to find jobs. Legal exceptions were also made to allow youth, under certain circumstances, to work in industries from which they had been barred during peacetime.

But the major new source of labor reserves to be brought into the paid labor force was women. Over 6 million women were employed during this period—about 4 million of whom were added during the war years. The major change in labor force behavior came with the entry of married women in general and white married women in particular into the civilian labor force. Black married women had already been in the labor force in disproportionate numbers relative to white married women. While many women were employed in entry-level occupations, it is also true that many old stereotypes about what types of jobs women could do or could not do were quickly put aside. Among these were notions that women should not work in factory occupations, in occupations where men were the major proportion of the workers, or in jobs that required arduous physical exertion. "Rosy the Riveter" became a popular national symbol of the patriotic contribution of women to the war effort. It was not a phrase of derision. The roots of the social revolution involving women workers in the workplace that was to explode on the American scene in the 1970s (and continue since) can be traced directly to the precedents established in the 1940s.

It was also in this context that significant public policy steps were initiated to attack the issue of racial discrimination in employment. As Ray Marshall has written, "despite years of hostile racial discrimination by employers and unions, until the Second World War America's governments generally adopted very few measures to counteract discrimination in employment."[26] But when the prospect of war became a reality, tightening labor markets opened up opportunities for government to address this long-neglected aspect of American life. These pioneering governmental initiatives of the 1940s paved the way for the passage of the Civil Rights Act of 1964 with its historic Title VII (i.e., the equal employment provisions) that would come a generation later.

At the federal level, President Roosevelt in September 1940 publicity condemned employment discrimination. This public rebuke of prevailing attitudes and practices was not effective in changing practices. But the following year, on June 12, 1941, Roosevelt issued the President's Nondiscrimination Order, in which he advised industry "to take the initiative in opening doors to all loyal and qualified workers regardless of race, national origin, religion, or color." This action is regarded as "a milestone" in the history of equal employment opportunity.[27]

Black leaders, who had been pressuring the president to act on this issue, were not satisfied with this gesture. A. Philip Randolph, the president of the Brotherhood of Sleeping Car Porters union and a pioneer civil rights leader, stated that far stronger steps were required. He initiated plans for a protest march on Washington to force stronger action. As the leaders of the nation were openly criticizing the rise of Nazism, in part for its avowal of racial superiority principles, it would have been a source of national embarrassment if the same charges were made of racial practices in the United States. Consequently, President Roosevelt issued Executive Order 8802 on July 25, 1941, which created a federal Committee on Fair Employment Practices (FEP). It was empowered to investigate employment discrimination in defense industries. Because there was a conservative coalition of Southern Democrats and Northern Republicans in Congress who were adamantly opposed to any legislative action in this area, there was no way at the time to pass any legislation at the federal level to address this issue. Consequently, the steps taken by the president were as strong as possible at the time.

This original FEP committee met widespread resistance as it sought to engineer social change. Indeed, the entire membership of the committee resigned in January 1943 in protest of the resistance it encountered. They were replaced in June 1943 by a new committee with a stronger mandate as the result of the issuance of another executive order on the subject. This second FEP committee also met defiance, especially by the companies and unions in the railroad industry, but it also had a number of important pioneering successes. There were also numerous changes in employment practices undertaken voluntarily by the private sector during this period of tight labor markets. When the war ended, congressional opponents succeeded in killing the federal FEP committee by cutting off its funding. In the immediate postwar years, however, twenty-four states (all in the North and West) passed FEP laws.

Thus, the era of labor shortages did have the positive effect of at least opening the door for wider job opportunities for racial minorities even though the issue of employment discrimination itself was still far from resolved. The labor shortages of the World War II period and the lack of an immigrant alternative provided the leverage needed to launch the economic plank (i.e., the equal employment opportunity goal) of the broader civil rights agenda that would later come to a head as a full-scale movement in the late 1950s and early 1960s.

Thus, on the domestic front, the World War II era was a period of full employment. Labor shortages forced the nation to reach out to segments of the population that had not been previously encouraged to work and to members of the labor force who had been hitherto underutilized or denied opportunities to use and develop their latent human resource abilities. It is true that this task of providing labor market access and opportunities to these subgroups—most of whom were untrained and poorly educated—was greatly facilitated by the nature of most of the jobs that were created. Continuous process production remained the basic technology of the era. The military needed vast amounts of standardized products. Steel and wheeled vehicles were the backbone of the military procurement requirements. It was the automobile industry that was the dominant manufacturer of the metal products required by the war effort, and it manufactured these items in almost limitless quantities. Thus, Detroit became "the greatest center of war production."[28] But there was also the need for mass produced items such as uniforms, food, tents, armaments, and aircraft. Hence, other established industrial centers in parts of the Northeast, Midwest, and West Coast also became deeply involved in war production. Normally, the factories previously used to make civilian goods were converted to production of military goods, but new factory construction also occurred on a huge scale.

Thus, it was the manufacturing industry that sustained the largest increase in employment during the war years. At its high point in 1944, manufacturing had added over 6 million jobs over its employment level in 1940. With over 17 million workers in 1944, manufacturing accounted for 41 percent of the employed nonagricultural labor force of the nation. Prior to this period, the manufacturing sector had not experienced any net increase in employment since the 1917–18 era (i.e., since World War I). The other goods-producing industries—mining and construction—both sustained absolute decreases in employment during this war period.

Most of the occupations that sustained the greatest growth in the manufacturing industry during the period were in the unskilled and semiskilled job categories. While it is true that there were significant advances made in public and private training initiatives, and there were extensive efforts made by employers to redesign job requirements so less skilled workers could do them, it remained the case that the applicable technology in manufacturing did not require extensive education, training, or literacy from most of its workforce. Indeed, the motto of the job recruiters of the Detroit manufacturers who were sent into the rural South during these years for the first time has become legendary: "If he or she is warm and breathing, we hire them." Job credentials could not get any lower. Moreover, most of these manufacturing jobs were unionized and provided good wages, job protection, and fringe benefit packages. They were among the best available jobs for blue-collar workers anywhere in the nation.

The tight labor markets of the war years forced employers and government to look inward to the nation's domestic population and labor force for workers. Market pressures, combined with creative employment policies by the private sector and assisted by a strong prod from the public sector to abandon artificial barriers to employment, proved that there was a viable alternative to mass immigration as a means to find workers in a growing economy.

A Fateful Wartime Shift in the Administration of Immigration Policy

The advent of World War II also served as a pretext for a critical shift in the administrative responsibility for the nation's immigration policy. It has had lasting consequences. As noted in the previous chapter, immigration policy was assigned to the U.S. Department of Labor (DOL) when this agency was created as an independent entity in 1913. The two immigration functions—administering the immigration laws and supervising the naturalization of aliens—were performed by two separate bureaus within the DOL. On June 10, 1933, President Roosevelt issued Executive Order 6166, which combined both functions into a single agency known until 2003 (see Chapter 2) as the Immigration and Naturalization Service (INS). It remained within the U.S. Department of Labor.

By the late 1930s, however, the relationship of immigration to the welfare of U.S. society had come under close scrutiny for a new reason. The prospect of U.S. involvement in a war in Europe raised concern that immigration might be a way for enemy saboteurs and subversive elements to enter the country. Hence, a fateful short-run decision that has had lasting long-run consequences was initiated. On May 20, 1940, President Roosevelt recommended to Congress that the INS be shifted from the Department of Labor to the Department of Justice as part of the President's Reorganization Plan No. V.[29] He urged that "quick action" be taken on his request.[30] On June 14, 1940, Congress approved the transfer.[31] In his message to Congress, President Roosevelt stated:

> In normal times much can be said for the retention of the Bureau [sic] of Immigration and Naturalization in the Department of Labor where it has long resided. . . . Today however, the nation is confronted with matters relating to aliens in our midst. It is more than necessary to exercise, for national safety, certain measures and controls over aliens, which are not demanded in normal days.[32]

In subsequently published background papers, the specific rationale was explained as follows:

> The Immigration and Naturalization Service was originally placed within the Department of Labor because of the historical reason that it was, formerly, mostly concerned with problems pertinent to American labor.
>
> In recent years, however, there has arisen a dangerous threat from abroad in the form of the fifth column and other activities. It seemed expedient, therefore, to transfer the Immigration and Naturalization Service, to the Department of Justice in order to cope with this danger, as a matter of national defense.[33]

It is of consequence to note that the original draft of this presidential message concluded with the following sentence, which the president crossed out in his own writing before issuing the formal message: "After these days of emergencies have passed, the Congress can and should, of course, consider whether the Bureau [sic] of Immigration and Naturalization should remain in the Department of Justice or be returned to the jurisdiction of the Department of Labor."[34]

In the place of this sentence, a sentence is written in his own handwriting in which President Roosevelt simply urges "quick action" on his recommendation. Why Roosevelt struck out the above sentence is unknown. It may have been that he just wished to shorten the message and not raise the issue of later reflection on the wisdom of the decision. It is known, however, that Attorney General Robert H. Jackson opposed the idea of making this shift to his agency and that the Bureau of the Budget was not consulted about the actual change until after it was about to be made public.[35] Secretary of Labor Frances Perkins, however, strongly favored the move. As she wrote in her autobiography:

> I had been recommending for five years that the Immigration Service be taken out of the Department of Labor and put in some more appropriate place. During the war the opportunity came to do this. Because the main

problems of immigration during the war period were the recognition and apprehension of spies and foreign agents, it seemed appropriate to move it to the Department of Justice near the FBI. The Immigration Service had for many years swamped the Labor Department. Immigration problems usually have to be decided in a few days. They involve human lives. There can be no delaying. In almost every administration the Secretary and his principal assistant had functioned chiefly in the immigration field. That is, I think, one of the reasons there had been, until the New Deal, so much neglect of the true function of the Labor Department.[36]

Apparently, it was the work burden placed on her agency that caused her to favor this critical administrative change. She suggests that immigration functions were overshadowing the chronic need for the Department of Labor to address the urgent issues of unemployment, collective bargaining, and work standards that were confronting the nation's labor force. Nonetheless, she felt the Department of Justice was not the appropriate permanent home for this vital responsibility, as indicated by her following retrospective thoughts:

The President decided to transfer the Immigration Service to Justice for the duration of the war. Whether that is the appropriate place for it in years to come has not been decided. I doubt that it is. It deals with human affairs and, I should say, is more properly related to the Federal Security Agency or the Department of the Interior. It should not be a permanent function of the Labor Department or the Department of Justice, and certainly not of the FBI.[37]

When the war ended, however, there was no effort made to return the INS to the DOL or to shift it anywhere else. It remained in the Department of Justice until 2003.

There are multiple reasons why the Department of Justice was an inappropriate agency to oversee immigration policy. To begin with, the Department of Justice had a multiplicity of major governmental divisions (e.g., criminal justice, civil rights, and antitrust), all pleading for attention from the U.S. attorney general. In this context, immigration matters tended to be neglected or relegated to a low order of priority. Moreover, the Department of Justice is the most politically sensitive of all federal agencies. When confronted with difficult decisions, it often looks for politically expedient solutions that overlook long-term consequences. With regard to immigration matters, this agency seldom manifested interest in the economic effects of immigration policy, and it never saw fit to establish any ongoing research program to monitor the influences of immigration on the labor market or the economy.

An important ancillary administrative consequence of the shift of the INS to the Justice Department was that the Senate and House judiciary committees gained the responsibility for formulating immigration policy and for overseeing immigration affairs. Traditionally, membership on these committees has been reserved almost exclusively for lawyers. The result is that immigration law in the United States has become obsessively complex and procedurally protracted. It also has meant that immigration lawyers and consultants have found a flourishing business—a "honey pot"—in the intricacies of immigration law. In this legalistic atmosphere that typically focuses on individual situations, the broader economic considerations that affect the collective welfare of society have seldom become a concern.

The Wartime Exception: The Use of Foreign Workers in Agriculture and Its Postwar Legacy

With the approach of World War II, growers in the Southwest anticipated that there would be a worker shortage in the region's labor intensive agricultural industry. Even before the Pearl Harbor attack, growers had begun to lobby the federal government to meet their anticipated needs by allowing them to tap the supply of cheap farm labor available in Mexico.[38] A precedent had been set during World War I whereby the federal government had authorized such a temporary worker program. The growers were optimistic that a request for a similar program would be approved if they agitated for it.[39] Their initial petition, however, was denied in 1941, but the next year, the government reversed its position in the wake of changing world events. In August 1942, following bilateral negotiations between the governments of the United States and Mexico, legislation was adopted that created the Mexican Labor Program. It is more popularly known as "the bracero program" (a term that literally means "one who works with his arms"; the word is a corruption of the Spanish word *brazos*, which means "arms").

The grower argument was that, with both the military draft and the expansion of the nation's manufacturing sector to fill war contracts, the southwestern agriculture industry could not retain or attract a sufficient number of unskilled workers to feed the nation. It is of consequence to note that the legislation that authorized the program, Public Law (P.L.) 45, was part of an omnibus appropriation bill. It was not an amendment to the nation's immigration statutes. Indeed, the recruited workers were not immigrants—they were workers who were legally allowed to be employed temporarily in the United States even though they were foreign nationals. After the planting and harvest seasons were over each year, they were expected to return to Mexico. In the case of the braceros, they could work only in agricultural jobs. The legislation specified that they were to be afforded specific protection with respect to transportation, housing, meals, medical care, and wage rates. P.L. 45 authorized the program's continuance until the war ended. It was subsequently extended by law for two more years until 1947 and was continued informally, without regulation, until 1951, when it was again formally reauthorized during the Korean Conflict by P.L. 78. This law, in turn, was extended, after the war ended in 1953, on three separate occasions by Congress, until it was finally terminated unilaterally by the United States at the end of 1964. Thus, what was supposed to be a temporary wartime measure ended up lasting twenty-two years. Indeed, the years in which it had the largest number of participants—when it was averaging almost half a million farm workers a year in the late 1950s—were years when peace prevailed.[40]

Without going into a prolonged discussion on this controversial program, it is important to note that the program was continually immersed in charges that U.S. employers did not honor their commitments. They did employ the Mexican workers, but they often ignored or circumvented the labor protection and wage rate provisions.[41] The workers were exploited. There were also numerous charges of corruption—in the form of kickbacks and favoritism—in the selection process of workers by government officials in Mexico before they got to the United States.

The extension of the bracero program beyond the dates of its original mission as a temporary wartime measure resulted in its becoming a subject of extensive political controversy. The availability of bracero workers exerted a narcotic effect on the agricultural employers of the Southwest. They became addicted to cheap Mexican labor that entered under contractual terms that bound the braceros to work for them or be returned directly to their homeland. The effects of the bracero program on citizen workers were the reduction of agricultural worker wage levels in some localities where they competed, the moderation of wage increases that would have occurred in the program's absence, and the shortening of the duration of seasonal employment, which reduced citizen worker incomes.[42] In essence, the program functioned as a public subsidy to the private agricultural sector. For this reason, its continuance after the war years spawned protracted criticism from various Mexican-American citizen groups and an array of other organizations that were empathetic with the plight of low-income citizen workers in rural areas. It was not until the Kennedy administration took office, in 1961, that sufficient political support could be garnered to terminate the program. In response to a plea from the Mexican government, it was agreed to phase out the program gradually. On December 31, 1964, it ceased to exist. But, as will be explained later, the program exposed hundreds of thousands of impoverished rural Mexican workers to the U.S. labor market. When the program ended, its effects did not. Many former braceros simply kept coming—albeit as illegal immigrants.[43]

Paralleling the Mexican Labor Program in the Southwest was a similar program known as the British West Indies (BWI) program along the East Coast. Also initiated as a temporary wartime measure, it was the product of intergovernmental agreements negotiated between the United States and Jamaica, the Bahamas, St. Lucia, St. Vincent, Dominica, and Barbados that were signed in April 1943. The BWI program was also created in response to concerns voiced by employers in East Coast states that they, too, were experiencing labor shortages for unskilled workers—especially in agriculture. But as these employers were generally unfamiliar with Spanish, they needed English-speaking workers. The surplus of black workers on the islands of the BWI provided a convenient labor supply to tap.

Originally, the BWI program was authorized under the same legislation as the bracero program, namely, P.L. 45. But when P.L. 45 ended in 1947, the BWI program was converted into a temporary worker program as authorized under a provision in the Immigration Act of 1917 to meet emergency situations.[44] The BWI program, because its scale was much smaller than the bracero program, never attracted the same amount of scrutiny. It was, however, criticized for its abuse by employers of its worker protection provisions.[45] There were also constant charges of favoritism and corruption in the selection process by the officials on the islands. At its height in 1945, it supplied 19,391 workers. Most were employed in agriculture—especially in Florida—but there were also instances during the war years when BWI workers were permitted to work in some nonagricultural occupations. In 1951, when the bracero program was reconstituted under P.L. 78, the East Coast employers requested not to be included in its ad hoc authorization, because it functioned outside of the immigration statutes. They wanted a program that would be less subject to quick termination. The following year, they got what they sought. Congress passed the Immigration and Nationality Act of 1952, which will be discussed in detail shortly. Among its multiple features was a new provision (Section H-2) that created a nonimmigrant category for the admission of temporary unskilled foreign workers (popularly called "H-2 workers"). The BWI program was subsumed under this section of the new immigration law, where it has continued to function to this day (although since 1986, the agricultural workers from foreign countries have been separated from other nonimmigrant temporary workers into a new category and are now referred to as "H-2A workers"). In the process of authorizing such temporary worker programs within the immigration statutes, the Immigration and Nationality Act repealed the Alien Contract Act of 1885, which had banned such recruitment arrangements of foreign workers. This seemingly small change in public policy has had enormous labor market consequences in later years, as will be detailed in Chapter 10.

The Postwar Prosperity and Low Levels of Immigration

With the end of World War II in 1945, there were dire predictions by some prominent economists and policymakers that the anticipated massive reductions in military spending would lead to a return of another era of mass unemployment. It did not happen. To the contrary, the nation entered into a period of unprecedented economic prosperity that, with the exception of a short recession in the late 1950s, extended over the next twenty-five years. The pent-up demand and the forced savings by consumers that occurred during the war years led to a veritable explosion in consumer spending when the war was over. In addition, fully one-third of the nation's population moved up into the middle class during the 1940s, which brought additional demand for durable goods. The return of the troops also resulted in a "baby boom" that would last into the early 1960s, adding further fuel to the mounting tide of consumer spending. In the short run, the Servicemen's Readjustment Act of 1944 (the so-called "G.I. Bill") provided funds for veterans to enter training and education programs rather than to immediately seek to re-enter the labor force. Over 7 million veterans availed themselves of the opportunities provided by this historic human resource development program. Also, of course, the outbreak of the Cold War in Europe between the Soviet Union and the Western democracies in the late 1940s, the victory of communist forces in a civil war in China over the nationalist government in 1949, as well as the three-year war in Korea in the early 1950s meant that the anticipated reductions in defense spending did not materialize. Indeed, the opposite occurred. Defense spending rose, and the military draft of young men was continued in peacetime for the first time in U.S. history until 1971.

The complacency of the nation that was bred by this prolonged period of postwar prosperity was, however, severely shaken in 1957 when the Soviet Union successfully launched the world's first space-orbiting satellite, Sputnik I. The adequacy of the nation's education system was immediately called into question. The preparation of students and the quality of teaching in mathematics and sciences were found to be seriously wanting. In the name of national defense, the federal government enacted pathbreaking legislation in 1958 to provide funds for higher education to prepare teachers and to assist students seeking careers in these fields. Furthermore, a new era of technology—based on the use of the computer and the principles of automatic control—was dawning. As will be discussed in Chapter 11, entirely new demands would be made on the preparation of the labor supply. There were other indications in the late 1950s that the structure of the economy was changing and that there might be difficult adjustments for workers in the future, but the signals were not altogether clear at the time.[46]

It was also in 1957 that another major social event began to unfold that would have lasting consequences on U.S. society and its labor force. It was the establishment of the Southern Christian Leadership Conference that year, led by the Rev. Martin Luther King. Its formation grew out of an incident in which Rosa Parks, a black woman in Montgomery, Alabama, refused, in December 1955, to sit in the back of a public bus as required by state law. This simple act of defiance, along with the ensuing consumer boycott led by Rev. King, ignited the civil rights movement in the heart of the Old Confederacy. Initially, it was focused on the social and political treatment of blacks in the South. But in short order it moved to the national level, spread to include economic concerns, and was joined by other racial and ethnic groups as well as by women in a full-scale assault on inequality of opportunity throughout society and the workforce. This movement quickly revealed that the nation had huge reservoirs of human talent that remained marginalized or excluded from the development of their human resource abilities. It would not be until the mid-1960s, however, that this movement and its goals would finally make it to the top of the nation's domestic political agenda. But the process had begun.

Against this postwar backdrop of unprecedented general prosperity, along with the gradual revelation that the status quo was being undermined by major changes in international trade, technology, and social relations, immigration slumbered in a state of relative dormancy. As shown in Table 8.2, the annual levels of immigration from the mid-1940s to the late 1960s rose only to the levels of the late 1920s.

The low levels of immigration in the postwar era, however, do not mean that controversy over immigration policy had abated. To the contrary, immigration policy was under virtually constant attack throughout this period. The criticisms, however, were not directed at the limits on the level of immigration. There were few who wished for a return to the unregulated days of pre-1924 mass immigration. Rather, the focus of attention was on the discriminatory screening restrictions and differing ethnic quotas that affected the composition of the immigrant flow.

By far, the most immediate conflict in the postwar years between the prevailing immigration policy and the national interest dealt again with the quandary of refugees. As noted earlier, the Immigration Act of 1924 made no provision for refugees or for any exceptions to its terms. When the war ended in 1945, the refugee issue, rather than lessening, worsened. There were millions of Europeans who had been displaced from their native countries during the years of conflict. Since many had come from eastern European nations that were now being taken over by communist governments, many of these refugees refused to return voluntarily to their homelands. Moreover, the wartime refugees were soon joined by many others who were continuing to flee from these same eastern European countries. The western European nations, however, had themselves been devastated by the war. They were in no position to absorb or to support such an enormous and growing refugee population while they sought to reconstruct their economies.

In this situation, it was imperative that the United States take some humanitarian action to relieve the human suffering. President Harry Truman felt compelled to act, so he bent the letter of the law while adhering to its spirit. In December 1945, he ordered that 80,000 refugees, mostly from eastern and southern European countries, be admitted to the United States. He accomplished this feat by using the accumulation of unfilled quota slots that these countries had not used during the war years to admit them. Truman was then successful in having the Displaced Persons Act of 1948 passed, which admitted another 205,000 refugees originally from eastern European nations. This legislation also stretched the intentions of the existing immigration law by allowing these countries, which mostly had low annual immigration quotas, to mortgage one-half of their future admission slots for various numbers of subsequent years for a large number of immediate admissions. In the long run, therefore, the ethnic composition of the nation that the national origins law sought to preserve would not be altered. In 1950 and 1951, the Displaced Persons Act was amended again to admit another 188,542 European refugees under essentially the same entry arrangement.

There were, however, only so many such contortions of the existing immigration laws that could be performed. The refugee problem was one of the paramount reasons that President Truman pressed Congress to overhaul the nation's immigration system.

False Start: The Immigration and Nationality Act of 1952

From the time that the national origins quotas had actually been put into place, in 1929, until 1949, only 27 percent of the available quotas were actually used. Even with the inclusion of the nonquota immigrants from the Western Hemisphere who entered during this period, the total immigration for the period was only 75 percent of what the overall quota would have permitted. Given the considerable emigration that also occurred—especially in the 1930s, net immigration averaged only about 22,000 a year over the twenty-year time span. Simply put: Immigration had ceased to be a prominent feature of the American economy. Indeed, its significance was diminishing with each passing year. Indicative of this state of affairs, the reception facilities at Ellis Island—the historic immigrant gateway to America—were closed in 1954. But the low level of immigration was not the issue that bothered reformers. Rather, it was the fact that the ethnic and racial discrimination of the national origins admission system was distorting both the composition of the immigrant stream and the actual administration of the entire immigration system. Some countries with large quotas, such as Great Britain, had many unused quota slots each year, while other countries with low quotas, such as Italy and Greece, accumulated massive backlogs of applicants. Still other nations, such as some of those in Asia, were precluded from sending any immigrants despite the significant interest of people from these countries in coming. Supporters of reform, both in the Truman Administration and in Congress, as well as many in the general populace, felt that it was time for the nation to move away from an admission system based on ethnic and racial selectivity. They favored a system based on the potential human resource contributions that immigrants could make to the nation's labor market as well as one that, recognizing the refugee crisis in the world, would also have a humanitarian component designed to assist those persons actually confronted with a threat of political persecution. In other words, immigration policy should be designed to meet defined national interests.

In response to President Truman's pleas for policy reform, the Senate initiated a study of the immigration system in 1947 and, based on its findings, issued a report in April 1950.[47] Prepared by its Committee on the Judiciary, the Senate report dismissed most of the goals that were favored by the Truman administration and other proponents of reform. Instead, the report argued essentially for the maintenance of the status quo. It stated: "Without giving credit to any theory of Nordic superiority, the Committee believes that the adoption of the national origins quota formula was a rational and logical method of numerically restricting immigration in such a manner as to best preserve the sociological and cultural balance of the United States."[48] Thus, the committee dismissed the issue that most reformers sought to make the core of legislative change.

The subsequent legislation adopted by Congress was the Immigration and Nationality Act of 1952 (also known as the McCarran–Walter Act). It was enacted by Congress over a stinging veto by President Truman. The new law perpetuated the national origins system and the prevailing ceiling on immigration from the Eastern Hemisphere. It did, however, make important modifications with respect to Asian immigration. All of the exclusions against Asian immigration were eliminated, and the countries of this vast region were each given a small annual quota (plus admission of immediate relatives). To accommodate these additions, the Eastern Hemisphere ceiling was raised to 156,700 admissions a year. But several restrictive provisions for administering these new quotas were retained (e.g., Asian immigrants were charged against the quota of the country designated as the person's ancestral nation and not against the nation of actual birth, as was the case with non-Asian immigrants from other Eastern Hemisphere nations). Thus, with respect to admission eligibility and the annual admission level, the Act was essentially a reaffirmation of the selective and restrictive policy principles that had been in effect since the 1920s.

But the Senate committee's report and the subsequent legislation also raised a new concern that communists might use the immigration system to infiltrate the country. It was, after all, a time when the Cold War was in its deep-freeze phase. The Iron Curtain had only recently fallen over Eastern Europe; the Soviet Union had blockaded Berlin for almost a year (from mid-1948 to mid-1949); the Nationalist government in China had fallen in 1949; and the United States was again at war, this time in Korea against the communist-led nations of North Korea and the People's Republic of China. It is not surprising, therefore, that the new legislation added membership in the Communist party to the list of exclusionary categories that applied to all would-be immigrants and nonimmigrants. Thus, the hesitancy to make major changes was, in part, due to the political environment of the era. As historian Robert Divine has described the passage of the Act, it was "in essence, an act of conservatism rather than of intolerance."[49]

President Truman was infuriated by the unwillingness of Congress to enact a reform measure commensurate with the nation's emerging international leadership responsibilities. In his veto message, he stated:

> . . . The Countries of eastern Europe have fallen under the Communist yoke—they are silenced, fenced off by barbed wire and minefields—no one passes their borders but at the risk of his life. We do not need to be protected against immigrants from these countries—on the contrary we want to stretch out a helping hand, to save those who have managed to flee into western Europe, to succor those who are brave enough to escape from barbarism, to welcome and restore them against the day when their countries will, as we hope, be free again. . . . These are only a few examples of the absurdity, the cruelty of carrying over into this year of 1952 the isolationist limitations of our 1924 law.[50]

Nevertheless, Congress responded by overriding his veto by substantial margins in both houses.

Although the new law made only minor changes in the quotas, it made major changes in how priorities were assigned to those who were admitted.

To be precise, it introduced a preference system to distribute visas within the quota allotments assigned to each country. Four categories were established and placed in order of significance. The first category, which meant it had the highest priority, was for immigrants with levels of education, technical training, special experience, or exceptional abilities that were deemed by the attorney general to be of benefit to the United States. By creating this category, Congress gave official recognition to the idea that immigration policy could be used as a human resource instrument to select immigrants on the basis of their training and in accordance with the needs of the nation's labor market. Half of the visas were to be granted on this basis. The other three admission criteria assigned priorities to various categories of adult family relatives of citizens or permanent-resident aliens.

The McCarran–Walter Act also introduced the concept of labor certification as a prerequisite for the admission of immigrants admitted for work-related purposes. This certification, however, was to be administered in a purely passive manner. The secretary of labor was empowered to certify that the admission of non–family related immigrants would not adversely affect the wages and working conditions of citizen workers who were similarly employed. The Department of Labor was obligated to refuse certification if it anticipated any adverse economic impact that might occur as a consequence of their admission. This agency of government, however, was not staffed in subsequent years to carry out such a vital task. In practice, it acted only in response to formal complaints or when immigrants were used in a blatant manner such as to break a strike or bring about a drastic alteration in prevailing work standards. As a consequence, this certification authority was rarely used.

The Immigration and Nationality Act of 1952 did not alter the status of immigrants from the Western Hemisphere. They remained immune from coverage by either the overall ceiling on immigration or the national-origin quotas and were still called "non quota immigrants" who were subject only to the various exclusionary categories that applied to all immigrants.

A Vision for Change

In his message vetoing the Immigration and Nationality Act, President Truman proposed that Congress create a bipartisan "commission of outstanding Americans to examine the basic assumptions of our immigration policy."[51] Congress ignored his request.

With only a few months left in his term in office and smarting from the rebuff by Congress, Truman issued Executive Order 10392 on September 4, 1952, which established the President's Commission on Immigration and

Naturalization. It was empowered to make recommendations for policy changes that would be "in the interests of economy, security, and responsibilities of this country" and to complete its work by January 1, 1953. Philip Perlman, a former solicitor general of the United States, was appointed as its chairman. When issuing its final report, the commission said that the newly enacted legislation "should be reconsidered and revised from beginning to end."[52] It charged, among other things, that the new legislation represents "an attitude of hostility and distrust of all aliens"; it perpetuates "discrimination against human beings on account of national origin, race, creed, and color"; and it ignored the economic needs and foreign policy interests of the country. The Perlman Commission stated that "the major disruptive influence in our immigration law is the racial and nationality discrimination caused by the national origins system."[53] It recommended that this admissions system be abolished and a totally nondiscriminatory system be adopted in its place. It called for immigration levels to be increased to an annual level of one-sixth of 1 percent of the U.S. population as determined by the most recent census (this would have been 251,162 immigrants a year for the decade of the 1950s—about 100,000 immigrants more than the fixed level under the prevailing law). It suggested that a new admission system be created that was based on five criteria: the right of political asylum, the reunion of families, the economic needs of the country, the special foreign policy requirements of the leader of the Free World, and a recognition of the benefits of increased immigration in general. It also recommended that the administration of immigration policy be removed from the U.S. Department of Justice and the U.S. Department of State and be consolidated into a newly created agency with sole responsibility for administering the nation's immigration policy.

The report of the Perlman Commission had, however, no immediate impact on U.S. immigration policy. Congress simply ignored its recommendations. But as will be shown, many of its proposals were ultimately accepted in the changes that were enacted by post-1965 legislation. In the interim, however, the Eisenhower and Kennedy administrations were forced to make major immigration policy decisions outside the framework of the nation's existing immigration statute.

Continuing Frustration with an Outdated Policy

As a consequence of the failure to address the refugee issue, the only other option for the executive branch of government would be to seek special legislation from Congress to admit refugees outside normal immigration channels. This is what the Eisenhower Administration did when it came into office in 1953. The Refugee Relief Act of 1953 was enacted, and it authorized the admission of 215,000 refugees from Europe and China (the Nationalist Chinese government had been defeated in 1949 by communist forces that had formed the People's Republic of China). Similarly, in 1956 when a flow of refugees suddenly poured out of Hungary after the Soviet Union sent troops into the country to suppress a civilian uprising, urgent action was required. President Dwight Eisenhower introduced yet a new twist to refugee admission policy. Namely, the Immigration and Nationality Act of 1952 contained a provision that authorized the attorney general to "parole" persons for admission to the United States for "emergent reasons" that were in the "public interest." The parole authority was never intended to be used for the admission of groups of persons, and there was never any stated intention that it be used to admit refugees.[54] But in the continuing tradition of creative ad hoc responses to the refugee issue, Eisenhower used this loophole to admit 21,500 Hungarian refugees in 1956 and another 10,000 such persons in 1958. The use of the parole authority clearly stretched the intentions of the law, and it greatly added to the discretionary powers of the presidency.

In early 1959, following the successful overthrow of the Cuban dictator Fulgencio Battista by revolutionary forces led by Fidel Castro, there was an immediate exodus of Battista supporters from the island—mostly to the United States. By the spring of 1959, Castro had made known the fact that not only was he replacing the Battista regime, but he intended to create a Marxist socialist state. Private property was confiscated, political trials were initiated, and summary executions were administered. Against this backdrop, there was a mass departure of members of the middle and upper economic classes. Those Cubans who made it to the United States were given paroles by the attorney general that allowed them to remain. Over 65,000 Cubans were given such paroles by the Eisenhower and Kennedy administrations before travel between the two countries was halted by Cuba in 1962.

In 1960, under the United Nations' banner of "World Refugee Year," a concerted effort was made to finally close the refugee camps in Europe that still contained refugees from World War II and that had been swelled by "refugee escapees" from the Iron Curtain countries of eastern Europe since then. Under this legislation, Congress authorized the attorney general to use the parole authority to admit another 19,700 persons to meet this particular situation. Similarly, in 1962, the same procedures were used to parole 15,000 Chinese refugees who had fled to Hong Kong for admission to the United States.

By the early 1960s, it was obvious that the refugee issue was not a temporary problem, that it was not confined to developments in Europe, and that the prevailing U.S. immigration policy had to come to grips with this issue in a legislative manner. Ad hoc remedies could not be applied indefinitely to what had become an ongoing occurrence.

In terms of their human capital characteristics, the post–World War II refugees of the 1945–62 period essentially replicated the characteristics of the refugees admitted to the United States prior to and during World War II. Germany continued to be the nation that was the largest source of immigrants during the decade of the 1950s. The postwar European refugees were disproportionately from the professional, technical, managerial, and business occupations. Such was also the general case for many of the Chinese and most of the Hungarians.[55] Likewise, the Cuban refugees of the 1959–62 period have been called the "golden exiles" because of the high levels of education and skills they brought with them to the United States.[56]

The relatively high human capital endowments of the refugees in the 1945–62 era and their large numbers (about 1 million people) exerted a disproportionate effect on the characteristics of the total immigrant flow of this entire period. This is because between 1945 and 1952, only about one-third of the available quota slots of the legal immigration system were actually used, as were only about 60 percent in the period from 1952 to 1965. When it is recalled that the legal system was distorted in favor of western European immigrants, it can be seen that the combined effect of the legal immigrants and the refugee flows further skewed in an upward skill direction the human capital characteristics of the immigrant admissions. The fact that the immigrants and especially the refugees of this period were generally skilled and well educated meant that the adjustment to the U.S. labor market was relatively easy. Learning the English language was often a problem that took time to overcome. Once English was acquired, however, most already had the skills, talent, and work experience that were commensurate with the needs of the labor market. It is also true, of course, that the unemployment levels in these postwar years were relatively low when compared to the higher rates of the 1970s, 1980s, and early 1990s, which, no doubt, facilitated their locating jobs. The occupational data for those admitted during these postwar years were similar to those of immigrants of the 1930s and 1940s, but they, too, represented a very sharp departure from the occupational characteristics of the pre-1924 waves of immigration (see Table 8.3). The unique methods of admitting the postwar immigrants—mostly outside the provisions of the legal immigration system—also complicate the interpretations of econometric studies that purport to compare these decennial cohorts of immigrants with those who came before or after and relate the results to prevailing immigration policies.[57]

Concluding Observations

The rapid decline in the level of immigration from the late 1920s through to the mid-1960s provided the opportunity for the nation to look internally to unused and underused subgroups of the population to draw on for its labor force needs. During this lengthy period, the economy was confronted with periods of mass unemployment (the 1930s), full employment (the 1940s), and unprecedented prosperity (most of the 1950s and early 1960s). It was also a period of continuing high tariffs that protected American industries and their employees from foreign competition. Tariffs were raised in 1921, 1922, and again in 1930 by the infamous Smoot–Hawley Act to historic new heights. There was some tinkering with tariff reductions by the Roosevelt Administration in the 1930s, but the efforts were interrupted by World War II, which greatly reduced all foreign trade. It would not be until the early 1960s that any serious attempt would be initiated, by the Kennedy administration, to actually lower tariffs.

While the aggregate demand for labor fluctuated over these forty years, human capital requirements to secure available jobs did not appreciably change until the late 1950s. The goods-producing industries, with their extensive blue-collar occupational structure, dominated the labor market needs for most of this period. Only by the late 1950s were there signs that the skill requirements for labor were changing, but, at the time, there was no consensus yet as to whether the new patterns reflected long-term structural shifts or were merely short-term cyclical swings.

On the labor supply side of the equation, however, this forty-year period witnessed a major departure from the past. For the first time in over 100 years, the nation had to rely on the domestic labor supply to respond to employer needs. As a consequence, subgroups of the population who had been previously underutilized, ignored, or purposefully excluded from participation in the labor market became utilized, sought after, and included. It was not a utopian period in which the changes occurred without resistance, hostility, or hardship. But the combination of events and circumstances created a climate for change, and it was seized. In later years, these changes would become institutionalized features of the nation's labor force characteristics and its related public policies. Perhaps these changes would have eventually occurred without the reduction in mass immigration that occurred over this time span, but that is a philosophic question for idle speculation. The reality is that, with immigration levels sharply reduced from all previous experience, women, minorities, disabled persons, older persons, youth, and rural migrants did enter occupations and industries as well as move to geographical areas where they had not been significantly present before.

It was also in this context of low immigration that conscientious efforts to develop the employability of the nation's actual and potential labor force were launched. Public and private investments in human resource development were initiated on a scale not previously experienced.

Although there were serious ethical and political problems with the discriminatory nature of the nation's immigration laws in this era, the low level of immigration was highly appropriate to the national interest. There was no need for immigrants in the depression economy of the 1930s, and even when labor markets tightened in the 1940s, it was time for the nation to turn its attention toward previously excluded and underutilized segments of the domestic population. Black Americans, in particular, but also other excluded or marginalized groups needed a chance to enter the workforce and to develop their latent human resource abilities. Likewise, it was also in the national interest that the lengthy period of a generally pauperized and unskilled labor force associated with the initial building phase of the nation come to an end. For on the horizon lay the era of postindustrialism when the quality rather than the quantity of labor inputs would become the basic requirement for advancement in this new stage of economic development.

9

The Redesign of Immigration Policy: Replacing Social Goals with Political Goals

Entering the 1960s, immigration policy represented a classic example of how laws and practices, enacted in a bygone era, become out of step when applied to the needs of a later period. The famed economist Thorstein Veblen has aptly described this social phenomenon: "institutions are the products of the past process, are adapted to past circumstances, and are, therefore, never in full accord with the requirements of the present."[1] Times had changed but immigration policy had not. As President Harry Truman exclaimed in 1952, "in no other realm of our national life are we so hampered and stultified by the dead hand of the past as we are in this field of immigration."[2]

The United States had emerged from World War II as the most politically, economically, and militarily influential nation in the world. It was precisely because of this position of international leadership that President Truman viewed immigration reform as being a national imperative. Despite his valiant efforts, Congress refused to make significant changes. The Eisenhower and Kennedy administrations that followed Truman were similarly stymied. It remained for President Lyndon Johnson to accomplish this monumental feat with the enactment of the Immigration Act of 1965. The goal was to end the national origins admissions system; it was not to increase the level of immigration. But its passage triggered a series of unexpected events over the ensuing years that served to revive the phenomenon of mass immigration from out of the nation's distant past. For this reason, it is critical to understand what was intended before turning attention to what actually occurred.

Laying the Foundation for Change

Between 1952 and 1965, the immigration system found itself in a paradoxical situation. Over this thirteen-year period, only 61 percent of the system's quota visas were issued. Yet tens of thousands of persons sought to immigrate to the United States but were ineligible to do so only because they were from the "wrong" country. During this interval, as previously discussed, Congress did enact a series of ad hoc admission programs for various refugee groups to circumvent the barriers imposed by the extant immigration laws. Most of those admitted were refugees from western Europe and Mainland China or escapees from various Communist-dominated nations of eastern Europe and Cuba. In sum, almost half a million persons were admitted through channels other than through the immigration system in this thirteen-year period. Moreover, nonquota immigration from the Western Hemisphere was rapidly approaching the scale of total immigration from the Eastern Hemisphere. Expressed differently, only about one of every three immigrants legally admitted to the United States between 1952 and 1965 was admitted under the terms of the national origins system. Clearly, public policy was out of step with the events it sought to regulate.

The continuation of the national origins system was also crippling the operation of the new preference system created by the Immigration and Nationality Act in 1952 that sought to regulate Eastern Hemisphere admissions. As already noted, the first preference under that law and 50 percent of all the available visas were reserved for immigrants who had skills, talent, work experience, or educational backgrounds that were in short supply in the labor market. But over the thirteen-year period in which this priority was in effect, only about 1 percent of those admitted came as first-preference immigrants.[3] The reasons were, first, that neither the preference system nor the ceiling on immigration created by that law applied to Western Hemisphere immigrants and their immediate family members. Second, those immigrants from Eastern Hemisphere countries that had large quotas (e.g., Great Britain) often had large numbers of unfilled quota slots, so there was no need to apply the preference system to order the applicants. Thus, the only nations to use the first-preference slots were those Eastern Hemisphere nations that had skilled workers who wished to emigrate and that also had a backlog of applications for visas. Most of these nations, however, had very low overall quotas available to them. Thus, the national origin system was seriously distorting the immigrant admission system. The vast majority of immigrants were being admitted on grounds other than that they specifically possessed needed labor market abilities. Hence, the whole notion that the major purpose of the legal immigration system should be to meet labor market needs was being undermined. Most of those being admitted were granted entry on grounds that were incidental to what was supposed to be the highest priority and the primary source of legal immigrants to the nation. If they possessed needed skills or abilities, it was purely accidental to the conditions of their entry.

From this experience, the lesson to be learned is not that the goal of using immigration policy as a conscientious element of national human resource development failed. Rather, it is that the attempt to impose such a worthwhile goal while retaining the restraints of the national origins admissions system was a monumental mistake.

The Spillover Effect of the Civil Rights Movement to Immigration Reform

In the early 1960s, the major domestic issue was not immigration reform, but the drive for a national civil rights policy. But the destinies of these two issues became intertwined. The civil rights movement had evolved into an activist stage that used demonstrations, marches, and boycotts to protest in nonviolent manners the perpetuation of overt segregation against black citizens in the South. The primary focus at the time was on the abuses of social dignity (e.g., segregated public facilities) and the denial of political rights (e.g., restrictions on the right to vote).

The culmination of these activities came with the passage of the Civil Rights Act of 1964. In the wake of the Kennedy assassination in November 1963, the political logjam that had blocked his attempts to address a multitude of domestic policy concerns was finally broken. The new president, Lyndon Johnson, was one of the most politically astute men ever to hold the position. Shortly after taking office, he announced his intention to enact a broad social program under the rubric of building "The Great Society." Between 1964 and 1966, the most ambitious domestic reform agenda in the nation's history was proposed and enacted. Pathbreaking legislation spanning such diverse topics as poverty prevention; federal aid to elementary, secondary, and higher education; environmental protection; public broadcasting; food stamps; job training; tax cuts; regional economic development; urban renewal; voting rights; Medicare for the elderly; Medicaid health coverage for the poor; civil rights; and immigration reform were passed in rapid-fire succession. People dedicated to the accomplishment of these objectives were appointed to head the various government agencies to implement this social agenda. It was a brief period when serious governmental efforts were made to confront an accumulation of national issues that, for too long, had been ignored.

With regard to the subject of immigration reform, there was a direct link to the success of the civil rights legislation. For to invoke in legislation the explicit principle that overt racism could no longer be tolerated in the ways citizens treated each other implicitly meant that there could no longer be overt discrimination in the nation's laws that governed the way future citizens would be considered for immigrant admission. As Secretary of State Dean Rusk testified before Congress in support of immigration reform in August 1964: "The action we urge . . . is not to make a drastic departure from long-established immigration policy, but rather to reconcile our immigration policy as it had developed in recent years with the letter of the general law."[4] It was the passage of the Civil Rights Act, therefore, that created the political climate needed to legislatively end the national origins system. Thus, as it has been observed, "the 1965 immigration legislation was as much a product of the mid-sixties and the heavily Democratic 89th Congress which produced major civil rights legislation as the 1952 Act [i.e., the Immigration and Nationality Act] was a product of the Cold War period of the early 1950s."[5]

There was, however, an ironic twist to the linkage of civil rights legislation to immigration reform. While it is true that both issues came to the forefront of the national agenda because of political and social concerns, it is also the case that both had significant economic effects with regard to their labor market impacts. The economic aspects, however, were not foreseen at the time, nor was the possibility that they could conflict with each other.

The Civil Rights Act of 1964 contained Title VII, which prohibited discrimination in employment on the basis of race, color, gender, religious belief, or national origin. When it actually went into effect on July 1, 1965, its terms applied to employers, labor unions, and private employment services. As opposed to the other sections of the Act that focused on social and political practices largely occurring in the South, equal employment opportunity was an economic issue, and it had nationwide implications.

Literally within months after its enactment, a rash of civil disturbances broke out in urban areas across the nation.[6] They continued over the ensuing years, reaching a level of nearly 150 such civil disorders in the summer of 1967. To identify the causes of these riots, a presidential commission, composed of eleven distinguished members from both the public and private sectors, was established in July 1967. A year later, the National Advisory Commission on Civil Disorders issued its historic report. It found, among other things, that the issue of employment discrimination was a far more complex issue than the drafters of the Civil Rights Act had envisioned. The manifestations of such discrimination were more likely to be covert (i.e., built into the way labor market institutions function) than overt in nature. Accordingly, the public policies needed to overcome the past denial of job opportunities, and to provide employment preparation would entail far more programmatic action and public funds than the mere issuance of a ban on future discriminatory behavior.

If past patterns of employment for black Americans were not to be replicated in the future, affirmative action policies would be needed to reach out and to include *already qualified* blacks for jobs. But too many blacks were unqualified for the high-skilled, high-income jobs that were expanding in number and were disproportionately concentrated in the low-skilled, low-income occupations and industries where jobs were declining. To change these patterns, it would be necessary to address the extensive human capital deficiencies of blacks that were the accumulated legacy of centuries of stifled aspirations, unequal educations, and inadequate training opportunities. The civil disorders, after all, had occurred at a time when full employment prevailed (i.e., the national unemployment rate was in the mid-3 percent range). But, because the black population had become highly urbanized and disproportionately concentrated in central cities, unemployment in these areas remained much higher than the overall national unemployment rate. Moreover, the black labor force was beset with inordinately high incidences of working poor, discouraged workers, underemployed workers, involuntary part-time workers, and female-headed households. Finding jobs and preparing blacks, through extensive human resource development programs, for jobs in growth sectors of the economy were the only ways to keep the past employment patterns of inequality from being perpetuated. There was no thought at the time that many of these same urban labor markets where blacks were concentrated were about to receive a mass infusion of new immigrants—most of whom would themselves be from minority groups and many of whom also had human capital deficiencies.

The Advisory Commission on Civil Disorders boldly stated that the nation had unfinished business to address if it was serious about fulfilling the domestic goals of the Civil Rights Act. There was the economic imperative that it was in the national interest to upgrade the capabilities and expand the utilization of the available pool of black workers. Otherwise, many blacks would be condemned to lives in a permanent underclass—with all of the attended hardships of welfare dependency, crime, alcoholism, prostitution, and irregular work habits that scar the individuals involved and burden society as a whole. But with respect to blacks, there was also a clear moral imperative that recognized that their collective fate had been greatly influenced by external institutional forces over which they had only marginal control.

As the Commission on Civil Disorders pointedly stated, "white racism is essentially responsible for the explosive mixture" that led to these riotous outbursts.[7] The moral imperative was for policymakers to initiate and carry through a programmatic agenda aimed at bridging the past period of denial of opportunities and a future period of equal opportunity. No one expected immediate correction of existing economic inequalities. What was anticipated, however, was that there would be a concerted effort made over the ensuing decade to give priority to the urgent needs of black Americans. Given the general economic prosperity of the era, it was clear beyond question that addressing the human resource development needs of blacks was the nation's most pressing domestic issue.

Who could have seen that immigration reform was about to become a new example of the institutional policies adversely affecting blacks that the commission had condemned? In earlier times, immigration policy had kept blacks in the rural South after slavery ended, by providing an alternative source of workers to meet the industrial expansion needs of the North and West in the late nineteenth and early twentieth centuries. In the late twentieth century, immigration policy once more provided an alternative to providing the momentum for the pursuit of inclusive policies needed to alter the economic status of blacks in U.S. society. Immigration reform in 1965 was not designed to have this impact, but the consequences have been no less damaging than if it had been purposely planned to prevent progress.

The Immigration Act of 1965: The Intentions of Its Proponents

The intent of the supporters of immigration changes in the mid-1960s was the same as that of reformers for the past several decades. President John Kennedy stated, "the most urgent and fundamental reform I am recommending relates to the national origins system of selecting immigrants."[8] He recommended that it be replaced by a system that would give "the highest priority" to "the skills of the immigrant and their relationship to our need" and it should not "matter where they are born."[9] He acknowledged that a skills preference existed under prevailing law, but, as discussed earlier, it could not accomplish this purpose within the restrictive confines of the national origin system. His proposal did not call for any significant increase in the level of immigration. Indeed, he specifically pointed out that "there is, of course, a legislative argument for some limitations upon immigration. We no longer need settlers for virgin lands."[10] Thus, he reiterated that "the clash of opinion arises not over the number of immigrants to be admitted, but over the test for admission."[11] It was the test (i.e., the national origins selection criteria) that he sought to change.

On July 23, 1963, the Kennedy administration formally forwarded its immigration reform proposal to Congress. As promised, it sought to change the character of immigration policy—that is, to abolish the national origins system. The goal was *not* to increase the level of immigration. Indeed, there were widespread fears in Congress at this time that increasing the number of immigrants in general would lead to adverse employment and wage effects in the labor market. Indicative of these concerns was the fact that the Johnson administration, which took office on November 22, 1963, following the assassination of President Kennedy, followed through with the earlier decision made by the Kennedy administration to terminate the Mexican Labor Program (i.e., the bracero program) in 1964 after twenty-two years of existence. The rationale of both the administration and Congress for this action was that the program was depressing wages, retarding improvements in working conditions, and causing unemployment for low-income citizen workers (who were mostly Mexican Americans) in the agriculture industry. Furthermore, the Republican party raised the specter of massive job displacement consequences from the pending immigration reform in its unsuccessful quest to unseat President Johnson in the election campaign of 1964.[12] It is also worthy to note that the massive labor market effects of the postwar baby boom were just beginning to manifest themselves in 1965. One million more people turned eighteen years of age in 1965 than did so in 1964. The age of eighteen years was the primary labor force entry age for full-time workers at that time. Thus, the tidal wave of young labor force entrants—which would continue at this high level of annual entries until 1980—meant that there would be a substantial growth of new labor force entrants even if there were no additional increase in the level of immigration. Thus, not only was there no intention by reform advocates to increase the level of immigration, but there was absolutely no need to do so. As Secretary of State Dean Rusk aptly stated to Congress in 1965, "the significance of immigration for the United States now depends less on numbers than on the quality of the immigrants."[13] Indeed, the U.S. Department of Labor estimated that the labor force would increase by only about 23,000 persons a year if the administration's proposed immigration legislation was enacted.[14]

It was not until early 1965 that Congress responded in a serious manner to the administration's proposals. The original bill had called for a five-year phase out of the national origins system and the immediate termination of the last traces of discrimination against Asian immigration. In place of the use of national origin as the primary admission criteria, the bill proposed that the preference system created by the Immigration and Nationality Act of 1952 to govern admissions be retained. This would have meant that 50 percent of admissions would be based on preferences given to immigrants who had skills and work experience that were currently needed by the U.S. economy. The other half would be granted on the basis of various adult family relationships of would-be immigrants to U.S. citizens or permanent resident aliens. As before, the preferences would apply only to Eastern Hemisphere immigrants. But, as usual, it would be Congress that would have the final say concerning the actual content of the legislation.

Given the times, political agreement to end the overt racism of the national origins system was relatively easy. Finding common ground for a replacement criterion was much more difficult. It was the Judiciary Committees of Congress—which had remained under the control of politically conservative influences—that would set the actual legislative framework. In particular, it was members of the Judiciary Committee in the House of Representatives who had the greatest influence on the final product, especially Representative Michael Feighan (D-Ohio), chairman of the subcommittee with original jurisdiction on immigration matters. From the onset, Congress made it known to the Johnson administration that any new legislation in this area must contain two new components.

First, there must be a ceiling on Western Hemisphere immigration. Congress feared that with the extraordinarily high population-growth rates in Latin America, the absence of a limit would lead to an uncontrolled influx of immigrants from this region in the near future. Hence, the inclusion of a ceiling on the Western Hemisphere in the enacted bill "was a necessary *quid pro quo* in exchange for abolishment of the national origins quota system."[15] The Johnson administration opposed this change, contending that it would adversely affect the United States' relations with Latin America, but soon realized that, without it, the bill would not pass. Thus, an annual ceiling of 120,000 immigrants from the Western Hemisphere was included in the final version of the legislation.[16] It took effect on July 1, 1968. It was the first restriction ever to be placed on Western Hemisphere immigration.

Second, congressional leaders felt that the labor certification requirements for non–family related immigrants had to be strengthened. Prior to 1965, as noted earlier, the ability of the United States to protect citizens from any adverse effects on the wages and working conditions of nonrelative immigrants was restricted to purely a negative role. The secretary of labor could deny labor certification only if such immigrants would have an adverse labor market impact. The Immigration Act of 1965 reversed this logic. Under its terms, immigrants who were admitted on any basis other than family reunification or refugee status must receive certification in advance from the U.S. Department of Labor that their presence would not adversely affect employment opportunities or the prevailing wage and working conditions of citizen workers. This important change also reinforces the conclusion that

Congress had no intention in 1965 of causing any significant increase in the level of immigration as the result of its actions.

Under other provisions of the Immigration Act of 1965, an annual ceiling of 170,000 visas was imposed on immigration from all the nations of the Eastern Hemisphere. This figure was slightly higher than the limit in effect since the 1920s, which had been slightly modified in 1952 (i.e., the 156,700 annual ceiling). The rationale for the slight increase was recognition that refugees from Europe and Asia were likely to be a continuing reality and not just a temporary post–World War II phenomenon. It was hoped that the increase of about 14,000 visa slots a year in the Eastern Hemisphere ceiling would absorb such persons. Combined with the new Western Hemisphere ceiling of 120,000, the total number of visas to be issued in any year was 290,000. The 1965 legislation also set an annual ceiling of 20,000 visas for any single country in the Eastern Hemisphere. No such country limit was applied to any Western Hemisphere nation. Under the new law, the country of origin of immigrants remained a basic policy component, but no preference could be given on the basis of race, sex, place of birth, or place of residence. The legislation also eliminated the last elements of discriminatory treatment against Asians.

To determine which individuals were to be admitted within the framework of the numerical ceiling set for the Eastern Hemisphere, a seven-category preference system was created (see Appendix B). Within each category, visas were available on a "first come, first served" basis. The preference categories and the labor certification provisions of the law, however, did not apply at the time to Western Hemisphere nations. Subject to the various general exclusions that apply to all immigrants, persons from nations in this region had only to comply with the total hemisphere ceiling.

The adoption of the new preference system represented a dramatic shift in policy emphasis away from the human resource development considerations (that had been in place since 1952) toward one that relied largely on family reunification as its priority concern. The new system did not alter the admission status of "immediate family" relatives (i.e., persons defined under the Act as being spouses and minor children, although it did add parents of U.S. citizens over the age of twenty-one to this category). Immediate family members were not counted as part of the hemispheric or the individual country ceilings. Thus, the term "family reunification," in this case, referred to the admission of adult children over the age of twenty-one, of U.S. citizens, spouses and unmarried children of permanent resident aliens, and adult brothers and sisters of U.S. citizens (see Appendix B). Collectively, they accounted for 74 percent of the annually available visas. Thus, family reunification became the "cornerstone" of U.S. immigration policy, and it has remained so ever since.[17]

It is of vital consequence to recall that the Johnson administration had strongly supported the termination of the national origins system, but it favored the retention of labor market need as the highest preference and held the position that most of the available visa slots should be reserved for such admissions. During the legislative process, however, Congress reduced the occupational preferences share of the available visas to no more than 20 percent. Moreover, the previous single occupational preference grouping for work-related immigrants was split into two separate categories that were downgraded from being the first priority to the third and sixth levels of priority: The third preference was reserved for professionals and persons of exceptional ability, and the sixth was for skilled and unskilled workers (see Appendix B). Ostensibly, the rationale for these changes was that between 1952 and 1965, the occupational preference category—for the reasons cited earlier—had been underutilized, while the family preference groupings were chronically backlogged. The most significant shift in admission priorities, however, occurred as a result of the addition of a new fifth preference group for adult brothers and sisters of U.S. citizens and the assignment of 24 percent of the available visas to this new family grouping. Under the earlier Immigration and Nationality Act of 1952, would-be immigrants in this new category had been eligible to compete only for the system's limited number of unused visas (i.e., nonpreference visas, if any were available).

These drastic changes in the priorities of the admission system were made in response to the lobbying of various groups (e.g., the American Legion and the Daughters of the American Revolution) that were strongly opposed to abolition of the national origins system. Recognizing that they could not block the reform drive on this fundamental issue, they sought to make the changes in the admissions criteria more symbolic than real. These groups and their congressional sympathizers on the House Judiciary Committee believed that by stressing family reunification, it would be possible to retain essentially the same racial and ethnic priorities that the national origins system had fostered, even if this mechanism itself was abolished. It seemed unlikely, for instance, that many persons from Asia or from southern or eastern Europe would be admitted under the new system, because the prohibitions imposed during the national origins era had prevented the entry of many of their relatives for the past forty years. Conversely, those favored in the past would most likely have the most family relatives who could use their citizenship status to admit others like them. Representatives of various Asian-American organizations, indeed, vigorously testified against the shift to family reunification as the primary entry criterion.[18] The Department of Justice, which was also opposed to this inordinate shift to family reunification, estimated that under this legislation, Asian immigration might hit a high of about 5,000 immigrants a year before subsiding to an even lower level.[19]

Bearing these thoughts in mind, the House Judiciary Committee succeeded in its efforts to make family reunification the primary factor for determining eligibility for legal immigration to the United States. As the price for ending the national origins system, the Johnson administration ultimately conceded to Congress and accepted the new admissions priority system. Satisfying the private interests of some citizens rather than serving the public interest would become the distinguishing feature of the new immigration system.

Thus, the principle of family reunification, which political supporters have strongly defended in subsequent years, does not rest on a strong moral foundation. It should not be overlooked that, aside from making nepotism the dominant attribute of the legal immigration system, family reunification was based on the nefarious belief that it would perpetuate past discrimination into the future but under a more politically acceptable mantle. As Congressman Emanuel Celler (D-N.Y.)—the cosponsor of the legislation—stated on the floor of Congress during the final debate on the bill in which he urged its passage, "there will not be, comparatively, many Asians or Africans entering the country . . . since the people of Africa and Asia have very few relatives here, comparatively few could immigrate from those countries because they have no family ties to the U.S."[20]

In addition to seeking compromises that would make the new law politically palatable, Congress also sought to address issues about which the old law had been silent. Most prominent of these concerns was the troublesome issue of refugee accommodation. The addition of a seventh preference category—specifically for refugees—in the Immigration Act of 1965 marked the first time an explicit provision dealing with this issue had been included in the nation's immigration law (see Appendix B). It represented an acknowledgment that refugee accommodation will be a continuing issue for the nation. The 6 percent of the available visas (or 17,400 slots) set aside for refugees was far below the annual average of refugees admitted during the preceding thirteen years. As discussed in the previous chapter, those refugees—largely from eastern Europe and Cuba—had been admitted under ad hoc arrangements involving both temporary admission legislation and the use of the parole authority of the attorney general. Continuation of both of these practices, however, was seen to be an unsatisfactory method of dealing with what had proved up until this time to be an ongoing issue. Thus, the Immigration Act of 1965 was the first effort to address this critical issue in a consistent manner. The statutory definition of refugees under this legislation, however, reflected prevailing foreign policy goals of the United States rather than an objective assessment of the actual dimensions of the refugee issue itself.

That is to say, refugees were defined in this law as being only persecuted persons who had escaped from a communist country, or a communist-dominated area, or persons fleeing from countries in the Middle East. Political ideology and political influence, rather than persecution per se, were the dominant features of this new venture in public policymaking.

Thus, under the new law, 74 percent of the immigrant visas were reserved for family reunification (plus their immediate family members), 20 percent for meeting labor market needs (which required a labor certification), and 6 percent for refugee admissions. Only if any of these visas were unused could someone else who did not fit into one of these three categories be legally admitted as a nonpreference immigrant.

On October 3, 1965, President Lyndon Johnson signed the Immigration Act of 1965 into law. Technically speaking, this statute was an extensive series of amendments to the Immigration and Nationality Act of 1952, which remains the basic immigration law of the nation to this day. In fact, however, it was "the most far-reaching revision of immigration policy" since the imposition of the first numerical quotas in 1921.[21] Its focus was on changing the character of the immigration flow by eliminating its overtly discriminatory features. While it is true that it raised the annual immigration ceiling from 156,700 visas (plus immediate relatives) to 290,000 visas (plus immediate relatives), it was not intended to dramatically increase total immigration. Indeed, part of the increase in numbers was simply due to the fact that this legislation sought to have all refugees admitted to the United States included within the overall legal immigration ceiling of 290,000 a year. As the Senate floor manager for the legislation, Senator Edward M. Kennedy (D-Mass.) reiterated during the final debate on the pending legislation: "this bill is not concerned with increasing immigration to this country, nor will it lower any of the high standards we apply in selection of immigrants."[22] Earlier in a committee session, he stated that, "our cities will not be flooded with a million immigrants annually," "the ethnic mix of this country will not be upset," and "it [the pending bill] would not cause American workers to lose their jobs."[23] But, as will be seen, the new law did, in fact, set into motion the process whereby none of these assumptions proved to be valid. Thus, the reemergence of immigration once more as a significant labor market influence dates from the implementation of this historic legislation in 1965.

The Achievement of a Unified Immigration System

In the 1970s, two important amendments were added to the Immigration Act of 1965 that have also had long-term implications for the evolution of U.S. immigration policy. They both were also logical policy progressions.

Following the imposition of the ceiling on Western Hemisphere immigration on July 1, 1968, a massive backlog of applications for immigrant visas quickly developed from persons living in nations (especially from Mexico) in this region. The backlog gave credence to earlier arguments that population pressures in Latin America were so strong that, if restrictions were not imposed, a massive migration from these nations to the United States would eventually take place. By 1976, there was a waiting period of more than two and one-half years for eligible new applicants from this region.

There was little congressional support for removing the ceiling itself. Nonetheless, because of the size of the backlog, the speed with which it developed, and the fact that it was causing hardship to some families who were separated because of it, efforts were initiated to implement some sort of mechanism to regulate admissions under the new ceiling requirement. Accordingly, in 1976, an amendment was adopted that extended the seven-category preference system and the labor certification requirements to would-be applicants from Western Hemisphere nations as well. The effect of this extension was that, for the first time, it would be very difficult for any person from the Western Hemisphere who did not fit into one of the seven preference categories to enter legally. Indeed, there were no residual nonpreference admissions to the United States from 1978 until 1987, when Congress added a special provision to the Immigration Reform and Control Act of 1986 that specifically permitted a lottery to be used to choose 5,000 immigrants a year for two years (later extended to four years) to enter as nonpreference admissions. The 1976 amendments also imposed, for the first time, the annual ceiling of 20,000 immigrants from any single nation in the Western Hemisphere that already applied to nations in the Eastern Hemisphere. The extension of annual visa ceilings to all countries of the world marked the legal manifestation of an important ideal: that the people of all nations should be treated equally in terms of their opportunity to immigrate to the United States. On the other hand, it further exacerbated the backlog problem for countries in the Western Hemisphere, such as Mexico, that had previously been sending an annual number of immigrants far in excess of the new country ceiling figure.

In 1978, another amendment was added to the Immigration Act of 1965, which finally gave the United States the unified immigration system that reformers had sought for over three decades. The two separate hemispheric ceilings were merged to give a single worldwide quota of 290,000 visas a year.

Concluding Observations

The Immigration Act of 1965 was a turning point in the history of U.S. immigration policy. On one hand, all remnants of past overt discrimination on the basis of race and ethnicity were eliminated from the admission process. On the other hand, immigration had been converted into being a political policy designed largely to serve narrow special interests. Congress "created a policy aimed primarily at fulfilling the private interests of its legal residents and their alien relatives and it simultaneously delegated to these individuals (and to a limited number of its employers) much of the power to select future citizens and workers in the nation."[24] The opportunity to redesign the nation's immigration system to serve the public interest was lost. In place of a system that had been premised largely on racial and ethnic discrimination, a new form of discrimination—nepotism—became the driving force of the legal admission system. Moreover, whatever human capital characteristics the vast majority of legal immigrants possess at the time of their entry is purely incidental to the reason they are admitted. Only minimal concern was manifested about any possible broad economic effects that might be the product of its provisions and that might have national implications. If the scale of immigration had remained small, as its supporters had promised, the consequences of such an ill-designed law would have been of little consequence. But, as will subsequently be explained, such was not to be the case.

Likewise, the humanitarian provisions of the Immigration Act of 1965, which gave the nation its first statutory recognition that refugees are going to be a continuing part of the nation's immigration experience, were primarily intended to further prevailing foreign policy objectives. With such a built-in bias, refugee policy also lacked a positive definition of national purpose. The mitigation of human suffering due to persecution was clearly a secondary objective to the realization of foreign policy goals.

Unfortunately, the focus on placating political interests served to divert attention away from the fact that none of the assumptions made by supporters of the Act that had economic implications proved to be valid. As will subsequently be discussed, the size, the human capital endowments, and the characteristics of post-1965 immigrants have all differed significantly from what was anticipated. Moreover, the fourth wave of mass immigration that it unleashed has taken place when domestic labor force growth was more than able to provide an ample supply of workers and precisely when it was imperative that the nation turn its attention to the correction of internal inequities in economic opportunities within its native-born population. Under these circumstances, it should be no surprise that the post-1965 immigration policy was destined to collide with the national interest.

10

Unexpected Consequences: The Revival of Mass Immigration

Nothing in the reform movement that culminated in the passage of the Immigration Act of 1965 was intended to cause a significant increase in the scale of immigration. The primary goal had been to change the criteria for legal entry. Over the ensuing years, as the unanticipated consequences of rising immigration were revealed, no attempt has been made to restrain it. The launching and perpetuation of the "fourth wave" of mass immigration, therefore, has been more the product of omission by policymakers than an act of commission.

Table 10.1 shows the dimensions of the resurgence of immigration since the Immigration Act of 1965 went into full effect in mid-1968 (compare Table 10.1 with Table 8.2). The data show those who, as immigrants, have been granted permanent resident status in each fiscal year. It includes: (1) those who entered through the legal immigration system; (2) those who entered as refugees and who, after one year of residence, actually applied to adjust their status; (3) those who entered illegally but who were made legally eligible to adjust their status under various amnesty programs authorized in the 1980s and 1990s and who, after a waiting period, actually adjusted their status; and (4) those who entered as nonimmigrant aliens and have subsequently been allowed to adjust their status.

It is equally important to note that the data in Table 10.1 do *not* indicate the "true" annual flow of foreign-born persons into the U.S. population and labor force. It excludes: (1) persons admitted as refugees who have been in the country for less than a year or those who have been for more than a year

Table 10.1

Immigration to the United States, 1961–2000

1961–1970	3,321,677	1981–1990	7,338,062
1961	271,344	1981	596,600
1962	283,763	1982	594,131
1963	306,260	1983	559,763
1964	292,248	1984	543,903
1965	269,697	1985	570,009
1966	323,040	1986	601,708
1967	361,972	1987	601,516
1968	454,448	1988	643,025
1969	358,579	1989	1,090,924
1970	383,326	1990	1,536,483
1971–1980	4,493,314	1991–2000	9,101,443
1971	370,478	1991	1,827,167
1972	384,685	1992	973,977
1973	400,063	1993	904,292
1974	394,861	1994	804,416
1975	386,194	1995	720,461
1976	398,613	1996	915,900
1976 TQ	103,676	1997	798,378
1977	462,315	1998	660,477
1978	601442	1999	646,568
1979	460,348	2000	849,807
1980	530,639		

Source: U.S. Immigration and Naturalization Service.
TQ = Transitional quarter.

but who have yet to file for permanent resident status; (2) illegal immigrants who were eligible but did not apply for the various amnesty programs offered to them; (3) illegal immigrants who were ineligible for the amnesty programs; (4) illegal immigrants who have entered subsequent to the various eligibility cutoff dates prescribed by the various amnesty programs; (5) applicants for political asylum who are already in the United States and are awaiting the disposition of their backlogged cases and/or appeals; and (6) the more than half a million nonimmigrant aliens who, in an average recent year, availed themselves of the legal opportunity to work in the country for temporary periods of time.

Indeed, when allowances are made for these additional categories of entrants, the "real" inflow of foreign-born persons into the United States for permanent settlement during the 1990s was in far excess of the 9.1 million immigrants who were "officially" reported by the INS. Regardless of what the precise number may have been, it was the decade that experienced the largest inflow of immigrants for permanent settlement in the nation's history.

Table 10.2

Foreign-Born Population and the Percent of Population Foreign Born, 1965–2000

Year	Foreign-born population (millions)	Percent of population foreign born
1965	8,549	4.4
1970	9,619	4.7
1980	14,079	6.2
1990	19,767	7.9
2000	31,100	11.1

Sources: (1) For 1965: Jeffrey S. Passel, "30 Years of Immigration and U.S. Population Growth," Paper presented at the annual meetings of the Association for Public Policy Analysis and Management (Washington, DC, November 1995), unnumbered chart. (2) For 1970–1990: U.S. Bureau of the Census, "Historical Census Statistics on the Foreign Born Population of the United States, 1850–1990," Working Paper No. 29, (Washington, DC: U.S. Department of Commerce, February, 1999), Table 1. (3) For 2000: U.S. Bureau of the Census, "Number of Foreign Born Up 57 Percent Since 1990 According to 2000 Census," Commerce News (Washington, DC: U.S. Department of Commerce, 2002), p. 1.

Unless policy changes are enacted, the first decade of the twenty-first century can be expected to set a new decennial record. In terms of the stock of immigrants in the country, Table 10.2 shows that, as of the year 2000, there were 31.1 million foreign-born persons living in the United States, and they represent 11.1 percent of the total U.S. population. These numbers, too, are conservative, as the Census Bureau itself acknowledges that at least 1 million illegal immigrants are believed to have been missed by the 2000 census.

If the intention of the reform legislation of 1965 had been to significantly increase the level of immigration (with its derivative effects on the size, distribution, and composition of both the nation's population and labor force), the legislation would be deemed a smashing success. There would be no need for an analysis of a policy intervention that accomplished what it promised.

But the reality is just the reverse. The outcome was not expected—even by the legislation's strongest advocates. Hence, the experience requires careful scrutiny. How did immigration reform designed to eliminate discrimination lead to a quantum increase in the subsequent level of immigration? It would be unfair to say that the revival of mass immigration was the product of purposeful deception. But this does not mean that its actual consequences should simply be rationalized in retrospect. How it happened is vital to understand—not only because of the unanticipated changes it has wrought on U.S. society, but also because the fourth wave shows no evidence of imminent decline.

There are four factors that explain what happened. They are: the politicalization of the process of admitting refugees and asylum seekers, the explosion of illegal immigration, the unexpected acceleration in family-sponsored legal immigration, and the escalation of the numbers of nonimmigrant foreign nationals legally permitted to work temporarily in the country each year. Each requires individual discussion.

The Politicalization of Refugee Policy and the Advent of Mass Asylum

Hardly had the Immigration Act of 1965 been signed before events once more swamped its new refugee provisions. Developments in Cuba in 1965 initiated the process by which the attempt by Congress to limit the use of the parole authority as a means to accommodate the mass entry of refugees was literally nullified. But this was only the beginning of what has become a seemingly unending story of policy abuse.

The Cuban Refugee Crisis of 1965–1973

Due to economic stagnation and civil turmoil in Cuba, Premier Fidel Castro unilaterally announced on September 28, 1965, that any Cubans wishing to leave—except young men of military age—could do so. On October 3, 1965 (the same day that the Immigration Act of 1965 was signed into law), President Lyndon Johnson announced that any of these Cubans who desired to come to the United States could do so. His invitation was humanely generous, but it was also strongly motivated by political considerations. President Johnson was willing to sacrifice adherence to a coherent immigration policy for the opportunity to embarrass the communist dictator of Cuba before the world community.

Cuba, in the meantime, announced that the port of Camarioca would be open for Cuban exiles in Florida to come by boat to pick up their relatives. A flotilla of such boats brought about 5,000 persons to the United States over the next month. As this procedure was deemed to be unsafe, it was announced in November that the two governments had reached a mutual accord. An "air bridge," involving daily chartered flights, was established to transport Cuban refugees directly to the United States. From the time these "freedom flights" began until they were unilaterally stopped by Cuba in 1973, about 270,000 Cuban refugees were admitted to the United States under this arrangement. Many were relatives of Cubans who had previously sought refuge in the late 1950s and early 1960s (see discussion in Chapter 9).

Like the earlier era, those who came via the "air bridge" were typically members of "the upper socioeconomic class of pre-revolutionary Cuba." Because they were "the able, the educated, and the successful," their migration has been described as being "the biggest brain drain the Western Hemisphere has ever known."[1] They have also been referred to as the "golden exiles" because of their extensive human capital endowments.

The legal authority used to admit the Cuban airlift refugees was, once again, the parole authority of the U.S. attorney general. In 1966, a special law, the Cuban Refugee Adjustment Act, was passed to enable these refugees to become permanent resident aliens without first leaving the country and applying for the appropriate visa.[2] Cuban refugees who entered the United States were allowed to adjust their status to become permanent resident aliens after they had been in the United States for two years (subsequently reduced in 1980 to one year). These Cubans were originally counted as part of the new annual ceiling of 120,000 quota immigrants from the entire Western Hemisphere, but this practice was subsequently declared illegal.[3] As a result of a court order, 145,000 additional visas above the established ceiling were issued to other persons from the Western Hemisphere who had sought entry to the United States but had been denied entry because these visas had been diverted for use by Cuban refugees.

By the time the Cuban airlift ended in 1973, a total of 677,158 Cuban refugees had entered the United States since 1959. Despite initial efforts to disperse them around the country, a disproportionately high number of these persons returned or remained in the Miami-Dade County area of south Florida. While there can be no question that the mass influx of Cubans into this area brought a new vibrancy to a local economy that had long been stagnant, it has also caused tension and conflict between and among the various native-born and foreign-born segments already residing in that community.[4] During the 1980s, for instance, there were four significant civil disorders in Miami—each of which had clear racial overtones.

The Southeast Asia Refugee Issue

No sooner had the Cuban "air bridge" ceased, than the ending of the war in Vietnam set in motion a new refugee stream. In April 1975, the government of South Vietnam, which the United States had supported, collapsed. With the withdrawal of U.S. military forces, "the largest emerging mass immigration of refugees to the United States" yet known commenced.[5] Many of the initial refugees had been closely associated with the war effort. Between April and December 1975, 130,000 Indochinese refugees were admitted to the United States under the parole provisions as authorized by President Gerald Ford. Most of these persons were either related to U.S. citizens or had been closely allied with the war effort itself. These Vietnamese refugees were soon joined by refugees from other parts of Indochina who also sought to be admitted to the United States. In 1976, another parole program was undertaken to admit 11,000 refugees who had escaped from South Vietnam, Kampuchea (formerly known as Cambodia), and Laos and who had relatives living in the United States. Included in this grouping were some of the first "boat people" (most of whom were ethnic Chinese), who had been forcibly expelled from Vietnam by the new communist government and who were having difficulty finding any country that would allow them to disembark.

With events clearly spinning out of control, President Ford decided that "relying upon the parole provision was not a desirable means of formulating U.S. refugee policy."[6] He announced in mid-1976 that he would no longer use this authority and called for new legislation to establish a systematic admission procedure. His administration, however, was voted out of office in November of that year. When President Jimmy Carter assumed office in January 1977, he made it known that he did not feel compelled to refrain from using the parole authority, but he did express a preference for new refugee legislation.[7]

As economic conditions continued to deteriorate and as factional fighting broke out in Vietnam, Laos, and Kampuchea, the outpouring of refugees accelerated. Against this backdrop, President Carter announced that he would use the parole authority to accommodate a substantial portion of the human outflow in excess of those permitted to enter under the existing immigration law. On April 13, 1979, the attorney general authorized the parole admission of 40,000 Indochinese refugees over the next six months. In July 1979, it was announced that an additional 14,000 Indochinese refugees a month—or a total of 210,000 such refugees—would be admitted under the parole authority between July 1, 1979, and September 30, 1980. As these mass admissions were taking place outside the preference limits of the prevailing immigration law, special legislation (similar to that given to Cubans) was temporarily enacted that permitted them subsequently to adjust their status to become permanent resident aliens. A disproportionate number of the refugees from Southeast Asia (about 40 percent) settled in the urban areas of California, especially in the Los Angeles–Long Beach area.

The Refugee Act of 1980

By this time, it was apparent that the prevailing refugee provisions of the Immigration Act of 1965 "were totally inadequate as the basis for a fair and coherent refugee policy."[8] Both President Carter and Congress agreed that a new refugee policy had to be formulated. In 1979, a bill was drafted in the

Senate. It embodied many of the recommendations for reform that were under discussion by the Select Commission on Immigration and Refugee Policy during this same time period and that were contained in its subsequent final report. This bill became the Refugee Act of 1980. It was signed by President Carter on March 17, 1980, and went into effect on April 1, 1980.

The new legislation had the effect of removing refugee admissions from the legal immigration system. It did this by abolishing the seventh preference admission category for refugees that had been created by the Immigration Act of 1965 (with its 17,400 visas reserved for refugees). To compensate for its removal, the annual number of immigrant visas under the legal immigration system was then reduced from 290,000 to 270,000, which were allocated among the remaining six preference categories that were left in place (see Appendix C).

The new legislation then created a separate admission system for refugees. Under this law, a refugee is defined as "any person who is outside any country of such person's nationality . . . and who is unable or unwilling to avail himself or herself of the protection of that country because of persecution or a well-founded fear of persecution on account of race, religion, nationality, membership in a particular group, or political opinion." The intention was to remove the overt ideological bias of the definition of who was a refugee in the 1965 legislation and to make the actual threat of persecution to an individual the determining eligibility factor. This definition meant that the United States had now accepted the same wording as an earlier protocol on refugees adopted by the United Nations (UN) in 1967. The language of the Refugee Act of 1980, however, went further than the UN protocol by stating that the term "refugee" also includes persons who are *within* their country of nationality and who are also subject to persecution. This grouping—those who were "within their country of nationality"—was restricted, however, to persons who were specifically designated as "refugees" by the president and could not be self-proclaimed by the individuals. Otherwise, it was felt, endless numbers of persons living in many nations could lay claim to refugee status. Persons who had contributed to the persecution of others were declared to be ineligible to later become refugees themselves.

Thus, having broadened the definition of the term "refugee," the critical question for policymakers was how many persons to admit each year under these new terms. There was disagreement between Congress and the Carter administration as to whether a certain number should be specified in the law by Congress or whether the president should have the discretion to decide the number that he felt was in the national interest to admit each year. Ultimately, a compromise was reached. From 1980 to 1982, up to 50,000 refugees could be admitted each year by the president. This ceiling was considered to be "the normal flow" for those years. The number was arbitrarily selected on the basis that between 1956 and 1979, the average annual number of refugees admitted to the United States under the parole provision was 44,670 persons. With the exception of the Indochinese refugees, the ceiling of 50,000 refugees a year would have accommodated all of the yearly refugee admissions that occurred between 1956 and 1979. The president could admit additional refugees above the 50,000 figure in an "emergency situation," after consulting with Congress.

After October 1, 1982, the law specified that a new procedure would take effect. Prior to the beginning of each fiscal year, the resident is required to state in advance the total number of refugees he wishes to admit in the coming year, and he must consult with Congress through "personal contact" with specifically designated representatives as to the appropriateness of the requested number. Congress, in turn, is required to hold a hearing on the number. In addition, the law requires that the president assign geographic allocations to refugees from different parts of the world in order that no one group or region could use all the available refugee slots. It is important to note that these assigned figures are ceilings. They are not goals. Although it is widely misunderstood, there is no implied obligation to reach the annually authorized refugee figure or the specific geographic allocations. The refugee program was created in such a way as to be deemed satisfactory if the ceilings are not achieved, for "the underlying principle is that refugee admission is an exceptional *ex gratia* act provided by the United States in furthering its foreign and humanitarian policies."[9]

For present purposes, it is of significance to note that there was no intention by Congress at the time of the passage of the Refugee Act of 1980 to increase the total number of legal immigrants and refugees to be admitted over what had been the actual level prior to its passage. Elimination of the seventh preference category and the simultaneous reduction of the worldwide immigrant ceiling to 270,000 visas meant that, with the addition of up to 50,000 refugees a year, a new total of up to 320,000 legal immigrants and refugees would be admitted each year. This new total, however, was approximately the same as the previous aggregate total of immigrants (i.e., the old 290,000 quota of immigrants a year, 17,400 of whom were refugees) plus the remainder of the prior average annual number of refugees admitted as parolees between 1956 and 1979 (i.e., 44,670 refugees a year). In other words, the 320,000 figure is the sum of 270,000 plus 50,000. Hence, supporters of the 50,000–refugees-a-year figure in the Refugee Act of 1980 argued that, in fact, "there would be no actual increase in the immigration flow as a result of the Refugee Act."[10] Having enacted what it believed was a more flexible admissions procedure for accommodating refugees, Congress sought assurances that the parole authority of the attorney general would be used only as it had originally been intended—for individual emergency cases. Thus, an amendment was included in the Refugee Act that said that after May 15, 1980, the attorney general would be forbidden to use the parole authority to admit refugees unless a "compelling reason" that was in "the public interest" with respect to a particular individual dictated that this person be admitted as a parolee rather than as a refugee.[11]

As for what has actually happened, Table 10.3 indicates the authorized admissions from 1980 to 2002. The first complete year in which the Refugee Act of 1980 was in effect was fiscal 1981. The range of authorized admissions extends from a high of 217,000 (in 1981) to a low of 67,000 (in 1986).

Since the consultation process began in 1982, the authorization level has become the annual subject of immense political pressure. As the president sets the numbers, special interest groups annually seek to influence each administration to enlarge the number of persons about whom they are the advocates—usually a particular ethnic, racial, or religious group. These interest groups typically show little concern for the national interest when they conduct their lobbying efforts, and they do not worry about the accommodation requirements imposed on the local communities who actually receive the subsequent inflow.[12]

The Achilles Heal: Asylum Policy

Prior to the Refugee Act of 1980, the immigration statutes contained no provisions for granting asylum to individuals who were already in the United States and who feared they would be persecuted if they were required to return to their homeland. Assistance to refugees was restricted to persons who were temporarily residing in some other nation of "first instance" after fleeing their homeland. Under these circumstances, refugees could be screened with respect to their eligibility for admission before being physically allowed to enter the United States. Prior to 1980, the only existing authority that came close to being an asylum policy was a section in the Immigration and Nationality Act of 1952. It allowed the attorney general to issue an Extended Order of Departure (EOD) to voluntarily block the deportation of an alien already in the United States, if it was believed that the alien would be subject to persecution on the basis of race, religion, or political opinion if forced to return home. The EOD authority was a manifestation of a long-standing diplomatic practice among nations known as *nonrefoulement* (i.e., a practice whereby no nation should force the return of an individual to his or her homeland if it is known that the individual will be persecuted).

Table 10.3

Refugee Authorizations, Approvals, and Admissions to the United States, 1980–2002

Year	Authorized admissions	Approvals	Admissions
1980[a]	273,700	206,912	N.A.
1981[a]	217,000	155,291	N.A.
1982	140,000	61,527	93,252
1983	90,000	73,645	57,064
1984	72,000	77,932	67,750
1985	70,000	59,436	62,477
1986	67,000	52,081	58,329
1987	70,000	61,529	66,803
1988	87,500	80,282	80,382
1989	104,500	95,505	101,072
1990	110,000	99,687	110,197
1991[b]	116,000	107,962	100,229
1992[b]	123,500	115,330	123,010
1993[b]	116,000	106,026	113,152
1994	117,500	105,137	114,471
1995	111,000	78,936	98,520
1996	90,000	74,491	77,600
1997	78,000	77,600	69,276
1998	88,000	73,198	N.A.
1999	78,000	67,761	N.A.
2000	90,000	N.A.	N.A.
2001	80,000	N.A.	N.A.
2002	70,000	N.A.	N.A.

Source: U.S. Immigration and Naturalization Service.

[a]Data for these years do not include the approximately 123,000 Cubans and 6,000 Haitians of the "Mariel Boatlift" era of 1980–1981 who were later given the opportunity to apply for amnesty under the Immigration Reform and Control Act of 1986.

[b]Does not include Amerasians (i.e., persons born in Vietnam between January 1, 1962, and January 1, 1976, if the alien was fathered by a U.S. citizen) who were allowed to enter the United States as legal immigrants during these years.

Note: Admissions in a given year may be higher than approvals because of the actual arrival in a given year of persons who were approved in previous years.

N.A. = Not available.

Under the Refugee Act of 1980, however, the attorney general was authorized to grant asylum protection to an alien who was already in the United States, if the individual applied for such status and if the attorney general determined that the individual could be otherwise classified as a refugee. The asylum status could be revoked at a later time if it was determined that the conditions in the alien's homeland had changed such that the status was no longer warranted. As the policy was intended to address the needs of individuals, the Refugee Act of 1980 specified that only 5,000 asylees each year could adjust their status, after one year, to apply for permanent resident status. In 1990, the number was raised to 10,000 asylee adjustments a year. Asylee admissions do not count as part of the annual ceiling on worldwide immigration or the individual country ceiling as specified under the legal immigration statutes.

Within weeks after passage of the Refugee Act of 1980, events quickly demonstrated that the asylum section was the weakest link of the new legislation. Its implications had not been thought through. As usual, the legislation had been formulated on the basis of past experiences. The possibility that the United States itself might become a country of "first instance" for massive numbers of persons—all arriving within a very short time frame and all claiming asylum—had never been contemplated. This, however, was precisely what happened.

The Mariel-Haitian "Boatlift" Experience

Once more, events in Cuba caused U.S. refugee policy to fall into disarray. In the early months of 1980, declining economic conditions in Cuba culminated in "a rising tide of dissatisfaction, particularly among those Cubans with relatives in the United States."[13] A number of violent outbursts occurred as increasing numbers of Cubans sought asylum in various foreign embassies located in Havana. Suddenly, in a moment of peevishness, Fidel Castro announced on April 4, 1980, that anyone who wished to leave Cuba could do so. In response, thousands accepted his offer, and they descended on various foreign embassies to apply. Initially, some were allowed to fly on chartered flights to Costa Rica, where they were given temporary safe haven. But as the planes landed, they became the center of worldwide publicity, and the media interviews with those who fled cast a disparaging image of contemporary life in Cuba. In reaction, on April 18, 1980, the Cuban government suspended the refugee flights. Two days later, Castro unilaterally announced on the radio that all Cubans who wished to emigrate to the United States were free to board boats at the port city of Mariel and go.[14]

Within hours of the broadcast, which was received in southern Florida, a flotilla of boats streamed toward Mariel from Florida, and on April 21, the first boat returned to Key West. Many of the persons who left Cuba were relatives of persons already in the United States, but it was also the case that "a deliberate policy of forcing acceptance of several non-relatives for every relative on board" was also in effect.[15] Many of the nonrelatives were persons who had been committed to various state mental and penal institutions. Reflecting both the declining educational and training opportunities in Cuba over the preceding decade, as well as the types of nonrelatives included in the outflow, the human capital attributes of the Mariel people were considerably below those of the Cuban refugees of the 1960s. Indeed, in contrasting the two human outflows, one account has referred to the Cubans of the 1960s as the "promising ones" and those of the early 1980s as the "frightening ones."[16]

The number of Cuban refugees quickly soared, from several hundred a day in late April to over a thousand a day by early May. In a speech on May 5, 1980, President Carter stated: "Ours is a nation of refugees. We will continue to provide an open heart and open arms to refugees seeking freedom from Communist domination brought by Cuba."[17] The next day, however, responding to an urgent request by the governor of Florida, the president declared that "a state of emergency" existed in south Florida. By May 9, 1980, 30,127 persons had arrived in south Florida, and the massive scale of the movement was finally recognized. Moreover, the dangers of overcrowding, as well as the lack of sufficient safeguards on what were essentially pleasure boats designed for families, became apparent. Thus, on May 14, 1980, President Carter moved to halt the sealift. Ostensibly, his reason was that he wanted to find a safer way of conducting the transfer. No doubt the request was also an effort to reduce the size of the flow and to allow the government more time to develop an appropriate policy of accommodation and to seek international assistance in distributing the people to other nations as well. An international conference was hastily convened in San Jose, Costa Rica. At that meeting, eighteen nations agreed to accept some of the Cubans, but none agreed to take more than a few hundred persons.[18] Thus, the burden of trying to stop the flow of refugees as well as to accommodate the Cubans who were already ashore fell squarely on the United States.

Technically speaking, the Cubans who were boatlifted to south Florida were illegal immigrants, and the citizens who conveyed them were "smugglers." The Carter administration did not treat them as illegal aliens, and, initially, no action was taken against those who transported them. Indeed, the INS immediately accepted their applications for a status classification, granted them visas, and authorized them to seek work. Deciding what status to assign to the Cubans, however, proved difficult. The administration declined to classify all of them as refugees. They were already in the United States, and the administration wanted to avoid setting a precedent that might lead persons from other countries to think they could simply enter the United States without documents and claim to be refugees.[19] Thus, the 3,500 Cubans who entered the United States by way of Costa Rica, which was the number the United States agreed to accept as its share of the initial Cuban outflow, were classified, as a group, as refugees. This was because they were actually screened for refugee eligibility in Costa Rica before being allowed to enter the United States. But those who had come directly to Florida from Cuba by boat were classified as "applicants for asylum." The Refugee Act of 1980 had provided for the assignment of asylee status to persons already in the United States, but the use of that classification had been intended for individuals, not for massive groups of persons. Declaring the flotilla Cubans to be "applicants for asylum" meant that each person would have to be interviewed individually to determine his or her eligibility for asylee status. The situation in May 1980 was deemed by the administration to be "a very special emergency situation."[20]

Meanwhile, the Carter administration continued to be unsuccessful in its efforts to arrange for U.S. officials to interview persons in Cuba to determine their eligibility for refugee status or to arrange for an orderly process that might regularize the flow. Thus, the "freedom flotilla" continued despite efforts that began in mid-May to crack down on those who were providing the transportation. The government impounded the private boats that were being used as they arrived and levied fines against their captains. By mid-June, the deterrents imposed by the U.S. government as well as a change in the attitude of the Cuban government toward the exodus resulted in a sharp reduction in the number of Cubans who reached the United States, although the process continued at a much reduced level through early October 1980.

As if the flow of persons from Cuba was not enough for policymakers to worry about, the entire situation was further inflamed when a number of boats crowded with people from Haiti also began to arrive. Such boats, with their human cargoes, were not new—they had been arriving in south Florida on a sporadic basis since December 1972. But their arrival in the midst of the massive Mariel exodus ignited a long-simmering dispute. Since Cuba and Haiti were neighboring islands and both had long been ruled by dictators (albeit that one was a left-wing dictator and anti-American, and the other was a right-wing dictator and pro-American), it was unavoidable that comparisons of the treatment of persons fleeing from each would be made. Successive U.S. administrations had consistently contended that most Haitians were illegal immigrants while virtually all Cubans were refugees and asylees.[21] This difference in treatment has caused countless legal and political difficulties. It has also evoked charges of racism because the Cubans tended to be white whereas the Haitians were exclusively black.

Over the years following 1972, several hundred Haitians had been returned to their homeland by the INS. The position of the U.S. government had consistently been that, with relatively few exceptions, most Haitians were fleeing from the general economic conditions of poverty and unemployment on the island rather than from specific political persecution. Those able to prove political persecution on an individual level were granted refugee status.

But the vast majority of the Haitians were treated as illegal immigrants, a status that some challenged in protracted legal proceedings. When the number of Haitians increased during the Mariel era, the Carter administration initially refused to exercise its parole authority for Haitians as a group. Instead, they were given the same entry status as the Cubans who entered in this period. Thus, on June 20, 1980, the U.S. attorney general administratively established a new temporary status, "Cuban-Haitian Entrant (Status Pending)," for the boatlift people from both countries who had arrived by that date, and issued them a temporary six-month parole into the United States. Eligibility for this status was later extended to all persons who had arrived as of October 10, 1980. During this interval, the administration sought to have Congress give a statutory basis to this emergency classification, but Congress declined to do so. In total, about 123,000 Cubans and over 6,000 Haitians arrived in the United States during this six-month period and were now in a legal limbo as to their immigration status.

In November 1980, President Carter was unseated by Ronald Reagan. In part, the large influx of Cubans and Haitians had contributed to the charge by the Republican party during the campaign that the Carter administration was ineffectual in its ability to govern. The Reagan administration did not want to fall victim to the same accusation in the future. Hence, in 1981, it initiated a controversial two-pronged policy of deterrence to prevent more Haitians from arriving en masse by sea. The U.S. Coast Guard was ordered to begin interdicting refugee boats on the high seas and to turn them back before the Haitians could actually touch U.S. soil and lay claim to being asylees. The government of Haiti formally agreed to accept back all such persons and to do so without reprisals. At the same time, the Department of Justice also adopted a policy of placing all subsequent mass arrivals of people in detention centers rather than, as had been the practice up until this time, releasing them to private sponsors while their status was determined or while subsequent appeals were pending. There was a protracted legal challenge to the detention policy, partly on the basis of a claim that it was racially discriminatory against Haitians. Ultimately, after a series of conflicting decisions by lower courts, the U.S. Supreme Court upheld the legality of the detention policy on June 25, 1985, and ruled that the action was not discriminatory.[22]

As for those classified as "Cuban-Haitian Entrants," the Reagan administration announced in 1984 that all of the Cubans whose status was pending could adjust their status to become permanent resident aliens because they were covered by the Cuban Adjustment Act of 1966, which essentially gave blanket refugee status to most Cubans who reached U.S. soil (the exceptions would be for those who fell into any of the specific exclusionary categories that apply to all would-be immigrants and refugees). Many people believed that the Refugee Act of 1980 had superseded this specific legislation, but the administration said it was not so. A congressional effort made in 1984 to repeal the Cuban Adjustment Act failed, so the preferential treatment for Cubans remained in effect. There were also unsuccessful efforts made to introduce special legislation in 1984 to allow the Haitians of the Mariel era to adjust their status, but it did not pass. Ultimately, however, the controversy over the status of the "Cuban-Haitian Entrants" ended with the passage of the Immigration Reform and Control Act (IRCA) of 1986. Among its multiple provisions were four amnesty provisions for various groups of people already in the United States who had entered outside the terms of existing policy. One of these amnesties permitted all of the 129,000 persons classified as "Cuban-Haitian Entrants" (and not excludable) to immediately apply to adjust their status to become permanent resident aliens. About 3,000 Cubans were found to be excludable due to criminal histories. They were placed in prisons until Cuba would agree to their return.

The Ongoing Dispute over Disparate Treatment

The issue of the differential treatment afforded to Cubans has remained a topic of controversy—especially in the Miami area where Cubans and Haitians have continued over the years to arrive by various means. Cubans, unless excludable, are automatically given refugee status whereas Haitians and others must prove they would be specifically subject to persecution in their homelands. In the ten-year period from 1981 to early 1991, over 23,000 Haitians were intercepted by the Coast Guard and immigration officials as they attempted to enter the United States without proper documents. Only eight Haitians were granted political asylum over this period.[23] Most of the remainder were put in detention camps or returned to Haiti. In contrast, between 1988 and 1991, over 8,000 Cuban balseros (a name given to Cubans who arrive in south Florida aboard anything that will float) were given official refugee status. As a consequence, the bitterness over the differential treatment continued to percolate. In one widely publicized incident that occurred in mid-July 1991, for example, a boatload of 161 Haitians had picked up 2 Cubans they found floating on a raft off the Florida coast before the boat was intercepted by the U.S. Coast Guard. The 2 Cubans were brought to shore and immediately given refugee status and allowed to remain in the United States; only 9 Haitians were brought to shore (6 of them because they were seriously ill; the other 3, after being interviewed at sea, were allowed to file for asylum) while the boat and the other 152 people were returned to Haiti under escort of the Coast Guard. INS officials, speaking of this highly publicized incident, stated "there is nothing perverse or discriminatory about it; it is the law."[24]

Efforts to establish a regularized procedure for the admission of Cubans have passed through numerous iterations. On December 14, 1984, the U.S. Cuban Migration Agreement was signed, which permitted a number of former Cuban political prisoners (and their immediate family members) to enter the United States in return for Cuban willingness to accept the excludable aliens from the Mariel era.[25] The accord also provided for "the normalization of immigration procedures" between the two countries. This meant that persons in Cuba could apply to immigrate and, if they fell into one of the established preference categories of the legal immigration system, they could do so up to the 20,000 annual visa ceiling that applied at the time to all countries. Although widely misunderstood by many Cuban Americans, the agreement did not say that 20,000 Cubans would be admitted each year. It said that within the scope of the existing worldwide ceiling on annual immigrants, Cubans would be granted visas as their eligibility to be considered occurred under the existing immigration system that applies to all countries. It also meant that Cubans could once more enter the United States as nonimmigrant visitors, as can persons from other countries. Hardly had this agreement become operational before it was unilaterally suspended on May 20, 1985, by Castro. His action was a form of protest when a radio station (i.e., Radio Marti) that was authorized and funded by the U.S. government to broadcast freedom messages from Florida to Cuba went on the air. The agreement was reinstated, however, on November 20, 1987. On May 20, 1988, as a result of an unprecedented agreement between a private political organization, the Cuban American National Foundation, and the Reagan administration, 4,000 Cuban refugees who had been settled in Panama and Costa Rica during the earlier Mariel era were permitted to resettle in the United States. The cost of the resettlement of these "third country" Cuban refugees was borne by the foundation rather than by the federal government. During that same year, the U.S. Catholic Conference also worked out an accord with the Cuban government to admit another 3,000 political prisoners and their family members to the United States.

By mid-1991, as the strength of communism in the Soviet Union—which had been a benefactor to Cuba—was rapidly disintegrating, Cuba again experienced mounting economic weakness and political unrest. As a result, the number of persons fleeing Cuba on rafts or small boats began to rise. In addition, applications for nonimmigrant visas from Cubans in 1991 to visit the United States began to soar (i.e., they were approaching an annualized rate of 100,000 persons), and over one-third of those who came as of mid-1991 elected not to return. As Cuba continued to relax its travel restrictions, there was worry among immigration officials in the United States that a "slow-motion Mariel" was developing.[26] Fearing that Castro was again using immigration as a means to reduce the domestic pressure that was opposed to his rule, the Bush administration in August 1991 froze the issuance of any new nonimmigrant visas to Cubans. Before the freeze went into effect, however, thousands of Cubans who had entered the country as nonimmigrants were given blanket refugee status just by asking for it.

Haiti Deja Vu: The Aristide Crisis

Against this backdrop, the differential treatment of Haitians again resurfaced in a major way. Namely, on September 30, 1991, the president of Haiti, Jean-Bertrand Aristide, was overthrown by a military coup and sent into exile. Aristide, who took office in February 1991 after winning a landslide victory, was the first duly elected president in Haiti's 187-year history as an independent nation. In response to his ouster, the United States declared a trade embargo, and Venezuela immediately imposed an oil embargo on Haiti. A month later, the U.S. Coast Guard intercepted the first of what would soon be many boats packed solid with Haitians fleeing the worsening economy and civil unrest on the island. In accordance with prevailing policy, the Haitians were taken aboard and interviewed to determine if any of those picked up wished to apply for asylee status and, if so, whether or not they were eligible. Some did not ask for asylum. The majority, however, were found to be ineligible because they were deemed to be fleeing economic deprivation, not political persecution.[27] Only 200 of the 6,000 Haitians picked up as of December 1, 1991, were found to actually be eligible to apply for asylum. But instead of taking those who were denied asylum to Florida, the Bush administration ordered that they be held on board the Coast Guard cutters. This was done until there was no room left on any of the thirteen vessels initially involved. The Bush administration did not want to do anything to encourage a mass exodus from the island on overcrowded boats that were only marginally seaworthy. Hence, on November 18, 1991, the Bush administration ordered that those denied asylum be returned to Haiti. The administration contended that repatriation would save lives by deterring others from attempting such dangerous voyages. A total of 538 Haitians were, in fact, returned before officials at the Haitian Refugee Center in Miami secured a temporary court order from a federal district judge on November 19, 1991, that suspended the practice.[28] On December 4, the court order was extended pending an appeal to the 11th Circuit Court of Appeals. In issuing this second ruling, the district judge dismissed a claim by the federal government that he lacked jurisdiction because the actions were being taken hundreds of miles beyond U.S. territorial waters, but he made no provision for those in custody to be brought to the United States. In the meantime, the several thousand Haitians who had been held on ships were taken to the U.S. naval station located at Guantanamo Bay, Cuba. A tent city was set up with provisions made to accommodate 10,000 persons while the court drama was played out. Several hundred others were taken to camps in regional countries (Honduras, Venezuela, Belize, Trinidad, and Tobago) that agreed to provide temporary safe haven.

The Bush administration made it clear during this period that it felt that most of the Haitians were ineligible for asylum status. If the Haitians were taken to the mainland of the United States while their status was unclear, the administration felt it could trigger a massive exodus from Haiti of other impoverished persons. As experience has shown, it has proven very difficult to make asylum applicants leave once they are actually in the country. For these reasons, the administration declined to offer "temporary protected status"—a classification authorized under the newly enacted Immigration Act of 1990—to these Haitians who were not found to be eligible for asylee status.

While this was happening, of course, any Cubans picked up at sea were taken immediately to Florida, and, as usual, most were granted automatic refugee status. The difference in treatment once more aroused the bitter charge of racism. Congressman Charles Rangel (D-N.Y.) charged that "this would not have happened if the refugees were Europeans," and Senator Connie Mack (R-Fla.) said "returning Vietnamese, Russian Jews, Cubans, Nicaraguans and others back to the countries they were fleeing would be unthinkable; how can we justify it for Haitians?" [29] The INS acknowledged the differential treatment but rejected the implications of racism by simply pointing out once more that it is Congress that has required the special mandated treatment for Cubans. As INS Commissioner Gene McNary stated, "the simple fact is that because of the Cuban Adjustment Act, Cuban nationals are treated differently under the law."[30]

On December 17, 1991, the 11th Circuit Court of Appeals dismissed the Miami District Court's injunction and held that Congress and the executive branch alone have the authority to set foreign policy.[31] Furthermore, the appeals court ruled that the events had entirely taken place beyond the boundaries of U.S. territorial waters, so the district court lacked jurisdiction. On December 20, 1991, however, the same district court issued another injunction, saying that lawyers have a right to speak to the Haitians before they can be returned to Haiti. No immediate action was taken by the administration to return the Haitians, but negotiations did proceed with the military government to restore the Aristide government while the ruling was appealed to the U.S. Supreme Court. On January 31, 1992, the Supreme Court ordered that the stay issued by the district court be lifted. Two days later, the process of returning those Haitians deemed to be ineligible for asylum to Haiti began. By this time, there were about 12,000 Haitians in custody, of whom only about 1,400 had been found to have plausible asylum claims.

On June 21, 1992, the Supreme Court voted 8–1 to uphold the policy of interdicting Haitian boat people on the high seas.[32] The decision held that such actions that are taken in international waters do not violate federal immigration law or any international treaties pertaining to refugees or would-be asylum seekers. The obligation to consider requests for political asylum does not apply outside of U.S. territory and its foreign embassies.

Meanwhile, as more boats of Haitians were interdicted, the Bush administration, on May 24, 1992, moved to stiffen its policy. It ordered the U.S. Coast Guard to return all Haitians subsequently encountered at sea directly back to Haiti without first determining if they faced persecution. Those Haitians seeking asylum were directed to apply for such status at the U.S. embassy in the capital city of Port-au-Prince. Overruling a federal appeals court decision that temporarily blocked its implementation, the Supreme Court upheld the administration's policy on August 24, 1992, by a 7–2 vote. With these actions, the outflow of Haitians came to a halt, albeit only temporarily.

Of the approximately 40,000 Haitians who had been intercepted at sea and processed on boats or at Guantanamo Bay since the coup, about 10,000 Haitians were found to have a possible basis for filing a claim for political asylum. They were transferred to Miami to pursue their cases. The others were voluntarily or forcibly returned to Haiti.

The Bush administration's policy regarding the treatment of Haitians became involved in the presidential campaign in 1992. The Rev. Jesse Jackson called the policy of forced repatriation "an immoral act of genocide," and he promised to force candidates for office to take a position on the subject.[33] During the subsequent campaign, candidate Bill Clinton attacked Bush's policy toward the Haitians as being "immoral" and "cruel." Bush, in turn, continued to hold to his position that most Haitians were seeking to escape poverty and not political oppression. In a speech in Georgia, he affirmed his policy: "I will not, because I have sworn to uphold the Constitution, open the doors to economic refugees from all over the world. We can't do that."[34]

But after the election in November 1992 in which Bush was defeated, thousands of Haitians began building boats to set sail for the United States immediately following Clinton's inauguration. Economic conditions on Haiti had continued to deteriorate, due to the effects of the prolonged embargo. There were frequent civil disorders in protest of the military rule as well as assassinations of dissident leaders. Against this backdrop, President-elect Clinton suddenly announced on January 14, 1993—just days before his inauguration—that he would continue the Bush administration's policies of at-sea interdiction and in-country processing of would-be Haitian applicants for asylum. He would, however, step up pressure on Haiti's military leaders to allow Aristide to return to office. He felt this was the only way to end the episode. On Clinton's taking office, this policy was pursued, but the issue was not resolved. The military leaders of Haiti refused to allow Aristide to return, even as other nations joined in the tightening of the economic embargo. As boatloads of Haitians continued to be interdicted and those aboard returned to Haiti, the protests of black political leaders in the United States mounted (especially as political conditions in South Africa improved in the spring of 1994). Haitian policy came to the fore of their international political agenda. Consequently, the Clinton administration announced in June 1994 that it would commence shipboard processing of Haitian asylum seekers rather than automatically returning all those persons picked up at sea to Haiti.[35] This action, of course, was exactly the same as the initial policy of the Bush administration. Immigration officials were stationed on a 1,000-bed hospital ship moored in the harbor of Kingston, Jamaica. Those deemed to have a plausible claim for political asylum were transported to the Guantanamo Bay Naval Station for medical tests and further evaluation. Those without valid claims were returned directly to Haiti. The government of the Turks and Caicos Islands agreed to allow some of the Haitians to be held and processed on their territory, but Panama, which originally agreed to do so, changed its mind and refused to be of assistance.

Meanwhile the pressure by the Clinton administration on the military leaders of Haiti to leave was stepped up. U.S. Marines were placed on naval vessels positioned just outside of Haiti's territorial waters. Ultimately, under threat of imminent invasion and with the negotiation assistance of former President Jimmy Carter, the leaders of the coup agreed to go into exile and President Aristide returned to the island and to his position of authority on October 15, 1994. With this accomplished, the process of returning the Haitians still held in detention at Guantanamo Bay proceeded over the next several months. At one point, there had been as many as 21,400 Haitians housed in the camps at the U.S. naval base.

Cuba Deja Vu: A Policy Reversal After More Turmoil

On August 5, 1994, Fidel Castro once again announced that he would not stop anyone who wished to leave Cuba by sea and go to the United States. It led to yet another mass outpouring of people. His action was precipitated by several days of serious rioting in Havana in protest of continuing food shortages and a declining quality of life. Castro blamed the protests on the ongoing economic embargo imposed by the United States and now supported by many other nations. Permitting dissidents to leave has been an effective way for Castro to reduce pressures against his rule. As long as U.S. policy will accept these persons, he has little to lose. Moreover, these actions had, in the past, proven to be an embarrassment to a series of U.S. presidents as it high-lighted the fact that the United States could not control its own borders. Several hundred Cuban refugees a day began to arrive in south Florida over the following week.

The governor of Florida, Lawton Chiles, requested that President Clinton declare an "emergency" situation that would have required the mobilization of funds and services to accommodate an expected surge in refugee claimants. The Clinton administration, however, resisted this proposal for fear it would signal Castro and Cubans in general that the door to the United States was wide open. The administration vowed that it would not permit "a replay of the Mariel exodus." The Coast Guard was ordered to increase its patrols and to seize any boats coming from Florida to pick up refugees. Those Cubans who made it to U.S. shores were initially treated as those before: They were automatically given refugee status and released to sponsors. But suddenly, on August 18, 1994, President Clinton announced an end to the policy of granting political asylum automatically to Cubans, which had been in effect for twenty-eight years. Instead of bringing them ashore to the United States, all future Cubans intercepted at sea by the Coast Guard would be transported to the U.S. naval base at Guantanamo Bay, Cuba (where they would join over 15,000 Haitians who, at that time, were also there—as discussed in the preceding section). Once there, they would be treated the same as the Haitians. Only those who could prove they were subject to persecution could expect to be admitted to the United States. Those fleeing poverty and poor quality of life would be considered economic refugees and would be denied entry. Attorney General Janet Reno, in an effort to stem the outflow, stated that "the odds of ending up in Guantanamo are very great, the odds of ending up in the United States are very, very small."[36] President Clinton firmly stated that the reason for this shift in policy was that he wanted to prevent another Mariel experience. Specifically, he said, "we tried it that way once, it was wrong then, it's wrong now, and I am not going to let it happen again."[37] Those Cubans who somehow avoided being intercepted at sea would not be released on arrival to U.S. shores, but, instead, they would be put in detainment camps in Miami and processed as any other claimant for political asylum.

Initially, the policy shift did not stop the flow of Cubans into the Straits of Florida. But as those intercepted were taken to Guantanamo rather than Florida, it became obvious that the United States was holding firm in its resolve. Unless Castro stopped the outflow, however, it would not be long before there would be no more room at Guantanamo to accommodate both the thousands of Haitians already there and the thousands of Cubans who were now arriving.

To force Castro to stop this process, the administration announced, on August 26, 1994, additional economic sanctions. No longer could Cuban Americans send cash or gifts to friends and relatives in Cuba, and tighter restrictions were imposed on travel between the two nations. Shortly afterward, Panama agreed to permit up to 10,000 Cubans picked up at sea to be kept in detention camps on its territory but kept under guard by U.S. troops.

Many Floridians cheered the new policy stance.[38] Cuban–American leaders were divided in their support and criticism of the fact that, for the first time in almost three decades, Cubans would be treated not as a privileged group, but like everyone else from other countries in their ability to claim political asylum. Attorney General Reno had announced the new policy on August 24, 1994, in a radio broadcast over Radio Marti beamed to Cuba, saying that, "you will not be processed for admission to the United States" if you are taken to Guantanamo or to Panama.[39]

The crisis, however, continued to build. More Cubans took to the sea. On August 23, 1994, over 3,000 Cubans were intercepted and taken to Guantanamo. The Cuban government said it would be willing to enter into broad negotiations that included immigration with the United States but that it would also seek to ease the economic sanctions on Cuba. One Cuban official warned that "if the hostilities continue, we are prepared for no obstacles to be placed in the way of those who leave Cuba."[40] The administration responded that it would talk only about immigration issues.

Ultimately, a meeting was arranged at the United Nations headquarters. The United States, believing that increased immigration would allow Castro to rid Cuba of dissidents, proposed a special agreement with Cuba that would assure that at least 20,000 Cubans a year could immigrate to the United States and maybe as many as 27,845 persons—the annual ceiling under the Immigration Act of 1990 on the number of visas permitted for any one nation that year. It was proposed that the word "family" in the immigration admission process be broadened for Cubans to include cousins, aunts, and uncles of U.S. citizens and permanent resident aliens. The attorney general would use her "parole authority" to guarantee that the full number of Cubans be admitted each year beyond the number who would competitively qualify under the established admission system. Thus, unlike all other countries of the world in which the number of immigrants must competitively qualify for the limited number of worldwide visas (675,000 in 1995, as will be discussed in Chapter 12) so that very few countries ever hit the ceiling of 27,845 for any one nation, Cuba alone would be guaranteed the full amount of annual immigrants (even though most would not otherwise qualify for admission). The parole authority would be used to accomplish this feat because there are no numerical limits on its usage. If the administration wanted to admit more

Cubans under existing law, it would have had to go to Congress and ask for an increase either in the number of refugees to be admitted or in the number of visas available under the Immigration Act of 1990. Both of these options were rejected because, it was felt, it could set off a protracted political fight whose outcome was uncertain. Cuban officials, in a futile effort to broaden the negotiations to include lifting the economic embargo publicly, chided the United States by pointing out the irony of the situation. Namely, for years the United States had been pressing Cuba to allow free emigration, and now that it was happening, the United States was trying to stop it.[41]

Nonetheless, on September 9, 1994, an agreement was reached between the United States and Cuba to end the crisis.[42] Cuba agreed to renew its beach patrols in order to stop the outflow. Cuba also agreed to take back any of those who had fled (now totaling close to 30,000 persons) and who were housed at camps at Guantanamo Bay, Panama, and Honduras or still on U.S. ships, if they voluntarily sought to be repatriated. The United States, in turn, agreed that at least 20,000 Cubans a year would be allowed to immigrate to the United States, and the number could go as high as 27,845, where, as indicated earlier, it was capped by law. If fewer than 20,000 Cubans actually qualify to be admitted, the attorney general will use her parole authority to admit the number of immigrants needed to meet that higher floor. All Cubans on an immigrant waiting list (about 19,000 persons) compiled in Havana by U.S. immigration officials stationed there would be given the opportunity to enter. In the future, all Cubans seeking political asylum must apply to U.S. officials stationed in Havana for in-country processing. Only those meeting the definition of individual persecution will be approved for possible entry to the United States as refugees. The economic embargo against Cuba remained intact. The agreement went into effect on September 13, 1994. There was a flurry of rafters setting sail over the seventy-two-hour period between the signing of the agreement and the time it became effective. At the appointed time, Cuban officials began confiscating boats along the shore, and this phase of the crisis ended. What to do with the 30,000 detainees, however, remained to be settled.

Some of the detainees at the various camps over the next month did seek to go back to Cuba, and they were repatriated. Most, however, did not. In October 1994, the United States agreed to let all unaccompanied minors under the age of thirteen in the camps, as well as all detainees over seventy years of age, to be brought to Miami. In late October, a federal district judge in Miami issued an injunction against any forced repatriation of Cubans. In early December 1994, riots broke out at three of the detention camps in Panama. Over 200 U.S. soldiers were injured as they sought to quell the disturbances, and 1,000 detainees escaped for a short period. In response, the Panamanian government directed that the camps be closed. Beginning in early January 1995, 7,000 of the detainees still in these camps were transferred to Guantanamo Bay. As the cost of the confinement continued to soar and the fear that riots could break out at Guantanamo intensified, it soon became apparent that something must be done. Moreover, the number of pregnancies among the female detainees began to rise—a condition that for medical reasons justified transfer to Miami.

Against this backdrop, the Clinton administration announced, on May 2, 1995, a dramatic policy shift.[43] All 20,916 Cubans still at Guantanamo Bay would be allowed to enter the United States over the following few months. They would be allowed to apply for political asylum. All future Cubans intercepted at sea, however, would be returned directly to Cuba. They could apply with U.S. consular officials stationed on the island, but they would have to qualify on the same grounds as any other would-be refugee claimant. The era of automatically being brought to the United States and receiving refugee status was over. A White House spokesman described the new policy as follows: "We're rescuing people at sea and doing what we do with anyone—return them to their country when they are trying to immigrate illegally."[44] The new policy was both praised and condemned. On the day after it was announced, the first test came when thirteen Cubans were picked up at sea and returned by the Coast Guard to Havana. The governor of Florida heralded the new policy, saying that it "will insure that Florida should never again confront a massive wave of uncontrolled immigration from Cuba."[45] Some Cuban–American political groups, however, pledged to seek a policy reversal in the future. One said "as soon as Americans see on CNN a bunch of Cubans crying as they've been returned to Castro, the Administration will have to re-evaluate its policy."[46]

The 1995 agreement, however, has a loophole that in subsequent years has allowed Cuban refugee flows to continue—albeit at a very slow pace—but that has often had tragic consequences. Namely, since the Cuban Adjustment Act of 1966 has not been formally repealed by Congress, the 1995 agreement has been interpreted by practice to say that any Cubans who can defy being intercepted at sea by the U.S. Coast Guard and actually set foot on U.S. soil are allowed to stay. They are granted refugee status automatically. This arrangement is popularly referred to as the "wet foot, dry foot policy." It means that, if Cubans are caught at sea, they are returned to Cuba; if they elude capture and reach U.S. soil, they are automatically given refugee status and can remain. Thus, the situation has generated an organized human smuggling process whereby Cuban family members living in Florida pay smuggler networks significant sums (reportedly about $8,000 per person in 2001) to pick up relatives clandestinely in Cuba and use high-powered speedboats to transport their human cargo to the nearest Florida shore (often to any of the string of islands known as the Florida Keys that protrude into the Florida Straits). If detected, the crews on the boats do everything they can to evade capture. If they are stopped and efforts are made to force the people to board U.S. Coast Guard cutters for return to Cuba and to confiscate their boat, those aboard often resort to physical violence. All of the boats are overcrowded, which sometimes causes individual accidents; others have sunk with the loss of life of all aboard. In 2001, over 800 Cubans made it safely to shore; how many perished will never be known.[47]

The politicalization of Cuban refugee policy, with its mass asylum consequences, has been one of the contributing factors to the return of mass immigration since 1965. In the process, the differential treatment of Cubans and Haitians has caused what should be seen as a genuine humanitarian gesture to become unnecessarily a cause of bitterness and a subject of derision.

The "Politicalization" of Human Rights: The Case of Central America

Throughout the 1980s, there were numerous other examples of the distortion of refugee policy to conform to foreign policy goals. The most striking of these instances was in the differential treatment of persons from certain countries in Central America. Beginning in 1981, the Reagan administration concluded that "human rights"—which the preceding Carter administration had championed—was a threat to its foreign policy goals in Central America. Hence, the U.S. Department of State decided that "human rights" should be defined as "political rights" in order to convey "what is ultimately at issue in our contest with the Soviet Bloc."[48] Thus, U.S. foreign policy in this region shifted from a focus on the sanctity of human life to a concern for political freedoms and civil liberties. As Charles Maechling observed, the Reagan administration's policy sought "to divert public attention from the atrocities and abuses of 'friendly' governments to the constitutional imperfections and civil liberty infractions of adversaries."[49] Little attention was to be given to the cruelties committed by constitutional governments in this region against the native Indian populations and political dissidents by right-wing governments that had been elected into power in Guatemala and El Salvador. Conversely, major opposition was mounted by the Reagan administration against the Marxist Sandinista government that had seized power in Nicaragua. The implementation of this policy created grotesque problems for the administration of the nation's refugee policy in Central America.

The origins of the instability of most countries in Central America are as much social as they are political. The rapid rate of population growth is a persistent negative influence on efforts to stimulate economic development.[50] Rapid population growth is the fundamental source of the region's political turmoil and violence because it is linked to the problems of health, housing, education, nutrition, and land use. Thus, it is not surprising that many people would want to leave. For most Central Americans, the legal immigration system of the United States—with its visas largely restricted to those with family ties or who possess specific job skills—offered no opportunities. But when civil war broke out in El Salvador and in Nicaragua, and when "death squads" and guerrilla fighting flared up in Guatemala, U.S. refugee policy offered a possible way out for many people in this region—if they qualified.

Under the prevailing policy of the 1980s, however, refugee status could not be given to individuals simply because they were caught in the midst of fighting or because civil authorities could not maintain domestic order. Refugee status could be given to only those individuals confronted with persecution for one of the five grounds specified in the Refugee Act of 1980. Otherwise, those who entered the United States without a visa, or who overstayed a visa, were considered to be illegal immigrants and subject to deportation if apprehended. It was in this context that several hundred thousand people from these three countries entered the United States during the 1980s by whatever means they could. The issue was whether they were legitimate asylum seekers who should be permitted to stay or illegal immigrants who, if caught, should be returned to their homelands.

To the Reagan administration, most of those fleeing from El Salvador and Guatemala were perceived as being persons who were fleeing from poverty and related economic adversities. Therefore, they did not qualify for asylum status. On the other hand, a far more lenient position was taken with regard to persons fleeing from Nicaragua where a left-wing government had seized power through the use of force. Indeed, on July 8, 1987, Attorney General Edwin Meese went so far as to issue an order that no Nicaraguan in the United States who had "a well-founded fear" of persecution would be deported and that they were to be immediately issued work authorizations if they requested them. He directed INS officials "to encourage and to expedite" such Nicaraguans to file such requests and also to "encourage Nicaraguans whose claims for asylum . . . have been denied to reapply for a reopening or rehearing."[51] It was essentially a declaration of "safe haven" for Nicaraguans for as long as the fighting between the Contras (the guerrilla forces supported by U.S. foreign policy) and the Sandinistas (the unelected Marxist government) continued.

In making this policy declaration, Meese indicated that the Department of Justice was simply implementing a U.S. Supreme Court decision rendered earlier in 1987. In that decision, the Court held that the Refugee Act of 1980 required only that an asylee applicant have "a well-founded fear of persecution" rather than "a clear probability of persecution," which had been the previous stricter standard.[52] Meese's statement, however, said nothing about the status of persons from El Salvador who were entering the United States in droves. Nor did he indicate that the Court's decision applied to all asylum requests regardless of the nation involved—which, of course, it did. Indeed, in May 1987, the Reagan administration denied a specific request from the president of El Salvador, Napoleon Duarte, that Salvadorans apprehended without proper documents to the United States not be deported, because of the rapidly declining economic conditions and the reign of violence within the country. The number of such Salvadorans in the United States at the time, who had entered without inspection, was estimated to be about 450,000.[53]

When asylum requests were filed during the 1980s, the approval rate was over 80 percent for Nicaraguans while being only about 2 to 3 percent for requests from Salvadorans and Guatemalans. It was in this context of seeming unfairness that a grassroots protest movement, known as the Sanctuary Movement, was spawned in the Southwest, in 1982, and briefly flourished across the country.[54] Without going into detail, the supporters of this movement argued that refugee policy was being twisted by the Reagan administration from being a politically impartial policy to being one designed to further its foreign policy agenda. They argued that asylum protections were readily available to refugees from "left wing" dictatorships (like Nicaragua and other countries at the time like Afghanistan, Poland, the Soviet Union, Vietnam, and Cuba) but seldom available for those fleeing "right wing" governments (like Guatemala, El Salvador, or Haiti). The Sanctuary Movement involved political and religious activists who created an "underground railroad" that physically transported Salvadorans and Guatemalans from the U.S. border region through a series of loosely associated churches and safe houses into the interior of the nation. Leaders in Texas and Arizona were subsequently arrested, tried, and convicted of smuggling illegal immigrants into the United States. Following their trials (in which they usually received suspended sentences), these leaders vowed to continue their activities until the policy inequities were ended, but in a less publicized way.[55]

As for Nicaraguans, the "Meese directive" of 1987 was widely interpreted as a green light to enter the United States en masse because there seemed to be little chance of being deported if apprehended. And they did. In April 1988, the administration added support to this perception when the INS announced it would allow aliens crossing the U.S.–Mexico border to obtain asylum applications in Harlingen, Texas (the nearest U.S. land entry point to Nicaragua), but they would not have to file them until they reached their final destination (usually Miami but also, in significant numbers, Los Angeles and New York City) in the interior. As one might expect, asylum applications soared as thousands of Nicaraguans, mostly impoverished persons and families who were fleeing the declining economic opportunities and falling standards of living in their homeland, crossed through Mexico and into the United States. Many other Nicaraguans simply entered illegally and made a claim for asylum only if they were apprehended. Unlike the original outflow of the Nicaraguan business class that had fled to Miami after the Sandinistas took control of the government in Nicaragua in the early 1980s, those who came in the late 1980s were from the countryside and were typically poor, unskilled, and illiterate.[56] As it had been before with the Cubans and then the Haitians, it was the native-born black population that bore most of the ill-effects of the flood of Nicaraguans into the Miami-Dade County labor market. Their negative reactions to the onslaught of new refugees contributed to a series of violent racial riots in Miami.[57]

By late 1988, the folly of the Reagan administration's political policy had become apparent. Over 27,000 Nicaraguans had requested asylum petitions at Harlingen, Texas, over the preceding ten months and moved inland. Hence, following the presidential elections in November, the INS, on December 16, 1988, revoked its April 1988 order and reverted to its earlier policy that asylum requests had to be actually filed and processed at the first port of entry in the United States. But the word that the "open door policy" was no longer in effect could not stop those already in transit. Hence, several thousand Central Americans (mostly Nicaraguans) quickly found themselves trapped in south Texas while still others continued to arrive. They were required to remain there until their claims for political asylum were acted on. Detention camps were set up by the INS to hold those whose requests were denied, while others, whose applications were pending, set up a "tent city" or moved into various abandoned buildings in the area to await decisions. Local social services were quickly overwhelmed by the associated food and medical costs. At its height, there were about 3,600 people living under such dire conditions. On January 9, 1989, a federal district judge issued a temporary restraining order that directed the INS to desist from its policy of keeping the applicants in south Texas while their claims were reviewed. The immediate effect was that most of these asylum applicants moved inland to cities like Miami and Los Angeles as had their fellow countrymen before them. Another 5,200 asylum applicants crossed into south Texas (including some Mexican nationals who felt they, too, had found a loophole in U.S. immigration policy) over the next five weeks before the judge lifted his restraining order. The INS policy of receiving and processing applicants at the point of entry was reinstated. Plans to establish detention camps in south Texas were announced where applicants would be placed while their papers were processed.[58] As a consequence, the flow of asylum seekers declined sharply. A year later, in February 1990, the Sandinista government was voted out of office and replaced by a government more sympathetic to U.S. interests. Nonetheless, the economy of Nicaragua did not improve, so the exodus of Nicaraguans continued, but there was no longer a political advantage to be gained from granting refugee status to those who fled to the United States. They were considered to be illegal immigrants, which, had it not been for Attorney General Meese's interference, most of those who entered earlier would have also been so classified. Indeed, the majority of those Nicaraguans who requested asylum applications during this episode did not show up for subsequent hearings on their applications. They simply "disappeared" into the large Hispanic communities in their destination cities. Even many of those who did show up for hearings and, after adjudication, were denied asylum protection simply stayed in the United States, albeit as illegal immigrants. Only some of those who became involved in criminal activities sometimes found themselves deported out of the country.

As for those who fled from El Salvador and Guatemala during the 1980s, the fact that virtually none of their applications for political asylum were granted during this period became the subject of a class action suit that was filed in May 1985 by a number of church groups—many of which had been associated with the aforementioned Sanctuary Movement. The suit alleged that during the Reagan years, the federal government had not acted in a neutral, nonpolitical manner as required by the Refugee Act of 1980. As a consequence, it was alleged that many persons from these two countries concluded it was futile even to apply for asylee status through administrative channels and that many of those apprehended were falsely classified as being illegal immigrants.

On December 19, 1990, the U.S. Department of Justice reached an out-of-court settlement with these churches. The government agreed to stop detaining and deporting aliens from El Salvador and Guatemala until it granted a hearing to 150,000 persons from these countries who had been declared illegal aliens because their asylum requests were denied over these years or whose final decisions on such requests were pending.[59] Moreover, the settlement also required the INS to offer hearings to another estimated 350,000 persons from these countries who were believed to have entered illegally during these years and who did not file for asylum became of possible beliefs that the procedures were weighted against them.

Meanwhile, the blatant distortions of refugee policy had led Representative Joseph Moakley (D-Mass.) and Senator Dennis DeConcini (D-N.M.) to introduce bills in Congress to provide safe haven for Salvadorans. Their proposal was included in the Immigration Act of 1990. It created for the first time a Temporary Protected Status (TPS) for persons fleeing from disorder in their homelands but who do not qualify for refugee status because they are not the specific target of persecution. The expectation was that, when matters settled down in their home countries, these persons would return to their countries. In the meantime, they could register with the INS and be given documents that permitted them to work temporarily in the United States. Over 187,000 Salvadorans came forth to do so. In 1992, however, a peace treaty was signed in El Salvador between the warring factions, which made it difficult to press pending claims for refugee status and meant that TPS would soon be withdrawn.

Meanwhile, the aforementioned court victory against the Department of Justice in 1990 and the adoption of a formal TPS policy that same year gave legal advocates and other activist groups the opportunity to pursue steps to allow these various Central Americans to remain permanently in the United States.[60] By this time, many of these persons had been in the country for a number of years. Some had married U.S. citizens. Some had had children born in the United States and who were now U.S. citizens. Many others claimed that they had now been acclimated to America and would find it difficult to readjust to life back in their homelands. To make a long story short, advocates used highly publicized vigils, fasts, and demonstrations as well as broad political alliances with other immigrant organizations that culminated in the passage of the Nicaraguan Adjustment and Central American Relief Act of 1997. Essentially, its provisions granted amnesty to approximately 150,000 Nicaraguans who had entered the United States before December 1, 1995, and to 50,000 Guatemalans and 200,000 Salvadorans covered by the 1990 court decision who applied for asylum before April 1, 1990, as well as most of their family members. They could have their status adjusted to become permanent resident aliens.

Soviet Emigres: International Relations Collides with Domestic Politics

Still another, highly contentious refugee issue of the 1980s centered on the status of émigrés from the Union of Soviet Socialist Republics (USSR). Throughout the Cold War era, the Soviet Union was criticized for its restrictions on the emigration rights of its people. Over these years, there were individual cases of Soviet citizens who sought asylum (or Extended Orders of Departure) after they were already in the United States. Usually they involved musicians, athletes, dancers, students, or scientists, but sometimes they were former government officials or secret agents in the United States or who had defected in another free nation and sought to resettle in the United

States. But always there was the larger issue of the plight of individuals and groups within the Soviet Union who were not free to leave. Among these were leaders of various dissident groups but also there were the general groupings of people, usually religious in nature, who were unable to pursue the practice of their faiths (e.g., Jews, Ukrainian Catholics, and various Evangelical Protestants). There were also members of various ethnic groups who felt they, too, were singled out for persecution due to their resistance to assimilating.

Prior to the passage of the Refugee Act of 1980, there was a brief period of liberalization in Soviet emigration policy during the 1970s. It was associated with the era of political "détente" in U.S.–Soviet relations. In 1979, for instance, over 70,000 persons were permitted to leave the Soviet Union. Some went to other western European nations, some to Israel, but most were admitted to the United States through the use of the attorney general's parole authority. In December 1979, however, Soviet troops entered Afghanistan in an ill-fated attempt to suppress a coup against its puppet government. The era of détente ended, and an immediate casualty of this renewal of the Cold War was emigration. The number of Soviet émigrés fell to about 20,000 in 1980, and it continued to decline until 1985 when it numbered just over 1,000 persons. Most who were allowed to leave were Jews, Armenians, and ethnic Germans.

Throughout the 1970s and the first half of the 1980s, the very act of applying to emigrate had the effect of turning applicants and their families into internal refugees. "The applicant was identified as someone disloyal to the Soviet system who lost his or her employment, apartment, and frequently, suffered social and political ostracism."[61]

But, beginning in 1987, another reversal in Soviet attitudes occurred as the policy of "glasnost" began to take hold. A number of Jews (8,000 persons) and Armenians (3,000 persons) were permitted to leave that year. Most entered the United States. Another 14,500 ethnic Germans were allowed to move to West Germany. Discriminatory actions against those who applied for exit visas rapidly diminished. In 1988, the liberalization trend continued in the Soviet Union, and it was accompanied by similar actions in many eastern European nations under Soviet control. Over 108,000 persons from the Soviet Union were permitted to leave, which made 1988 a record year. Most of the successful Soviet applicants in 1987 and 1988 who applied to the U.S. Embassy were required to be persons who had some family ties to U.S. citizens. The majority did, in fact, immigrate to the United States directly. Other Soviet Jews without such family ties were allowed to apply to the Dutch Embassy for visas to immigrate to Israel or to West Germany. When these émigrés arrived in Vienna, Austria (the usual railroad exit point from the USSR), the majority then changed their travel plans, tore up their

Israeli visas, and proceeded to Rome, where they applied directly to the U.S. Embassy to seek entry to the United States as refugees. Their requests were usually granted, with the attorney general using the parole authority to accomplish the feat with little attention given to whether or not the applicants were actually experiencing any persecution that would qualify them for refugee status.

This policy quickly led to a strange international confrontation over the application of U.S. refugee policy. Namely, the government of Israel requested that the United States cease giving refugee status to the Soviet Jews.[62] The Israeli government actually proposed that all Soviet Jews be required to go to Bucharest, Rumania (still a communist-dominated country) to pick up their Israeli visas rather than to exit in Vienna. They would then have to travel directly to Israel and could not get to Rome to file for refugee admission to the United States. This Israeli action, in turn, was bitterly criticized by Jewish groups in the United States (who felt Soviet Jews ought to be free to choose where they wish to resettle) and by various Arab groups (who did not want more Jews to settle in Israel). U.S. refugee policy had once more become a subject of external political manipulation. Pushed to the background was the more fundamental issue. Were these persons actually qualified to be political refugees because they were the targets of individual persecution, or were they economic migrants who were looking for a way to improve their economic conditions as the Soviet economy was collapsing?

As 1988 was again a presidential election year, the Reagan administration chose to maintain the status quo with respect to the status of Soviet Jews and to leave a solution to its successor.[63] In the first nine months of 1989, 46,000 Soviet émigrés were admitted to the United States, and the international tension over the issue continued to mount. Groping for a resolution, the newly elected Bush administration announced that, as of October 1, 1989, all Soviet applicants who intended to apply for admission as refugees while still in the Soviet Union would have to apply at the U.S. Embassy in Moscow. The "Vienna–Rome pipeline" was closed as of that date. In the following months, over 600,000 applications were distributed, of which over 300,000 were completed and returned. In the fiscal year 1990, about 50,800 Soviet refugees were admitted to the United States (of whom 8,000 were "third country refugees" whose expenses were privately funded by Jewish organizations under the same arrangement with the U.S. government that had been reached with private Cuban organizations in 1988). In May 1991, the Soviet Union adopted a new emigration law that eased the ability of persons to leave the country to resettle elsewhere.

Thus, there was a complete reversal of the emigration situation. Whereas in the early 1980s the policy concern of many of the nations of the free world had been directed to persons who wished to leave the Soviet Union and its eastern European satellites but could not, the concern had switched in the early 1990s in western Europe to a fear that far too many would actually elect to do so.[64] It became also a vital concern for policymakers in the United States.

With the formal breakup of the Soviet Union in December 1991, it has been more difficult over the succeeding years to make the case that émigrés from these countries qualify as political refugees. Given the transitional difficulties associated with the conversion to market economies that ensued, it is likely that most who sought to leave were economic refugees. If so, they were not much different in their quest for better living standards and economic opportunities than were the persons from the myriad Third World nations who annually seek to enter the United States and western Europe. Just because the United States and other free nations supported the right of people to leave their homelands, it does not mean that those people must be automatically admitted to the United States or these other nations. As Senator Alan Simpson futilely protested in 1996, "we ought to stop this gimmickry of the use of the word 'refugee.' We must distinguish between the right to leave the Soviet Union and the right to enter the United States. They are not the same thing."[65] Yet, from 1996 to 2002, almost 100,000 persons have been admitted from the former Soviet Union as "refugees" even though there is no evidence of any generalized persecution involved in their circumstances. Political considerations largely explain the perpetuation of this policy distortion.

China: Politics Cause Policy Chaos

On his last day as attorney general before resigning from that office, Edwin Meese sought to add a new wrinkle to the "politicalization" of refugee policy. On August 5, 1988, he issued policy guidelines for asylum requests that instructed the INS to consider requests from individuals from China who cited the possibility of persecution on the grounds that they violated that country's "one couple, one child" family-planning policy if they were forced to return home. Meese requested that, on a case-by-case basis, the INS consider whether such a refusal to follow government population policy constitutes political dissent and would, therefore, be a proper grounds for granting asylum.

There was immediate opposition to this arbitrary action. Critics pointed out that if the population policy of China applies uniformly to everyone, it cannot be a form of individual persecution. After all, the purpose of China's policy is to reduce the nation's population growth rate for an equally compelling humanitarian reason: to provide a higher standard of living for the future generations of Chinese citizens. In the first test case of this decision, the INS rejected an asylum request, in May 1989, by a married couple from China who entered the United States illegally.[66] The policy itself, however, was not revoked.

Subsequently, on November 30, 1989, President George Bush issued a directive that permitted asylum to be granted to people fleeing pressure in their native lands to have abortions or to be sterilized. The following May, the Department of State ruled that a Chinese couple who fled China ostensibly for these reasons qualified for refugee status.[67] The Department of State, however, refused to elaborate on the basis for its decision. Yet the precedent for creating an administrative category of "reproductive refugees" was established.

In 1993, however, the newly elected Clinton administration reversed the Bush policy of offering political asylum to women who showed evidence of being subjected to compulsory abortion. This led to a move in Congress to write the Bush policy into the nation's asylum law. This attempt caused Undersecretary of State Tim Wirth to say that if such action is taken by Congress, "we could potentially open ourselves up to just about everybody in the world who says 'I do not want to plan my family, therefore I deserve political asylum.'"[68] Nonetheless, in 1996, the Illegal Immigration Reform and Immigrant Responsibility Act of 1996 was passed and signed into law by President Clinton. It contained a provision that stipulates that a person qualifies as a refugee or asylee persecuted for political opinion if forced to undergo, or who has a well-founded fear of being compelled to undergo, or who resists a coercive population control procedure. A cap, however, of 1,000 annual asylum admissions under this provision was specified in the law. In 1999, a total of 185 such asylum requests were granted—mostly to claimants from China. Because this provision involves the politically volatile issue of abortion, it has the potential to have major ramifications on the conduct of immigration policy in the years ahead.

But population control policy was only one issue in which refugee policy became entangled with U.S.–China relations. Ironically, when the Bush administration was confronted with another situation in China in which refugee status seemed logical, it refused to grant it. Namely, after the failed student-led democracy movement in China in June 1989 that culminated in the Tiananmen Square massacre, there were as many as 40,000 Chinese students studying at U.S. universities. Many had openly supported the protests. The Bush administration, however, refused to grant their asylee requests and President Bush vetoed a bill passed by Congress that would have allowed these Chinese students to remain in the country after their visas expired. President Bush, however, did issue on November 30, 1989, an executive order that permitted all such students to remain in the country until June

1994. It was his view that this action, at least for the time being, accomplished the same result, but it did not offend the Chinese government to the same degree as grants of asylum on the grounds of persecution would have. Subsequently, the House of Representatives voted to override the president's veto, but it was narrowly sustained when the Senate failed to vote for an override.[69]

In the next session of Congress, however, the Chinese Student Protection Act was adopted in 1992, which allowed all of these designated students to adjust their status. Beginning July 1, 1993, they could become legal immigrants who would be admitted as skilled workers under the employment-based admission category of the newly enacted Immigration Act of 1990. These applicants were not counted as part of the overall country ceiling for China. Technically speaking, therefore, the 26,915 Chinese students who actually availed themselves of this opportunity were not granted political asylum, so the Chinese government did not lose face. On the other hand, they were all admitted without having to prove that any of them, as individuals, would have been persecuted on return to China. Immigration policy had been again distorted for political purposes.

While the Chinese student drama was being played out in the early 1990s, a more insidious immigration problem involving people from China surfaced, and it led to a direct perversion of asylum policy. Namely, the U.S. Coast Guard discovered that large freighter ships were transporting cargoes of human beings from the People's Republic of China to the West Coast of the United States. These ships, in turn, were met by smaller boats or yachts several miles offshore, where the people were transferred and brought ashore in a clandestine manner. It was a process whereby organized criminal elements in China were smuggling illegal aliens into the country. Typically, these persons had paid large sums for this service and were obligated on arrival to work off these sums under terms of virtual bondage in Chinese-owned business enterprises in the United States. How many such drop-offs occurred is, of course, unknown. But when boats were intercepted by the Coast Guard and the people brought ashore, they typically requested political asylum based on China's "one couple, one child" policy and usually were released.[70] In most instances, they simply disappeared into the large illegal immigration population of the Chinatowns of San Francisco, Los Angeles, and New York City, where they must work for years in essentially a state of indentured servitude to pay off the cost of their transportation.[71]

As the number of interceptions began to mount, what was originally perceived as being an isolated incident was soon recognized as being an organized process that was part of an ongoing criminal phenomenon that continues to this day. The issue received national attention when, in the early hours of June 6, 1993, an aging freighter (called the *Golden Venture*) ran aground on a beach near New York City. It had 286 Chinese nationals aboard. It had been at sea for four months, but, unlike the earlier vessels that had been intercepted on the West Coast, it had sailed around India and Africa to get to the East Coast of the United States. Those aboard were forced to jump into the water, and ten died. The others were rescued but, as they came ashore and were apprehended, they all asked for political asylum. All (either as individuals or their families) were obligated to pay $30,000 to an international criminal network to cover their transportation costs.[72] President Clinton directed the INS to put all of those from the *Golden Venture* in a detention camp for processing, unlike most of the Chinese caught on the West Coast, and he pledged that his administration would work to stop the human smuggling process. Holding the smuggled Chinese in these camps was intended to underline the toughening attitude of the government. Twenty-one crewmembers, shipboard enforcers, and members of the criminal network were subsequently convicted of alien smuggling and sentenced to short prison terms. As for the human cargo, only twelve were granted political asylum shortly after they were detained; about one-third were returned to China, one-third were voluntarily deported to various Central American countries, and the remaining fifty-three were released after almost four years of detention and given paroles to remain in the United States.[73] These released persons, it is reported, were met by the representatives of the smuggling gang to remind them that they still had years of indentured work to perform to repay the original smuggling charges.[74]

Only one month after the *Golden Venture* ran aground, three other freighters, crammed with over 600 persons from China, were intercepted in international waters south of San Diego, California. The freighters were prevented from entering U.S. territorial waters by U.S. Navy vessels. The government of Mexico—after much coaxing from the U.S. government—agreed to allow the ships to be escorted to its territorial waters, where it then allowed the ships to dock. Mexican officials immediately transported those aboard to the airport in nearby Ensenada, and they were then flown directly back to China.[75] In explaining the willingness to perform this task, an official of the Mexican government explained: "We know very well that none of these people who are coming here are being persecuted. The U.S. knows that, too. The only difference is that in the United States the only thing you have to do is step on American soil and cry asylum and you get a hearing."[76]

Obviously, this smuggling process is, in reality, an illegal immigration issue. But it is facilitated by the terms of the nation's political asylum policy should they get caught. In essence, the process is contributing to the creation of a human slavery system in the United States. This is because the Chinese aliens who are not apprehended, and those who are apprehended but are released because they claim political asylum, are typically kept as virtual prisoners while they work for years in restaurants or in "sweatshop" garment factories in urban Chinatowns, at very low wages, to pay off their debts.[77] Others are forced into criminal activity such as prostitution or drug running. If they break the terms of these arrangements, their relatives still in China are killed or tortured by other members of the smuggling organizations.

Asylum Abuse at International Airports

As the mass asylum crises involving Cubans, Haitians, and Chinese captured the headlines of the media and the attention of the courts, another egregious abuse of the nation's asylum policies was occurring. It involved the accumulation of individual requests for asylum of persons, mostly from Third World countries, who showed up at border entry points—usually airports—with false documents or stolen documents or, increasingly, no documents at all and claimed they would be killed or tortured if they were returned home.[78] For a period in 1993, their numbers were averaging almost 10,000 persons a month. In most situations, the individuals were released after making their claim, because there was no available detention space locally available to hold them. They were simply told to show up at a hearing on their request at some future date. Most never appeared.

Under procedures in effect at the time, any person who arrived at such an entry point and made such a request was entitled to a protracted legal process to determine the validity of their asylum claim. As one frustrated immigration official said, "it is so easy to defeat the system that a 10-year-old kid could do it."[79] Nonetheless, efforts to address this abuse of policy met stiff opposition—especially from the immigration bar. The INS did establish, in 1993, pre-inspection screening stations at several foreign airports that have a high volume of U.S.-bound air traffic. These INS officials were given the authority to examine travel documents for their authenticity and to ensure that all persons boarding planes at these foreign airports possessed the required entry documents. All that was required for these stations to be set up was that permission be negotiated with the designated countries. INS officials, however, feel that pre-inspection is a costly procedure for an underfunded agency and not very effective. Only a handful of nations permit the INS to perform this function on their soil. Hence, it is felt that such asylum abusers have simply shifted their departures to airports in other countries where pre-inspection stations do not exist.

In response to these mounting abuses of asylum policy, legislation was enacted in 1996 that authorized summary exclusion (i.e., removal) without the right to a hearing if an alien who arrives at a port of entry without any documents or with false documents is determined by an INS inspector to be inadmissible. A total of 69,309 persons received such expedited removals in the year 2000. Also, the legislation stated that an alien may not apply for asylum if it is determined he or she could be removed to a "safe third country" or if an alien has not filed for asylum protection within one year after arrival in the United States, and an alien who has been previously denied asylum may not apply again unless it can be demonstrated that changed circumstances have occurred since the first application.

The Continuing Weakness of Asylee Policy

As the preceding discussion suggests, asylum policy has taken on a life of its own. It has become a separate immigration admission system. What was originally perceived in 1980 as being an ancillary addition to the nation's overall immigration system has become itself a major contributor to the overall influx of immigrants. Each year, tens of thousands of asylum applications are filed. As only a few thousand requests are actually approved, it would seem on its surface that the issue is not really important. But nothing could be further from the truth. The vast preponderance of the individuals who file asylee applications never show up for the scheduled interviews with INS officials. They simply fade into the local communities and become illegal immigrants. The likely reason for this behavior is that many, if not most, of these applicants are fleeing their homelands not because they fear individual persecution, but because they are in search of a better life in economic terms. Many also expect that there may be another amnesty given to illegal immigrants in the future if they just bide their time.

Even those cases that are fully adjudicated give a false picture as to the consequences. Just because the applicant's request is rejected, it does not mean that he or she leaves the country. Most stay, albeit as illegal immigrants. The reason for not immediately escorting those who lose their cases directly back to their homelands is, in part, a lack of funds to do so. But it is also the case that throughout the 1980s, many of the asylum requests that were denied were from people fleeing from countries that were dominated by communist governments (e.g., Cuba, Nicaragua, Poland) or where tyrannical regimes were in power (e.g., Iran) or where civil unrest was widespread (e.g., El Salvador and Guatemala). Under those circumstances, there was little disposition by the federal government to force people to leave even though they had no right to be in the United States.

With the dismantlement of the Berlin Wall in 1989 and the subsequent breakup of the Soviet Union in 1991, however, the dynamics of refugee and asylee issues were radically altered. In the new world order, differences in political ideology have given way to differences in economic conditions between nation states as the prompting force for the outflow of would-be refugees and asylum seekers. In part, these pressures are associated with the political disintegration of the poorer republics of the former Soviet Union and its former satellite nations into ethnic enclaves. But the most endemic of the new contributory pressures are emanating from North–South economic differences between the "have" and "have-not" nations. Refugee and asylee pressures are increasingly being linked with the broader worldwide issues of population growth and unbalanced economic development.

Rather than reassess the chronic shortcomings of asylum policy in light of the changing world circumstances, the political response has been to tinker with procedures. On July 18, 1990, the Bush administration initiated administrative steps to neutralize the asylum review procedures. The action was, in part, a response to the legitimate criticisms of the biased application of asylum policy that occurred during the years of the Reagan administration. It announced that the INS would establish an Asylum Corps composed of 150 officers who would be specially trained to judge whether an applicant actually had "a well-founded fear" of persecution in his or her homeland. New rules were also promulgated directing these officers to give the benefit of the doubt to asylum requests by aliens. The officers were also empowered to make independent decisions about the merits of such claims without necessarily following recommendations made by the U.S. Department of State on their validity. Moreover, an alien may qualify for asylum on the basis of the applicant's own statements, without corroboration, if the testimony appears "credible in light of general conditions" in the alien's home country. The applicant does not need to prove that he or she was being singled out individually for persecution if "there is a pattern or practice of persecuting the group of persons similarly situated." A new documentation center was created to gather and to hold information about political conditions in various countries for use by the asylum officers. In praising this action, Senator Edward Kennedy stated that "too often in recent years we have tolerated a double standard, under which asylum has been unfairly denied to legitimate refugees for fear of embarrassing friendly but repressive governments."[80] He added that the new rules "are fairer and more generous."

Although these policy changes provided an "even playing field" for all asylum applicants, these procedural changes added to the existing disarray of asylum policy. They constituted an enormous loophole to any quest to establish a comprehensive national immigration policy. If one could reach the United States, all one had to do, if apprehended or detained at a border, was make a request for political asylum. While the case was pending, the applicant could legally work. If the request was approved, he or she was on the road to becoming a legal immigrant. If the request was denied, or if the applicant did not show up for the adjudication hearing, he or she often remained as an illegal immigrant and hoped for a future amnesty. This is not the way asylum policy was intended to work. Its real mission is to serve as a humanitarian outlet for individuals who are actually threatened with death or torture due to the exercise of their human rights. It is not intended to be an alternative entry channel that invites mass abuse by economic migrants.

Recognizing that the political asylum system was linked to the problem of illegal immigration, the Clinton administration proposed significant procedural changes for adjudicating asylum claims in 1994. At the time, the backlog of pending asylum requests totaled 340,000 cases, and some of these cases involved more than one person. The perceived explanation for the acceleration in such requests was "the procedural requirements imposed by current regulations."[81] Moreover, the administration contended that "a significant and growing percentage of current receipts [i.e., applications] are claims that appear on their face to be non-meritorious or abusive."[82] The major object of the revised procedures was to decouple the work authorization from the asylum authorization and to streamline the decision-making process to expedite the lengthy review process in place at the time.

These changes went into effect on January 4, 1995.[83] Under these procedures, members of the Asylum Corps either grant the requests or refer the request to an immigration judge who will actually decide the more difficult cases. No longer is the Asylum Corps involved in writing denials of such requests (which in the past were usually appealed anyway). Hence, meritorious cases can be quickly decided and the difficult cases can be taken up more quickly by immigration judges in the Department of Justice. More importantly, under these rules, asylum applicants are not eligible to apply for an authorization to work until 150 days after the asylum application is accepted for filing. The INS then has 30 days to adjudicate the request and issue an employment authorization document. In total, therefore, it will be 180 days before an asylum applicant is permitted to work, unless the asylum application is granted before that time. If at any time in that period the application is denied, the applicant is not eligible to apply for work authorization, even if the initial decision is being appealed.

By the time the new procedures were put in place in 1995, the pending backlog of asylum requests totaled 425,000 cases. The Asylum Corps was doubled in size (to 300 officers), but the problem remains. At the end of 2001, there were 330,000 cases pending. But of greater consequence than the backlog is the fact that only a small portion of those appeals that are denied lead to actual deportations from the country. Only a policy of detention of all questionable applicants until their cases are decided can ensure that such results occur. Detention, however, is very costly, and it can be quite inhumane treatment for those who are subsequently found to have legitimate cases.

It is also the case that an entirely new agenda of political issues has become the subject of asylum requests. These requests have involved such claims of being persecuted because of one's homosexuality, being a battered wife, fear of female genital mutilation, and being subject to gender discrimination. These are not the concerns that led to the creation of asylum policy during the Cold War era, but the widening agenda has enormous implications for policy evolution in the twenty-first century.

Lastly, in the 1990s, the permissiveness of asylum policy took on a more sinister dimension. It became a vehicle for exploitation by terrorists. In 1993, Sheik Omar Abdel Rathman—an Egyptian cleric who had fled his homeland because of involvement in the assassination of Egyptian president Anwar Sadat in 1981 and for being a member of the militant Egyptian Islamic Jihad movement—masterminded a network of terrorists who detonated a truck bomb inside the World Trade Center in New York City. Rathman had filed a claim for political asylum but did not appear at the scheduled hearing on his claim and, like many others, was not pursued for deportation.[84] The identical abuse of asylum procedures provided the opportunity for Mir Aimal Kansi, a Pakistani Islamic militant, to assassinate two employees of the Central Intelligence Agency in Langley, Virginia, as they arrived for work in 1993.

Thus, the refugee and asylum policies of the nation have become a significant explanation for the post-1965 resumption of mass immigration. Unlike the legal immigration system, the refugee and asylum systems do not have fixed ceilings, and they do not consider the labor market effects as part of their operational features. Like the legal immigration system, however, the refugee and asylum systems have been highly politicized and massively abused.

The Explosion of Illegal Immigration

Although the problem of illegal immigration dates back to the 1870s when the first screening restrictions were imposed, it was not considered a serious problem until after the Immigration Act of 1924 went into effect. Even then, the coming of the depression decade followed by the outbreak of World War II subsequently dampened such tendencies before they got out of control. During the war years of the 1940s, for example, apprehensions averaged only about 12,000 persons a year. There was a significant spurt of illegal immigration from Mexico following the war, but illegal immigration then receded from the mid-1950s to the mid-1960s.[85] The sharp decline was largely the result of a "border sweep" of Mexican nationals conducted by the INS (called "Operation Wetback") in 1954 along the southwestern border, and the residual publicity of that infamous endeavor.[86] But, following the passage of the Immigration Act of 1965, illegal immigration quickly soared.

There are two distinct categories of illegal immigrants. The first involves the foreign nationals who enter the United States by crossing a border in a clandestine manner in order to avoid inspection. Such entries are criminal actions. The second involves foreign nationals who enter with legitimate nonimmigrant visas that allow them to remain in the United States for a limited period of time, after which they are expected to leave. Those who overstay their visas or who violate the terms of their visas (e.g., by working at a job when the visa prohibits such persons from doing so) are also committing an illegal offense.

Table 10.4 shows the rapidity of the escalation in illegal immigration as measured by actual apprehensions by the INS. It shows almost a twentyfold increase in the number of apprehensions between 1965 and 2000. To be sure, there are serious problems associated with the use of apprehension data as a measurement standard. For example, the data contain multiple counts of repeated captures of the same individuals. But there is no reason to believe that this statistical problem is proportionately more serious at the present time than it was in 1965. Hence, apprehension data can serve as a general indicator of changes in illegal immigration trends. Conversely, apprehension data do not include what is believed to be a larger number of persons who enter illegally but who avoid apprehension. It is also the case that over 90 percent of those who are apprehended each year are Mexicans who are physically caught crossing or who are found within close proximity to the border. Thus, non-Mexicans, who are more likely to be visa "overstayers," are significantly undercounted in this data. But debates over the adequacy of the illegal immigration statistics are endless and usually fruitless.[87] Because it is an illegal activity, precise annual flow data will never be available. Thus, the apprehension data are the best indicators that are presently available of the directional trends in illegal immigration. No one contests the fact that the number is large, and few disagree with the view that the trend has been toward annual increases.

As for the accumulated stock of illegal immigrants in the United States, the Census Bureau estimated that they numbered a startling 8.7 million persons in 2000.[88] The previous estimate from the 1990 census was 3.7 million persons.

An immediate explanation for the increase in illegal immigration in the late 1960s was the fact that the aforementioned bracero program (see Chapter 8) was unilaterally terminated on December 31, 1964, by the United States. Over the following years, many of these same agricultural workers from

Table 10.4

Apprehended Illegal Immigrants, Fiscal Years 1961–2000

1961–70	1,608,356	1981–90	11,883,328
1961	88,823	1981	975,780
1962	92,758	1982	970,246
1963	88,712	1983	1,251,357
1964	86,597	1984	1,246,981
1965	110,371	1985	1,348,749
1966	138,520	1986	1,767,400
1967	161,608	1987	1,190,488
1968	212,057	1988	1,008,145
1969	283,557	1989	954,243
1970	345,353	1990	1,169,939
1971–80	8,321,498	1991–2000	14,667,092
1971	420,126	1991	1,197,875
1972	505,949	1992	1,258,650
1973	655,968	1993	1,327,259
1974	788,145	1994	1,094,718
1975	766,600	1995	1,394,554
1976	875,915	1996	1,649,958
1976TQ	221,824	1997	1,536,520
1977	1,042,215	1998	1,679,439
1978	1,057,977	1999	1,714,035
1979	1,076,418	2000	1,814,729
1980	910,361		

Source: U.S. Immigration and Naturalization Service.

TQ = Transitional quarter when the fiscal year was shifted from starting on July 1 to October 1.

Mexico simply returned to seek work as they had done for the preceding two decades. This time, however, they were illegal immigrants and those apprehended were so treated. But it was also the provisions of the Immigration Act of 1965 that contributed to the acceleration of illegal immigration. The Act, it is to be recalled, placed a ceiling on immigration from the Western Hemisphere that went into effect in 1968. This action legally capped the fastest-growing component of the overall legal immigration stream. Likewise, when the annual country limit of 20,000 immigrants a year was extended to Western Hemisphere nations in 1976, it meant that Mexico—which was annually supplying over three times that number of immigrants to the United States—quickly accumulated a massive backlog of would-be emigrants who could not legally leave. The application of the preference system for admission to all Western Hemisphere nations in 1976 also meant that, for the first time, the only ways one could qualify for legal immigration were if one had a relative who was already a U.S. citizen or resident alien; if one had the specific skills, education, or work experience needed by U.S. employers and could, therefore, qualify for the limited number of work-related visas; or if one was a refugee. Once the single worldwide ceiling on immigration went into effect in 1978, there were no nonpreference visas available to anyone for the next ten years. Hence, the only channel available for people determined to immigrate but who did not meet the preference requirements was to enter illegally. Hundreds of thousands of persons from the Western Hemisphere—especially from Mexico but also from various Caribbean islands—did just this. Meanwhile, illegal immigration (in the form of visa "overstayers") began to increase from nations in the Eastern Hemisphere with which the United States had close commercial and/or military relations (e.g., Korea, Taiwan, Iran, the Philippines, and Nigeria).

But the power of the factors that "push" people on a mass scale to leave their homelands (e.g., poverty, overpopulation, unemployment, political corruption, human rights violations, and the lack of economic opportunity) cannot alone explain the scale of illegal immigration to the United States. After all, aside from Mexico and some of the countries of the Caribbean region, there are other industrialized nations that are often nearer to the homelands of those persons from other countries who have instead illegally immigrated to the United States. The answer lies with the fact that the U.S. immigration policy in the post-1965 era up until 1986 lacked any semblance of credible deterrence.

Other industrial nations of the free world typically had in place work permit systems and national identification systems, and they quickly adopted legal sanctions against employers who hired illegal immigrants, when confronted with their presence.[89] The United States did not. It was illegal for aliens to enter the United States without inspection or to "overstay" nonimmigrant visas, but it was not illegal for an employer to hire such persons (knowingly or not). The Immigration and Nationality Act of 1952, as a concession made to Texas agricultural employers, included a specific provision that exempted anything that employers did in their role as employers from constituting the illegal act of "harboring" an illegal immigrant. This was known as the "Texas Proviso." Moreover, when illegal immigrants were apprehended in the United States, they were given the right to contest the charge (but they would have to post bail); to remain in custody and, if found guilty in a legal proceeding, face formal deportation (which usually precludes any future right to legally immigrate to the United States); or to elect to take "a voluntary departure" from the country. About 95 percent of those apprehended at the time elected the latter option. If they chose voluntary departure, and if they had been apprehended near a border (usually the Mexican border), they were escorted to the border and released. Frequently this meant that they simply turned around and sought to re-enter, which made the whole process a farce. If they were actually apprehended in the interior of the nation and chose the voluntary departure option, they were usually released and told to leave, unless some criminal activity was also involved. It is unlikely that many did. In some cases, if the INS had available funds, it would pay the transportation costs of these persons back to their homelands, but such funds were often not available. Again, the whole process had the appearance of being more of a sad joke than a serious deterrence policy. Furthermore, throughout this period, the Border Patrol, which was responsible for monitoring the border region, was chronically underfunded and understaffed (having fewer than 2,000 members, no more than 400 or so who were on duty on any eight-hour shift or any given day but who were expected to patrol the lengthy borders with Mexico and Canada).

Legislative Reaction to Mounting Illegal Immigration

The initial political reaction to the rapid escalation in the number of apprehensions of illegal immigration was to do nothing. Indeed, for ten years following the passage of the Immigration Act of 1965, the powerful chairman of the Senate Judiciary Committee (who had also appointed himself chairman of its Subcommittee on Immigration and who championed the causes of agricultural employers in Congress), James O. Eastland (D-Miss.), refused even to convene a meeting of the subcommittee, where any reform legislation had to originate. Thus, efforts in the House of Representatives in the early 1970s, led by Peter W. Rodino (D-N.J.), to repeal the Texas Proviso and to enact sanctions against employers who hire illegal immigrants were to no avail. Both times the House passed such legislation, the bills died in the Senate.

Perceiving that illegal immigration was reaching a crisis stage, President Jimmy Carter sent to Congress a legislative proposal on August 4, 1977, "to help markedly reduce the increasing flow of undocumented aliens in this country and to regulate the presence of millions of undocumented aliens already here."[90] It included an employers sanction program, enhanced funding for border enforcement, temporary legalization status for illegal immigrants who had been in the country for over five years, and a proposal to increase the country ceiling for legal immigrants from 20,000 a year from Canada and Mexico to a combined level of 50,000 based on demand (which at the time would have meant about 42,000 visas a year for Mexico because Canadians were using only about 8,000 visa slots a year). Lacking a consensus on the merits of these ideas, the Carter proposals were not acted on by Congress. Instead, when Congress established the aforementioned single worldwide ceiling on legal immigration in 1978, the legislation included a provision to establish the Select Commission on Immigration and Refugee Policy (SCIRP).

The Report of the Select Commission

SCIRP was given the mandate to examine all elements of the nation's immigration policy. Illegal immigration, it was felt, could best be addressed as part of a comprehensive examination and possible overhaul of the entire immigration system. Many believed, however, that Congress simply wanted to bide time rather than to react to the Carter proposals to restrict illegal entry, which powerful special interest groups opposed.

When SCIRP released its final report on March 1, 1981, it proposed significant changes in all facets of the nation's immigration policy.[91] But the recommendations pertaining to illegal immigration drew the most reaction. Succinctly stated, SCIRP called for the enactment of civil and criminal sanctions against employers who hire illegal immigrants (i.e., the repeal of the Texas Proviso), the coupling of sanctions with some form of secure identification system for job applicants (but the commission could not agree on what the nature of the identification system should be), enhanced border enforcement to preclude illegal entry, and an amnesty for those illegal immigrants who were in the United States as of some unspecified date set several years prior to the actual enactment of employer sanctions (in order not to set off any massive onslaught of persons seeking to qualify for a future eligibility deadline).

By the time that SCIRP issued its report, however, the Carter administration had been voted out of office. The incoming Reagan administration had not considered immigration reform to be a high priority. Its initial reaction was to be wary of the subject. Hence, it set up its own task force to study the SCIRP recommendations. Ultimately, a legislative package was put forth by the administration, but its provisions were far more timid than those of SCIRP.[92] Consequently, the Reagan proposals were put aside by Congress, and a bipartisan bill was drafted by Senator Alan Simpson (R-Wy.) and Representative Romano Mazzoli (D-Ky.). It embraced the key recommendations of SCIRP and also proposed a number of other policy changes.

The original Simpson–Mazzoli bill was comprehensive in its design. It sought changes in all of the component parts of the nation's immigration and refugee policies. Nonetheless, the proposals pertaining to illegal immigration attracted the most critical attention. In particular, two key elements— employer sanctions and amnesty—were the targets of attack. In general, people who supported one, opposed the other, but the key to the bill's passage rested on their linkage. Other controversial amendments were added to the bill during the legislative process, pertaining to attempts to add a foreign worker program for agricultural workers and new provisions to prohibit employment discrimination on the basis of alienage (i.e., citizenship). These controversial amendments contributed to the strident nature of the subsequent debate.[93] The upshot was that the bill passed the Senate but died on the floor of the House of Representatives in December 1982. Another attempt to pass a similar bill in the next Congress also failed in the House of Representatives, in 1984, after passing in the Senate.

The Immigration Reform and Control Act of 1986 (IRCA)

With the perception that the problems of the immigration system were worsening, a new tack was taken in 1986: piecemeal reform. Illegal immigration was selected as the first issue to be addressed. This time, different bills were introduced in the Senate and the House of Representatives. In the Senate, Alan Simpson introduced a bill that had three key provisions: employer sanctions, amnesty, and enhanced border enforcement. His bill did include revisions in the existing H-2 provisions (see Chapter 8) that would make it easier for agricultural employers to employ temporary foreign workers as nonimmigrant workers. The hope was that the availability of H-2 workers would ameliorate some of the opposition of southwestern agribusinesses who feared the loss of a substantial number of workers if they could no longer hire illegal immigrants from Mexico. On the Senate floor, Pete Wilson (R-Cal.) offered an amendment to add an entirely new temporary worker program for agricultural workers, and it was adopted. It permitted up to 350,000 temporary harvest workers of perishable commodities to be admitted for each of three years after the proposed bill went into effect. The program contained no provisions for worker housing or other worker protections as required for H-2 workers. The amended bill passed the Senate in September 1985.

In the House, a bill cosponsored by Representatives Peter Rodino and Romano Mazzoli was introduced in September 1985. It, too, contained provisions that were similar to those in the Simpson bill. It also had provisions to make it easier for H-2 workers to be brought into the United States. It did not contain any provisions for any new temporary worker program, although it provided for a transitional temporary worker program for agriculture whereby the number of such illegal immigrant workers who would be permitted to temporarily work in that industry would be annually reduced over a three-year phaseout period.

For the next ten months, there was no visible action taken on the House bill. Behind the scenes, lengthy negotiations took place over the issue of the temporary foreign worker provisions. Involved were proponents of farm workers, supporters of agricultural business interests, and advocates of a compromise solution between these two contending groups in order that the broader immigration reform bill could be debated. Finally, in early June 1986, Congressman Charles Schumer (D-N.Y.), a leader of the compromise group, announced that agreement had been reached on a plan to end the stalemate.[94] His amendment stated that the attorney general could grant lawful permanent resident status to all illegal immigrants who could prove that they had been working in perishable agriculture for at least twenty full days between May 1, 1985, and May 1, 1986. Called the Special Agricultural Worker program (SAW), it was, in essence, another amnesty program. It also provided that, if a substantial number of SAW workers subsequently quit working in agriculture, their numbers could be "replenished" by other workers recruited from foreign countries who could subsequently apply for permanent resident alien status if they worked in agriculture for a set time period. These persons would be known as Replenishment Agricultural Workers (or RAW workers).

The rationale for providing the opportunity for illegal immigrants recently employed in agriculture to become permanent resident aliens was multifold. It overcame the opposition of southwestern growers as to the possibility that employer sanctions would make several hundred thousand of their current employees ineligible to be retained. These agricultural employers had been adamant in their assertions that citizen workers could not be attracted to meet their seasonal demand for workers to pick perishable crops in rural areas. Of equal importance was the fact that the SAW program also overcame the fears of supporters of immigration reform who strongly opposed the idea of a guestworker program (e.g., the Wilson Amendment to the pending Senate bill). By allowing those illegal immigrants who had been employed in agriculture to have a right to obtain permanent resident alien status by virtue of their past employment record and, if they chose, to become naturalized citizens later, these workers would quickly acquire most of the protections and freedoms available to nonagricultural citizen workers. Given resident alien status, SAW workers would be able to qualify for some social entitlement programs in the off-season. Moreover, they would not be forced to remain agricultural workers (i.e., they would not be tied to particular employers as "serfs") if better job opportunities elsewhere should become available to them. For those who remained in agriculture, it would be easier for them to be unionized if they knew that they could remain permanently in the United States. Thus, this ingenious compromise provided a balance between the demands of growers for an adequate supply of labor and the insistence of unions and various Hispanic groups that agriculture workers be protected from the opportunities for exploitation that were traditionally associated with temporary worker programs in the agricultural industry in the past (i.e., during the bracero era).

The immediate reaction to the Schumer Amendment, however, was far from positive. It became a subject of intense controversy. Nonetheless, it accomplished its primary purpose: It broke the logjam in the House Judiciary Committee that had prevented IRCA from reaching the floor. On June 25, 1986, the committee voted to add the Schumer Amendment, with only slight modification, to the bill. The revised version specified that permanent resident alien status would be provided to illegal immigrants if they had worked in agriculture for not less than sixty days during the twelve months that preceded May 1, 1986. At this point, however, Congressman Mazzoli threatened to abandon the entire bill. Calling the amendment "unparalleled, unprecedented, and unacceptable," he pessimistically predicted that "passage of the Schumer Amendment ensures that bill's doom."[95] Nonetheless, the next day the Judiciary Committee voted to send the amended bill to the floor of the House.

For a time, it seemed that Mazzoli's prediction would prove true. The bill was not taken up by the House Rules Committee until late September 1986. When it was, House minority whip, Trent Lott (R-Miss.), called the Schumer Amendment "the most controversial issue" in the entire bill, and Representative Dan Lungren (R-Cal.), a strong supporter of immigration reform, called the amendment "an abomination" that would "kill the bill."[96] When the debate rules were established, however, they forbade any amendments to be made from the floor to the fragile terms of the Schumer Amendment. Other key provisions of the bill—employer sanctions and amnesty—could be debated on the floor and were subject to possible deletion—but no feature of the SAW and RAW programs could be discussed. Their fate was linked to the passage of the overall bill.

A resolution to adopt the debate rules, however, was defeated on the floor of the House of Representatives on September 26, 1986. With the Congress planning to adjourn during the next week, the prospects for an immigration reform bill appeared to be lost again. All fingers of blame were immediately pointed to the provision in the rules that prohibited debate on the Schumer Amendment.

Amid an outcry of critical editorials from the nation's print media in the days that immediately followed, a completely unexpected window of opportunity for the resurrection of immigration reform was suddenly created. The Congress had not yet passed a military appropriation bill that contained several controversial foreign policy provisions. In addition, President Reagan had not yet signed another controversial bill pertaining to the creation of a large environmental "superfund," and there was congressional fear that, if Congress adjourned, he would kill the bill with a pocket veto. It was at this point that officials in the White House suddenly announced on October 7, 1986, that President Reagan would meet personally with Soviet Premier Mikhail Gorbachev in Reykjavik, Iceland, on October 11 and 12. Hence, Congress could not force the showdown on the appropriation bill while the president was preparing for this critical meeting or was actually out of the country at a summit meeting on the possibility of setting an agenda for nuclear disarmament. Thus, an unexpected pause in its planned activities was forced on Congress. Adjournment had to be postponed. With nothing else to do, behind-the-scenes negotiations on the immigration bill were quickly renewed. A minor change was made in the provisions of the Schumer Amendment. The number of days an illegal immigrant who had worked in agriculture in the year preceding May 1, 1986, to be eligible for status adjustment was increased from sixty to ninety. The House of Representatives then reversed itself on October 9, 1986, and voted to accept the debate rules it had rejected only the week before. Fourteen amendments to IRCA would be allowed to be debated (four of which were subsequently adopted), but there could not be any debate on any portion of the Schumer Amendment. A marathon session began, and, late in the evening of October 9, 1986, the House passed IRCA.

A Senate–House conference committee was hastily convened, and it reached agreement on October 14, 1986. In the conference, the Senate proposal for the Wilson guest-worker program and the House proposal for a three-year transitional farm worker program were both deleted; the House proposal with the Schumer provisions was retained. Both houses of Congress then voted to accept the conference report, and the historic bill was signed into law by President Reagan on November 6, 1986.

From the day it was signed, IRCA affected every employer and every jobseeker in the country. Among its major provisions were strictures designed to prohibit employers from hiring illegal immigrants. The Texas Proviso was repealed. An escalating series of civil penalties (i.e., fines), with provisions for criminal penalties for employers who repeatedly violated its provisions, was established. Every time a new worker is hired, the employer must verify that the worker is eligible to be employed. Only U.S. citizens, permanent resident aliens, and foreign nationals with a valid nonimmigrant visa allowing them to work temporarily in the United States can be hired. The employer must see two forms of identification from each job seeker: one identifying the person (e.g., a driver's license) and one proving that the individual is eligible to be employed (e.g., a social security card, a naturalization card, or a valid nonimmigrant visa). The worker must sign an I-9 form stating he or she is eligible to work and that the employer has checked the required identification papers.

IRCA also provided four separate amnesty programs. The largest was the general amnesty that stated that any illegal immigrant who had lived continuously in the United States since January 1, 1982, and who did not fall into any of the excludable categories could register within a twelve-month period that began six months after the Act took effect (i.e., after May 5, 1987). Applicants who could prove their eligibility were granted a temporary resident alien status. After eighteen months in that status, they had one year to file to adjust their status to become permanent resident aliens. As of December 1, 1991, 1,760,201 persons filed for coverage by the general amnesty. Of these, 94.8 percent were approved and granted temporary resident status. Of the 1,580,558 persons who had followed through with an application for permanent resident status as of that date, 1,526,814 were approved (or 96.6 percent).[97]

The second amnesty was the aforementioned SAW program, whose applicants had to have worked in perishable agriculture for ninety days in the year ending May 1, 1986. The number of SAW applicants far exceeded what anyone expected. A total of 1,272,978 persons filed for the SAW amnesty, of which 997,429 (or 88 percent) were approved. SAW applicants who had worked in the United States in the years 1984–86 were immediately eligible for permanent resident status; those who had worked only in 1986 were granted temporary resident alien status for a year, after which they automatically acquired permanent resident status.

The other two amnesties were smaller scale. One provided specific amnesty to the 129,000 persons previously discussed as being the "Cuban–Haitian entrants" who entered during the Mariel era. The other involved an update in the legal registry date from June 1, 1948, to January 1, 1972. The registry date provision allows the attorney general, at his or her discretion, to adjust the status of persons who had illegally entered prior to that date to become permanent resident aliens without having to meet the various eligibility standards of the other amnesty programs.

In addition to the substantial number of persons who were the direct beneficiaries of the amnesty programs, there were substantial family reunification obligations associated with each person who was granted permanent resident alien status. Many spouses and children of such amnesty recipients were already in the United States. The general amnesty under IRCA, however, did not cover any persons who had entered after 1982, so there was concern that some family members who arrived after that date could be deported. In February 1990, the INS reversed its initial position that made no exceptions to enforcing the letter of the law. The INS announced that a "family fairness" policy would be administratively put into place that modified its original stance.[98] Children and spouses of amnesty recipients would be granted a temporary resident status and be permitted to work if they were residing in the country prior to November 6, 1986. The change did not affect the status of children over the age of eighteen or family members who arrived after that cutoff date. But even most of these persons were eventually eligible to legally immigrate to the United States once the amnesty recipient received permanent resident status or, later, when they qualified to become a naturalized citizen.

IRCA also included provisions that strengthened the existing law on employment discrimination on the basis of national origin as it expanded the nation's civil rights law by prohibiting discrimination on the basis of alienage (i.e., citizenship). An interesting feature of this provision, however, is that it specifically states that employers may always give hiring preference to a citizen job applicant if the citizen and noncitizen applicants are viewed as being equally qualified. Such absolute preferences for one group relative to another are not available under the other protected categories specified in the Civil Rights Act. The protection against citizenship discrimination applies to the public as well as to the private sector. But in the public sector, an important exception is made that limits its scope. Namely, in government employment, certain jobs may be designated by law, regulation, executive order, or government contract to be filled only by citizens. There are many such occupational restrictions at the federal, state, and local levels of government that legally remain in effect.[99] In New York, for example, public school teachers and state troopers are required to be U.S. citizens. In California, all "peace officers" (which include occupations ranging from state troopers to welfare investigators to members of the state Board of Dental Examiners) must be U.S. citizens. In 1976, President Gerald Ford issued Executive Order 11935, which requires most civilian federal workers (except those employed by the U.S. Postal Service) to be U.S. citizens. In the wake of the terrorist destruction of the World Trade Center, on September 11, 2001, the Aviation and Transportation Act of 2002 requires that all airport security screeners must be both federal employees and U.S. citizens.

Lastly, IRCA did include provisions to make it easier for employers to hire temporary workers under the H-2 provisions for nonimmigrant admissions. Agricultural workers were separated into a new H-2A section in the hope that, in the future, agricultural employers, when confronted with real labor shortages, would make use of this program rather than to agitate for any new temporary worker program as they had done throughout the debates on immigration reform in the 1980s. Section H-2B was reserved for requests from nonagricultural employers who had similar requests for temporary foreign workers to meet specific labor market shortages.

The Continuation of Illegal Immigration

Despite the enactment of IRCA, there are no signs that illegal immigration to the United States has abated. As noted in Table 10.4, apprehension rates only slightly declined after IRCA went into effect, but by 1990, they were back at pre-IRCA levels. Since then, as also indicated in Table 10.4, illegal immigration has soared. Aside from the substantial "push" factors involved in the process of generating illegal immigrants in the source countries that IRCA did not address, it has remained the case that enforceability of the nation's immigration laws is still a problem. The employer sanctions program contained an enormous loophole. IRCA did not require that a counterfeit proof identification system be established to verify eligibility to work. Employers were not responsible for the authenticity of the documents that were offered by job applicants. They were required only to make a "reasonable" effort to attest to their validity. As a consequence, producing counterfeit documents— which was always a problem—has become a thriving urban enterprise. The INS has had to devote an inordinate amount of its staff and limited resources toward document validation, which has never been the agency's strong suit.

It is also the case that the amnesty created by the SAW program was massively abused. The legislation placed the complete onus on the INS to prove that the documents that were presented by applicants were fraudulent, rather than on the applicant to prove they were valid. As the number of SAW applicants far exceeded any of the pre-IRCA predictions of the number of eligible agricultural workers, it is not surprising that the SAW program has been aptly described as being "one of the most extensive immigration frauds ever perpetrated against the United States Government."[100]

There is one other counterproductive aspect of IRCA that has contributed to the ongoing issue of illegal immigration. Namely, prior to its passage, it was legal for the INS to go into open farm fields that were the private property of growers without first obtaining a search warrant from a court specifying that there was "probable cause" that illegal immigrants were at work. The legal premise was that fields were open space and are different from buildings and homes where privacy protections require the issuance of warrants before they may be entered by authorities. IRCA responded to the pressure of agribusiness by requiring that the INS had to secure such a warrant in advance of entry onto such open fields. But in rural areas that are distant from courts, it is simply not feasible to locate farm workers who may be illegally employed, go back to a city where a court is located, make a case for a warrant, and return to the original rural location and expect to find the illegal immigrants still there. Hence, the use of "field raids"—which, prior to 1986, had been a highly successful strategy for apprehending large numbers of illegal immigrants—has essentially been abandoned. With these barriers to enforcement, it is not surprising that Gary Thompson and Philip Martin found that IRCA has failed "to convert the agricultural labor market into a legal market."[101]

IRCA was the first legislative step to attempt to control illegal immigration. But, as events were quick to show, it was not the last. By the early 1990s, with apprehension levels exceeding those of the pre-IRCA years, the Commission on Immigration Reform (CIR), in its 1994 interim report, concluded that "enforcement efforts have not been effective in deterring unlawful immigration."[102] Among its multiple recommendations was a proposal for a better system for verifying work authorization. Recognizing the main flaw in IRCA is that work documents are too easily counterfeited, CIR recommended the creation of a computerized registry, using existing data from the Social Security Administration and the INS. Using the Social Security numbers that each citizen and permanent resident alien already possesses, employers would be required to call in the number of each person they hire to verify that the number is valid and that it has been issued to someone who is authorized to work. The advantages of this system are that it reduces the potential for fraud (since it uses data on file with the government rather than documents provided by the worker), it reduces the potential for discrimination on the basis of citizenship and national origin (since employers would no longer have to decide, on the basis of a document review, whether the person is eligible to work), and it would significantly reduce the paperwork requirements required under IRCA to verify employer compliance. CIR also recommended that fraudulent access to "breeder documents"—particularly birth certificates—be reduced by regulation of requests for birth certificate procedures and the creation of interstate and intrastate matching of birth and death records. It called for imposition of stiffer penalties on those persons who produce fraudulent documents. Likewise, it noted the need for vigorous enforcement of existing fair labor standards and the employers sanctions law as an integral part of a strategy to reduce illegal immigration. In order to reduce some of the attractiveness of illegal entry for persons who are not just seeking jobs, the commission also stated that "illegal aliens should not be eligible for any public services or assistance except that made available for compelling reasons to protect public health and safety . . . or to conform to constitutional requirements."[103] Furthermore, it added that "should illegal aliens require other forms of assistance, their only recourse should be return to their countries of origin."[104] This recommendation preceded by a month the passage of Proposition 187 by the voters of California on November 8, 1994, pertaining to exactly the same issue.

Thus, illegal immigration has been a major contributor to the mass immigration that has occurred since 1965. Discussion of the half-hearted and grossly inadequate responses made by Congress in 1996 to CIR's recommendations as to how to make the nation's immigration laws enforceable will be taken up in Chapter 12.

The Accelerating Increase in Non–Employment-Related Legal Immigrant Admissions

One of the many unexpected consequences of the Immigration Act of 1965 has been the steady increase of legal immigrants who are admitted on grounds unrelated to the specific employment needs of the labor market. Table 10.5 vividly reveals this trend. The column labeled "occupational preference" (or "employment related" admissions) shows the annual number of persons admitted under the two preference categories reserved for labor market needs between 1965 and 1991. Table 10.6 shows the data for the four such family preferences in effect since 1992 (after passage of the Immigration Act of 1990). Clearly, the "employment based" preference remains a small component of the total admission flow. In fact, the actual number of needed workers admitted under the "occupational preference" (see Table 10.5) and the "employment based" preferences (see Table 10.6) over the years has been even far smaller than these numbers indicated. This is because "accompanying family members" of those admitted under these preferences are counted individually in these same statistics. For example, the 77,517 persons admitted in 1998 under the "employment based" preferences include not only the persons who are admitted because they qualify to meet the specific skill requirements, but also their spouses and all minor children who accompanied the visa recipient. In this case, 39,283 of the 77,517 persons (i.e., 51 percent) admitted under the "employment based" category were spouses and minor children. Hence, the aggregate data significantly overstate the actual number of persons admitted because they have needed skills or are qualified to be employed in a shortage occupation.

As is clear in Tables 10.5 and 10.6, the vast preponderance of the legal admissions to the United States since 1965 have entered under the "relative preference" (i.e., "immediate relatives" and "family preferences"). They have been allowed to legally immigrate because they are in some way related to someone who is already a U.S. citizen or permanent resident alien. This does not automatically mean, of course, that those admitted under the "relative preference" are lacking in needed skills, educational abilities, or work

Table 10.5

Legal Immigration to the United States by Major Immigrant Categories, Fiscal Years 1965–1991

Year	Total	Immediate relatives[a]	Relative preference[b]	Occupational preference[c]	All other
1991	1,827,167	237,103	216,088	54,949	1,319,027
1990	1,536,483	231,680	214,550	53,72	1,268,204
1989	1,090.924	217,514	217,092	52,775	603,543
1988	643,025	219,340	200,772	53,607	169,306
1987	601,516	218,575	211,809	53,873	117,259
1986	601,708	223,468	212,939	53,625	111,676
1985	570,009	204,368	213,257	50,895	101,489
1984	543,903	183,247	212,324	49,521	98,811
1983	559,763	177,792	213,488	55,468	113,015
1982	594,131	168,398	206,065	51,182	168,486
1981	596,600	152,359	226,576	44,311	173,354
1980	530,639	151,131	216,856	44,369	118,283
1979	460,348	138,178	213,729	37,709	70,732
1978	601,442	125,819	123,501	26,295	325,827
1977	462,315	105,957	117,649	21,616	217,093
1976	398,613	102,019	102,007	26,361	168,226
1976-TQ	103,676	27,895	28,382	5,621	41,778
1975	386,194	91,504	95,945	29,334	169,411
1974	394,861	104,844	94,915	28,482	166,620
1973	400,063	100,953	92,054	26,767	180,289
1972	384,685	86,332	83,165	33,714	181,474
1971	370,478	80,845	82,191	34,563	172,879
1970	373,326	79,213	92,432	34,016	167,665
1969	358,579	60,016	92,458	31,763	174,342
1968	454,448	43,677	68,384	26,865	315,522
1967	361,972	46,903	79,671	25,365	210,033
1966	323,040	39,231	54,935	10,525	218,349
1965	296,697	32,714	13,082	4,986	245,915

Source: U.S. Immigration and Naturalization Service.

Note: The categories listed are generally used to describe large groups of immigrants. During 1965–91, minor changes were made in the qualifications for some immigrant classes making up these categories.

[a]Spouses of citizens, children (unmarried and younger than 21) of citizens, and parents of citizens 21 or older.

[b,c]See Appendices B and C for the preferences that made up these categories under the Immigration Act of 1965 that were in effect over this period.

experiences that are consistent with emerging labor demand requirements. Rather, it means that, if they have these abilities or characteristics, it is entirely incidental to the reason they were admitted. Likewise, the local labor market where those admitted for family reasons seek to find employment is more likely to be located where their U.S. relatives live, rather than determined by prevailing local labor market conditions or actual employment trends.

Table 10.6

Legal Immigration to the United States by Major Immigrant Categories, Fiscal Years 1992–1998

| Year | Total | Family sponsored immigrants | | IRCA legali-zation | Employ-ment based | Diversity | All others[b] |
		Immediate relatives[a]	Family preferences				
1992	973,977	235,484	213,123	163,342	116,198	33,911	157,531
1993	904,292	255,059	226,776	24,278	147,012	33,468	160,325
1994	804,416	249,764	211,961	6,022	123,291	41,056	136,365
1995	720,461	220,360	128,122	4,267	85,336	40,301	132,075
1996	915,900	300,430	294,174	4,635	117,499	58,245	140,917
1997	798,378	321,008	213,331	2,548	90,607	49,360	121,524
1998	660,477	283,368	191,480	955	77,517	45,499	61,658

Source: U.S. Immigration and Naturalization Service.

Note: See Table 12.2 for the preferences that make up these categories under the Immigration Act of 1990, which became effective for Fiscal Year 1992 (i.e., as of October 1, 1991).

[a]Spouses of citizens, children (unmarried and younger than 21) of citizens, and parents of citizens 21 or older.

[b]Amerasians, parolees (former Soviet Union countries and Indochina), refugee and asylee adjustments, and other miscellaneous admissions.

The number of immediate relatives, as shown in Tables 10.5 and 10.6, in the "fourth wave of mass immigration" has also revealed a significant growth trend. In part, this pattern indicates an increasing trend for whole families to immigrate together (in contrast to the immigration pattern of single men that dominated the earlier waves of mass immigration that were discussed in Chapters 5, 6, and 7). This means that there is no longer any proper analogy with the "birds of passage" phenomenon that characterized those earlier waves of mass immigration.[105] Fourth wave immigrants are more likely to settle permanently. Figure 10.1 shows the trends of the component groups that comprise the "immediate relatives" category from 1970 to 1998. Spouses are by far the largest segment of this group, with parents of adult U.S. citizens increasing rapidly. A substantial number of children are also part of the legal immigrant flow of the fourth wave, which means greater pressure on local communities to provide educational, health, and housing opportunities in the local labor markets where their parents have settled. There are also large numbers of parents of U.S. citizens entering, many of whom are elderly and in need of income, support, and medical care.

As for the last column of Tables 10.5 and 10.6, titled "all others," it reflects the growing scale of adjustments to permanent resident alien status of persons originally admitted as refugees and asylees, or as nonimmigrants who have subsequently become eligible for immigrant status (e.g., they may have married a U.S. citizen or been a beneficiary of a change in legislation), or who have become eligible for any of the various amnesty programs created for persons who entered illegally. Here again, virtually all of these admissions have been made without any concern for the human capital endowments of those admitted or the prevailing labor market conditions in the local labor markets where they have settled.

The Immigration Act of 1990

In accordance with the political strategy of pursuing piecemeal reform, the legal immigration system became the next component to be addressed after IRCA was passed in 1986. SCIRP, in its aforementioned report in 1981, stated that "we recommend the closing of the back door to undocumented/illegal immigration" and "the opening of the front door *a little* more to accommodate legal immigration in the interest of this country."[106] The commission, however, called for a "cautious approach" to the topic and specifically stated that "this is not the time for a large scale expansion in legal immigration."[107] It proposed that the number of legal immigrant visas granted each year be raised to 350,000 (plus immediate family relatives who would remain exempt from the numerical ceiling). Included within the slight increase in the

Figure 10.1 **Immigrants Admitted as Immediate Relatives of U.S. Citizens, Fiscal Years 1970–2000**

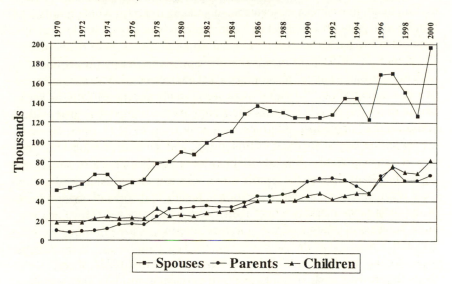

Source: U.S. Immigration and Naturalization Service.

number of visas was the recommendation that a new category of "independent immigrants" be created and that it be assigned a proportion of these new visas (no specific number was proposed). This new category would allow some legal admissions of persons who could not otherwise qualify on the basis of having either family relatives in the United States or having needed work skills.

In 1987, steps to reform the legal immigration system were begun by Congress. In sharp contrast to the common definition of the issues involved in addressing the problem of illegal immigration, there was no clear agreement among policymakers about the ideal composition or the desirable level of legal immigration. Given the preference system created in 1965, family reunification considerations dominate the admission flow. But as immigration scholar John Higham has observed, the dominance of the family reunification preferences is "discouraging the diversity, fluidity, and innovation that immigration traditionally fostered."[108] He has explained:

> In the name of family reunification, the new preferences have given a high claim on admission to certain relatives of immigrants already legally established in the United States. The family reunification preferences have tended to preempt the annual quotas. In doing so they reinforce and

perpetuate existing patterns of migration. Instead of opening a way for prospective leaders, striking out on their own to make a new life, we have with the best of intentions granted a preference to followers, pursuing the family chain.[109]

In searching for alternatives, there were some who felt that it was time to give greater emphasis to the economic effects of the level of annual immigration and the human capital endowments of those who are admitted. But others were far more concerned with another of the unexpected consequences of the 1965 legislation. Namely, the fact that its country-neutral and family-based features had led to a major shift in the immigrant-sending regions away from Europe in favor of a small number of Asian and Latin American countries. By the late 1980s, about 85 percent of all the legal immigrants to the United States were coming from Asia and Latin America. The countries of Mexico, the Philippines, Korea, Cuba, Vietnam, India, the Dominican Republic, and China had become the dominant source countries. Only about 10 percent of immigrants were coming from Europe, the continent that had dominated all earlier mass immigrant flows. Nothing in the earlier debates in 1965 had anticipated such a possible outcome. Thus, one of the leaders of the new reform movement, Senator Edward Kennedy, candidly stated at the beginning of the hearings, in 1987, on prospective changes, that: "One of the issues . . . that I am particularly concerned with is . . . how we correct the unexpected imbalances stemming from the 1965 Act—the inadvertent restriction on immigration from the 'old seed' sources of our heritage."[110]

The ensuing bill, coauthored by Senators Kennedy and Simpson, sought to address these concerns. Their bill, which overwhelmingly passed the Senate on March 15, 1988, sought to place a cap on legal immigration at 590,000 a year. The cap would be on the sum of both the number of family-related immigrants admitted under the preference system and the number of immediate family members. The two had never before been linked in law. It proposed a separate admission track for "independent immigrants" be created for those who could not be otherwise admitted under either the family or the occupational preferences. A total of 50,000 visas was suggested to be made available for such immigrants, and they would be granted on the basis of a point system that rewarded certain factors such as training, age, occupational demand, and English-speaking ability. Originally, there were points to be given if the applicant came from a list of thirty-four countries that had been "adversely affected" by the Immigration Act of 1965 (i.e., mostly European countries). This latter consideration was subsequently dropped after it was publicly criticized for reintroducing national origin considerations. The Senate bill, however, was not acted on by the House of Representatives, although it did hold hearings on the subject.

In the next session of Congress, the Kennedy–Simpson Bill was reintroduced and passed on July 13, 1989, by the Senate. Among its multiple provisions, this revised version called for raising the ceiling on legal immigration to 630,000 persons a year, and it also proposed that a cap be placed on the total number of family-related immigrants and immediate family members who could be admitted.

In the House of Representatives, a different bill was prepared by the Subcommittee on Immigration, now chaired by Representative Bruce Morrison (D-Conn.) of the Judiciary Committee. The House bill was even more expansive in its provisions than the Senate bill was. It called for an increase in legal immigration to 844,000 for two years before falling back to a level of 776,000 a year with no cap on family-related and immediate relatives. It also sought to expand the coverage of the definition of "immediate family members" who could be admitted each year without limits to members of families of permanent resident aliens. It had provisions for the admission of 75,000 "diversity immigrants" (i.e., persons from countries that have had low levels of immigration in recent years) as well as for "investor immigrants" (i.e., persons who agreed to invest in job creating business ventures as a condition of their entry). There were also extensive changes in the various nonimmigrant worker programs as well as a host of other changes in the prevailing immigration statutes that ranged from concern for battered spouses of immigrants to tighter antidiscrimination provisions under IRCA as well as a proposed extension in the time that potential beneficiaries of IRCA's amnesty program could have to convert from temporary to permanent resident status. On October 3, 1990, the House of Representatives passed, with some floor modifications, the Morrison bill.

With enormous differences between the bills that had been separately passed in the Senate and the House, it did not seem that a compromise was likely. It was an election year, and Congress was anxious to adjourn. Moreover, a key supporter of the legislation in the Senate, Alan Simpson, announced on September 24, 1990, that he could no longer support the key feature of both bills—the substantial increases in the level of legal immigration. Simpson noted that recently released apprehension data showed that illegal immigration was again soaring. He reiterated the fact that SCIRP (of which he had been a member) had proposed only "slight" increases in legal immigration and that the recommendation was predicated on the assumption that the "back door" of illegal immigration would be closed. He stated that "we must face the fact that we have not yet closed the back door."[111] He added that "in fact, we are still leaving the back door open while considering prying open the front door much wider," and he concluded that, "I just do not believe it would presently be in the national interest to approve of the increase in legal immigration that we are now contemplating by proposed legislation." He then introduced a bill that provided for the strengthening of IRCA's provisions by addressing the issue of the use of false documents by illegal immigrants and requiring the INS to construct new physical barriers or to upgrade existing barriers at key entry points for illegal immigrants on the southwestern border. He indicated that these concerns should be the quid pro quo for passage of the pending legislation with its proposed substantial increases in legal immigration levels. His proposals, however, were ignored.

It was at this point that politics once more overwhelmed any rational examination of the goals of the legal immigration system. With two bills as diverse as those pending in the Senate and the House, there seemed to be little chance that the differences could be reconciled in the few weeks remaining in the 101st Congressional session. Moreover, the dominant issue that laid claim to national attention at the time was the fact that Congress and the Bush administration were at loggerheads over the federal budget for Fiscal Year 1991 that had already begun on October 1, 1990. The Democrats in Congress were determined to force President Bush to accept a series of tax increases as part of a budget package that included some restraints on government social spending. President Bush threatened to shut down the federal government if his budget proposals—which did not include new taxes— were rejected. When the new fiscal year began and no budget agreement had been reached, some federal agencies were briefly closed, only to be reopened for short periods when the president accepted temporary budget extensions. Without going into prolonged detail, the point is that the media and public attention were riveted on the terms of the budget fight while, behind the scenes, attempts were being made to craft a new legal immigration law from the separate immigration bills that each chamber of Congress had passed. On October 19, 1990, an informal agreement was reached between the leaders of the legal immigration reform movement.[112] In the traditional spirit of the political process, when time pressures forced closure, differences were split and whole sections of one bill were accepted on the condition that whole sections of the other bill were accepted. Efforts to tighten illegal immigration provisions of IRCA were dropped. Several new provisions that had not been part of either of the previous bills were added in an effort to gain quick support (e.g., the repeal of a number of exclusionary provisions for immigrants and nonimmigrants and the addition of a new temporary "safe haven" provision for foreign persons who might need such protection but who do not qualify as refugees). In the following week, the compromise bill, which was 277 pages long, was hastily crafted, and, before the bill had even been voted on by either chamber, a conference bill was pasted together on Octo-ber 24, 1990. The resulting product, which it is doubtful that any member of Congress had actually read, was passed by the House of Representatives on October 26, 1990, and by the Senate on October 27, 1990—the same day that Congress finally passed the Budget Reconciliation Act of 1990 and ad-journed. President Bush signed the Immigration Act of 1990 into law on November 29, 1990, with its effective date set for October 1, 1991.

In terms of historical significance, the Budget Reconciliation Act, which was the focal point of public attention throughout the early weeks of October 1990, will not even warrant a footnote. The Immigration Act of 1990, how-ever, received virtually no public scrutiny at all during those critical weeks, yet it is destined to make landmark changes in U.S. society. It ranks as one of the major legislative actions of the decade of the 1990s. The Immigration Act of 1990 not only expanded the scale of legal immigration by 35 percent over the already high level in existence at the time of its passage, but it also cemented into existence the phenomenon of mass immigration as an ongo-ing feature of American life for as long as it remains in effect.[113]

As this chapter is devoted to a discussion of how mass immigration was revived, a discussion of the major provisions of the Immigration Act of 1990 and the findings of the CIR, which was created under its auspices, will be deferred until Chapter 12.

The Increasing Utilization of Nonimmigrant Workers

Paralleling the increases in legal immigrants, refugees, asylees, and illegal immigrants in the population and labor force since the mid-1960s, there has been a less publicized growth in the use of foreign nationals as temporary workers in the U.S. economy. Since the Immigration Act of 1924, each non-citizen entering the United States must be classified as either an "immigrant" or a "nonimmigrant." The "immigrant" classification is straightforward. It consists essentially of permanent resident aliens who have been abroad for a temporary period for business or pleasure. It can be more complicated in the special case of border commuters, who are permanent resident aliens but actually live in either Canada or Mexico and commute on a regular basis to jobs in the United States.[114] But since 1929, the U.S. Supreme Court has upheld the notion that border commuters are to be treated as "immigrants" when they enter the United States, even though everyone knows it is "ami-able fiction" that they are returning from a temporary trip abroad.[115]

But putting aside the border commuter anomaly, the "nonimmigrant" classification is a residual grouping. It collectively embraces all other per-sons who are not U.S. citizens but who seek to enter the United States for a temporary period of time, not for permanent residence. Nonimmigrants were first defined in U.S. law in 1819, but it was the Immigration Act of 1924 that set forth the process of defining separate admission classes, which were expanded in number and broken into subclasses of nonimmigrants by the Immigration and Nationality Act of 1952. This latter legislation also created an unofficial convention whereby entrants under each of these separate classes and subclasses are now identified by the letters and numbers of the sections and subsections of this Act under which they are defined.

The number of nonimmigrants entering the United States each year is staggering in its size. Virtually every year, a new record high is set. In 1999, entries totaled 31,446,054 persons. In most instances, the presence of nonimmigrants in the United States is encouraged. For example, the largest grouping by far is composed of tourists (i.e., B-2 visa holders) who come for pleasure. Another important visitor grouping is foreign persons who come to conduct business (i.e., B-1 visa holders). Collectively, these two classifications account for about 85 percent of all the nonimmigrant visas issued each year. For most nonimmigrant admissions classifications, the policy of the United States is one of an "open door," which means there are few restrictions on their numbers, although there are strict limitations on how long they can remain, whether they can extend their stays, and, in some cases, who is eligible to receive such a visa. Most nonimmigrants are not allowed to be employed while in the country, so there are no adverse labor market effects associated with their presence except for the stimulative effects on domestic employment opportunities that their spending provides.

Like most elements of the nation's immigration system, however, the B-1 visa has been a subject of employment abuse. As indicated, B-1 visa holders are granted so that foreign business officials can travel in the United States in the conduct of their affairs. In 1992, it was disclosed by several investigative journalists (and later in 1993, the subject of a *60 Minutes* television segment) that several major U.S. firms that hire large numbers of engineers and computer programmers were using the provisions of the B-1 visa as a means to dismiss their regular employees and replace them with B-1 visa holders (usually from India) at a fraction of the wage costs.[116] This circumvention of U.S. law was accomplished by using U.S.-based consulting firms that usually also had offices in the foreign country. The consulting firms entered into contracts with U.S. firms to do certain work. They then recruited already-trained foreign nationals, who were sent to the U.S. consulate offices in their home countries and told to tell U.S. officials that their company wants to send them to the United States on a business trip. When they arrived in the United States, they went directly to a computer keyboard in the offices of the U.S. firms and did the programming work the consultant firm had contracted to do. This is, of course, illegal, but it is a costly process for the INS and the State Department to ferret out, given the massive number of requests of B-1 visas that are received each year and the limited staff available to both agencies to monitor the rules.

In addition to work abuses, the fact that sixteen of the nineteen terrorists who flew their hijacked planes into the World Trade Center and Pentagon on September 11, 2001, entered the United States with B visas was a tragic wake-up call for more vigilance as to their ease of issuance, usage for re-entries, and abuse by overstaying.[117]

Some other nonimmigrant classifications do permit such persons to be employed, but, because of the nature of their work, they do not compete with domestic workers. These are nonimmigrants who work, for example, for foreign governments (e.g., ambassadors, diplomats, consular officers) and their attendant employees, or officers and employees of international organizations (e.g., the United Nations), or members of the foreign news media who cover events in the United States.

But there are also certain groups of nonimmigrants who are permitted to work under specified conditions in the United States in occupations and industries where the domestic workforce is employed. Most of these nonimmigrant workers can be admitted only if qualified citizen workers cannot be found. But, typically, merely perfunctory checks are made to test for citizen availability. Supposedly the nonimmigrant workers are admitted only for temporary periods, but their visas can be extended in some cases for up to five or six years. Table 10.7 shows these selected classifications and the dramatic growth in the number of entries in each category admitted in 1974 and in 1999. It should be noted, however, that just because they are permitted to be employed does not mean that all of these nonimmigrants actually exercise that option. But it is a safe assumption that most do. Furthermore, because many of these nonimmigrants have visas that last for more than one year, the actual number of foreign nationals legally permitted to work in competition with citizen and permanent resident workers is actually some unknown multiple of the annual number of such visas issued each year.

Some nonimmigrant classifications, such as foreign students (i.e., F-1 visa holders), have restrictions on the number of hours and the circumstances under which they may work. Treaty traders and investors (i.e., E visa holders) are not technically considered to be "employed," but it is widely acknowledged that, for all intents and purposes, many are, because they are permitted to establish business enterprises in the United States. Others, as exchange visitors (i.e., J visa holders), are permitted to study, teach, conduct research, or participate in cultural exchanges, all of which often involve a substantial paid-work component. There is also a student exchange program, administered by the

Table 10.7

Nonimmigrants Admitted to the United States Under Classifications that Permit Nonimmigrants to Be Employed, Fiscal Years 1974 and 1999

Category	Classification	Number in 1974	Number in 1999
Treaty trader or investor	E-1 and E-2	36,853	151,353
Student	F-1	109,197	557,688
Temporary worker			
Of distinguished merit or ability[a]	H-1	15,074	302,860
Other temporary worker[b]	H-2	40,883	68,187
Industrial trainee	H-3	4,414	2,568
Exchange visitor	J-1	50,911	275,519
Intracompany transfers	L-1	12,478	234,443
Worker with extraordinary ability	O-1 and O-2	N.A.[c]	2,568
Internationally recognized athletes and entertainers	P-1	N.A.[c]	36,228
Artists and entertainers in reciprocal or unique programs	P-2 and P-3	N.A.[c]	12,243
Workers in international cultural programs	Q-1	N.A.[c]	2,485
Workers in religious occupations	R-1	N.A.[c]	12,687
Professional workers— North American Free Trade Agreement	TN	N.A.	68,354
Total		278,058	1,728,077

Source: U.S. Immigration and Naturalization Service.

[a]As a result of legislative changes in 1989, an H-1A classification was created for registered nurses (6,512 visa holders in 1995). As of October 1, 1995, the H-1A classification ceased to exist. In 1991, the same legislation created the H-1B category and called it "specialty occupations."

[b]As a result of legislative changes in 1986, the H-2 classification was divided into two subclassifications, H-2A for agricultural workers (32,372 visa holders in 1999) and H-2B for nonagricultural workers (35,815 visa holders in 1999).

[c]These categories in 1974 were included in the H-1 and H-2 categories. Beginning in 1992, these separate categories were created.

Department of State, operating under the auspices of the J visa, whereby some foreign students are allowed to live in U.S. homes where they do household and childcare duties while allowed to live free in the household for a period of time. Due to scant monitoring, this program (also popularly known as the au pair program) has had its share of abuses. Indeed, it has been sarcastically referred to as being a "work program masquerading as a cultural program."

There are two other nonimmigrant classifications that have sustained substantial growth and about which there has been considerable concern with respect to their direct impact on the U.S. workforce. One of these is intracompany transfers (i.e., L-1 visas), who are permitted to provide temporary managerial, executive, and technical services to international corporations operating within the United States. As foreign ownership of U.S.-based firms—often previously owned by U.S. enterprises—has soared, there has been concern that many foreign enterprises are filling the top jobs in these newly acquired firms with L-1 visa holders brought on a rotational basis from their homelands.[118] Responding to these charges, congressional hearings were held on the subject. Extensive testimony was given to the fact that a "glass ceiling" existed in Japanese-owned companies operating within the United States whereby U.S. citizens can see top management jobs in these enterprises but are not allowed to hold them. These accounts led Representative Tom Lantos (D-Cal.) to conclude that U.S. workers are "crying out in anguish as American citizens are discriminated against within their own country."[119] This phenomenon is not restricted to only Japanese-owned enterprises.

The other nonimmigrant classification that has sustained consistent growth and become a major source of controversy is that of temporary workers (i.e., H visa holders). These visa holders span the gamut of occupations that include all levels of skill. Beginning in 1952, there were two classifications of H visas. The H-1 visa was for temporary workers of "distinguished merit or ability." It included such diverse categories of workers as professors, athletes, and entertainers, but, over the years, it was expanded to include engineers, therapists, and nurses. With the passage of the Immigration Act of 1990, a number of groups that were formerly included in the H-1 category were split off into new and separate visa classes—such as for professional workers, athletes, entertainers, and artists (see Table 10.7, with further discussion in Chapter 12). The H-2 visa, on the other hand, was usually reserved for less prominent and less skilled workers who were, ostensibly, "performing services unavailable in the U.S." It was frequently used in certain labor-intensive segments of the agricultural industry along the East Coast (e.g., apple pickers and sugarcane cutters).

There has been extensive debate, however, over the need to use nonimmigrant workers in unskilled and low-wage labor markets. It is difficult to argue in these circumstances that there are not members of the domestic labor force who need jobs but who are unable to meet the minimal hiring standards associated with such jobs. Employers, however, argue that the very fact that they are temporary jobs, often seasonal in nature, and that they are located in specific geographical areas (sometimes isolated rural settings as in the case of agriculture or seasonal tourist resorts) makes it impossible to retain or to depend on domestic workers to fill them. The central issue of concern is whether the availability of these foreign workers reduces the incentives of employers to raise wages in order to attract domestic workers. To better monitor and regulate those admitted under this H-2 visa category, it was split in 1986 under IRCA into two separate groupings: H-2A visas for temporary workers in the agricultural industry and H-2B visas for all other industries.

In one industry, the extensive use of H-1 workers as a means of supplying foreign nurses to work in the United States set off a firestorm of protest throughout the 1980s. Nursing was identified at the time as a growth occupation that has been associated with the anticipated future expansion of the health care industry. It is also an occupation in which, it was alleged, there was an extreme shortage of labor. Consequently, many hospitals and other health organizations turned to the H-1 program in the 1980s as a means to find trained nurses from abroad. On the supply side, there are a number of foreign countries that have turned the training of women as nurses into an export industry. The principal such country is the Philippines. Other countries—such as Ireland, Canada, the United Kingdom, and Jamaica—where English is also the primary language and that also had surplus female labor also proved to be fruitful sources of recruits. As a consequence, in 1989, there were 24,417 foreign nurses in the United States working under H-1 visas (of these, 72.6 percent were from the Philippines).[120] It was believed that 60 percent of all such foreign nurses were employed in the New York City and northern New Jersey areas in 1989. In New York City, one of every three nurses was believed to be working with an H-1 visa. At the time, H-1 workers could work for up to five years before their visas expired, after which they were expected to return to their homelands. As more hospitals hired H-1 workers, and as the years passed, the inevitable time came when the visas were about to expire for a large number of these foreign nurses. There was an outcry from the employers in the health care industry about the possible dire effects of such a substantial loss of trained personnel.

While it is sometimes the case that nonimmigrant workers use their entry as an opportunity to adjust their status to become a permanent resident alien, this was not possible for most of the Philippino nurses. The reason was that, if they applied for such a change of status, they would have to wait until there was an opening in the two occupational preference categories of the legal immigration system at that time. Also, the availability of visas was subject to the annual ceiling on immigration from any one country. In the case of the Philippines—which consistently has a massive backlog of would-be immigrants to the United States for all of the preference categories, the waiting time for status conversion in 1989 was estimated to be 16.3 years in the professions category (i.e., the third preference) and 4.5 years in the skilled or unskilled category (i.e., the sixth preference) of the Immigration Act of 1965, which was in effect at that time.[121] The only other entry option was if they married a U.S. citizen or permanent resident alien while they were in the country (which some did).

As a consequence, the Immigration Amendments of 1988 were enacted, which allowed foreign nurses, who were facing the expiration of their five year H-1 visas, to remain in the country for one additional year. In 1989, the Immigration Nursing Relief Act was passed, which provided special permanent resident alien status to all individuals (as well as accompanying spouses and children) who had entered the United States prior to January 1, 1988, with H-1 visas and were employed as registered nurses. In other words, the foreign nurses were allowed to convert their status without being subject to the lengthy waiting times, and they would not be charged against the existing worldwide or individual country ceilings.

To qualify for future access to foreign nurses, however, the medical facility for which the foreign nurses work is required to certify that the employment of such foreign nurses will not adversely affect the wages and working conditions of registered nurses similarly employed. Furthermore, it must certify that it has taken and will continue to take significant steps to recruit and to train registered nurses who are U.S. citizens or permanent resident aliens. A new H-1A temporary visa classification was established for foreign registered nurses to use when recruited by a qualifying health institution in the United States. This special visa category for nurses expired on September 30, 1995. Since then, foreign nurses are still admitted, but now under the H-1B program, which has significantly fewer labor protections for U.S. workers in this profession.

Without prolonging the discussion, there are other instances where U.S. firms have felt it advantageous to recruit H-1 workers (called H-1B visa holders after 1989) in various scientific, professional, and technical occupations. They claim that they are unable to find similarly qualified workers from the available labor force, and, because the waiting times are so long, it is not possible to recruit someone through the limited number of occupation preferences available each year under the legal immigration system. Whether these claims are valid has proven to be a subject of extreme contention. On one hand, industry advocates claim that they need certain specialized workers who are not sufficiently available. On the other hand, critics have argued that the H-1B classification is being used to circumvent the labor protections that supposedly guarantee jobs for U.S. workers at prevailing wages and working conditions.

The computer software industry in particular became the subject of ongoing controversy over its extensive reliance on the H-1B program as a source of skilled workers in the 1990s. Critics have charged that the use of H-1B workers in the computer industry is linked more to the fact that they can be had for lower wages rather than any shortage of qualified would-be citizen and permanent resident applicants.[122] Moreover, the H1–B workers cannot quit their jobs if a better job becomes available, as that would violate the conditions of their visa. The abuse of the program derives from the fact that the regulatory rules are lax, and enforcement of what is specified in the law is inconsistent. As Demetrios Papademetriou, formerly an official who specialized in international labor issues in the Department of Labor, said of the program's protections, "Do you want me to call it a hoax? Sure it is. This program never has worked and it never will."[123] As this chapter is concerned with how public policy went awry, further discussion of policy responses to the use of H-1B workers will be deferred to Chapter 12 .

Nonetheless, given the sizable increase in the presence of nonimmigrant workers in the labor market, the reliance by employers on nonimmigrant workers is symptomatic of the fact that something is grossly wrong with the legal immigration system. Either the legal system—which gives dominant preference to family reunification as the principle entry route—forestalls efforts by employers to meet legitimate shortages of skilled labor through the use of the legal immigration system, or the nonimmigrant system is being abused by employers who seek to violate the law by using it to recruit foreign workers at wage rates and working conditions below those required to assure an adequate supply of citizen and permanent resident alien workers, or both.

There is also another way to interpret the increasing tendency of U.S. employers to rely on nonimmigrant workers for skilled jobs. Namely, given the declining quality of the nation's educational and training systems as well as its paucity of adequate occupational preparation opportunities available for young people, many employers are simply finding it easier to recruit foreign workers who are already trained and who may already have relevant work experience. The employment of nonimmigrant workers can serve as a preferential alternative to setting up their own training systems or waiting for elusive educational and training reforms promised by politicians to be initiated to upgrade the nation's human resource development capabilities. Nonimmigrant workers are proving to be an attractive option, but their increasing use does not augur well for the future employment opportunities for the nation's labor supply—especially its youth—which could be prepared for these same jobs.

Concluding Observations

Without the benefit of careful design and with little congressional regard for the unexpected consequences that ensued, all of the major components of the nation's immigration policy contributed to the return of mass immigration since 1965. As will be discussed in Chapter 12, the subsequent policy responses enacted under the banner of "immigration reform" during the 1980s and 1990s did not address any of the fundamental policy deficiencies. Indeed, the main consequence of these reform measures is that they make certain that mass immigration will continue into the twenty-first century.

Of equal significance is the issue of the skill composition of the inflow. Immigration policy has been written largely to placate special interest groups. It has become a playground for ambitious politicians to gain and retain elected offices. It has, in the process, become essentially a political policy that manifests little concern for any of its economic consequences. But paralleling the years since 1965 in which mass immigration has resumed, the labor market of the United States has entered a period of radical transformation. Both the demand and the supply of labor are being buffeted by unprecedented pressures of change. As will be discussed in the next chapter, the failure to appreciate the scope of these change-creating forces and to adjust immigration policy to fit this new American reality has turned immigration into a source of problems instead of answers.

11

Oversight: The Economic and Social Transformation of the U.S. Labor Market

Paralleling the time span marked by the post-1965 revival of mass immigration, the labor market of the United States entered a period of economic transformation. Both the nature of the demand for labor (i.e., the evolving employment patterns) and the supply of labor (i.e., the evolving labor force) have been significantly altered. The gradual pace of labor market changes that characterized past stages of economic development has given way to abrupt new trends. In such an economic environment, the old, comfortable assumption that the labor market can easily adjust to such changes is no longer valid.

Immigration policy, as discussed in the previous chapter, has been implemented since 1965 in a manner that is totally oblivious to these new economic trends. The fourth wave of mass immigration was spawned and is perpetuated by public policies designed primarily to serve political goals. Only by pure luck would such a politically driven immigration policy produce consequences congruent with the profound economic changes in progress over this same time span. But, the nation has not been so fortunate.

As if the economic adjustments were not a sufficient challenge, the post-1965 era has been a period of social transformation as well. New public attitudes have been created concerning the labor market participation of various population segments in the economy. The year 1965 marked not only the time when the nation's immigration laws were revamped but it was also the year in which the equal employment opportunity provisions (i.e., Title VII) of the Civil Rights Act of 1964 actually went into effect (i.e., on July 1, 1965). That historic legislation sought to end the overt racial discrimination haunting the nation since its birth. It was originally conceived as a response to the demonstrated needs of black Americans for equal inclusion into the nation's economic life. But as its goal is to achieve equal employment opportunity, the language of the Act does not specifically mention blacks. Instead, it is written in broad terms so as to protect all groups from the pernicious effects of unequal hiring and unfair employment practices. Consequently, other racial, ethnic, and religious groups as well as women in general quickly seized its provisions as a source of leverage for social change.

In its ongoing quest to stretch the boundaries of freedom, the nation also enacted the Age Discrimination Act of 1968 to protect older workers and the Americans with Disabilities Act of 1990 to protect physically and mentally impaired workers in their respective efforts to find and to maintain employment. Thus, as the nation has striven to provide greater access to the labor market for groups that were hitherto largely ignored or purposely restricted from achieving such opportunities, it has also been dramatically enlarging the flow of immigrant workers into the same labor market. There has been no recognition in the immigration reform debates of any need to reconcile efforts to afford greater opportunities for these citizen groups with the increased competition for employment and job preparation opportunities of the expanded immigrant flow over these same years. Indeed, the Immigration Reform and Control Act (IRCA) of 1986—as discussed in Chapter 10—created yet another protected group. It extended antidiscrimination protection in employment to cover alienage—that is, to include noncitizens who are eligible to work (e.g., permanent resident aliens)—for the first time in U.S. history.

Thus, the period of labor market transformation—with its efficiency concerns for labor market adjustment—has exactly paralleled the time period in which the United States initiated its equal employment opportunity endeavors that are intended to achieve equity goals. Under such circumstances, immigration policy should have been designed to assist the nation to achieve both of these domestic objectives. Such was not the case. Instead, it has become a policy "wildcard" that is unaccountable for its economic or social consequences.

Postindustrialism and the Changing Patterns of Employment

Although most social scientists feel it is risky to place exact dates on when social systems move into entirely new eras, sociologist Daniel Bell has written that "symbolically at least" the "birth years" of the "post-industrial society" were from 1945 to 1947.[1] It was in these years, beginning with the dropping of the atom bomb on Hiroshima, encompassing the development of the first electronic computer in 1946, including the publication of Norbert Wiener's classic book *Cybernetics* (which set forth the mathematical foundations of electronic communication and automatic control that launched the computer revolution), and embodying the pioneering work by Vannevar Bush and his associates that began in 1945 and that culminated in the creation in 1950 of the National Science Foundation (which institutionalized the massive federal government financial support for scientific endeavors over the ensuing years), that this new era was spawned in the United States.

Although sociologists may wrangle over the precise timing and which events were the most prominent contributions to the beginning of postindustrialism, the economic indicators do show that in the years following World War II, the employment patterns of the nation have been fundamentally altered from anything that had hitherto existed. These years mark the inflection point whereby entirely different employment patterns from the past began to emerge. These manifestations of a new era of labor market transformation are in full stride as the twenty-first century commences.

Industrial Shifts

The most significant sign of the advent of postindustrialism has been the general stagnation (in absolute terms) and the sharp decline (in relative terms) of employment in the goods-producing sector of the economy. This sector (which includes agriculture, manufacturing, mining, and construction) had been the historic employment base since the nation was born. It should be recalled from earlier chapters that it was the growth of the goods-producing sector that attracted and accommodated the preponderance of the immigrants of the previous three waves of mass immigration that occurred in the nineteenth and early twentieth centuries. Since the 1950s, however, the goods-producing sector has virtually ceased providing increases in employment opportunities. While continuing to be a vital source of value added to the nation's gross national product, the high levels of output in the goods producing sector no longer require the input of increasing numbers of workers.[2] Most goods-producing industries now require fewer production workers to produce expanded levels of output.

Agriculture, the only goods-producing industry that was in long-term employment decline prior to World War II, has continued to sustain employment shrinkage. In 1948, there were 7.6 million agricultural workers; by 2001, their ranks had fallen to 3.1 million farm workers. The decline has been the greatest for those workers in the unskilled farm worker occupations.

As a consequence, this critical industry—once the sponge for the absorption of mass numbers of unskilled and poorly educated workers—has not produced a net new job in almost sixty years. To the contrary, it has been a negative source of employment. The displaced agricultural workers—who far outnumber those workers displaced to date from other goods-producing industries but for whom no publicly supported displaced worker policy was ever enacted—have been forced to seek employment on a catch-as-catch-can basis in the nonagricultural sector. Most of those who have been displaced have been non-Hispanic whites, but a disproportionate number have been blacks from the rural Southeast and Mexican Americans from the rural Southwest.

Aside from the agricultural sector, Table 11.1 shows that manufacturing employment has essentially stagnated, mining has declined (except for the period around 1980 when energy shortages briefly revived the industry), and only the construction industry has shown any long-term growth trend. But construction is notoriously sensitive to cyclical swings, so it cannot be counted on to provide increasing numbers of jobs at any particular time. Collectively, Table 11.2 shows that employment in the goods-producing industries has fallen dramatically from 41.6 percent of total nonfarm employment in 1950 to 19 percent in 2001. This trend is the key employment indicator of the advent of the postindustrial society.

The rapid fall-off in employment in the goods-producing sector has been caused by the confluence of several economic forces. First, there has been a shift in spending patterns. Since the demand for labor is derived from the demand for goods and services, changes in expenditure patterns can alter industrial employment patterns. Indeed, employment projections based on the assumption that employment trends follow spending trends are the safest of all economic forecasts.

In its first century as a nation, the expenditure patterns of the economy of the United States were primarily spent on nondurable goods (food and fiber). Agriculture, as a result, was the major employment sector. During the last quarter of the nineteenth century and throughout the first half of the twentieth century, the economy shifted its expenditures toward durable production. Manufacturing emerged in the 1920s as the major employment sector. In terms of its percentage of total nonfarm employment, manufacturing peaked during the World War II years at about 41 percent. By 1953, manufacturing was employing about the same absolute number of workers as during World War II, but its percentage of total nonfarm employment had fallen to 35 percent.

Following World War II, the United States entered a new phase of economic development. It is the mature stage of being a mass consumption society.[3] One of the most distinguishing features of such a society is the

Table 11.1

Employees on Nonfarm Payrolls by Major Industry, 1950–2000 and 2001
(in thousands)

Industry	1950	1960	1970	1980	1990	2000	2001
Goods-producing							
Mining	901	712	623	1,027	735	543	563
Construction	2,333	2,885	3,536	4,346	5,205	6,698	6,891
Manufacturing	15,241	16,796	19,349	20,285	19,064	18,469	17,697
Service-producing							
Transportation, communications, and public utilities	4,034	4,004	4,504	5,146	5,838	7,019	7,069
Wholesale trade	2,518	3,004	3,816	5,275	6,361	7,024	7,014
Retail trade	6,868	8,388	11,255	15,035	19,790	23,307	23,484
Finance, insurance, and real estate	1,919	2,669	3,687	5,160	6,833	7,560	7,624
Personal services	5,382	7,423	11,641	17,890	28,209	40,460	41,024
Government	6,026	8,353	12,561	16,241	18,295	20,681	20,874
Total	45,222	54,234	70,920	90,405	110,330	131,759	132,210

Source: U.S. Department of Labor.

Table 11.2

Total and Percent of Employees on Nonfarm Payrolls by Goods-Producing and Service-Producing Sectors, 1950–2000 and 2001
(in thousands)

Sector	1950	1960	1970	1980	1990	2000	2001
Goods-producing	18,775	20,393	23,508	25,658	25,004	25,709	25,121
Service-producing	26,447	33,841	47,412	64,747	85,326	106,050	107,089
Total	45,222	54,234	70,920	90,405	110,330	131,759	132,210
Percent in goods	41.6	37.6	33.1	28.4	22.7	19.0	19.0
Percent in services	58.4	62.4	66.9	71.6	77.3	81.0	81.0
Total (%)	100.0	100.0	100.0	100.0	100.0	100.0	100.0

Source: U.S. Department of Labor.

expansion of personal consumption beyond levels required to provide basic food, shelter, and clothing requirements and into a vast array of new economic wants. In the process, there was a perceptible shift in consumer expenditures toward services, and the growth in service employment began in earnest. By 2001, 81 percent of the nonagricultural labor force were employed in the service industries (see Table 11.2). Moreover, it is projected that "virtually all" (i.e., 94 percent) of the jobs to be created in the decade 2000–2010 will be in the service industries.[4]

In addition to spending shifts, the advent of computer-controlled technology in the decade following World War II has created automatic production systems that have reduced the demand for unskilled and semiskilled workers in the goods-producing sectors.[5] An electronic "mind" has been created for coordinating, guiding, and evaluating most routine production operations. With the introduction of a vast array of mechanical and electrical substitutes for the human neuromuscular system, computer-driven machines have been linked into self-regulating systems that can perform an enormous variety of work tasks. Norbert Wiener, the intellectual father of the cybernetic revolution, described in 1950 what the anticipated employment effects of computer technology would be. He wrote:

> Let us remember that the automatic machine, whatever we may think of any feelings it may or may not have, is the precise economic equivalent of slave labor. Any labor which competes with slave labor must accept the economic conditions of slave labor.[6]

Thus, Wiener observed, "in all important respects, the man who has nothing but his physical power to sell has nothing to sell which is worth anyone's money to buy."[7] His words have proven prophetic. Indeed, the technology of manufacturing production has changed so rapidly that even the descriptive word "manufacturing" itself has become obsolete. For as the linguist Bill Bryson has observed, "manufacture, from the Latin root for hand, once signified something made by hand; it now means virtually the opposite."[8] Moreover, the application of computer technology has not been restricted only to the goods-producing sectors. It has also made extensive inroads into the service sector of the economy as well.

What a far cry are the evolving employment patterns associated with the era of computer technology from those of the nineteenth and early twentieth centuries when the nation last experienced periods of mass immigration. In those times, the need was for manual labor to do the physical work associated with the needs of an expanding goods-producing sector. But the mass immigration of the post-1965 era is occurring against an entirely different economic backdrop. With the new technology, high-paying jobs for poorly skilled and inadequately educated workers are largely becoming a thing of the past. As former secretary of labor William E. Brock has aptly said, "the days of disguising functional illiteracy with a high-paying assembly line job that simply requires a manual skill are soon to be over. The world of work is changing right under our feet."[9] The new technology is creating additional

Table 11.3

Employees in the Private Sector Employed in Nonproduction or Supervisory Occupations, 1950–2000 and 2001 (in percent)

Industry	1950	1960	1970	1980	1990	2000	2001
Goods-producing							
Mining	9.4	19.9	24.1	25.8	28.0	23.3	21.7
Construction	11.1	14.7	16.7	21.3	23.0	22.7	22.8
Manufacturing	17.8	25.1	27.5	29.9	32.1	31.7	32.7
Service-producing							
Transportation, communications, and public utilities	N.A.	N.A.	13.3	16.6	16.9	18.8	16.1
Wholesale trade	9.6	13.9	16.6	18.2	19.8	20.3	20.4
Retail trade	5.6	7.5	9.1	10.2	11.5	12.0	12.3
Finance, insurance, and real estate	17.1	18.4	21.0	24.3	27.4	26.9	26.7
Personal services	N.A.	N.A.	9.2	11.0	12.8	12.8	12.8

N.A. = Not available.
Source: U.S. Department of Labor.

jobs, but the preponderance of employment growth is in occupations that reward extensive training and education in both the goods-producing and service-producing sectors of the economy.[10] Conversely, technology is reducing the need for workers in occupations that lack such credentials in both employment sectors.

Occupational Shifts

Looking specifically at the rapidly changing occupational structure of the U.S. economy, the effects of the transformation process are startlingly apparent. Table 11.3 shows the percentage of employees in the private sector who were employed in nonproduction or supervisory occupations for selected years from 1950 to 2001. In rough terms, these figures indicate white-collar employment. The ratio of employment in nonproduction occupations to total employment has dramatically increased in every industry. The changing percentages are especially noteworthy in the goods-producing industries. Conversely, of course, these trends mean that production and nonsupervisory jobs, which are often described as being blue-collar occupations, are vanishing. Such jobs in the past often provided high pay, good fringe benefits, and job protections for workers with relatively low human capital endowments. In many instances, the workers in these jobs benefited from being unionized. In fact, from the mid-1920s until the mid-1960s, these blue-collar jobs in the goods-producing sector were the heart of the union movement in the private sector of the economy. Unionism, which had flourished after earlier waves of mass immigration ended, had soared to 35.8 percent of the employed nonagricultural labor force in 1945. It was still as high as 30.1 percent in 1965 when the fourth wave of mass immigration began. Since then, union membership has fallen off precipitously. By 2001, the percentage was only 13.5 percent. Moreover, almost half the unionized labor force is now in the public sector. The decline of unionism has been massive in the private sector. The changing industrial and occupational structure is one reason for the rapid decline in unionism in the United States, but so has been the return of mass immigration as well as increasing management resistance to unions.[11]

Looking more specifically at occupational growth in the U.S. economy from 1978 to 2000 (a time span when the number of employed persons increased by 30 percent), the executive, professional, and technical occupations experienced the greatest growth by far. As shown in Table 11.4, these three occupations accounted for a phenomenal 52 percent share of the total employment growth between 1978 and 1990 and 57 percent between 1991 and 2000. On the other end of the spectrum, the relatively unskilled occupations of private household workers, laborers, and farm workers all sustained negative growth rates and declining shares of the nation's workforce between 1978 and 1990, and only the laborer occupation experienced mild growth between 1991 and 2000. The semiskilled occupation of machine operators has experienced declining employment opportunities over the entire time span from 1978 to 2001. Thus, the types of jobs that are disproportionately increasing are those with the highest education and skill requirements, whereas those jobs that are declining (or only marginally increasing) are overwhelmingly the ones that require the least in the way of human capital preparation.[12]

A confirmation of the adverse effects of these occupational shifts has been the widening wage inequality that the nation has experienced. Between 1980 and 1995, the real earnings (i.e., the inflation adjusted) of an adult worker at the top tenth of all full-time workers rose by 10.7 percent whereas those for the bottom tenth declined by 9.6 percent.[13] For all adult workers over this period, the median real wage declined by 3.6 percent.[14]

The emergence of the service economy has imposed an entirely different set of job requirements on the actual and potential labor force. While the technology of earlier periods of U.S. economic history stressed physical and manual skills for seekers (when the goods-producing industries were expanding), the emerging service-producing economy creates jobs that stress mental, social, linguistic, and communication skills. A premium is placed on cognitive skills such as reading, writing, numeracy, and fluency in spoken

Table 11.4

Growth and Share for Major Occupational Groups in U.S. Economy Between 1978–1990 and 1991–2000 (percentage terms)

Major occupation	Percentage increase (or decrease)		Percentage share of total employment increase (or decrease)	
	1978–1990	1991–2000	1978–1990	1991–2000
Executive, manager, and administrator	56.7	32.2	25	26
Professional	42.3	31.4	22	28
Technical	45.8	15.5	5	3
Sales	36.7	17.0	18	13
Administrative support	18.4	2.0	13	2
Protective services	35.9	15.8	2	2
Private household	−26.1	0.6	−1	0
Other sevices	24.3	14.9	12	11
Precision production and craft	13.9	13.1	8	9
Machine operators	−10.0	−4.9	−4	−2
Transportation operators	7.9	13.9	2	4
Laborers and handlers	−3.9	18.4	−1	5
Farm, forestry, and fish workers	−7.9	−2.7	−1	−1
Total occupational growth for U.S. economy	22.1%	16%	100%	100%

Sources: (1) 1978–1990: John Bishop and Shani Carter, "How Accurate are Recent BLS Occupational Projections?" *Monthly Labor Review* (October 1991), p. 38. (2) 1991–2000: U.S. Department of Labor (same data source as used by Bishop and Carter).

English. Thus, the emerging employment structure is in the process of debunking a pervasive myth that service sector jobs are dead-end and low paying. Some are, of course, but so are some jobs in the goods-producing sector (e.g., many in agriculture as well as in textile and garment manufacturing). The reality is that 80 percent of the professional and managerial jobs in the entire economy are to be found in the service sector. While it is true that there are growing employment opportunities in such low-paying service industries such as fast foods and nursing home care, there are also substantial employment increases being realized in high-paying jobs in computer services, legal services, business services, and advertising as well as in average-paying jobs in insurance, wholesale trade, and auto repairing.

In its forecast of occupational growth for the decade of 2000 to 2010, the

U.S. Department of Labor summed up its findings by stating that "occupations requiring a post-secondary award or an academic degree, which accounted for 29 percent of all jobs in 2000, will account for 42 percent of the total job growth from 2000 to 2010."[15] In other words, the occupations growing the most in the first decade of the twenty-first century are expected to continue to be those requiring the most education and training as prerequisites.

It is true, however, that all occupational groupings are expecting some absolute growth by 2010. Low-skilled jobs will increase, too, but, because they start from high bases, they will grow much more slowly (and, therefore, decline relatively) over this time span. Thus, the shift to a service-based economy is leading to a general upgrading of the skill and educational requirements of the labor force from what had ever previously existed. Conversely, those occupations that require minimal skills and education are contracting in proportional terms and are projected to continue to do so.

Geographical Shifts

The U.S. economy is also in the midst of a major geographic shift in its employment patterns. The distribution and growth of nonagricultural employment in the United States is uneven.[16] The areas of greatest employment growth since the 1970s are in the South Atlantic (from Delaware to Florida), the West South Central (from Arkansas to Texas), and the Pacific Coast regions. The areas of greatest decline are in the mid-Atlantic (New York, New Jersey, and Pennsylvania) and East North Central (the Great Lakes area from Wisconsin through to Ohio) regions. The employment shifts reflect the broader movement of the population away from the Northeast and Midwest to the South and West.

These geographic shifts are the product of a number of forces. Among these are differences in regional income, wages, costs of living as well as changes in the importance of certain geographic features and natural resource endowments. Nonetheless, within the context of these long-term influences, there are also several specific change-creating pressures at work. The rapid shift to a service economy has implications for the location of jobs. Goods-producing industries tend to cluster in specific geographic areas. During their growth phase, for instance, employment in the automobile industry was concentrated in Michigan—especially in the Detroit area; the steel industry was concentrated in western Pennsylvania, western New York, northern Ohio, and northwest Indiana; and the rubber industry was in Ohio. Thus, if workers wished to find jobs in these industries, they had to migrate to these areas. But the key characteristic of services is that they must be produced locally. Thus, the shift from goods to service industries has contributed to a general decentralization of employment away from the historic concentration in the urban Midwest and urban Northeast to other regions.

It is also the case that the urban cities of the interior regions of the United States were not only tied heavily to many manufacturing industries, but their economies were also linked disproportionately to agriculture. When these goods-producing industries began to decline in terms of their employment needs, these urban labor markets also felt the impact of the employment erosion. On the other hand, the coastal cities of the nation were more dependent on service industries (e.g., banking, insurance, finance, legal services, and advertising) in particular and have disproportionately benefited from their rapid growth since the 1970s.

Shifting national defense expenditures have also affected the geography of jobs within the manufacturing sector. Historically, through the Korean Conflict of the 1950s, major nonpersonnel defense expenditures were made on steel and wheeled vehicles as well as armaments. Their production was typically concentrated in the existing manufacturing centers in the urban Midwest and urban Northeast. Since the 1960s, however, the bulk of nonpersonnel expenditures has shifted toward missiles, rockets, and aircraft. These weapons often require that some phase of their construction be accomplished out-of-doors and that they be tested either over water or in remote areas with low populations. The result has been a shift in employment opportunities in the defense industries to the Southeast and Southwest. California, in particular, has been the greatest beneficiary of the growth in defense spending in this era and is expected to continue to be. Because present-day military weaponry has become so dependent on electronics, much of the related production costs are associated with research and development expenditures as well as highly technical production techniques. The wars in the Persian Gulf with Iraq in 1991 and 2003 and in Afghanistan against the Taliban in 2001 clearly proved the superiority of "silicon over steel" as the weapon technology for the future. These defense contractors, however, are not the same industries as those that were prominent in the World War II and Korean Conflict eras. They disproportionately require more highly skilled workers, and they tend to be located along the coastal states of the Southeast and the Southwest.

The Internationalization of the U.S. Economy

The post–World War II era has also witnessed the introduction of another, entirely new force that is exerting unprecedented influences on the U.S. economy, its workforce, and its communities. It is the rapid increase in international competition. In 1946, the dollar value of merchandise trade for the United States was $11.7 billion in exports and $5 billion in imports, for a favorable net balance of $6.7 billion. By 2000, these figures had risen to $772.2 billion in exports versus $1,224 billion in imports, for a staggering deficit trade balance of $452.2 billion.[17] The lion's share of the increase in all of these numbers has occurred since the mid-1970s. Prior to 1971, the United States had been a net creditor nation for over seventy years; since then, it has become the world's largest debtor nation. The accumulated trade debt of the U.S. economy in 2000 was over $3 trillion.

Explaining the sharp growth in international trade is the fact that the United States has now embarked on a foreign trade policy that departs from anything that it had pursued before. The U.S. economy was not built on the principles of free trade. Indeed, the nation's rise to world dominance was based precisely on the fact that it did not depend on the control of foreign markets but, rather, on production for its vast home market. The pace of U.S. economic development was also greatly stimulated in the twentieth century by the expanded production demand associated with two world wars that were fought on foreign shores. In the process, the U.S. economy generated a disproportionate number of high-wage and high-income jobs that became the envy of the world and developed a mass domestic market, especially for expensive and technologically advanced goods and services that were produced by the highly heterogeneous industrial structure.

As discussed earlier, high protective tariffs were a fact of life throughout the nation's history up until the 1930s. The lack of any numerical ceiling on immigration prior to the 1920s meant that the labor market had been subject to extensive worker competition, but the product market was securely protected from competition throughout that entire period. With the enactment of the Smoot–Hawley Tariff in 1930, U.S. tariffs reached their highest levels in history. As a direct consequence of the tariff's passage, twenty-five other countries quickly retaliated by raising their tariffs on U.S. exports. This legislation has been blamed, in part, for the worsening and prolonging of the Great Depression that began only a few months before its passage.

With the election of President Franklin Roosevelt in 1932, U.S. tariff policy underwent a dramatic revision. Protectionism per se was repudiated. A new era of reciprocal trade agreements was launched. It allowed bilateral agreements to be arranged whereby favorable tariff reductions of up to 50 percent of existing levels were permitted by the United States on a reciprocal basis with other nations. World War II, however, soon interrupted this trend. Foreign trade came to a virtual halt in 1940. During the war years, however, the productive capabilities of the U.S. economy were increased dramatically. Moreover, the economies of all other major industrial powers at the time were devastated by the destruction of the fighting. The United States emerged from the war as the leading industrial power in the world. In 1950, the United States accounted for 50 percent of the world's total production of goods and services.[18] It was from this position of unrivaled economic strength that the United States slowly began the process of abandoning its protectionist tradition. It was in the national interest to do so. The United States was instrumental in the adoption of the General Agreement on Tariffs and Trade (GATT) in 1947, whereby the twenty-three original signatory nations of the free world pledged to reduce the tariff barriers to trade among them. Support was also given during these years to the creation of the International Monetary Fund and the International Bank for Reconstruction and Development as well as to a host of other aid programs to assist the economic recovery of countries in Europe as well as Japan.

The initial GATT system was based on the precepts of reducing tariff barriers to trade, the establishment of fixed currency exchange rates, and the maintenance of domestic autonomy for the participating nations. Initially, almost all trade was in commodities and manufactured goods that were transported by sea. The specific barriers to enlarged trade were either tariffs or import quota restrictions on such goods. Between 1947 and 1967, tariffs were reduced by 73 percent among the GATT nations (from an average of about 40 percent in 1947 to about 7 percent in 1967).

By the mid-1960s, the concerns gradually shifted to a broader array of trade barriers. In particular, these included a host of nontariff practices that had been devised to circumvent the system of formal tariffs that were being reduced. The subjects of coverage were also expanded to include such issues as intellectual property, technology-sensitive goods, and a wide array of services.

By this time, the economies of western Europe and Japan had revived and the system of fixed international exchange rates of currencies came under mounting pressure. The integration of world capital markets meant that balance of payments deficits of individual countries raised the prospect of currency devaluations, which, in turn, triggered speculative capital outflows from such countries. In response, governments often felt the need to take restrictive actions to stop the outflows or be forced to formally devalue (or, in some instances, revalue) their domestic currencies, which most were reluctant to do. Also, in 1971, the United States (confronted with its first trade deficit in the postwar era) unilaterally announced that it would no longer convert dollars into gold at a fixed price of $35 an ounce (which it had done since 1933). As a consequence of these developments, the era of fixed exchange rates ended, and world trade relationships entered a new era of uncharted waters. World currencies would hereafter float and be determined by market pressures. Economic volatility has often been the result as domestic prices and production levels of nations can now be affected by developments outside the control of individual governments. Indeed, in some instances, international financial speculation by private groups has been able to influence the values of some national currencies (and the standards of living in these countries).

By this time, many firms around the globe began to establish subsidiaries in their major overseas markets. Under these circumstances, the definition of what constituted a domestic enterprise became blurred. Consequently, the rules governing foreign investment as well as relationships with foreign consumers became entwined with trade itself. Trade now involved multilateral negotiations. By 1993, the number of participating GATT countries had grown to 125. That year, the Clinton administration led the international movement for freer trade by completing the so-called "Uruguay Round" of negotiations that had been dragging on for seven years and that had missed two earlier agreement deadlines. Not only did these negotiations lead to a 34 percent average reduction in the product tariffs in place at the time, but they "capped" these reductions so that member nations agreed to give up the possibility of future increases above these bounded levels. The agreement also limited the ability of signatory nations to place restrictions on permissible trade imports and many existing restraints—such as those on apparels and textiles—were targeted to be phased out by 2005. With regard to agricultural import restrictions and subsidies, they, too, are also supposed to be phased out and replaced by tariffs of mutual restrictiveness. But final agreements on these ever thorny matters have yet to be reached.

The GATT was administered over the years through little more than talk by government officials until it was amended in 1994 by the creation of a formal bureaucracy known as the World Trade Organization (WTO), which is headquartered in Geneva, Switzerland. The WTO is intended to be a referee in disputes over trade practices among nations, but it has the ability to impose financial sanctions to enforce its rulings. These rulings, made by specially convened panels of trade experts who meet in secret, can only be reversed by a consensus of the WTO member nations themselves, which is quite unlikely. A country, therefore, can refuse to abide by a WTO ruling (so as to retain the appearance of maintaining its sovereignty), but it must negotiate compensation with the aggrieved nation or absorb any retaliatory trade sanctions imposed by the aggrieved nation that the WTO approves. By 2001, 144 nations had joined the WTO.

The Clinton administration also succeeded in gaining approval Congressional of the North American Free Trade Agreement (NAFTA) in 1993 pertaining to trade between Canada, the United States, and Mexico. Effective January 1, 1994, these three nations agreed to phase in the elimination of tariffs pertaining to both industrial and agricultural products as well as to protect intellectual properties and to liberalize financial, land transportation, and tele-communication services between them.

The result of these trade agreements is that the nation's employers (and, by derivation, the nation's workforce) are now subject to the effects of direct foreign competition. Unlike domestic competition whereby the ground rules (i.e., environmental standards, worker protections, and safety regulations) are essentially uniform, the nations of the world have vast differences in the meanings of all of these concerns. To what degree these differing perspectives can be reconciled with these evolving trade mechanisms is yet unknown.

When the WTO met in Seattle, Washington, in December 1999 to set the agenda for the next round of negotiations, the meetings became the target of extensive and violent street demonstrations. No formal agreements were reached. Protestors claimed that the WTO was providing a means for multinational corporations to escape strict accountability for their conduct and to avoid adherence to strong labor protections as well as collective bargaining requirements in the major industrial economies. Corporations can now flee to less developed nations where similar laws are either nonexistent or only minimally enforced and then export back to the United States the output they once produced domestically.[19] Critics saw WTO and NAFTA as both being a means of exporting jobs—especially those involving low-skilled and semiskilled U.S. workers—and importing cheaper goods, often produced by lower paid and less protected workers. The ultimate objective of all economic policies should be to raise the standard of living for everyone, not just for those few on the higher rungs of the nation's economic ladder. Moreover, many of the critics of globalization (e.g., the nation's organized labor movement) are concerned about the use of prison labor, slave labor, and child labor to produce products as well as the practices in some countries that tolerate rampant discrimination and prohibit free unions from functioning. They contend that these actions are not derived from any natural comparative trade advantage based on legitimate productivity differences. These are artificial advantages that are the results of practices created and perpetuated by man-made institutions that exploit labor for corporate gain, not human betterment. In other words, they believe that free trade is not always fair trade.

International trade of goods and services can be linked directly to immigration because they both alter the supply of labor and change the skills mix of the economy.[20] With respect to imported trade, it is the output produced by foreign labor that comes to the United States rather than the foreign workers themselves. But the employment effects are essentially identical. The imported goods are the embodiment of the labor required to produce them abroad. Hence, enhanced trade can reduce the demand for domestic labor with similar occupational skills of those workers who produce the actual imports. Conversely, enhanced trade can also stimulate exports that can increase domestic employment for workers in certain industries. Thus, to the degree that there is truth in the proposition that exports create jobs, it is also the case that imports destroy jobs and the United States has been running a trade deficit every year since 1976. Likewise, the types of jobs created by expanded exports are not the same as those eliminated by expanded imports. There are winners and there are losers. Hence, certain industries, workers, and localities benefit from enhanced international trade while others are adversely affected. It has been low-skilled and semiskilled workers—especially those in manufacturing—who have been the principal losers of jobs.

The rapid internationalization of the U.S. economy has meant that this is the first generation of U.S. businesses and workers who have had to compete in such a global environment. When GATT was originally signed in 1947, it was anticipated that a parallel agreement on the protection of work standards in signatory nations would be adopted at a later date. It has yet to happen. Subsequent trade legislation such as the Caribbean Basin Initiative of 1983 and the Trade and Tariff Act of 1984 usually contains general homilies requiring that "internationally recognized worker rights" are to be assured as a consequence of reducing trade barriers, but there is no effective agency or mechanism in place to enforce such a principle and, to date, little political will to find such a means.[21] Confronted with mounting competition from foreign imports, cost cutting has become the order of the day for many domestic enterprises. Such endeavors usually involve efforts to cut employment levels, to reduce worker benefits, and to invoke higher productivity requirements on those employees who remain or who are subsequently hired.[22] Thus, the advent of the era of international competition has contributed to a dramatic reshaping of the workplace.

The United States is the largest single marketplace in the world, and it serves as a natural magnet to attract the exports of other nations. Most other major industrial powers have comprehensive trade policies in place that encourage export industries while affording protection to nonexporting industries.[23] Most of the major industrial nations also have parallel human resource development strategies that provide retraining, educational upgrading, and relocation assistance to workers, along with general community readjustment assistance programs to ease the transitional process for the members of their local labor forces who are adversely affected by trade policy. Lacking such formal public policies and with little historical experience to provide guidance, many U.S. communities and U.S. workers have had to fend largely for themselves.

The Growing Size and Changing Composition of the Labor Force

As for the supply side of the U.S. labor market, the labor force is also in the midst of a prolonged period of unprecedented growth in its size and radical

Table 11.5

Civilian Labor Force by Sex, Age, Race, and Hispanic Origin, 1980, 1990, 2000, and Projected 2010

Group	Level				Change		
	1980	1990	2000	2010	1980–1990	1990–2000	2000–2010
Total, 16 years and older	106,940	125,840	140,863	157,721	18,900	15,023	16,858
16 to 24	25,300	22,492	22,715	26,081	−2,808	223	3,366
25 to 54	66,600	88,322	99,974	104,994	21,722	11,652	5,020
55 and older	15,039	15,026	18,175	26,646	−13	3,149	8,471
Men	61,453	69,011	75,247	82,221	7,558	6,236	6,974
Women	45,487	56,829	65,616	75,500	11,342	8,787	9,884
White	93,600	107,447	117,574	128,043	13,847	10,127	10,470
Black	10,865	13,740	16,603	20,041	2,875	2,863	3,439
Asian and other	2,476	4,653	6,687	9,636	2,177	2,034	2,950
Hispanic origin	6,146	10,720	15,368	20,947	4,574	4,648	5,579
Other than Hispanic origin	100,794	115,120	125,495	136,774	14,326	10,375	11,279
White non-Hispanic	87,633	97,818	102,963	109,118	10,185	5,144	6,155

Source: U.S. Department of Labor.

change in its composition. The fourth wave of mass immigration, as discussed in Chapter 10, is significant for both its numerical size and the diversity of its participants. Both forces reinforced similar trends already at work in the domestic economy.

Beginning in the mid-1960s, the labor force of the United States entered a period of protracted growth. From 1965 to 2000, the civilian labor force of the United States increased from 74.4 million workers to 140.8 million workers (by 90 percent over the thirty-five-year interval). On average, over this time span, the size of the labor force increased by almost 2 million workers a year. No other industrialized nation that competes with the United States has been confronted with such pressure to accommodate annually so many new job seekers.

During the 1990s, the labor force grew by 15 million workers (or by 11.9 percent) and it is projected by the U.S. Department of Labor to increase by another 17 million workers by the year 2010 (or by 12 percent).[24] Although, as shown in Table 11.5, the annual growth rate of the labor force in the 1990s slowed slightly over the decade from the record levels of the 1980s, growth

Percent change			Percent distribution				Annual growth rate (%)		
1980–1990	1990–2000	2000–2010	1980	1990	2000	2010	1980–1990	1990–2000	2000–2010
17.7	11.9	12.0	100.0	100.0	100.0	100.0	1.6	1.1	1.1
−11.1	1.0	14.8	23.7	17.9	16.1	16.5	−1.2	0.1	1.4
32.6	13.2	5.0	62.3	70.2	71.0	66.6	2.9	1.2	0.5
−0.1	21.0	46.6	14.1	11.9	12.9	16.9	0.0	1.9	0.9
12.3	9.0	9.3	57.5	54.8	53.4	52.1	1.2	0.9	0.9
24.9	15.5	15.1	42.5	45.2	46.6	47.9	2.3	1.4	1.4
14.8	9.4	8.9	87.5	85.4	83.5	81.2	1.4	0.9	0.9
26.5	20.8	20.7	10.2	10.9	11.8	12.7	2.4	1.9	1.9
87.9	43.7	44.1	2.3	3.7	4.7	6.1	6.5	3.7	3.7
74.4	43.4	36.3	5.7	8.5	10.9	13.3	5.7	3.7	3.1
14.2	9.0	9.0	94.3	91.5	89.1	86.7	1.3	0.9	0.9
11.6	5.3	6.0	81.9	77.7	73.1	69.2	1.1	0.5	0.6

remained a significant feature of the U.S. labor force in the 1990s and is projected to continue to be as the twenty-first century commences. Accordingly, job creation will continue to be a significant challenge for public policy makers.

There have been three ongoing factors that have contributed to rapid growth of the labor force. Each of these pressures is also exerting significant influences on the gender, race, age, and ethnic composition of the labor force (see Table 11.5). In the process, a new labor force is being constituted with characteristics unlike any previous labor force in the nation's history and unlike that of any other major industrialized nation. The remaking of the U.S. labor force, however, is taking place in an era when older issues still remain unsolved but still have a powerful claim for both priority and remediation. It is in this social context that these new transforming forces are of special significance.

One of the new pressures is, of course, the return of mass immigration as a significant feature of the U.S. economy. As it was the subject of lengthy discussion in the previous chapter, its contributory influences will not be repeated here. The other two powerful forces for growth and change in the population and labor force are the unprecedented number of women who have sought entry into the labor market and the demographic positioning of the post–World War II baby boom population cohort.

The Growth in the Female Labor Force

More women in both absolute and relative terms have been entering and staying longer in the labor force than at any previous time in the nation's history. The movement has been so abrupt and so large that it can be fairly described as being a "social revolution" in its own right. As shown in Table 11.5, two out of every three new labor market entrants since 1980 have been women, and the same pattern is forecast to continue through to the year 2010. The labor force participation rate of all women has risen from 33.9 percent in 1950 to 60.2 percent in 2000. It is projected to rise even further, to 62.2 percent, by the year 2010. In total, women constituted 46.6 percent of the civilian labor force in 2000, and it is projected that this percentage will increase to 47.9 percent by 2010.

The contributing factors for this growth rest with the rapidly increasing participation rate of married women in general and women with children in particular. It is their labor market behavior that represents the dramatic departure from the past. Single adult women without children were usually in the labor market, but married women and women with children were not.

The reasons for the sudden acceleration of women in the labor market are still the subject of debate. The movement was completely unpredicted by demographers and labor market forecasters in the 1960s. The mechanization of housekeeping tasks since the end of World War II combined with the growing acceptance of family planning and the availability of new contraceptive methods to control both the occurrence and the timing of births created an opportunity for the social change to occur. The momentum to alter the status of women in the workplace was provided in the 1960s by the civil rights movement. Women were not initially included in the original version of the Civil Rights Act of 1964, but, as the result of an amendment offered on the floor of the House of Representatives by opponents of the bill as a possible ploy to defeat the legislation, prohibitions against sex discrimination in employment were included in the adopted version. The moral force of the law, combined with the creation of a legal enforcement mechanism, provided the emerging feminist movement with a lever to attack barriers that had previously prevented women from fully participating in the labor market. The pattern of change was subsequently enhanced by the prolonged period of high inflation that occurred during the 1970s and early 1980s. The decrease in real family incomes forced many women to find jobs in order to maintain their family's previous standards of living. Simultaneously, there has been a surge in the number of female heads of households. In 2000, 17.4 percent of all families were so constituted—up from 10.8 percent in 1970. Aside from single adult women, other factors such as widowhood, divorce, and pregnancies outside marriage have caused an increasing number of other women to be the sole breadwinners for their families. Many such women have been forced to seek employment whether they wished to do so or not.[25]

An important population corollary to the growth of female participation in the labor market is the decline in family size. The number of children per family in the United States has fallen from 3.2 in 1930 to 2.1 in 2000 (it had been as low as 1.8 children per family in the mid-1980s). The most significant encouragement to smaller families has been provided by the aforementioned entry of women with children into the labor force. In the future, it is highly unlikely that women will abandon the financial and personal independence that they have come to experience. This is especially the case since divorce has become so common. Thus, high labor force participation by women is certain to be a permanent feature of the U.S. economy, as will be the pattern of smaller families.

The Maturing of the Baby Boom Population

The rapid growth of the labor force has also been significantly affected by the age distribution of the U.S. population. Since the early 1970s, there has been a large "bulge" in the age distribution of the labor force as a direct result of the labor force entry of the post–World War II baby boomers (those born between 1946 and 1964). In 2000, the baby boomers constituted 49 percent of the labor force and numbered 66 million workers. As of 2000, the oldest of the baby boomers was fifty-four years old, and the youngest was thirty-six years old. For the most part, these are prime labor force participation years. Hence, the "bulge" has been a "good" problem for the economy.

It is also of critical significance to note that the racial and ethnic composition of the "baby boom" population is also affecting the composition of the labor force. Although family size is generally decreasing for all major racial and ethnic groups, the decline began earlier and has been more rapid for non-Hispanic whites than for minority groups. When combined with the effects of fourth wave mass immigration, the racial and ethnic composition of the U.S. population is undergoing rapid change. As shown earlier in Table 11.5, the annual labor force growth rates of blacks, Asians, and persons of Hispanic origin have all exceeded that of non-Hispanic whites since 1980 and are projected to continue to do so until 2010. Immigration has been the major explanation for the accelerated growth of persons of Asian and of

Hispanic origins. Indicative of this influence is the fact that 73.2 percent of the Asian origin population who were foreign born in 2000 entered the United States since 1980; for such persons from Latin America (including Mexico), the percentage was 72.1 percent.[26]

The Rise of Labor Force Participation

One of the most consequential results of the aforementioned growth of the labor force has been the rising overall labor force participation rate in the United States. In 2000, this overall rate reached the highest level to date in U.S. history—67.2 percent. No other major industrial country has a labor force participation rate of that magnitude. The Department of Labor projects that labor force participation will continue its upward momentum and projects that it will reach 67.5 percent by 2010. In layman's terms, this means that of the entire noninstitutionalized population over the age of sixteen, 67.5 percent will be in the labor force (i.e., they will either be employed or unemployed as "officially" defined). Thus, the rising labor force participation reflects the fact that the labor force will continue to experience substantial aggregate growth pressures.

The Major Exception: Male Blacks

Buried within the statistical data contained in Table 11.5 is one deeply worrisome exception. It pertains to the low labor force participation rate of black males relative to white males. Historically through the 1940s, the black male labor force participation rate consistently exceeded that of white males. But since the 1950s, the white male rate has passed the black rate and the gap has widened. In 2000, the white male rate exceeded the black male rate by 6.4 percentage points (75.4 percent to 69 percent). The wide gap exists for every age grouping. Indicative of the significance of this decline in black male participation is the fact that the absolute number of black women in the labor force in 2000 exceeded that of black men (8,787,000 black women to 7,816,000 black men). It is the only racial group in the U.S. labor force where this occurs, and it is projected to worsen throughout the first decade of the twenty-first century.

An inordinately high number of black males are incarcerated in federal and state prisons as well as local jails. Such persons, of course, are not even included in the labor force participation data because the data are based only on the noninstitutionalized proportion of the black male population. The low black male participation rate reflects, in part, the fact that black male unemployment is about twice that of white males. Low participation rates mean that a significant number of black males have simply stopped looking for work. The question, then, is, if these adult black males are not at work, or in school, or in the military, what are they doing to survive? The answer, of course, is that an urban subclass of adult black males who function outside the normal labor market has been formed and institutionalized.[27] It exists through reliance on irregular activities such as casual "off the books" work and antisocial behavior such as crime. It may also entail such self-destructive activity as alcoholism and drug abuse. Helping those black male adults who can be reached to enter the regular labor market and preventing many black male youth from succumbing to nonparticipation in the labor market remain urgent challenges for policymakers as the new century begins.

One reason why black male labor force issues have not been resolved—especially since they were highlighted in the 1960s by both the civil rights movement itself and the aforementioned findings of the National Advisory Commission on Civil Disorders (see Chapter 9)—has been the availability of the large flows of immigrant workers over the succeeding decades into many of these same urban labor markets where the urban black population is concentrated. Post-1965 mass immigration—like the earlier waves of mass immigration experiences—has been overwhelmingly an urban phenomenon. In 2000, 95 percent of the foreign-born population lived in metropolitan areas, compared to 79 percent of the native-born population.[28] Moreover, 78 percent of the foreign born lived in cities of more than 1 million people, as opposed to 52 percent of the native born.[29]

Given the scale of fourth wave immigration and, as matters now stand, the fact that the inflow is going to continue, the entry of immigrants into these central city areas has increased the competition for available jobs. Under these conditions, an inordinate number of black males apparently have despaired from seeking work in the regular economy. Competition from immigrants is not the only factor to explain the low labor force participation rates of black males, but it must be included within any such list of negative influences. Proving displacement, as discussed in the previous chapter, is a difficult chore because it is not possible to measure what would have happened absent the mass immigration that has occurred. Would blacks have continued to migrate into the cities to fill jobs if immigrants had not moved in? What is clear is that black migration out of the South—which began only after earlier waves of mass immigration ended prior to World War I—was reversed during the 1980s for the first time in U.S. history. As Raymond Frost has found, "there is a competitive relationship between immigration and black migration out of the South. . . . [W]hen the rate of immigration declines, black migration to the North and West increases; when the rate of immigration increases, black migration declines."[30] For the first decade in the twentieth century, black migration out of the South to the North was negative (–444,000 persons) during the 1980s (which meant there was a net outflow of blacks back to the South).[31] The return migration continued at a record rate in the 1990s, with a net movement of 368,000 blacks back to the South between 1990 and 1995 over the number who moved out.[32]

The worsening plight of black males is, of course, also affecting black females and black family structure in general. Up until the 1950s, black women married at higher proportions than did white women. By the early 1990s, the proportion of black women who do not ever marry had reached the incredible figure of 25 percent of all black women.[33] This figure is three times higher than the comparable percentage for white women. The major explanation for the disparity rests with the fact that the pool of black men who are able to earn a living through work in the regular economy that is sufficient to support a family is rapidly shrinking. The consequential effects on black family structure have been devastating. In 1999, 68.9 percent of all black births were born out of wedlock (compared to 26.8 percent for whites and 42.2 percent for Hispanics). Female heads of households with families, especially those who are from minority groups, are usually condemned to lives of poverty, as are their offspring.

The economic status of blacks is a complicated issue, but it is, given the legacy of slavery and de jure segregation, a problem that the citizens of the United States are obligated to resolve. Any public policy—including immigration policy—needs to be carefully examined to be certain that it does not in any way reduce the domestic pressures to address the needs of native-born blacks. To date, no comprehensive attempt has been made to do this. Because immigration policy has been designed primarily to meet political objectives, policymakers have largely ignored any concern of the economic impact of mass immigration on local labor markets. Not only have the economic interests of blacks been largely ignored, but so have the interests of the nation's workforce in general. Immigration policy was not purposely intended to harm black Americans, but it has, and the longer it is allowed to function as a political policy, the worse are the economic prospects for many urban blacks.

Labor Market Mismatch, the Economic "Bubble"
of the Late 1990s, and the Return to Reality

When the national trends representing the demand for labor (i.e., the evolving employment patterns) are combined with those portraying the supply of labor (the emerging labor force size and characteristics), there are ample indications that the labor market is in disequilibrium. Although adjustment

Figure 11.1 **U.S. Civilian Unemployment Rates, 1890–2001**

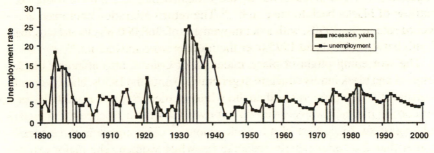

Source: U.S. Department of Labor.

problems are not restricted only to minorities, there are clear racial and ethnic patterns associated with who is having the worst difficulties.

While free markets have historically experienced cyclical fluctuation in economic activity that results in unemployment, Figure 11.1 shows that volatility of the economy has been far less of an issue since World War II than it was prior to it. On the other hand, Figure 11.1 also shows that much of the post–World War II period witnessed a gradual trend of rising unemployment rates associated with each succeeding period of economic prosperity (i.e., in each nonrecessionary period). Implicit in this pattern were indications that the effects of structural changes in the labor market were becoming more difficult to overcome. The national unemployment rate from 1970 through 1996 was never below 5 percent.

Beginning in 1997, however, the U.S. economy entered an unprecedented phase. There was a surge in productivity, spurred by the rapid spread of Internet technology, that enabled the stock market to soar in value while unemployment fell below 5 percent for almost five years and inflation rates declined despite the tightening of the labor market. Federal Reserve Board Chairman Alan Greenspan opined in January 2001 that, "analysts are struggling to create a credible conceptual framework" to explain the period that "has defied conventional wisdom based on our economic history of the past century."[34] Greenspan worried that this holiday from history might prove to be another of the "euphoric speculative bubbles" that have dotted past historical eras. By early 2001, in fact, the bubble had burst. Productivity rates collapsed as unemployment rose to above 5 percent, and, as shown in Figure 11.1, the economy entered into a period of recession.

Thus, the aforementioned long-run concerns about the tendency for there to be imbalances in the labor market were once again renewed. These worries had been articulated in a 1987 study done for the U.S. Department of Labor, which issued a report entitled *Workforce 2000*.[35] It warned that the

United States was facing the prospect of a serious crisis in the workplace. For the reasons outlined earlier in this chapter, a mismatch was foreseen between the requirements of jobs that were expanding and the qualifications of the future workforce to meet them. A follow-up study in 1989 concerned with how the nation should respond to this mismatch was conducted by the Commission on Workforce Quality and Labor Market Efficiency. This commission found that, in fact, "the crisis envisioned in *Workforce 2000* had already begun to emerge."[36] The commission spoke of a "skills gap" that was developing, due largely to the lack of "preparedness" of the new labor force entrants as well as the tendency toward rapid obsolescence of the skills of much of the experienced workforce. The retraining of the experienced labor force, however, was hindered by the fact that the basic reading and computational skills that an effective program requires have prerequisites that "are well beyond those currently possessed by many experienced workers." It further noted that "at least 20 million, and possibly as many as 40 million, adults today experience substantial literacy problems."[37] In accepting the report, Elizabeth Dole, then the U.S. Secretary of Labor, described the U.S. labor force as being "woefully inadequate" for the demands expected of it.[38] The commission warned that if comprehensive education and training reforms were not soon initiated, job vacancies for skilled workers would coexist with unemployed job seekers, a disproportionate number of whom would be minorities. Moreover, the report indicated that, under such circumstances, employers will actively recruit skilled immigrant and nonimmigrant workers or be tempted to relocate abroad where they can find the skilled workers they need. Such outcomes, the commission noted, "could lead to social and political conflict" within the nation by those individuals and groups who are left out.

In the same vein, another labor market analysis was issued in 1990 by the Commission on the Skills of the American Workforce for the National Center on Education and the Economy. It found that the economic expansion of the mid-1980s was due largely to the aforementioned growth in the size of the labor force, but that real wages for 70 percent of the workforce had actually declined considerably (i.e., by more than 12 percent) since 1969. Hence, in most families, it was essential that there be two wage earners to make ends meet. The commission's analysis blamed the decline in labor force productivity for the decline in real wages. It, too, had a warning that, if substantial changes in human resource development did not occur, "either the top 30 percent of our population will grow wealthier while the bottom 70 percent become progressively poorer or we will all slide into poverty together."[39] Interestingly, this commission found that many U.S. firms did not perceive there to be a skills shortage, although most, however, complained about the "quality" of job applicants (by which they meant their social behavior, reliability, appearance, personality, and work ethic). The commission blamed much of the low productivity on the organization of work in the United States that has been premised on breaking complex jobs into simple rote tasks that a worker is expected to repeat almost endlessly. Under this arrangement, little attention has been focused on educational quality of the workforce, and little attention is given to formal training. Indeed, the commission found that only one-half of 1 percent of U.S. employers accounted for 90 percent of all the funds spent on formal work training. Over two-thirds of these funds are spent on workers who already have a college degree. On-the-job training is the way most workers actually learn their jobs. The result is that a huge, multilayered bureaucracy is required to supervise what the workforce does. The result of such organizational structures is low productivity and an emphasis on low wages as the means to compete. As Co-Chairman William Brock stated in a separate interview about the commission's finding,

> The choice is between high skills and low wages. We [i.e., the United States] seem to be continuing to compete on the basis of wages, which means that the effort will constantly be to pull wages down instead of building skills up. We are making the wrong choice.[40]

The commission found that other industrialized nations place much greater emphasis on high educational standards for virtually all of their students; have superior school-to-work transitional systems; have comprehensive human resource development systems in place that provide training, labor market information, job search, and income maintenance programs for those who become unemployed; have generalized company-based training programs for upgrading workers and preventing skill obsolescence, financed by general tax revenues or payroll tax schemes; and all have achieved national consensus about the desirability of high-productivity work organizations and high-wage economies. None of these attributes are features of the U.S. economy. Moreover, none of these other industrialized countries saw immigration as a means of bolstering the skill and educational levels of their respective workforces. Instead, they have decided to invest in their citizens through these human resource development policies and have actually strengthened restrictions on immigration.

In 2000, still another report with similar conclusions was released by the 21st Century Workforce Commission, which was established by Congress. It concluded that by 2006, nearly half of all U.S. workers will be employed in industries that produce or intensively use information technology products and services.[41] Accordingly, the future demand for labor will increasingly require workers who can read and understand complex material. Thus, the "digital divide" is rapidly becoming "the big barrier," not only between those who are financially well-off and those who are not, but also between those who have knowledge and access to emerging technology and those who do not.

Thus, these comprehensive reports all come to the same policy conclusion. The Commission of Workforce Quality found that the employment prospects are bleak for the substantial number of persons who are inadequately educated and poorly trained. The Commission on Skills of the American Workforce concluded that this same segment of the workforce can expect only falling real wages if the prevailing organization of work, with its disregard of human resource development policies, is perpetuated. And, the vice chair of the 21st Century Workforce Commission, Kathy Clark, summed up its findings with the dire warning that, "the nation will struggle to meet the need [i.e., for an information–technology-literate workforce] because too many adults are entering the U.S. workforce with poor basic academic and workplace skills."[42]

Unfortunately, the prospect of a society characterized by widening income disparity has become a reality. As Secretary of Labor Robert Reich stated in 1994, "we are on the way to becoming a two-tiered society composed of a few winners and a large group left behind."[43] He explained that "most Americans are on a downward slide not because of some genetic deficiencies but because they lack the learnable skills to prosper in an economy convulsing with change."[44]

The U.S. Bureau of the Census has confirmed that the widening disparity in the distribution of family incomes within the nation began in 1968. Before then, the United States had experienced over the preceding two decades an unprecedented movement toward greater equality of income. From 1947 until 1968, there was a 7.4 percent decline in family income inequality. The greatest gains were made by the bottom 20 percent of American families. These were the last years of low immigration before the fourth wave of mass immigration commenced. Since 1968, mass immigration resumed, and income inequality among families has dramatically increased. By 1982, income inequality was back to the same level it had been in 1947, and by 1994, family income inequality in the nation had increased by 22.4 percent over the distribution that existed in 1968.[45] During the last half of the 1990s (during the "economic bubble" years), income inequality tendencies stabilized. Inequality did not worsen, but neither did it improve despite the booming economy.[46] But the economy went into a recession in 2001, which, in all probability, means that income disparity will remain the Achilles heel of the nation's well-being as it enters the twenty-first century.

The Counterproductive Impact of Immigration Policy

Given the preceding discussion of labor market transformation and the warnings concerning the mismatch between labor demand requirements and labor

Table 11.6

**Educational Attainment of the Foreign-Born Adult Population,
Age 25 and Older, by Region, 2000**

Region	Number (in millions)	Educational attainment (in percent)			
		Less than high school	High school graduate	Some college	Bachelor's degree or more
Europe	3.8	18.7	28.7	19.7	32.9
Asia	5.8	16.2	21.8	17.1	44.9
Africa	0.6	5.1	23.3	22.3	49.3
Latin America	10.9	50.4	24.9	13.5	11.3
Caribbean	2.3	31.9	30.0	18.9	19.3
Central America	7.1	62.7	21.8	10.0	5.5
Mexico	5.6	66.2	20.3	9.3	4.2
Other	1.5	49.2	27.8	12.5	10.5
South America	1.5	20.3	31.6	22.1	25.9
North America	0.6	14.5	27.0	22.3	36.2
Total	22.4				

Source: U.S. Census Bureau.

supply capabilities, it is incomprehensible that immigration policy is allowed to continue to function in a manner that is oblivious to these national concerns.

As shown in Table 11.6, the adult (age twenty-five and older) foreign-born population has a disproportionately low level of educational attainment at the very time when the job opportunities for such persons are rapidly declining. Whereas 84.4 percent of the native-born population had at least completed high school in 2000, only 67 percent of the foreign born had done so.[47] Worse yet, the immigrants from the region that accounts for the largest number of foreign-born adults (Latin America, with 49 percent of the total) had the highest percentage of adults who lacked even a high school diploma (50.4 percent).[48] Mexico, the nation that accounts for the largest number of adult immigrant workers, had the highest percentage of adults without a high school degree (66.2 percent). The counterproductive consequences of the nation's prevailing immigration policies could not be more obvious. At a time when the nation has been trying to reduce the adverse economic impact of low educational attainment among its population, immigration policy is flooding the low-skilled labor market with poorly educated immigrant workers. It is small wonder why the real wages of low-skilled workers have been declining and the income distribution of the nation has been worsening over the past three decades.

To be sure, not all foreign-born adults are poorly educated. Indeed, the percentage of foreign-born adults with a bachelor's degree or higher (25.6

percent) is the same as that of the native-born population (25.6). Thus, the nation's labor market has benefited from the fact that immigration has also supplied higher-educated workers at the same time that the nation has needed such workers. But the fact remains that the vast preponderance of the adult foreign-born population is at the bottom of the nation's educational distribution. Not only does such an inflow of so many poorly skilled workers make it extremely difficult to improve the overall educational quality of the nation's labor force, but it also means that the low-skilled workers who are native born are carrying the bulk of the burden of competing for the shrinking number of low-skilled jobs available with surging numbers of immigrant job seekers. Such a policy outcome is not only unfair; it is unjust.

It is in this context of economic and social transformation that the fourth wave of mass immigration continues.

12

The National Interest: Synchronization of Immigration Policy with Economic Circumstances

With its labor market in a state of transformation, immigration is the one element of change that can be designed to respond to emerging economic circumstances. While there will always be a need each year to admit foreign-born persons who are immediate family members of U.S. citizens as well as a number of refugees without regard to their skill levels, the raison de'etre for immigration policy should be to respond to labor market conditions. Immigration policy should never be permitted to make the economy's adjustment process to structural changes and business cycle fluctuations more difficult. Immigration policy is not a form of fiscal or monetary policy; it is a human resource policy. Since 1965, the potential benefits of immigration have not been utilized while its counterproductive tendencies have been allowed to run roughshod throughout the economy. The reason for the perpetuation of this incongruity is the reluctance of policymakers to acknowledge that immigration is, at its heart, an economic phenomenon. The annual inflow of immigrants affects the size and skill quality of the nation's labor force. Its regulation should be regarded as being primarily an instrument of economic policymaking and not an opportunity for political maneuvering to appease special interest groups without regard to societal consequences.

Upon entry, most immigrants (as broadly defined to include legal immigrants, illegal immigrants, refugees, and asylees) as well as those nonimmigrants who are legally permitted to work temporarily in the labor market each year must seek employment to support themselves and their families. Most of their accompanying spouses and children eventually seek employment if, indeed, they do not do so immediately following entry. Those immigrants who do not work must be supported by citizens and resident aliens who do. Hence, there are always labor market implications associated with the number of immigrants who enter, the human capital attributes that they individually and collectively bring with them, and the fiscal effects that their presence imposes on the people and communities where they settle.

The entry of mass numbers of immigrants into local labor markets also affects domestic labor mobility. It forces some native-born and resident alien workers who were previously employed in an immigrant-receiving locality to leave and go elsewhere to find employment. It also discourages the migration of native born and resident aliens into a particular local labor market where immigrants are congregating that might otherwise have occurred. Hence, immigration shapes local labor markets as well as responds to local conditions.

As there was no anticipation that mass immigration would rekindle in the mid-1960s or that it would be allowed to continue unabated ever since, its economic impact has been largely ignored. Unfortunately, the simultaneous transformation of the U.S. economy by rapid technological change and the pursuit of globalization policies has created entirely new patterns of employment over this same time span. Thus, comparisons about the adjustment experiences of earlier eras of mass immigration with that of fourth wave immigrants are largely irrelevant. The mass immigration of the nineteenth and early twentieth centuries disproportionately supplied unskilled, poorly educated, and non–English speaking immigrants just as is presently happening with fourth wave immigrants. What is different is the labor market. In the earlier periods, the economy needed unskilled workers to staff its emerging goods-producing industries; in the present era, the economy needs highly skilled workers to staff its evolving information-oriented industries. The U.S. economy has never before confronted such significant shifts in its industrial, occupational, and geographic employment while it is contemporaneously experiencing such growth and compositional changes in its labor force. Even greater changes are anticipated in the new millennium.

With immigration currently accounting for half (depending on what estimate of illegal immigration is applied) of the annual growth of the U.S. labor force, it is essential to know how the labor market transformation process relates to immigrants. The flow of immigrants is the one aspect of labor force change that public policy should be able to control and shape to serve the national interest.

The Incongruity of Fourth Wave Immigration with
Emerging Economic Trends

Up until this point, the focus of the discussion of post-1965 mass immigration has largely pertained to its size and growth—the foreign-born population has grown from 8.5 million people in 1965 (or 4.4 percent of the total population) to 31.1 million people in 2000 (or 11.1 percent of the population). But, because the foreign-born population is younger than the native-born population and it contains more men than women, the labor force impact of immigrants is significantly greater than is revealed by population statistics. Indeed, in 2000, the foreign born accounted for 12.4 percent of the labor force (or one of every eight workers).[1]

Aside from its sheer scale, the next most significant characteristic is the fact that the human capital characteristics of the immigrant flow are counter to evolving employment trends of the economy. As discussed in Chapter 11, the immigrants have tended to be bimodal in terms of their human capital attributes (as measured by educational attainment). The highest concentration of immigrants, by far, is at the lowest end of the nation's human capital distribution. The other concentration, although significantly smaller in size, is at the highest level of human capital endowment. Thus, it is at both ends of the skill ladder that existing immigration policy exerts its employment impacts.[2]

Furthermore, the ability to speak English in an increasingly service-oriented economy has been definitively linked to the ability to advance in the U.S. labor market of the post-1965 era, yet almost half of the foreign-born population (five years and older) report they do not speak English "very well."[3] Indicative of the scale of this issue is the fact that, in 1998, of the 12 million elementary and secondary level students identified by the U.S. Department of Education as being "low-achieving," 2 million were "limited English proficient."[4] How many others similarly situated in this age bracket who have dropped out of school and are unreported is unknown.

The paucity of human capital endowments of many immigrants can also be seen by examining data that show the occupations of the legal immigrants at the time of arrival for selected years since 1970. The administrative data shown in Table 12.1 are admittedly crude, but they show broad trends and rough orders of magnitude. The data reflect what an admission system that is not based on work-related needs has produced. When this immigrant occupational data is compared with the occupational growth data in Table 11.4, they are virtually mirror-opposites. Since the fourth wave of immigration began, the proportion of immigrants whose occupations at the time of arrival were in the professional, technical, or managerial occupations has generally declined, although it is precisely these occupations that have sustained the

Table 12.1

Percent Distribution of Immigrants by Major Occupation Group at Time of Arrival, Selected Years 1970–1999[a]

	Fiscal year							
	1970	1975	1979[c]	1985	1990	1991	1995	1999
Professional, technical, and kindred workers	12.3	9.9	8.6	7.3	4.4	3.2	8.2	5.7
Managers, officials, and proprietors (except farm)	1.6	2.6	4.0	3.6	3.0	1.5	3.6	2.4
Clerical and kindred workers	3.7	3.8	4.6	3.4	3.8	1.5	2.5	2.1
Sales workers	0.7	0.9	1.0	2.1	2.2	1.0	1.6	1.6
Craftsman, foremen, and kindred workers	7.5	5.5	4.4	4.6	7.3	2.9	2.5	1.3
Operatives and kindred workers	4.9	4.8	6.6	{8.5	{16.0	{5.4	{7.1	{3.9
Laborers (except farm and mine)	3.8	3.4	3.0					
Private household workers	2.7	1.5	1.9	{7.5	{15.0	{5.3	{6.4	{2.6
Service workers (except private household)	2.5	4.2	3.5					
Farmers and farm managers	1.0	0.2	0.2	{1.9	{6.6	{51.0	{1.7	{1.7
Farm laborers and foremen	1.2	1.6	2.1					
No occupation[b]	57.9	61.3	59.8	61.1	41.7	28.0	66.2	78.3
Total immigrants, in thousands (000)	373	386	531	570	1,536	1,827	720	647

Source: U.S. Immigration and Naturalization Service.

[a]As indicated, some occupational categories were consolidated by the INS in 1985.

[b]Includes dependent women and children and other aliens without occupation or occupation not reported.

[c]Occupational data for 1980 and 1981 were lost in data processing by INS (see 1981 *Statistical Yearbook of the INS* [Washington, DC: U.S. Government Printing Office, 1982], p. VII). Hence, 1979 data are used.

greatest growth over this time interval. Likewise, despite some fluctuations, the preponderance of the occupations of the new legal immigrants has tended to be in the blue-collar occupations (operatives, laborers, and farm workers) and service occupations. They are the occupations that have, in general, experienced the sharpest declines over this period.

Thus, precisely at the time that every labor market indicator shows that the nation needs a more highly skilled and better educated labor force, its immigration policy is pouring large numbers of unskilled, poorly educated job seekers with limited English-speaking ability into the central cities and metropolitan areas of many of its major urban labor markets. The perpetuation of such incongruence cannot possibly be in the national interest.

Having drawn this obvious conclusion, the difficulty is in trying to discern how to change prevailing policies. With regard to the legal immigration system, for instance, the majority of each year's legal immigrants have already been in the United States for two to seven years when their legal status is granted.[5] About 20 percent of those counted each year as legal immigrants originally entered the country illegally. Because of the series of amnesties granted since 1986, many have been able to subsequently adjust their status to qualify for permanent resident alien status and naturalized citizenship. Others originally entered the country on temporary visas but were also able later to qualify for entry because of marriage to a U.S. citizen or for an employment-based entry visa as certified by a U.S. employer. In addition, there is a clear bimodal distribution in the educational experiences of legal immigrants (as there was in the aforementioned foreign-born population data that includes entry from all sources). The proportion of adult legal immigrants with postgraduate education (21 percent) is almost three times higher than that of the native-born population.[6] But, at the other end of the skill spectrum, the proportion of adult legal immigrants (20 percent) who have less than a ninth-grade education is also about three times that of the native-born population.[7] As a consequence, when the data for adult legal immigrants is averaged together, it gives a statistical picture of a reality that does not exist, whereby the median years of schooling of foreign-born adults is almost one full year higher (thirteen years) than that of native-born adults.[8]

But, immigration to the United States is not just composed of those who enter legally. As previously discussed, there are other doors—illegal immigration, refugees, political asylum, and temporary work admissions. Hence, the collective impact is measured by the data on the foreign-born population. The National Research Council (NRC) has catalogued the fact that the educational attainment levels of post-1965 immigrants have steadily declined.[9] Consequently, foreign-born workers, on average, earn less than native-born workers and the earnings gap between them has widened over the years.[10] Those from Latin America, who account for over half of the entire foreign-born population of the nation, earn the lowest wages. The NRC, however, found no evidence of discriminatory wages being paid to immigrants.[11] Rather, immigrant workers are paid less than native-born workers because, in fact, they are less skilled and less educated. The relative declines in both skills and wages of the foreign-born population were attributed to the fact that most immigrants are coming from the poorer nations of the world (review Table11.6), where the average education, wages, and skill levels are far below those in the United States.[12] As a direct consequence, post-1965 immigrants are disproportionately increasing the segment of the nation's labor supply that has the lowest human capital endowments. In the process, they are lowering the wages of all workers in the lowest skill sector of the labor market.[13] The chief beneficiaries of immigration are the immigrant workers themselves, whose wages are usually considerably higher than if they had stayed in their homelands.[14]

The few available studies that have focused on determining the human capital characteristics of illegal immigrants have found them to be overwhelmingly employed in blue-collar and service occupations of the low-wage sector of the economy and to have minimal human capital endowments.[15] These findings have been confirmed in the data that have been collected on the 2.7 million illegal immigrants who benefited from the legalization of their status that was provided by the Immigration Reform and Control Act of 1986.[16] Likewise, the data on the human capital characteristics of the refugee and asylee flows since the late 1970s also reveal minimal human resource characteristics for the vast majority of those who have entered.[17] The occupational data for nonimmigrants, as could be expected, is quite mixed as they have been employed in a variety of occupations ranging from farm workers, to nurses, to athletes, to engineers, to scientists, to executives, to managers, and to professors. One reason for the growth in the use of nonimmigrant workers is that there have been so few work-based visas available under the prevailing legal immigration system. The increasing dependence of U.S. employers on nonimmigrant workers is, itself, a symptom that something is fundamentally wrong with the current system. It implies that the legal immigration system lacks the direction and the flexibility to respond to legitimate shortages of qualified workers needed to fill real job vacancies.

For these reasons, it should come as no great revelation that the incidence of poverty among families of the foreign born population in 2000 was 45 percent higher than that of native-born families. In 2000, foreign-born persons living in poverty accounted for 16.1 percent of the nation's total poverty population.[18] It is not surprising, therefore, that in 2001, foreign-born households had a considerably higher participation rate in means-tested social programs (i.e., food stamps, Medicaid, and housing assistance) than did native-born households: 21.2 percent versus 14.6 percent.[19]

The human capital and income-earning deficiencies of many adult immigrants has dire intergenerational consequences on the preparation of their children to become future workers. Studies of immigrant children indicate that they are "twice as likely to be poor as compared to all students, thereby straining local school resources."[20] Moreover, "many immigrants, including those of high school age, have had little or no schooling and are illiterate even in their native languages."[21] New demands for the creation of bilingual programs and special education classes have significantly added to the costs of urban education and have frequently led to the diversion of funds from other important academic programs for other needy children.[22] Overcrowding of urban school systems, already confronting enormous educational burdens, has frequently occurred with devastating impacts on the educational process.[23] Other educational costs to social policy are subtler, but equally as significant as the financial concerns. Namely, the societal goal of desegregated urban schools has been greatly retarded by the arrival of immigrant children because it has increased the racial isolation of inner-city black children.[24]

As for the racial and ethnic composition of the immigration phenomenon, immigrants from Asia and Latin America overwhelmingly dominate the current inflow.[25] Immigrants from Asia and Latin America account for over 80 percent of the post-1965 immigrants. As of 2000, 61.4 percent of the Asian population of the United States were foreign born, with 82 percent of such persons entering the United States since 1980. As for the Hispanic population, 39.1 percent were foreign born in 2000, with 72.7 percent of such persons entering since 1980. In contrast, only 3.6 percent of the non-Hispanic white population was foreign born, and only 6.3 percent of the non-Hispanic black population in 2000 were foreign born. Thus, the most distinguishing feature of the Asian and Hispanic labor forces is the inordinately high proportion of both groups that is foreign born. Immigration, therefore, is significantly altering the racial and ethnic composition of both the nation's population and its labor force.

If the revival of mass immigration since 1965 had been evenly distributed across the country, the incongruity of the immigrant inflow would have been less dramatic than it has been. A key feature of the post-1965 mass immigration, however, has been its geographic concentration. Six states (California, New York, Florida, Texas, Illinois, and New Jersey) accounted for 70.4 percent of the entire foreign born population in 2000.[26] It is also the case that the foreign born are overwhelmingly concentrated in only a handful of urban areas. Five metropolitan areas in 2000, Los Angeles, New York, Miami, Chicago, and San Francisco–Oakland, accounted for 49.8 percent of the foreign-born population in 2000 even though they accounted for only 20.5 percent of the total population of the nation.[27] The concentration in the central cities of the nation is even more extreme. The 2000 census revealed that 45.1 percent of the foreign-born population (versus 27.5 percent of the native born) lived in central cities in 2000.[28]

Accordingly, there has to be a parallel concern about the impact of immigrants on the employment opportunities of citizens and resident aliens who also seek employment in these same major labor markets. Unfortunately, the issue of job competition is the hardest to prove. Logic would indicate that, if immigrants are disproportionately concentrated in the nation's largest urban labor markets, and if foreign-born workers are disproportionately lacking in human capital attributes, and if they are overwhelmingly minority group members themselves, it would be similarly situated native-born workers who experience the greatest competition with immigrants for jobs. Consequently, as former U.S. Secretary of Labor Ray Marshall has pointed out, "there can be no doubt that immigration displaces workers since elementary economics suggests that increased labor supplies depress wages and reduce employment opportunities for legal residents unless you completely segregate labor markets."[29] But, developing a methodology to measure displacement has proven to be an insurmountable feat. Not only is it impossible to prove that if one person is hired, someone else has been displaced, but even if such a straightforward approach were feasible, it would not settle the issue. There is no way to ascertain who else would have moved to the high–immigrant impacted cities if the immigrants were not themselves pouring into those same labor markets. Research on contemporary labor mobility has found that the internal migration of the native-born labor force toward urban areas where immigrants are concentrated has been reduced.[30] Other research has found that the immigrants themselves are less likely to move out of states where they are concentrated than are the native born.[31] Both features cause an accentuation of the impact of immigration in those urban labor markets where immigrants are concentrated. As economist Lawrence Katz has summarized his work and that of others, "there is now evidence that where immigrants are going, natives are leaving" because the arrival of more unskilled immigrant workers means lower wages and fewer low-end jobs for those who were originally there.[32] In those urban cities in California that have experienced quantum increases in immigration, for example, there has been a "flight" of low-income, poorly educated citizen workers out of their former communities to the outer fringes of their metropolitan areas or to other states.[33]

This means that they have lost the competitive struggle for jobs with low-skilled, poorly educated immigrants, and that other labor markets are now confronted with trying to accommodate the ensuing inflows of unskilled citizen and resident alien job seekers.

While the direct displacement issue cannot be definitively measured, the substitution of immigrant workers for native-born workers can be described. For example, one excellent study in southern California clearly documented the situation whereby black janitorial workers, who had successfully built a strong union in the 1970s that provided high wages and good working conditions, were almost totally displaced and the union broken by Hispanic immigrants in the 1980s who were willing to work for far lower pay and with few benefits.[34]

Given these findings, and others, it comes as no surprise that post-1965 immigration has been found to be adversely affecting the distribution of income within the nation. As the Council of Economic Advisers to the President has summarized the effects, "immigration has increased the relative supply of less educated labor and appears to have contributed to the increasing inequality of income" in the United States.[35] This finding is, perhaps, the most significant indictment of prevailing immigration policy.

The Immigration Act of 1990

As indicated in Chapter 10, the Immigration Act of 1990 was "unexpectedly passed" on the last day that the 101st Congress was in session, behind the smokescreen of a protracted budget battle between President Bush and Congress.[36] It had been the subject of very little public debate, and the final version was the product of last-minute, behind-the-scenes political compromises over the terms of two different bills. The legislation was signed into law by President George Bush on November 29, 1990, and went into effect on October 1, 1991. The Congressional Research Service has stated that "the Immigration Act of 1990 represents a major overhaul of immigration law."[37]

Yet, despite the fact the new law made numerous procedural changes in immigration policy, its central feature is that it dramatically increased the level of immigration while maintaining essentially the same entry criteria as the law it amended (i.e., the Immigration Act of 1965). Moreover, the alleged responsiveness of the new law to labor market needs as championed by its advocates was illusory. As a consequence, the nation's immigration policy remains highly mechanistic, legalistic, nepotistic, and inflexible. It is still essentially a political policy. Its design continues to reflect a complete disregard for the economic transformation that is restructuring the nation's employment patterns and reconstituting its labor force.

The key provisions of the Immigration Act of 1990 are set forth in Table 12.2. As this legislation has formed the core of the nation's immigration policy ever since, its features require elaboration.

An Increase in the Level of Legal Immigration

The most distinguishing characteristic of the Immigration Act of 1990 is that it raised the annual level of legal immigration by about 35 percent over the levels occurring at the time of its passage. For fiscal years 1992 through 1994, the annual admission level was 700,000 persons. Beginning in 1995, the ceiling became 675,000 persons. The chosen numbers in no way reflect a recognition of the actual labor market needs of the nation, nor are they the product of any careful labor market studies. Rather, they were merely the consequence of a political compromise that "split the difference" between the two entirely separate bills that were pending at the time in Congress.[38]

Ostensibly, a unique feature of this legislation is that it places a "cap" on total immigration that was not present under the previous Immigration Act of 1965. But as will be discussed shortly, the new legislation also contains provisions that make the cap "pierceable" under certain circumstances. Moreover, there were special provisions in the legislation that enabled additional inflows of immigrants to take place outside the "cap." For example, additional immigrant visas were given to 12,000 Hong Kong nationals who worked for multinational firms in the United States, and for 1,000 displaced Tibetans. There also were mandated provisions for "safe haven" to be provided to 350,000 Salvadorans believed to be living "illegally" in the United States to remain for up to eighteen months. But, as discussed in Chapter 10, most were subsequently allowed to remain as a consequence of court decisions and special amnesty legislation enacted in 1997. The Act also created a potentially open-ended category of "safe haven" protection for people from any country to be granted by the attorney general to nationals from countries facing "armed conflict," natural disasters, or where other countries notify the United States that they cannot handle any large return of their citizens who fled from earlier armed conflicts. Hence, the immigration "cap" is anything but firm in its definition.

The law also replaced the previous annual country ceiling of 20,000 visas with a requirement that no one country can receive more than 7 percent of the family-based and employment-based visas issued in a single year. Hence, the number can vary slightly each year but it will be at least 26,620 visas a year, although this figure, too, has some exceptions (e.g., 75 percent of the visas allocated to spouses and minor children of permanent resident aliens are not counted toward a country's numerical limitation).

Table 12.2

The Preference System Created Under the Immigration Act of 1990 (in effect as of October 1, 1991)

Category and preference	Fiscal years 1992–1994	Fiscal years 1995 and beyond
Family immigration (total)	465,000	480,000
Immediate relatives	(unlimited)	(unlimited)
(projected)	239,000	254,000
Preference system	226,000[a]	226,000[a]
Unmarried adult children of U.S. citizens	23,400	23,400
Immediate family members of permanent residents	114,200[a]	114,200[a]
Married adult children of U.S. citizens	23,400	23,400
Brothers and sisters of U.S. citizens	65,000	65,000
Additional family legalizations (for relatives of IRCA amnesty recipients)	55,000	NONE
Independent immigration (total)	180,000	195,000
Employment based immigration	140,000	140,000
Priority workers (workers of extraordinary ability)	40,000	40,000
Professionals (with advanced degrees)	40,000	40,000
Skilled workers, professionals and other workers (unskilled)	40,000 (10,000 limit on unskilled)	40,000 (10,000 limit on unskilled)
Special immigrants	10,000	10,000
Investor immigrants	10,000	10,000
Diversity immigrants	40,000 (16,000 must be Irish)	55,000
Total immigration	700,000	675,000

[a]As the immediate family members are exempt from numerical limitation, the limitation on family immigration is determined by subtracting the immediate relative total of the previous year from the worldwide total of family-sponsored immigrants, but the family preference may not fall below 226,000. Hence, the indicated numbers are "pierceable"—they may be exceeded if the immediate family members are greater than is projected.

Family-Related Admissions Remain the Dominant Entry Route

As shown in Table 12.2, 465,000 of the immigrants from 1992 to 1994 were admitted on the basis of family reunification. Immediate family members (spouses, minor children, and adult parents) of each visa holder were admitted without limitation, as was the case under the previous law. The number of remaining visas went to four categories of family-related immigrants (these categories are the same as under the Immigration Act of 1965). The law stipulated that at least 226,000 visas each year were reserved for the four family preference categories (this was 10,000 more family-related visas than were available for these same categories under the immigration system it replaced). Moreover, for the initial three-year period, 55,000 additional visas were made available each year for spouses and children of aliens whose status was legalized by the amnesty provisions of IRCA in 1986. These persons would have eventually been eligible to adjust their status, but this provision expedited the process by several years. It simply recognized that many family members of newly legalized aliens were already in the country (albeit illegally), but, rather than force families to be broken up, they were allowed to adjust their status more quickly. It was in accord with the INS policy of "family fairness" that was administratively put into practice in 1990.

Beginning with fiscal year 1995, the overall number of family-sponsored immigrants was increased to 480,000 visas, where it has remained ever since. No more visas were made available for IRCA family members. The number of immediate family members of each visa recipient remains unlimited. Hence, the numbers of visas available to the family preference immigrants is determined each year by subtracting the number of immediate family members from the 480,000 figure. But, the number of family preference visas still may not be lower than 226,000 visas each year. If the number would be less than 226,000, then the overall cap of 480,000 is to be "pierced" to accommodate the required minimum of family preference immigrants. Hence, the law introduced a new oxymoron—the "pierceable cap"—into the nation's immigration lexicon.

Employment-Based Immigration Is Increased

Much of the political rhetoric surrounding the passage of the Immigration Act of 1990 dealt with allegations that the nation was facing the prospect of a general labor shortage in the 1990s. It was a myth. Nonetheless, the Immigration Act of 1990 increased the number of visas that could be issued based on employment needs. The number of such visas was increased from 54,000 to 140,000 visas a year over the levels in effect since 1965, and the number of work-related admission categories was increased from two to five (see Table 12.2 and compare with Appendix C).

The first employment-based preference provides 40,000 visas annually for "priority workers." These are persons of extraordinary ability as demonstrated by national or international acclaim, "outstanding" professors and researchers to enter senior positions, and executives and managers of multinationals who have at least one year of experience with such firms. A U.S. Department of Labor official explained that the priority workers will be "international superstars, your basic Einsteins."[39] With the exception of those of "national or international acclaim," the other groupings in this category must have a U.S. employer before they can be admitted.

The second preference provides 40,000 visas a year for professionals with advanced degrees and aliens of exceptional ability. These persons must have a U.S. employer, and they must receive a labor certification before they can be admitted, although both requirements can be waived by the attorney general.

The third preference provides annually for 40,000 visas for "skilled workers, professionals, and other workers." All such immigrants are required to have a U.S. employer and a labor certification before they can be admitted. A skilled worker must be in an occupation that requires at least two years of training in advance. Professionals must have at least a bachelor's degree. "Other workers" is a grouping for persons who are "unskilled," but their numbers cannot exceed 10,000 visas a year.

A fourth preference was created for "special immigrants" for whom 10,000 visas a year are reserved. Special immigrants are ministers of religion, persons working for religious organizations, foreign medical school graduates, retired persons from international organizations, and employees of the U.S. government abroad.

The fifth preference is for a new grouping called "investor immigrants." Of these, 7,000 visas are for investors of $1 million or more in urban areas, and 3,000 for investors of $500,000 or more in rural areas. The investment must provide jobs for at least ten U.S. workers.

The Addition of a New Entry Route: Diversity Immigrants

One of the legislative motivations that culminated in the Immigration Act of 1990 was concern that the "country-neutral but family-based" immigration system created in 1965 had inadvertently foreclosed entry from the nations that had provided the bulk of earlier waves of mass immigration (most particularly Europeans, but also Africans). Reflecting these concerns, the legislation created an entirely new admission category for "diversity immigrants." For the years 1992 through 1994, a transitional program provided 40,000 visas a year for natives of thirty-four specified countries that were identified as having been "adversely affected" by the 1965 legislation. The 40,000 visas were awarded each year by use of a lottery process. Of these, 16,000 (or 40 percent) were specifically reserved for each of these three years for persons from one country, Ireland. The legislative preference for Irish immigrants simply reflected the political influence of Senator Edward Kennedy (D-Mass.) who, as one of the authors of the Immigration Act of 1990, used his position to benefit his constituency.[40]

When the first lottery was held in October 1991, chaos ensued. More than 19 million applications were submitted (many were multiple applications from the same persons). [41] Over 7.4 million applications were disqualified because they arrived too early, and over 2 million were disqualified because they arrived too late. In subsequent years, only single applications have been permitted, but the total number of annual applicants remains in the millions. In 2000, for instance, 13 million entries were received for "the green card lottery."

Beginning in fiscal year 1995, the permanent diversity program went into effect that permits 55,000 eligible persons a year to be admitted. There no longer is any Irish-preference provision. Instead, a complex mathematical formula is used to allocate the 55,000 visas among six different regions of the world.[42] Only foreign nations in each region from which immigration was less than 50,000 over the preceding five years are eligible to be included in the applicant lottery pool. There is no fee to enter the lottery. Applicants from each eligible country are required to have a high school education or its equivalent or at least two years' work experience in a skilled occupation within the five years prior to the date of application. Moreover, no country may receive more than 7 percent of the total of 55,000 visas available in one year.

The Creation of "Safe Haven" Provisions

The Act of 1990 grants the statutory power to the attorney general to provide a "safe haven" and to issue work authorizations to foreign nationals already in the United States who do not qualify for asylum protection, but who are from countries facing ongoing armed conflict, suffering natural disasters, or whose governments are unable to handle the return of their nationals who fled and so notify the U.S. government of their presence. Also, as noted earlier, the Act specifically mandated that "safe haven" be provided to persons from El Salvador in the United States since September 19, 1990, for a period of up to eighteen months. An estimated 350,000 Salvadorans were eligible (most had entered in the mid-1980s). While in the United States, they were granted work authorizations. This special program was set to expire as of June 30, 1992. Just prior to that date, on June 16, 1992, a peace settlement was signed between the warring factions in El Salvador, which meant the legal basis for granting protective coverage no longer existed. Fearing that the peace treaty might not hold, however, the temporary protection provisions were arbitrarily extended by the Bush administration until June 1993. The peace agreement, however, did hold. Nonetheless, in June 1993, the Clinton administration again "deferred enforcement" that the Salvadorans depart. In 1997, as previously discussed, most of those who had not found a way to adjust their status were included in the amnesty granted by the Nicaraguan Adjustment and Central American Relief Act. Hence, despite the fact that they were supposed to be in the United States only temporarily, most Salvadorans—like others from Central America who received such a designation—have stayed. This is, of course, precisely what critics of the concept had predicted would happen.

Expanded Nonimmigrant Provisions

The legislation made major changes in the nonimmigrant categories that have employment implications (review Table 10.7). Some have marginal employment consequences, but others have significantly added to the competition for jobs between these foreign nationals and U.S. citizens and permanent resident aliens.

To begin with, the treaty trader or investor category (i.e., E visa holders) was expanded to include trade in services and technology industries. The foreign student category (i.e., F visa holders) was changed for a three-year period to permit work outside the student's field of study (as long as the student maintains good academic standing and his or her employers attest to the fact that they have sought to recruit citizens and that the wages and working conditions offered to foreign students are the same as those offered to citizens). This change has proven to be extremely controversial. Unofficially known as "the McDonald's program," after its primary corporate advocate, a study completed in 1994 of the effects found that the F-1 changes had "had pervasive adverse effects" on the job opportunities for citizens and resident alien students who also seek jobs in these same local labor markets surrounding their colleges and universities.[43] Furthermore, it found that the adverse effects were not limited just to unskilled jobs. Foreign students were also found to be working in highly skilled jobs as a result of faculty and foreign student advisers recruiting them to work on research projects undertaken by high-tech firms located in proximity to the colleges and universities, and there were even instances where foreign students had set up their own local computer software companies. As a consequence, the U.S. Department of Labor and the INS both argued that the F-1 provisions introduced in 1991 be terminated as of September 30, 1994. Congress, however, extended the program, despite these findings of extensive adverse impact on U.S. college students.

The fact that three of the terrorists involved in the attacks on New York and Washington, DC, in 2001 had used the student visa as one way to gain access to the United States caused the visa issuance process to be reassessed. Background checks, which had been perfunctory, have, in 2002, become formal. Furthermore, a computer tracking system has been put in place to be sure that students arrive at schools, remain in full status, and leave when their studies are complete.

The temporary nonagricultural worker category (i.e., H-1B visa holders) was redefined to apply to "specialty occupations" whose applicants are admitted on the basis of professional education, skill, or experience. For the first time, a cap of 65,000 visas a year was applied to these skilled nonimmigrant workers, but, as will be seen, it was lifted and greatly expanded later in the decade. A cap of 66,000 visas was also applied and remains in effect for nonimmigrant unskilled workers (i.e., H-2B visa holders). Furthermore, the intracompany transfers category (i.e., L visa holders) was expanded to include international accounting firms, and the procedures to process all such visa applications were made easier.

Several new nonimmigrant categories were also created that have direct employment implications. A new O visa was created for temporary foreign workers with "extraordinary ability" in the sciences, arts, education, business, and athletics. A new P visa was created for aliens who perform as athletes or entertainers for specific performances. It was originally capped at 25,000 visas a year, but the cap was removed in 1991 before it could go into effect after extensive criticism by business groups. Both of these new categories were formerly included in the H-1 visa category prior to 1991, which was then rewritten to exclude these groups from its provisions. A new Q visa was also added for participants in international cultural exchange programs. It is facetiously known as the "Disney provision" because it was the Walt Disney Company that lobbied heavily for its creation to facilitate the hiring of native performers for various international theme attractions at its amusement parks. Finally, a new R visa was established for temporary workers to perform work in religious occupations for established religious organizations. It was supposed to end on October 1, 1994, but it was subsequently extended by Congress.

In these nonimmigrant categories that have employment consequences for U.S. citizens and resident aliens, the new law greatly added to their already legalistic nature. There are numerous provisions for filing petitions, reviews, and appeals, all of which have made lawyers more involved in the application and review processes than they previously had been and have added to the paperwork of the already overburdened INS.

The Grounds for Exclusion Are Extensively Recodified

The Immigration Act of 1990 made important changes in the area of immigrant exclusions. As noted in earlier chapters, Congress began in the 1870s to add various categories for which persons are "excludable" from consideration to become immigrants to the United States regardless of what country they come from. By 1990, there were thirty-three such grounds, and they pertained to such broad issues as moral turpitude, political ideology, health, and economic self-sufficiency. The new legislation recodified these into nine broad categories. Some previous exclusions were modified (as those pertaining to former members of totalitarian regimes or former prostitutes), some were eliminated (as those pertaining to homosexuals and most of those that had barred persons with physical or mental disabilities), some were expanded (as the power to exclude terrorists), and some were altered (as provisions that shifted the authority to determine whether a person who has a communicable disease that is of "a public health significance," like AIDS, is excludable to the U.S. Department of Health and Human Services from the INS).

The Congressional Retreat from Economic Reality

Despite its numerous changes in procedures and the extensive media hype that exalted its alleged virtues, the Immigration Act of 1990 is essentially an expansion in scale of the previously existing immigration system that had been in effect since 1965. Its most important characteristic is that it significantly increased legal immigration over the level previously authorized. Like the law it replaced, the new law gives short shrift to the specific human capital endowments of those to be admitted or to the general labor market conditions that prevail in the nation at any given time. Thus, the new legislation largely perpetuated the illusion that immigration policy—despite its magnitude—has minimum economic consequences.

As with its predecessor, the Immigration Act of 1990 is inflexible with respect to the total number of immigrants it admits each year. The 675,000 immigrants (since 1995) are all admitted each year regardless of whether the economy is in a period of prosperity, recession, or depression. The level of admissions is functionally independent of the state of the domestic economy.

Indeed, its implementation on October 1, 1991, could not have been more poorly timed. The U.S. economy was struggling to pull itself out of a lengthy recession at the time, only to reel back again into a deeper recession in the fall of 1991. There were one million fewer workers employed at the end of 1991 than were employed at the beginning of the year. Certainly the last thing that the slumping economy needed was an infusion of an additional inflow of immigrant job seekers of this enlarged magnitude.

The increase in the level of immigration meant that both the number of family-related and the number of employment-based visas were increased. The addition of the new entry route for "diversity immigrants" means that another noneconomic admission route has been added to the nation's immigration system. As a consequence, the 140,000 visas a year that are made available for employment-based reasons represents virtually the same percentage (20.7 percent) of the total legal admissions (675,000 visas since 1995), as was the case under the Immigration Act of 1965 (20 percent). Hence, there is no real change in policy emphasis. Almost 80 percent of those admitted still enter each year without regard for their human capital attributes.

Even the 140,000 slots available for work-related immigrants is a gross overstatement of what the law provides. This figure includes not only the eligible workers themselves, but also their "accompanying family members." As a result, the number of needed workers admitted is far fewer—perhaps only one-third of the total annual figure of 140,000 admissions. The majority of those admitted under the work-related provisions are actually admitted only because they, too, are family members. Moreover, any work-related slots that are not used in any given year are to be added to those slots available solely for family-related admissions.

Thus, all of the contemporary labor market research that stresses the need to raise the skill, education, and communication abilities of labor force entrants is largely ignored when it comes to the issue of labor force entry via legal immigration.

In addition, the emphasis given to family reunification assures that most of the new immigrants will settle in the same geographic labor markets as have their relatives whose family ties were the basis for their admission. This means that kinship, rather than labor market needs, is still the primary basis for settlement. The effect is that most new immigrants settle in central cities of a selected number of metropolitan areas where earlier immigrants from the same ethnic background have established enclaves.[44] The anticipated result is that ethnic networking will continue to be a major feature of the hiring process in these labor markets.[45]

Ethnic network hiring was a distinguishing feature of the urban labor markets of the earlier waves of mass immigration of the nineteenth and early twentieth centuries. But, since the passage of the Civil Rights Act of 1964, hiring practices are supposed to be changed so that it is now illegal to hire (or to exclude) job applicants on the basis of their national origin. But such practices have again become common in those urban labor markets where immigrants have congregated. The casualties often are the native-born citizens who also reside in these cities (a disproportionate number of whom are minorities, youth, and women) who are denied the opportunity to compete for such jobs on an equal access basis. In a study of immigration in New York City, for example, Elizabeth Bogen noted that "there are tens of thousands of jobs in New York City for which the native born are not candidates."[46] The reasons she cites are that "ethnic hiring networks and the proliferation of immigrant-owned small businesses in the city have cut off open-market competition for jobs," and she suggests that the blatant "discrimination against native workers is a matter for future monitoring."[47]

Likewise, an investigative report by the *Wall Street Journal* in 1995 found that in Los Angeles, "many immigrant bosses are refusing to hire the nation's largest minority" (i.e., American-born blacks) for entry-level jobs in their enterprises.[48] These immigrant entrepreneurs feel that immigrants are "more dependable" because they are "not inclined to complain about low wages or lousy working conditions"; they are "unaware of labor laws"; that "blacks are less intelligent, less honest, and more prone to criminal acts"; and that blacks "don't mix well with workers of other backgrounds."[49] It was reported that "its like an unwritten law": Immigrant employers "won't hire blacks."[50] With immigrant-owned enterprises accounting for about one-quarter of all low-wage jobs in both Los Angeles and New York, this is a significant segment of the entry-level labor market in these cities that is essentially off-limits to native-born black job seekers. The report found, in addition, that the same pattern of behavior characterized other immigrant-owned enterprises in higher-paying industries, such as electronics, that pursue the same exclusionary hiring practices.[51] Given the racial tensions in many urban communities between citizens (especially African Americans) and recent immigrants, the need for corrective equal employment opportunity enforcement is long overdue.

Likewise, research in those rural labor markets where immigrant workers have become a significant factor (e.g., in the agriculture industry of the Southwest) has also noted the widespread use of ethnic networking in the hiring process.[52] The negative effect on the employment of native-born workers for these rural jobs is the same in its results as it is in urban labor markets. The concept of networking is highly praised by many scholars who study the current immigrant experience.[53] But what is overlooked in these studies is that most of these practices are absolutely illegal. What is the difference between "ethnic networking," which is often lauded, and "the old boy system" of hiring, which is roundly condemned by all antidiscrimination advocates?

In earlier waves of immigration, networking served to aid in the adjustment process of immigrants. But those immigrants entered the United States prior to the passage of the Civil Rights Act of 1964. Times in the United States have changed—hopefully for the better. Since 1965, any employment practice that purposely excludes opportunities for native-born workers on the basis of their national origin is illegal conduct and it should be stopped. Unfortunately, the politics associated with immigration policy at the federal, state, and local level has caused many elected officials to be reluctant to address this issue despite the fact that it is often a primary cause of racial tension in their communities.

As for the admission category of "diversity immigrants," it not only ignores the whole issue of human capital characteristics of immigrants, but it also reintroduces an array of highly questionable practices to the nation's immigration system. It resurrects the use of geography and national origin as a criterion for legal entry. The primary goal of immigration reform in the 1960s was to rid the immigration system of these very features. Furthermore, the use of a lottery as the mechanism for admitting immigrants is itself the antithesis of rational policymaking. It is a surrender of accountability for consequences that can make sense only to politicians. As a former commissioner of the INS, Alan Nelson said of the use of the lottery, "it sort of cheapens the immigration process."[54] Indeed, the major beneficiary of this program has been the nation's immigration lawyers and consultants—many of whom receive substantial fees from their clients "essentially to stamp and mail envelopes containing very simple application letters."[55]

As for the "investor immigrants" category, the entire concept should be viewed as a source of shame. It introduces the principle that the rich of the world can buy their way into the United States. But, as one immigration consultant boasted, "I believe we have done a great job with boat people [i.e., Southeast Asian refugees] and I think that a few yacht people are not going to hurt America."[56] Aside from the fact that its terms are almost impossible to enforce, this category represents a reward of privileged status for "yacht people" that is unworthy of legal protection. The major beneficiaries of this new entry category are the nation's immigration lawyers and consultants, who were its chief proponents.

Another dubious provision of the legislation is the "special immigrants" category that gives priority to "religious workers." While there may be some legitimate purposes for such a preference, it is a vague concept that lends itself to opportunistic abuse.

The Recommendations of the Commission on Immigration Reform

The Immigration Act of 1990 also contained a provision that called for a commission to study the implementation and impact of this legislation on the U.S. economy. As discussed in previous chapters, it was the U.S. Commission on Immigration Reform (CIR). Composed of nine members, all were chosen from the public-at-large (i.e., none were affiliated with the federal government at the time, although two commissioners were former members of Congress). President George Bush appointed the original chairman of CIR, Cardinal Bernard Law of Boston. The other members, chosen by Congress, were eight males (none of whom were black or Asian). In early 1993, President Clinton replaced Cardinal Law with Barbara Jordan, a former Congresswoman from Texas who also happened to be black. She chaired the commission until she passed away in January 1996. By that time, virtually all of the commission's work was done, so President Clinton appointed Shirley Hufstedler, an attorney from Los Angeles, to wind up its findings and issue its final report on September 30, 1997.

As controversial immigration issues were surfacing across the country in the mid-1990s, CIR elected to issue interim reports pertaining to its emerging findings. The first report, issued in June 1994, addressed the continuing mass abuse of the nation's immigration laws by illegal immigration. One of the rationales for the dramatic expansion of legal immigration by the Immigration Act of 1990 was the presumption that illegal immigration was being reduced as the result of the earlier passage of IRCA in 1986. The premise was found to be false. By 1994, it was clear that the "back door" to the U.S. labor market was still wide open and that the deterrent measures in IRCA needed to be strengthened and additional measures initiated. Apprehensions of illegal immigrants were soaring (review Table 10.4). CIR's report drew the logical conclusion: "enforcement efforts have not been effective in deterring unlawful immigration."[57] It correctly stated that "the credibility of immigration policy can be measured by a simple yardstick: people who should get in, do get in; people who should not get in, are kept out; and people who are judged deportable are required to leave."[58] The commission identified illegal immigration as being the "most immediate need" for public policy action.[59]

Among its multiple recommendations, the commission unanimously called for greater efforts to prevent illegal immigration by expanding the size of the U.S. Border Patrol, by acquiring improved technology such as field sensor alarms and nighttime infrared scopes to warn of illegal crossings, by improving data systems so as to permit expeditious identification of repeat offenders in order that they may be imprisoned, by obtaining more equipment such as vehicles and radios, and by erecting more fences to deter illegal crossings. At the worksite, CIR recognized that the current system of employer sanctions is flawed because of the widespread use of fraudulent documents. To address this issue, CIR recommended the introduction of a computerized national registry that would use data provided by the Social Security Administration and the INS. Employers would be required to validate by telephone that the Social Security number, required of all newly hired workers, has been issued to someone who is authorized to work in the United States. This would eliminate the uncertainty by employers of the validity of the other types of identification documents that were in use (of which there were twenty-nine). Furthermore, this call-in system would be used only after someone was hired, so as to preclude the possibility of any prehiring discrimination of "foreign looking" or "foreign sounding" job seekers. Because the Social Security number cannot be used to verify the actual identity of a person (i.e., it does not have a photograph or fingerprints), the commission also recommended that there be a second step in the employment approval process. Namely, after checking the validity of the Social Security number with the registry, the hired person would still have to provide identification verifying that he or she is, in fact, the rightful owner of the specified number. To this end, CIR also called for actions that would reduce the fraudulent access to so-called "breeder documents," such as birth certificates. This would be accomplished by adopting regulations to standardize birth certificate applications issued by states, by establishing interstate and intrastate matchings of birth and death records, by making certified copies of birth certificates issued by states the only forms that are acceptable by federal agencies, and by encouraging states to computerize birth certificate repositories.

Aside from making employment more difficult for illegal immigrants, CIR also sought to reduce the attractiveness of public benefit programs. CIR concluded that "illegal aliens should not be eligible for any publicly funded services or assistance except those made available on an emergency basis or for similar compelling reasons to protect public safety or to conform to constitutional requirements."[60] It also called for enhanced procedures to enforce the existing requirement (which is widely ignored) to ensure that legal immigrants do not use public assistance within five years of entry (i.e., they do not become a "public charge") and that any sustained use of such benefit programs should result in deportation.

In June 1995, the commission issued a second interim report.[61] It pertained to legal immigration. While few people object to efforts to reduce illegal immigration, there is far more controversy over efforts to change legal immigration—especially if the reforms call for reducing the level of legal immigration. Voting 8–1 (with the only dissenting vote being cast by the member of the commission who was also the executive director of the American Immigration Lawyer's Association), the commission recommended reducing legal immigration levels to 550,000 a year. This was approximately the level that existed prior to the passage of the Immigration Act of 1990 except that the CIR proposal also includes refugee admissions under the overall ceiling. Since 1980, refugees have been admitted outside the existing legal immigration system.

The proposed new system called for a three-category admission system: nuclear family immigration (400,000 visas), skill-based immigration (100,000 visas), and refugees (50,000 visas). In the process, the commission recommended the elimination of the extended family admission categories that have been part of the immigration system since 1965. These are the categories that admit adult unmarried sons and daughters of U.S. citizens, adult married sons and daughters of permanent resident aliens, and adult brothers and sisters of U.S. citizens. It also recommended the elimination of the diversity immigrant admission category.

On the other hand, because there was a backlog of over 1.1 million applications for spouses and children of persons granted permanent resident alien status as a result of the amnesty program adopted in 1986, the commission felt that this backlog was contributing in part to the problem of illegal immigration (i.e., the close family members were not waiting until they were actually eligible to enter). Consequently, it recommended that 150,000 additional visas be made available each year for such eligible persons until this backlog is eliminated (which would have taken from five to eight years as new applications were still being received). Thus, with this latter provision, the actual number of legal immigrants permitted to enter the United States would be about 700,000 persons—which, of course, is about what the existing legal immigration level is. Accordingly, there would not have been any real reduction in the level of legal immigration levels until early in the twenty-first century. But, by including a ceiling on refugees of 50,000 persons, total legal immigration could have been somewhat reduced before then. The commission did not make any recommendations to address the growth of political asylum requests, which, as discussed in Chapter 10, remain at annual levels that are unpredictable.

Looking at each of the three proposed entry categories separately it is obvious that family reunification would have remained the core of the U.S. immigration system. The only difference in content would have been that the nuclear family would have been the sole basis for family entry. The highest priority for the available 400,000 visas each year was reserved for spouses and minor children (i.e., those under the age of twenty-one). Their numbers were unlimited. The remainder of unused visas each year (if any) would have been made available to elderly parents of U.S. citizens and, if any unused visas still remained, they would have been made available for spouses and minor children of permanent resident aliens. For those elderly parents who were admitted, the U.S. citizens would have been required to sign a binding affidavit that they would be financially responsible for their parents for as long as they lived. Furthermore, the U.S. citizens would have been required to purchase lifetime health insurance for the parents they seek to have admitted. These latter provisions were intended to address what was perceived to be the mass abuse of the nation's Supplemental Security Income, food stamp, and Medicaid programs by citizens who were bringing in their elderly parents and putting them on the rolls of these public welfare programs as their means of income support. In 1994, for instance, the federal government estimated that the elderly parents of immigrants (who typically are not eligible for Social Security benefits since they did not contribute any funds to the program as their worklife was all done in their foreign homelands) were costing the federal government $1.2 billion in food stamp and Supplemental Security benefits each year, plus hundreds of millions more annually for Medicaid health costs that were being paid by both the federal government and state governments.[62]

Turning to the second entry category for skill-based immigrants, CIR proposed that it be set at 100,000 visas a year (a reduction from 140,000 visas available for employment-based immigrants). This number would, as now, include all "accompanying" family members (i.e., spouses and minor children), so the actual number of skill-based immigrants would be considerably less. The skill-based category would have been divided into two separate subgroups. The "normal case" would have been for workers who had a bona fide job offer from a U.S. employer and who had certified that qualified American workers were unavailable for such jobs. The other subcategory would have been exempt from such labor certification requirements. It would have been reserved for persons at the very top of their chosen fields who had already demonstrated "extraordinary ability" in the sciences, arts, business, or athletics. Also exempt would have been certain managers and executives of international businesses and certain entrepreneurs whose commercial ventures would guarantee a significant number of jobs for American workers. A limited number of exempt visas would also have been made available for individuals ordained by a religious denomination as well as for religious workers who have been employed in such vocations for at least two years immediately prior to their entry application and who were sponsored by a bona fide religious organization in the United States. The commission also recommended the elimination of all employment-based visas for unskilled workers (for whom up to 10,000 visas a year are presently available). As Chair Jordan explained, "in an age in which unskilled workers have far too few opportunities opened to them and in which welfare reform will require thousands more to find jobs, the Commission sees no justification to the continued entry of unskilled foreign workers."[63] Unskilled workers, of course, would still have been allowed to legally immigrate if they qualified under the nuclear family, refugee, or asylum provisions of the reformed immigration system.

Mounting Public Criticism of U.S. Immigration Policy

Paralleling the years in the 1990s when the commission was conducting its deliberations, the subject of immigration was constantly in the national headlines. Aside from the specific policy controversies that were discussed in Chapter 10, a groundswell of public protest developed over the general state of the nation's immigration policy. Only a few months after taking office in 1993, President Bill Clinton expressed his own concerns as he released his proposals to address the mass abuse of the nation's political asylum system. He said "our borders leak like a sieve" and that this issue "cannot be permitted to continue in good concience."[64]

A series of court suits were filed and reports were issued by most of the states that were heavily impacted by immigration over the mounting financial costs that they must bear as a result of federal immigration policies over which they have no control. In 1994, for example, the governor of California charged that immigration was costing his state $3 billion annually, and he filed suit against the federal government for compensation of the cost of incarceration of criminal aliens ($1.6 billion) and for providing health care to illegal aliens ($369 million); San Diego County, California, filed suit for an additional $59 million to cover the costs of incarcerating criminal aliens; the governor of Florida released a report claiming that illegal immigration was annually costing his state $884 million to provide education, health, and incarceration costs; the New York State Senate released a report claiming that immigration was costing the state $5.6 billion a year for social services, incarceration, and education, and the governor announced that he would begin negotiations with the federal government for reimbursement of these expenses; a study in Texas placed the annual costs of legal and illegal immigrants at $4.6 billion for its governmental services; and the attorney general of Arizona filed a federal suit for $121 million for reimbursement for the cost of criminal incarcerations.[65]

But it was the launching of a citizen-initiated petition movement in California, known as "Save Our State" (SOS), in 1994 that catapulted the subject of immigration to the national level.[66] Known as Proposition 187, it proposed to create a state-run system to verify the legal status of all persons who make use of public education, health care, and other public benefit programs provided by the state of California. It also sought to make public education (K through twelfth grade) a public service for which illegal immigrants were ineligible. It was estimated that there were 350,000 illegal immigrant children in the primary and secondary schools at the time who cost the state's taxpayers $1.5 billion a year to educate. The proposition was passed by California voters on November 8, 1994, by a 59 to 41 percent margin and became effective the following day. Its passage was a grassroots manifestation of public frustration in the state with the mass abuse of the nation's immigration laws. But before its terms could actually be implemented, its legality was challenged in a series of lawsuits in state and federal courts. Ultimately, five suits were consolidated into a single federal case. On November 16, 1994, the U.S. District Court in Los Angeles issued a temporary restraining order (that became a preliminary injunction a month later) that enjoined the implementation of the key sections of the initiative until the Court could rule on its terms. A year later, on November 20, 1995, the Court struck down most of the key parts of Proposition 187.[67] The Court held that the power to regulate immigration is exclusively a federal responsibility. Proposition 187's requirements for verification by state officials and its notification, cooperation, and reporting provisions were, according to the Court, intended to regulate immigration by creating a scheme to detect and report the presence of illegal immigrants for the purpose of their removal from the state. The Court held that California lacked that authority. Most of the judge's ruling centered upon the actual source of the public funds that were provided for specific services. If both state and federal funds were involved, the judge ruled, California could not unilaterally make illegal aliens ineligible for such benefits. If, on the other hand, only state funds are involved, the state could legally deny their availability to illegal immigrants. It is only in the case of public education for grades kindergarten through twelfth grade that the source of the funds is irrelevant. This is because in 1982 the U.S. Supreme Court held in *Plyler* v. *Doe* that states are required to educate illegal alien children as a matter of equal protection under the law.[68] With regard to higher education, however, the judge ruled that the state of California may deny admission and charge out-of-state tuition to illegal immigrants who attend state institutions. This is because the state is already required to ascertain the residency status of students, and it is permitted to charge nonresidents higher tuition than residents.

The state of California initially sought to appeal the lower court's entire decision. It contended, with regard to educational services, that the circumstances differed since the issuance of the *Plyler* v. *Doe* decision (which had been decided on a narrow 5–4 vote). Not only had the membership on the Court significantly changed since 1982, but Congress subsequently passed the Immigration Reform and Control Act in 1986, which explicitly stated that it is illegal for illegal immigrants to be employed in the United States. Unlike in 1982, public policy is now clear: Illegal immigrants are unwanted in the labor market. As attorney general at the time, Janet Reno bluntly described the prevailing goal of public policy toward illegal immigrants: "the issue is get them out of here if they do not belong here."[69] California also argued that providing public school education for people who are not supposed to be in the state is an "unfair financial burden" on the taxpayers of the state. California has over one-quarter of all the foreign-born persons in the nation. Hence, it is unfairly affected by the violations of the nation's immigration laws by illegal immigrants. It contended this legal consideration is as important as the "equal protection" argument on which the original decision was narrowly rendered.

In November 1998, however, the Democratic candidate for governor of California, Gray Davis, was elected. During the campaign, he indicated that he had opposed Proposition 187. He defeated the Republican candidate, Dan Lundgren, who had supported Proposition 187 and supported the appeal by the state. Davis, therefore, inherited the pending appeal to the Ninth Circuit Court of Appeals of the lower court's rejection of most of Proposition 187. He was aware, however, that Proposition 187 was a manifestation of the "will of the people" that he had sworn to uphold when he took office. Meanwhile, a separate lawsuit was filed by the American Civil Liberties Union and the Mexican American Legal Defense and Educational Fund challenging the appeal by the state of California.

In April 1999, Davis announced that he would put the fate of the appeal in the hands of a federal mediator appointed by the court of appeals to see if a compromise could be reached short of a formal appeal.[70] Usually mediators are appointed when a compromise seems possible, but mediation is seldom used to resolve whether an issue is constitutional.[71] In May 1999, Latino legislative leaders and supporters of the challenge to the appeal announced they would support the mediation effort.[72]

In July 1999, the results were announced. Governor Davis agreed not to appeal the lower court's decision.[73] School officials, social workers, and medical workers would not be required to turn in suspected illegal immigrants to federal or state authorities. All that would remain of Proposition 187 was an agreement that two relatively minor provisions that established state criminal penalties for the manufacture and use of false documents to conceal illegal immigrant status would remain effective. The agreement did specify that California was free to enforce any restrictions adopted by the federal government—such as the 1996 welfare reform law that made illegal immigrants ineligible for most nonemergency public aid. On September 13, 1999, Judge Mariana Pfaelzer, who had issued the original injunction in 1994, approved the agreement to drop the appeal of the decision. The five-year legal battle was over, but at the cost of suppression of the "will of the people."

Congressional Reaction

In the wake of these ongoing developments as well as the parallel issuance of CIR's interim recommendations for policy changes, five separate reform bills were introduced in Congress in 1995. Each called for extensive changes in the nation's existent immigration system. Two bills subsequently emerged. Both embodied many of the key proposals made by the CIR.

In the House of Representatives, a bill was introduced by Representative Lamar Smith (R-Tex.), chairman of the subcommittee on immigration of the House Judiciary Committee. He bluntly stated that "the nation's legal immigration system is broken and it no longer serves the national interest."[74] His bill called for the reduction in the number of legal immigrants and refugees to 595,000 persons a year by the year 2001. Family reunification would be limited to the same nuclear family categories recommended by the CIR. The "diversity immigrant" program would be eliminated. No employment-based visas would be issued to unskilled workers. The bill also included most of the aforementioned proposals to combat illegal immigration that were recommended by CIR, with the addition of fines to be placed on illegal immigrants who are found to be employed. It sought to also restrict access by illegal immigrants to most social benefit programs as recommended by CIR. The bill cleared the subcommittee on July 20, 1995.

When the full Judiciary Committee took up the bill, special interest groups began to exert their influences to minimize any reforms. Chipping away at its original terms, a number of changes were made. The proposal for a call-in verification worker eligibility system was restricted to being a pilot program in only five states. Before it could be extended nationwide, Congress would have to authorize its adoption and small employers (with three or fewer employees) would be exempted. The committee also voted to retain the controversial diversity immigrant admission category. Of greater consequence, however, was the addition of an antiabortion amendment by the chairman of the Judiciary Committee, Representative Henry Hyde (R-Ill.). It called for the expanding definition of a refugee to include any person who fears persecution on the basis of a country's coercive population policies. The amended bill cleared the committee on October 25, 1995, by an overwhelming margin (23 to 10).

In the Senate, a separate reform measure was introduced in June 1995 by Senator Alan Simpson, the chairman of the subcommittee on immigration of its Judiciary Committee. Initially, it addressed only illegal immigration. It contained most of the recommendations put forth by CIR, including the call-in registration system for employers. A second bill was later introduced following the issuance of CIR's interim report pertaining to legal immigration. It called for a reduction in the annual level of immigration to 450,000 a year by the beginning of the twenty-first century. Simpson stated that the reduction would provide "a breathing space" as the prevailing levels are more than can be "comfortably absorbed."[75] It embraced the idea proposed by CIR that the nuclear family should provide the basis for family reunification. Accordingly, it eliminated the other extended family–related entry criteria. It also sought to bring refugees back into the overall immigration ceiling. To address the backlog of spouses and minor children of permanent resident aliens, his bill allowed an additional 150,000 visas a year to be issued until this backlog was eliminated. It also required that the parents of U.S. citizens be at least sixty-five years old and have a majority of their children already being U.S. citizens before they would qualify for admission as an immediate family member. Moreover, their U.S. children would have to agree to be financially responsible for them and purchase long-term health insurance for them before they could be admitted.

The Simpson bill also called for reducing the number of visas available for employment-based immigrants to 90,000 a year and eliminating, as CIR proposed, all such slots for unskilled immigrants. Simpson explained that "when major U.S. employers like IBM, AT&T, and GM are laying off workers by the tens of thousands, when the defense industry has undergone a major downsizing, when we read of the difficulty so many American college graduates face finding a job in their field, it is time to reconsider the changes to legal immigration levels enacted in 1990."[76] Moreover, to ensure that all immigrants admitted as employment-based immigrants actually meet the conditions of their admission, the bill called for the creation of a two-year conditional residence status before they could remain permanently.

Simpson's bill also proposed the imposition of a fee equal to 25 percent of the annual compensation paid to nonimmigrant foreign workers employed by U.S. employers. The fee would be placed in a specific training fund to finance the training of U.S. job seekers. The goal would be to reduce employer dependence on foreign workers in those industries that now hire such workers in large numbers.[77] To say the least, employer opposition to this idea was extensive.[78]

The Undermining of Comprehensive Reform

The year 1996 was a presidential election year, and it appeared that immigration reform was high on the national agenda. The Clinton administration had endorsed many of the recommendations made by CIR in its interim reports of 1994 (on illegal immigration) and 1995 (on legal immigration—including the centerpiece that called for the level of legal immigration to be reduced to 550,000 a year and the elimination of the extended family admission preferences). But national political ambitions quickly intervened to undermine any chance of comprehensive reform.

In February 1996, a top fund-raiser for the Democratic National Committee (DNC), John Huang, passed a memo to President Clinton that Asian Americans strongly opposed the provisions in both pending reform bills that called for deleting the extended family admission criteria of the existing immigration system (the so-called "sibling" preference provisions).[79] This provision permitted naturalized Americans to bring their adult brothers and sisters and their respective families to the United States. Asian Americans use these preference provisions extensively. Huang let it be known that a group of prominent Asian Americans would be making a donation of $1.1 million to the DNC for the re-election campaign and that they strongly supported leaving the sibling preferences in the law. In early March, the Clinton administration suddenly reversed course. It announced in writing that it no longer supported the removal of these provisions.[80] The administration denied that it was the promised funds that caused the "flip-flop" in its position but, rather, that other Democrats and other interest groups were also opposed to the change.

Indeed, there was other strong opposition to the pending changes in the legal immigration system. The Christian Coalition as well as the Leadership Conference for Civil Rights joined the chorus by arguing that the changes were an attack on "family values." As a consequence, when the reform measure was brought to the floor of the House of Representatives in mid-March 1996, the proposal to reduce legal immigration by removing the extended family admission preference categories was stripped from the bill. The same thing happened in the Senate, when, in late March 1996, the similar provisions and other changes in admission criteria were deleted. In addition, the sections that would have required U.S. employers to contribute to a fund to train U.S. workers for every nonimmigrant foreign worker that they hired were also dropped. For the most part, only provisions pertaining to illegal immigration remained in each of the separate bills that passed each house of Congress. The House bill, however, did contain a controversial floor amendment by Representative Elton Gallegly (R-Calif.) that would have permitted state governments to deny children who were illegal immigrants free kindergarten to twelfth-grade education just as California was trying to do with its Proposition 187. Moreover, if it was adopted in the final bill, it would have made the Court's ruling against California's Proposition 187 moot because the federal government does have the unquestioned authority to adopt such a policy. President Clinton, however, let it be known he would probably veto any final bill if the Gallegly Amendment were in it.

Over the course of the summer of 1996, private efforts were made by legislators to find ways to reconcile the separate versions of immigration reform before a formal conference committee could undertake the task.

The Illegal Immigration Reform and Immigration Responsibility Act of 1996

Aside from the fact that virtually all of the significant reforms pertaining to legal immigration had been removed by the time the legislation had passed each chamber of Congress, there was increasing doubt that anything at all would be enacted. The congressional session was drawing to an end, and a presidential election was only weeks away. Nonetheless, the House of Representatives passed a revised reform bill on September 25, 1996, similar to the one it had already passed earlier in March. It was aimed primarily at reducing both illegal immigration and the access of legal immigrants to welfare programs. In the Senate, their pending bill was incorporated into a separate federal appropriation bill to fund most of the agencies of government. By consolidating these bills, the Clinton administration and Senate Democrats were able to negotiate the removal of many provisions of the House bill pertaining to the denial of welfare eligibility for legal immigrants. Along, the way the Gallegly Amendment (for a national Proposition 187) in the House bill was also removed. The Hyde Amendment (stipulating that persons qualify as refugees if they have a fear they may be subjected to coercive population control procedures), however, was retained but capped at no more than 1,000 entries a year. The House of Representatives then approved the final version of what was left of the immigration reform bill as included in the federal budget provisions on September 28, 1996. The Senate followed suit on September 30, 1996. Thus, tucked into the 3,000-page omnibus appropriation law for fiscal year 1997, was the Illegal Immigration Reform and Immigrant Responsibility Act (IIRIRA) of 1996. Many of its terms were the result of last-minute negotiation sessions between the political leadership of the Senate, the House of Representatives, and the White House. Legislators in both chambers of Congress were then given the opportunity to vote for a minimalist package of immigration reforms and the massive budget provisions or vote against the immigration bill and shut down most of the federal government as the new fiscal year began on October 1, 1996.

The IIRIRA provided for a virtual doubling of the size of the U.S. Border Patrol and an enlargement of the internal enforcement staff of INS investigators; it funded the construction of miles of physical barriers along parts of the nation's land borders; it required the replacement of paper border-crossing cards issued for a lifetime to Mexican citizens who live in border towns with biometric-laser identifier cards with photographs that are valid for ten-year periods (a system which, after years of delay, was finally activated on October 1, 2002 in the wake of mounting national security concerns); it imposed fines of from $150 to $250 on each illegal immigrant apprehended for illegal entry; it created an automated entry–exit control system to collect departure forms from every noncitizen leaving the country and match the information with his or her arrival records; it deemed any foreign national who used false documents to enter the country as being inadmissible to the United States for five years; and it states that the visa stamp in any passport of any nonimmigrant foreign national who overstays his or her visa by as little as one day is void, and he or she can renew his or her visa only by returning to his or her homeland and reapplying for an extension—any person who overstays his or her visa by six months to one year is excludable from entering the United States for three years, and anyone who overstays by one year or more is excludable for ten years.[81] The legislation also introduced a new legal concept known as "removal" (or "summary exclusion") whereby persons who show up at border entry points without credentials or with stolen or false credentials and who do not make a claim for political asylum can be turned away without administrative or judicial review.

In assessing the political debacle associated with the high expectations of the immigration reform movement at the beginning of 1996 and the passage of this watered-down legislation later that year, political scientists James Gimpel and James Edwards concluded: "The voice of the people has had little impact on the tone or direction of the immigration debate in Washington."[82] They pointed out that, despite the extensive research findings that showed the need for significant legislative changes and that public opinion polls consistently showed that the citizenry want these changes to take place, it makes no difference to professional politicians. Immigration policy had been captured by an unholy alliance that linked religious organizations, ethnic groups, libertarian economists, and the powerful immigration lawyer's association, who were all interested in maintaining the status quo with corporate America (ranging from agribusiness, the garment industry, the health care industry, to the computer industry), which has a vested interest in perpetuating cheap labor policies. Unfortunately, even the AFL-CIO—hitherto the presumptive custodian of the interests of the American workers—chose to oppose any significant legislative changes as its leadership pondered becoming an advocate of immigrants rights.[83]

Efforts to undermine even these limited deterrent measures were soon under way after the IIRIRA became law. Politicians in both political parties sought to ingratiate themselves with the rapidly growing immigrant communities in various parts of the country. One way to do this, they believed, was to support amnesties (i.e., legalization) for members of these communities who are illegal immigrants. At the time IIRIRA was passed, there was already in effect a "section 245i" provision in the Immigration and Nationality Act that was added in 1994. It created a three-year period in which foreign nationals who were illegally in the United States but who had a right—due to family ties or employer sponsorship—to eventually become legal immigrants could adjust their status now by paying a $1,000 fine without leaving the United States. Some 545,000 foreigners took advantage of that amnesty program. Included in this number were also participants in myriad sham marriages that occurred in order for illegal immigrants to obtain a green card by becoming a spouse of a U.S. citizen. Moreover, since the adjustment of status occurred in the United States, the usual background checks that are performed abroad of persons when they apply for immigrant visas in the U.S. consular offices were not done. The magnitude of the number of applicants greatly added to the workload of the already overburdened INS. Under IIRIRA, all persons who had illegally entered the United States ahead of when they were permitted would have had to leave the country after October 1, 1997. Hence, in December 2000, a pro-immigrant coalition in Congress sought to subvert this restriction by attaching a second "245i" amnesty—called the Legal Immigration and Family Equity Act—to another massive appropriation bill in a lame duck session that legislators could vote only "up or down" in its entirety. They succeeded. This second "245i" amnesty permitted an estimated 640,000 foreign nationals illegally in the United States, to adjust their status on the same terms as the original version had allowed if they did so between January and April 2001. When President George W. Bush took office in January 2001, he supported still another "245i" amnesty for another 200,000 illegal immigrants, with the same eligibility requirements for 2002. The Republican-controlled House of Representatives dutifully responded in May 2001 by voting for another four-month extension of the "245i" program to begin in 2002. The Senate was poised to give its stamp of approval to this extension on the afternoon of September 11, 2001, but that morning, Islamic terrorists flew three hijacked commercial airlines into the World Trade Center in New York City and the Pentagon in Washington, DC. Three of the attackers were visa overstayers. Suddenly, illegal immigration policy could no longer be so easily used as a political ploy. National security considerations dictated that the subject finally be taken seriously. Background checks of would-be immigrants are necessary before those individuals can be permitted to enter the country. Sleeper cells of potential terrorists, it was feared, may have already established themselves in the country. Efforts would probably be made to establish others. Blanket amnesties could legitimize their presence and permit them to bide their time to do harm.

But in addition to seeking a series of rolling amnesties as a way to weaken the effectiveness of IIRIRA, still another, more devious policy change was implemented. It was designed to undermine efforts to demagnetize the labor market from attracting illegal immigrants. In the spring of 1999, the INS announced that it would essentially abandon worksite enforcement of employer sanctions against hiring illegal immigrants.[84] Instead, the INS stated, it was going to focus on the prevention of human smuggling activities, enhanced border management (as required under IIRIRA), and the deportation of criminals. Worksite enforcement had always been a controversial enforcement strategy because it sometimes involved questioning citizens and permanent resident aliens. There had been charges that employer sanctions caused hiring discrimination against persons who "look foreign," or speak with accents, or who have certain types of names.[85] Because many leaders in the Asian and Hispanic communities oppose the use of sanctions at the worksite, there was an opportunity for politicians to believe they could curry their favor by seeking to neuter these requirements. Also, employers seeking cheap and exploitable labor had always opposed the use of these sanctions. They, too, were a large constituency that was glad to see this policy change.

This administrative change is a big mistake.[86] Without the enforcement of sanctions, there is no credible threat of removal of illegal immigrants who overstay visas or who evade border detection and make their way into the interior of the country. Without the internal enforcement at the worksite, there is no hope of deterring illegal immigration.

The High-Tech Industry Seeks H-1B Workers: Politics Triumphs—Again

In the later years of the 1990s, the economy of the United States experienced an escape from reality. An acceleration of computer technology, associated with the rapid spread of Internet technology throughout the business sector, triggered a wave of exuberant entrepreneurial and investment activity. The ensuing surge in productivity enabled unemployment rates to fall to levels not seen since the late 1960s without triggering inflationary pressures. In retrospect, the era is now recognized for what it was: a bubble that could not last.[87] In late 2000, it popped.

But before the bubble broke, the tightening of the labor market precipitated a major policy controversy in which immigration policy became a lead player. The high-tech industry was viewed as the engine driving this unprecedented prosperity. Industry officials sensed that only a shortage of programmers and computer technicians could dampen this expansionary euphoria. If the software industry and its related computer designers had to depend on the supply of U.S. workers, wage rates (which were rising) might soar. Some portions of the existing workforce in these industries needed to have their skills upgraded, which, employers feared, would require expensive training to help them learn the new computer languages. If labor shortages did occur, industry leaders feared, higher wages would be required to hold present workers and to entice younger workers to aspire to enter these skilled occupations. Facing the reality of such a free market outcome, industry leaders sought to find a way for government to artificially swell the skilled labor pool. The policy of choice was to use the H-1B provisions of the Immigration Act of 1990. As noted earlier in Chapter 10, the H-1B program permitted the issuance of nonimmigrant visas to skilled workers from foreign countries to fill occupations for temporary periods that could last up to six years. All that was needed was to make the case that qualified citizen workers were unavailable.

The H-1B program had practical advantages to U.S. employers. H-1B workers, the vast majority of whom would be recruited from India, not only had excellent academic preparation in the needed skills, but they also could be required to have had several years of actual work experience using these skills. No matter how well American students could be prepared by their universities, they could not be given the years of experience that H-1B workers allegedly had. Moreover, under the terms of the program, in the mid-1990s, H-1B workers were essentially contract workers (or, more frankly, well-paid indentured servants). Those who came under contracts, signed with employment agencies in their home countries, could not quit working for U.S. employers who had contracted with these agencies for their services. If they quit or were fired, they had to return home. H-1B workers who did not come under such contracts could, technically, quit working for a particular U.S. firm that had hired them and work for another if they received a better offer. But this freedom of choice was essentially a mirage. Many of these H-1B workers were seeking to use their temporary employment with U.S. employers as a way to apply for eventual legal admission under the employment-based provision of the prevailing immigration law. But to do this, the H-1B worker must have his employer certify that there are no similarly qualified U.S. workers available to fill the position. Furthermore, because of the backlogs and the restrictions on how many people from any one country can qualify for employment-based visas in one year, it can take a minimum of several years for all of this to happen. Hence, if the U.S. employer is going to actually sponsor a particular H-1B worker for such a visa, the H-1B worker dare not leave his original employer. For to do so, he (or she in a few cases) would have to start all over again with the new employer to qualify eventually for permanent resident alien status to remain in the United States. Furthermore, an H-1B worker could not move from one U.S. employer to another at that time without the specific permission of the U.S. Department of Labor. This approval process often took months to complete. So, for all intents and purposes, even these H-1B workers were de facto indentured servants, even if de jure they were not. For U.S. employers, this meant that these workers were essentially tied to them, and, unlike citizen workers, they could not quit and go elsewhere in the competitive work environment of those halcyon days.

As stated earlier, when the H-1B program was created in 1990, it was capped at 65,000 visas a year. In 1998, this ceiling was hit by midyear. The high-tech industry, therefore, initiated an immediate lobbying campaign to raise the number. Despite efforts to refute industry claims that there was a shortage that could not be filled by retraining older employees and by actively recruiting younger workers, Congress responded by passing the American Competitiveness and Workforce Improvement Act of 1998.[88] It raised the ceiling to 115,000 visas in both 1999 and 2000 and 107,000 in 2001.

The 1998 legislation also funded an independent commission to be set up by the NRC to assess the validity of the claims of the high-tech employers that there was a labor shortage versus the contentions of critics who said domestic supplies were available but these firms preferred cheap and dependant foreign workers tied to their enterprises. There were also charges that some H-1B workers used fraudulent academic credentials and lied about their actual work experience, but they were retained anyway by the firms because they were able to acquire the needed skills while working on the job (which, of course, is exactly what U.S. workers could do, if they could be hired). Known as the Committee on Workforce Needs in Information Technology, the fifteen-member panel was chaired by Alan Merten, president of George Mason University and, formerly, dean of the Johnson Graduate School of Business at Cornell University. The committee was composed of persons from high-tech firms (e.g., Microsoft and Intel), computer scientists (some with research ties to industry), and labor economists. Their final report, issued October 24, 2000, concluded that the high-tech labor market was tight and that all sources of talent—both domestic and foreign—would be needed to ensure an adequate supply of skilled labor. It concluded that, without the H-1B program, the industry would experience a slowdown. However, it also stated that there is "no analytical basis" available to set the "proper" level of H-1B visas that are needed. Hence, their report concluded that decisions to increase or decrease an annual cap would have to be "fundamentally political."[89] Chair Merten, in a subsequent news conference about the panel's work, candidly stated that "we feel [the number of H-1Bs] is so large that we are totally dependent on it and it depresses wages."[90] In a separate report on the issuance of H-1B visas in 2000, the inspector general in the U.S. Department of Labor found that there were "numerous instances of fraud" in the H-1B program committed by the applicants, companies, and immigration attorneys.[91]

Nonetheless, at the urging of the high-tech industry, Congress, in October 2000, raised the number of H-1B foreign workers to even higher levels. A new ceiling was set for 2001 of 195,000 visas a year, and this same level was set for 2002 and 2003. The Senate approved the increase by a vote of 96–1, and the House, a few days later, did the same by a voice vote (so no one's vote would be recorded). Shortly afterward, President Clinton signed the legislation. After the November 2000 elections were over, Senator Robert F. Bennett (R-Utah), who was a sponsor of the legislation, candidly explained the dominance of politics in the decision-making process. He said that once it was clear that the measure was going to pass the Senate, "everyone signs up so nobody can be in the position of being accused of being against high tech"; but, he added, "there were in fact a whole lot of folks against it, but because they are tapping the high-tech community for campaign funds, they don't want to admit that in public."[92] Speaking of the voice vote in the House, Representative Thomas M. Davis (R-Va.) frankly stated, "this bill may not be popular with the public but it's popular with the CEOs."[93]

By early 2001, the U.S. economy was in a recession. Amid revelations of corporate corruption and accounting fraud—often involving high-tech firms—there were extensive layoffs of skilled workers. H-1B workers, however, continued to be recruited, but in 2002, the number admitted (163,000) was less than the number permitted (195,000). Many citizen workers, however, felt that this number of admissions was still too high given these deteriorating employment conditions. Advocates of H-1Bs, however, claimed that the high-tech industry was decentralizing and that H-1B workers were often willing to settle in these new regions (e.g., in Iowa, Michigan, and Georgia) while laid-off citizen workers in California and Colorado in particular were not. It should be recalled, however, that the H-1B visas are good for up to six years, so in 2002 there were still upward of 750,000 H-1B visa holders in the United States, despite the fact that citizen workers (and some H-1B workers, too) were being laid off.

If no action is taken in 2003 to renew these high entry numbers, the ceiling on H-1B workers will revert to its original 65,000 level.

September 11, 2001: Terrorism Forces a Reality Check

As the summer of 2001 neared its end, U.S. immigration policy continued to be viewed as a political football to be tossed around for partisan advantage. In the presidential election of 2000, neither political party had addressed any of the chronic shortcomings of the nation's immigration system. The comprehensive reforms proposed three years earlier by the Jordan Commission had been safely buried from public memory. Six years of meticulous work had been for naught. The grassroots challenge to the status quo offered by Proposition 187 had been muffled. As 2001 commenced, the economy was faltering after five years of exuberance. A recession had begun, but no political leaders of either party were concerned when the Census Bureau's report released that year said there were at least 8.7 million illegal immigrants in the country, and their ranks were swelling annually by half a million persons. Indeed, Congress had found its own way to reduce the number of illegal immigration: grant amnesties every few years. As mentioned, the House of Representatives—at the behest of the newly elected President George W. Bush—had passed in May 2001 another "section 245i" amnesty proposal, and the Senate was poised to give its approval on September 11, 2001.

The newly elected Bush administration only a few weeks earlier had appointed a former Wall Street executive, James Ziglar, as commissioner of the INS. Ziglar had been serving, as a political appointee, as sergeant of arms of the U.S. Senate for the several months that Republicans were in control of that body in early 2001. When control shifted to the Democrats in June 2001, he needed a new job. His appointment to the INS was confirmed by the Senate on July 31, 2001. An acknowledged economic libertarian who believed in "open borders," Ziglar had absolutely no previous experience that would have qualified him for the post. The major political issue confronting him when he took office was the administration's belief that the INS should be kept in the Department of Justice but its functions split into two branches: one would handle service issues such as naturalization and the issuance of "green cards"; the other would be responsible for enforcement issues at the borders and inland.

During the first week of September, the president of Mexico, Vicente Fox, had addressed a joint session of Congress. In his speech, he reiterated what he had been saying since he had taken office in the beginning of 2001. Namely, immigration issues were the most important concerns affecting bilateral relations between Mexico and the United States. He had been asking for months that the United States grant a general amnesty to the estimated 3.4 million illegal immigrants from Mexico believed to be in the country in 2001. He also asked that an agricultural guest-worker program be established that would allow additional Mexican workers to legally work in the United States for a set period of time and, by doing so, earn the right to stay in the United States permanently. Fox also sought to have the United States exempt Mexico from annual visa quotas so that more Mexicans could legally immigrate in larger numbers. Speaking of this package of proposals, Mexico's foreign minister, Jorge Casteñeda, had publicly proclaimed in June 2001 that "it's the whole enchilada or nothing." But, just a day prior to the actual Washington visit, he backtracked and said "it's not an all-or-nothing deal."[94] Nonetheless, Mexico was trying to take the policy initiative and force the United States to react publicly.

President Bush, already receptive to such ideas in principle, had some qualms about specifics. In August, he said, "there will be no blanket amnesty for illegals."[95] U.S. Secretary of State Colin Powell, in a visit to Mexico early in August, prior to Fox's trip to Washington, announced that they were discussing a plan whereby "some Mexicans living illegally in the U.S.—those who have jobs, pay taxes, and rear children who are American-born United States citizens—would be included in an expanded amnesty—and that a new guestworker program would rest on a carefully worked-out partnership between the sending and receiving countries."[96] What was under consideration, therefore, may not have been a general amnesty, but it certainly was intended to be a generous amnesty. President Bush had already stated his view on the topic in July: "We will consider all folks. . . . When we find willing employers and have willing employees, we ought to match the two. We ought to make it easier for people who want to employ somebody, who are looking for workers, to be able to hire people who want to work."[97] This would mean, of course, that those labor markets where these illegal immigrant workers are employed—which are disproportionately unskilled—would find it difficult if not impossible for their wages to rise. Greater income inequality in the nation would be the price paid for diplomatic accord.

The pro-immigrant lobby both inside and outside of Congress was enthusiastic about these ideas. But some still argued that they did not go far enough. Arthur Helton, a senior fellow at the Council of Foreign Relations and longtime advocate for refugees' rights, made it clear that, the "emerging norm of nondiscrimination in immigration policy is why it will not be possible politically for President Bush to limit a legalization program explicitly for Mexicans."[98] Any amnesty program would have to include everyone from everywhere.

Then it happened: September 11, 2001. The United States was attacked by a group of Al-Qaeda terrorists—all of whom were foreign nationals (mostly from Saudi Arabia) who had used the nation's impotent immigration system to gain access to the country. More sympathizers were believed to be in the country. Suddenly, it was recognized that borders and immigration policies do matter. They are the foundation on which national security itself rests. Government has no greater rationale for its existence than to protect its citizens from attack by foreign forces. The nation's politicians had failed in their duty to do so. In the days that followed, many political leaders and the national media feigned ignorance of how inadequate the nation's prevailing immigration system was.

The Response to Terrorism

In the wake of the terrorist attack, immigration was suddenly front and center on the political agenda. In October 2001, the USA Patriot Act was passed. For the most part, it treats immigration policy as "an afterthought."[99] Among its multiple provisions was recognition of the need for more monitoring of the nation's northern border with Canada. Only two years earlier, Ahmed Ressam—an Al-Qaeda operative from Algeria who had sought refugee status in Canada—was apprehended using a fake Canadian passport when he tried to enter Washington State. He had a car full of explosives and was on his way to blow up part of the Los Angeles International Airport on New Year's Eve, 1999.[100] Congress had not responded to this near catastrophe, but, during hearings prior to the passage of the Patriot Act, it was revealed that there were only 350 Border Patrol agents assigned to this 4,000-mile international border (with only about 60 on duty on any given shift). This Act doubled this number. New powers were given to the attorney general to bar terrorists and their supporters from entering the United States. Noncitizens in the United States could be detained if they were suspected of being terrorists. As of the end of September 2002, none of 1,200 foreigners arrested and detained after September 11 had been charged with an act of terrorism. Many, however, had been deported for being in violation of immigration laws. As of the end of September 2002, the number still in custody had fallen to 81 persons.[101]

In May 2002, the Enhanced Border Security and Visa Reform Act was enacted. It requires greater care in the issuance of visas to enter the United States from countries deemed to be sponsors of terrorists. It expanded border management by enlarging the ranks of immigration inspectors at border entry points and of immigration investigators used for internal enforcement. Furthermore, as discussed earlier, this law requires the establishment of a tracking system for the 500,000 foreign students who annually attend universities and colleges in the nation. Background checks of such students must be completed before they can enter the country. Institutions of higher learning are now required to assure the federal government that foreign students actually enroll, make satisfactory progress toward their degrees, and depart when their studies are complete.

In July 2002, Assistant Secretary of State Mary Ryan (the senior member of the nation's foreign service, with thirty-six years of experience) was forced to resign by Secretary of State Colin Powell. Ryan had played an instrumental role in designing an expedited entry program for nonimmigrant visitors from Saudi Arabia. It was called "Visa-Express." It permitted travel agencies in Saudi Arabia to collect visa applications for its citizens and submit them to the U.S. Embassy in the capital city of Riyadh. But under immigration law, only U.S. government officials can issue such documents and then only after a personal interview with the applicant. Fifteen of the September 11 terrorists had come from Saudi Arabia—three of whom had used this entry system. Others, still undetected, may have.

Following a year of relentless criticism, James Ziglar resigned as commissioner of the INS in August 2002, and, in late October 2002, the pending bill to reactivate another "Section 245i" amnesty program was quietly removed from consideration in the Senate.

The Creation of the U.S. Department of Homeland Security

The third legislative reaction to terrorism has the potential to have the most significant impact on the formation and implementation of immigrant policy. The Homeland Security Act of 2002 established the U.S. Department of Homeland Security (DHS). Enacted in a lame duck session of the 107th Congress following the congressional elections, it represents the largest reorganization of the federal government since the establishment of the U.S. Department of Defense in 1947.[102] When the transfer is finally completed over the ensuing several years, twenty-two separate government agencies will be combined to form the new DHS. Among these will be the INS, which has been part of the U.S. Department of Justice since 1940. The INS itself will be split into two separate bureaus: one will deal with enforcement functions (at the border and in the interior of the country), and the other with services to legal immigrants and nonimmigrants. The DHS will have the legal authority to issue visas to foreign nationals seeking to enter the United States. But, somewhat surprisingly, the actual application process and issuance of visas to enter the country will still remain a function of the embassies and consular offices abroad that are administered by the U.S. Department of State (DOS). Logically, such duties would seem to be fundamental responsibilities of the DHS. But shifting these functions would have led to a significant diminishment in the functions, personnel, and budget of the DOS. Thus, for essentially status and political reasons, these critical duties will remain outside the DHS's domain.

As an antiterrorism move, there is logic to placing immigration issues in this new department. But it remains to be seen whether the numerous other immigration issues—most notably economic and labor market impacts—will receive the attention they desperately need in this massive new bureaucratic structure. The DHS, after all, will have 170,000 employees and will be the third-largest department of the federal government. It also has an extensive array of responsibilities other than those that pertain to immigration issues. The overriding mandate of the DHS is national security. Immigration is an intrinsic element of national security, but the preponderance of immigration issues and concerns are not.

What Needs to Be Done?

Aside from national security issues, there still remains the issue of congruency between immigration policy and national well-being. The employment trends associated with the transformation of the nation's labor market are patently clear. On the demand side, occupations that stress skill and educational achievement are expanding, and those that do not are contracting. The number of skilled and educated workers is increasing, and, despite extensive corporate downsizing in the early 2000s, the trend should be a need for more in the future. As for unskilled and poorly educated workers, their ranks continue to swell. With their unemployment rates being consistently double the national rate, there is no apparent shortage of unskilled job seekers now or on the horizon. To the contrary, the major domestic economic policy challenge confronting the nation is what to do with so many poorly skilled workers at a time when the demand for their services is contracting. Since 1990, immigration has increased the number of high school dropouts in the labor force by 21 percent while increasing the supply of all other workers by only 5 percent.[103] Immigration policy must cease being a contradictory force. To the maximum extent possible, it must reflect awareness of these basic realities. The so-called preparedness issue of the labor force to compete internationally is a quality issue, not a quantity issue.

To this end, the first issue that immigration reform must address is the inflexibility of the current system. Economic circumstances change. Annual immigration levels, however, are set by legislation. The overall number of legal immigrants admitted each year should be allowed to fluctuate annually (as it does in all other countries that actually admit immigrants on a sizable scale).[104]

Congress should set an overall annual ceiling that embraces all forms of immigration and that cannot be exceeded. The legislative ceiling should be seen as a maximum number allowed to enter but not an annual goal to be achieved. Within the context of the permissible legislative ceiling, the actual level of immigration for any given year should be set administratively by an agency of the executive branch of the federal government. The number could be anywhere from zero up to the authorized annual ceiling.

Permitting the annual number of admissions to be set administratively would provide the necessary flexibility to respond to different economic circumstances that is currently absent. The administrative agency could be required to defend its decision each year at public hearings before the appropriate committees of Congress. The check of the agency's power would be the fact that, if the agency's decisions cannot be defended in a credible manner, Congress can change the law.

Ideally, the agency responsible for setting the annual immigration level should have an employment mission. Since most immigrants and their family members will either immediately or eventually enter the labor force, such an agency is best suited to judge how many immigrants should be admitted and under what entry guise. It also would be better equipped to enforce internally the laws that apply to immigrants at the workplace (e.g., employment sanctions or antidiscrimination protections for resident aliens that are derived from the employment relationship).

Prior to the change in international affairs that led to the creation of the DHS, the logical agency to perform such duties would have been the U.S. Department of Labor (which administered immigration policy from the time it was founded in 1913 until 1940). With the assumption of immigration duties into the DHS, the best that could be hoped for would be that this agency would delegate to the DOL the responsibility to set the annual immigration number and to determine what types of skills should be sought from abroad. The DHS would still be responsible for screening all applicants.

Because the DOL also has enforcement responsibilities for wage and hour violations, child labor laws, occupational health and safety laws, and migrant farmworker protections, it could easily become the sole enforcer of employer sanctions. It could easily add antidiscrimination enforcement against aliens to its duties.

The issue of refugee and asylee accommodation, of course, is more complicated to incorporate in this administrative structure. An advisory role should also be established by the DHS with the U.S. Department of State, as well as agreements with it to perform certain delegated responsibilities required to ensure that these humanitarian roles are adequately performed—but within established ceilings.

The primary objective should be to establish a targeted and flexible immigration policy designed to admit primarily persons who can fill job vacancies for which qualified citizens and resident aliens are unavailable. The number of immigrants annually admitted, however, should be far fewer than the number needed. Immigration should never be allowed to dampen two types of market pressures: those needed to encourage citizen workers to invest in preparing for vocations that are expanding, and those needed to ensure that government bodies provide the requisite human resource development to prepare citizens for the new types of jobs that are emerging. As the Commission on Workforce Quality and Labor Market Efficiency has warned, "by using immigration to relieve shortages, we may miss the opportunity to draw additional U.S. workers into the economic mainstream."[105] It further counseled that, public policy, first and foremost, should "always try to train citizens to fill labor shortages."[106]

Because it takes time for would-be workers to acquire skills and education, immigration policy can be used on a short-run basis to target experienced immigrant workers for permanent settlement who already possess these abilities. But the skill and educational preparedness, or lack thereof, of the domestic labor force is the fundamental economic issue confronting the United States. Over the long haul, citizen workers must be prepared to qualify for jobs that have growth potential.

A shift in admission preference away from family reunification toward greater reliance on employment-based criteria can be expected to encounter fierce opposition despite the fact that the rationale for establishing the priority for family reunification in 1965 was anything but noble in its original intentions (review Chapter 9). As the eminent authority on immigration, John Higham, has written:

> This [the elimination of family preference] will be as difficult to change as were the earlier anomalies and deficiencies in American immigration policy. Like those earlier deficiencies, the family preference scheme will have a stubborn constituency in the ethnic groups that believe they benefit from it. Just as the national origin quotas suppressed variety in the alleged interests of the older American population, so the current law does the same in the supposed interest of the groups that have recently dominated the incoming stream.[107]

The proposal by the CIR to reduce the extended-family provisions of the current law was a step in the right direction. If adult brothers and sisters of U.S. citizens as well as adult children of citizens and permanent resident aliens wish to immigrate to the United States, they should be required to qualify on the same grounds as any other would-be immigrants.

Given the unprecedented forces that are reshaping the occupational, industrial, and geographic employment patterns of the nation, the United States can ill afford an immigration policy that runs counter to its best interests. The nation is at an economic crossroad. It must choose between being a nation of high wages, made possible by a highly productive labor force, or becoming a nation of low wages, the consequence of a lowly productive labor force.

The necessity to choose the former of these two options is made more imperative by the changes that are reconstituting the composition of the nation's labor force. As the world's first advanced industrial society to have a multiracial and multiethnic labor force, it is mandatory that the society not polarize along racial and ethnic lines as to who is employed in the growth occupations and industries and who is left to flounder in the declining employment sectors or forced into the underclass of the economy. Thus, equity considerations and the need for domestic tranquility demand that every effort be made to incorporate those segments of the population that are experiencing difficulties qualifying and preparing themselves for the job sectors that are expected to expand. The design of immigration policy must not be allowed to continue to increase competition in the existing low-wage labor markets nor be allowed to diminish the pressures needed to develop and upgrade the latent talents of those citizens and permanent resident aliens who are already disproportionately vulnerable to the changing employment trends.

As immigration policy can influence the quantitative size of the labor force as well as the qualitative characteristics of those it admits, it can shape labor market conditions as well as respond to its changes. As matters now stand, there is little synchronization of immigrant flows with the demonstrated needs of the labor market. While there is no prospect for a general labor shortage as the twenty-first century begins, there may be spot shortages. This is a normal byproduct of a dynamic economy. These shortages will most likely be in occupations that require extensive training and educational preparation. In the technologically driven and internationally competitive economic setting of contemporary times, no industrialized nation with as many functionally illiterate adults as the United States has need have any short-run fear of a shortage of unqualified workers. There is no need for immigration to add to this surplus of illiterate adult job seekers. Moreover, the prevailing immigration and refugee flow is distorting educational expenditures in many communities. Increasingly, there are demands for more funding for remedial education, basic training, and language literacy programs in those communities impacted by their arrival. Too often, these funding choices cause scarce public funds to be diverted from being used to upgrade the human resource capabilities of citizens and resident aliens.

In this economic environment, an immigration policy designed to admit a flexible number of highly skilled and educated workers is what is required. The Immigration Act of 1990 was ostensibly intended to move public policy in this direction. But, as has been shown, it actually expanded the nepotistic family reunification focus that had been the predominate feature of the law it replaced and only marginally increased employment-based immigration. The inordinate adherence to this principle of family reunification, the continuing entry of illegal immigrants, and the admission of substantial numbers of Third World refugees are the major contributors to this worsening mismatch between the qualifications of many job seekers and the actual needs of the labor market.

Already having an abundance of unskilled and poorly educated adults, the last thing that the nation needs is to continue to allow more such persons to immigrate into the United States. It is always possible for more highly skilled and educated persons to do unskilled work. Hence, in the unlikely event that all of the experts on labor force trends and projections are wrong, and the future demand is for unskilled workers with a contraction of need for skilled workers, the operation of normal market forces should be able to guide the excess supply of skilled workers to vacant unskilled jobs. This assumes, of course, that the operation of the market is not sabotaged by an immigration policy designed to admit unskilled nonimmigrant workers or that continues to tolerate massive illegal entry of unskilled workers. But the reverse is not possible. If skilled and educated workers are needed, they cannot readily be created. Unskilled workers cannot fill skilled jobs except at great financial cost associated with significant time delays for retraining and relocation or with significant productivity losses for the economy, due to inefficient operations. Moreover, the lack of sufficient educational foundations will prevent many currently unskilled adults from ever being trained for the types of jobs that are projected to be most in demand in the new century.

On the positive side, immigration can be used as a means of providing some of the experienced workers that are actually needed. Under present circumstances, these workers are those who already have skills, education, and work experience and who, for whatever reason, voluntarily wish to leave their homelands. It is in this capacity that immigration can find a justifiable purpose in this era. Immigration policy can serve as a short-run method to fill some of these jobs until the nation can enact the quality human resource development policies capable of meeting this emerging demand.

Largely by means of circumvention, the current immigration system is trying to perform this function despite the self-defeating burdens imposed on it. The nonimmigrant system is becoming a significant avenue into the country's labor market for skilled and educated workers. Indeed, the use of nonimmigrant foreign workers has emerged as a major domestic labor policy as the new century begins. Nonimmigrant policy is supposed to allow for the admission of foreign workers to fill temporary shortages. All nonimmigrants should be expected to return to their homelands eventually, and, over time, market forces combined with public and private training should generate the needed domestic labor supply. Nonimmigrant policy should mean precisely what the term suggests. It is not an avenue for permanent immigration or a source of long-term worker supply for U.S. employers. But, because 80 percent of the available visas each year are restricted to family-related admissions, and because there have been lengthy backlogs of applicants and country ceilings that have affected the availability of the employment-based visas, many employers have turned to the nonimmigrant system to find experienced workers or to serve as an alternative to training citizens to perform. This is, of course, a perversion of immigration policy. Many of the relevant nonimmigrant categories have no annual ceilings, and some permit workers to remain in the country for many years. Consequently, nonimmigrant workers are rapidly becoming as important as the existing legal immigrant system in terms of its annual labor supply infusions. This should not be allowed to continue. The imposition of a substantial fee—such as proposed by Senator Simpson and discussed earlier—for each nonimmigrant hired is one way to ensure that nonimmigrants are truly temporary.

A shift from a family-based to a labor market–oriented immigration policy, of course, does have its dangers. For even the use of immigration as a source of experienced workers should be viewed as a policy of last resort, not immediate recourse. It should be used only in consort with other public policy measures intended to develop the employment potential of the nation's human resources. Labor shortages, should they develop, should not be viewed as a problem to be solved immediately by immigration. Rather, labor shortages should be viewed as an opportunity to educate youth, to retrain adults, to eliminate discriminatory barriers, and to introduce voluntary relocation programs to assist would-be workers to move from labor surplus to labor shortage areas. Obviously, if skilled citizens and permanent resident aliens are available—due to changes in economic conditions such as defense cutbacks or corporate downsizing—there should be limitations on the entry of even skilled immigrant workers during such periods.

If the prevailing policy of mass and unguided immigration continues, it is unlikely that there will be sufficient pressure to enact the long-term human resource development policies needed to prepare and to incorporate these citizens from minority groups into the mainstream economy. Instead, by providing both competition and alternatives, the large and unplanned influx of immigrant labor will serve to maintain the social marginalization of many blacks and Hispanics who are citizens and permanent resident aliens. It will also mean that job opportunities will be reduced for the growing numbers of older workers who may wish to prolong their working years and for the vast pool of disabled citizens who were extended employment protection by the Americans with Disabilities Act of 1990. In other words, a substantial human reserve of potential citizen workers already exists. If their latent human resource development needs were addressed comprehensively, they could provide an ample supply of workers for most of the labor force needs in the foreseeable future.

The national interest dictates that priority must always be to prepare citizen and resident alien workers for jobs in the expanding employment sectors of the economy. To respond to labor shortages by using immigration policy to fill jobs in an economy that is not at full employment is analogous to choosing to take a shortcut through quicksand. Immigrants can fill the jobs, but the social cost to the nation is a loss of opportunities to build a better society with all of the attendant social and human costs that will result.

Adopting an employment-oriented immigration system is, of course, predicated on the assumption that every effort is made to reduce illegal immigration. It is impossible in a free society to stop illegal immigration entirely, but the goal should be to pursue actively every possible means to reduce its incidence. Illegal immigration, aside from the competition it provides with other low-wage citizen and resident alien workers, is a major explanation for the revival of sweatshops and the upsurge in child labor violations that have occurred since the mid-1980s in many urban areas.[108] Existing fair labor standards laws, child labor laws, and occupational health and safety laws should be vigorously enforced to end such practices regardless of whether such illegal aliens and their children are actually displacing citizen or resident alien workers. U.S. employers should not be permitted to use Third World wages and working conditions to employ immigrant workers from Third World countries under any circumstances.

The entire presumption that the nation can have a realistic immigration policy is predicated on the notion that its terms can be enforced. But the scale of illegal immigration over the years has completely undermined this premise. The use of employer sanctions must return to the forefront of the nation's deterrence posture, but its loopholes with regard to the use of fraudulent documents and the absence of a reliable proof of identification system must be corrected. More attention should also be given by national policies to addressing the push factors in the major source countries. More economic assistance should be made available and tailored to the particular factors in any country that cause so many of its citizens to leave their homeland. These may involve such concerns as excessive population pressures, mass poverty, corrupt governments, or widespread human rights violations. U.S. assistance could take the form of family planning assistance, limited trade concessions, economic development assistance, and technical assistance.

With regard to refugee policy, the goal should be to make the treatment of refugees ideologically neutral. All political refugees should be treated the same. The refugee concept should be applied to individuals and not generalized to groups.

Certainly the United States is obligated to participate in worldwide efforts to assist legitimate political refugees who are being persecuted, but there is more to be done than simply admitting such persons for permanent settlement. Attention should be given to other policy alternatives. Aside from the standard efforts to resettle refugees in other regional countries near their homelands or to provide financial aid to support refugees in camps while they remain in neighboring third-party countries (if conditions in their homelands are expected to change in the near future), the United States should link its foreign policy, foreign aid, and foreign trade policies to the strict adherence to human rights principles in those countries that generate mass numbers of political refugees. Nonetheless, when there is no other recourse, those refugees and their family members who have sustained persecution for their individual actions should—as now—be admitted in limited numbers. As proposed by the CIR, the link between the legal immigration system and refugee policy must be re-established (as was the case from 1965 to 1980). Otherwise, the political temptation is for the federal government to act in piecemeal fashion that often results in significant inflows of refugees for which local and state governments must bear most of the settlement costs. Indeed, it would be preferable if the federal government would absorb all of the financial costs associated with preparing refugees for employment and their families for settlement for at least three years. Refugees are admitted to the United States as a direct result of federal policy decisions. Consequently, all of the people of the United States should share the costs of refugee policy and not just those who live in the local communities that are impacted by their physical presence.

The political asylum issue raises the same questions as with refugees. There needs to be an expedited method to separate the legitimate claims for political asylum from the claims by persons who are simply using it as a pretext to enter the country for personal economic gain. The original Simpson–Mazzoli bill of 1982 proposed that negative decisions of asylee adjudication cases be appealable only to courts on the basis of procedural errors. Substantive rulings on the merits of the decisions would not be appealable. These provisions were bitterly opposed by immigration lawyers and by some civil rights organizations. But the current system of lengthy appeals, protracted cases, and high legal costs simply cannot be sustained. A way of bringing fair but rapid closure to these cases must be found. The policy enacted in 1995 that denies work authorization while decisions are pending, if Asylum Corps officials question the authenticity of an asylum request, is a big step in the right direction. Likewise, if an expedited decision-making procedure could be established, the practice of keeping asylum applicants in detention while their cases are resolved could be applied uniformly. Otherwise one is confronted with the present mockery to common sense whereby many applicants simply make an asylum request, are released on their own recognizance, and disappear before their adjudication hearing or soon after a hearing in which they receive a negative decision.

The United States needs to adopt an immigration policy that is consistent with its rapidly changing labor market trends. If congruent, immigration policy can provide a valuable tool to national efforts to enhance economic efficiency and to achieve societal equity. If contradictory, immigration policy can present a major barrier to the accomplishment of either or both goals. The luxury of allowing immigration policy to continue to be determined on political criteria (i.e., to placate special interest groups) and to achieve idealistic social dreams (i.e., to pursue diversity simply for its own sake) can ill be afforded. Making immigration policy primarily a human resource development policy would give immigration policy what it now lacks: economic accountability for most of what it does.

Appendix A

Means by Which Selected Nations Grant Citizenship

Country	Birth[a]	Notes
Algeria	No	Father must be Algerian or stateless.
Argentina	Yes	
Australia	No	Children of immigrants born in Australia are citizens.
Belgium	No	One parent must be a citizen of Belgium.
Brazil	Yes	
Cameroon	Yes	
Canada	Yes	Children born to foreign parents after February 1977 are citizens at birth.
Columbia	No	One parent must be a legal resident.
Czech Republic	No	One parent must be a citizen of Czech Republic.
Egypt	No	Father must be an Egyptian citizen.
France	No	A child of foreign-born parents must apply and be approved for citizenship.
Germany	No	Those born in Germany automatically acquire the citizenship status of their mother.
India	Yes	
Israel	No	If Jewish, a child is automatically a citizen, otherwise, must be the child of an Israeli National to be a citizen.

(continued)

Appendix A *(continued)*

Italy	No	One parent must be Italian.
Jamaica	Yes	
Japan	No	One parent must be a citizen of Japan.
Kenya	No	One parent must be a citizen of Kenya.
Kuwait	No	Father must be a citizen of Kuwait.
Mexico	Yes	
New Zealand	Yes	
Nigeria	No	One parent must be a Nigerian citizen.
Norway	No	One parent must be Norwegian.
Pakistan	Yes	
Philippines	No	One parent must be a citizen of the Philippines.
Poland	No	One parent must be Polish.
Republic of Korea	No	One parent must be a citizen of Korea.
Saudi Arabia	No	Father must be a citizen.
Spain	Yes	However, the child needs one year of residence to become a citizen if the parents are foreigners.
Sweden	No	If mother is Swedish, the child acquires citizenship at birth; if parents are resident aliens, the children acquire the citizenship of their parents.
Switzerland	No	If child was born before June 1, 1985, the father must be Swiss for the child to be a Swiss citizen; if the child is born after June 1, 1985, the child will be a Swiss citizen if either parent is Swiss.
Syria	No	One parent must be a citizen of Syria.
Taiwan	No	One parent must be a citizen of Taiwan.
Turkey	No	One parent must be a citizen of Turkey.
United Kingdom	No	One parent must be a citizen or a legal resident of the UK for the child to be a citizen.
United States	Yes	
Venezuela	Yes	
Zaire	No	Mother must be a citizen of Zaire.

Source: Center for Immigration Studies, Washington, DC.

ᵃ"Birth" refers only to whether or not a person is guaranteed citizenship simply by being born in that country. However, excluded from consideration are the children of diplomats or other persons on official government business in a foreign country.

Appendix B

The Preference System Created Under the Immigration Act of 1965
(in effect until 1980)

Preference	Category	Maximum proportion of total admitted
First	Unmarried adult sons and daughters of U.S. citizens	20 percent
Second	Spouses and unmarried adult sons and daughters of aliens lawfully admitted for permanent residence	20 percent plus any not required by first preference
Third	Members of the professions, scientists, and artists of exceptional ability	10 percent
Fourth	Married sons and daughters of U.S. citizens	10 percent plus any not required by first and third preferences
Fifth	Brothers and sisters of U.S. citizens	24 percent plus any not required by first four preferences
Sixth	Skilled and unskilled workers in occupations for which labor is in short supply	10 percent
Seventh	Refugees	6 percent
Nonpreference	Any applicant	Numbers not used by preceding preferences

Appendix C

The Legal Immigration System and Its Preference Allocations That Were in Effect from 1980 to 1991

Preference	Category	Maximum proportion of total admitted
First	Unmarried adult sons and daughters of U.S. citizens	20 percent
Second	Spouses and unmarried adult sons and daughters of aliens lawfully admitted for permanent residence	26 percent plus any not required by first preference
Third	Members of the professions, or persons of exceptional ability in the sciences and arts	10 percent
Fourth	Married sons and daughters of U.S. citizens	10 percent plus any not required by first and third preferences
Fifth	Brothers and sisters of U.S. citizens, 21 years of age and over	24 percent plus any not required by first four preferences
Sixth	Skilled and unskilled workers in occupations for which labor is in short supply	10 percent
Nonpreference	Any applicant	Numbers not used by preceding preferences

Notes

Chapter 1. Introduction: The Revival of Mass Immigration

1. Oxford Analytica, *America in Perspective* (Boston: Houghton-Mifflin, 1986), 20.
2. Ibid.
3. U.S. Bureau of the Census, "Number of Foreign Born Up 57 Percent Since 1990 According to Census 2000," *Commerce News*, CB02–CN. 117 (Washington, DC: U.S. Department of Commerce, June 4, 2002), 1–3.
4. National Research Council, *The New Americans: Economic, Demographic, and Fiscal Effects of Immigration*, ed. James P. Smith and Barry Edmonston (Washington, DC: National Academy Press, 1997), 95.
5. U.S. Bureau of the Census, *Population Projections of the United States By Age, Sex, Race, and Hispanic Origin: 1995–2050*, P25–1130 (Washington, DC: Government Printing Office, 1996), 5.
6. National Research Council, *The New Americans*, 95.
7. Paul C. Light, "Government's Greatest Achievements of the Past Half Century," *Reform Watch* (Washington, DC: The Brookings Institution, November 2000), 5.
8. Ibid., 7.

Chapter 2. Immigration Policy: A Determinant of Economic Phenomena

1. For another example, see Robert LaLonde and Robert Topel, "Immigrants in the American Labor Market: Quality, Assimilation, and Distributional Effects," *American Economic Review* (May 1991): 297–302.
2. For a discussion of the data limitations, see Vernon M. Briggs, Jr., *Immigration Policy and the American Labor Force* (Baltimore: Johns Hopkins University Press, 1984), 6–10, 131–37.
3. U.S. Congress, House Select Committee on Population, *Legal and Illegal Immigration to the United States* (Washington, DC: Government Printing Office, 1978), 48.

4. National Research Council, Panel on Immigration Statistics, *Immigration Statistics: A Story of Neglect* (Washington, DC: Government Printing Office, 1985), 3.

5. U.S. Commission on Immigration Reform, *U.S. Immigration Policy: Restoring Credibility: A Report to Congress* (Washington, DC: Author, 1994), 31 of the Executive Summary.

6. John C. Keane, "Statement of the Director of the Bureau of the Census before the Subcommittee on Governmental Processes of the Committee on Governmental Affairs of the U.S. House of Representatives" (September 18, 1985), 5.

7. U.S. Bureau of the Census, *Profile of the Foreign-Born of the United States: 2000*, P23–206 (Washington, DC: Author, 2001), 17.

8. Cf. U.S. Bureau of the Census, *Profile of the Foreign Born . . . 2000*, 1, with U.S. Bureau of the Census, "Number of Foreign Born Up by 57 Percent Since 1990 According to 2000 Census," *U.S. Department of Commerce News*, June 4, 2002, 1.

9. Peter Passell, "Can't Count on Numbers," *New York Times*, August 6, 1991, A-1, A-14.

10. U.S. Bureau of the Census, "Evaluating Components of International Migration: The Residual Foreign Born," Working Paper Series No. 61, March 1, 2001, 16.

11. Robert Warren and Ellen Percy Kraly, *The Elusive Exodus: Emigration from the United States* (Washington, DC: Population Reference Bureau, 1985).

12. U.S. Immigration and Naturalization Service, "Emigration," *Statistical Yearbook of the Immigration and Naturalization Service: 1998* (Washington, DC: Author, 2000), 238.

13. U.S. Immigration and Naturalization Service, *The Triennial Comprehensive Report on Immigration* (Washington, DC: U.S. Department of Justice, 2002), 33.

14. Ibid., 34.

15. William J. Baumol, "Sir John Versus the Hicksians, or Theorist Malgre Lui," *Journal of Economic Literature* (December 1990): 1715.

16. Ibid.

17. George J. Borjas, *Friends or Strangers: The Impact of Immigration on the U.S. Economy* (New York: Basic Books, 1990), 220.

18. Vernon M. Briggs, Jr., "International Migration and Labor Mobility: The Receiving Countries," in *The Economics of Labour Migration*, ed. Julian van den Broeck (London: Edward Elgar, 1996), 113–50.

19. Cf., George J. Borjas, *Heaven's Door: Immigration Policy and the American Economy* (Princeton, NJ: Princeton University Press, 1999); and Vernon M. Briggs, Jr., *Mass Immigration and the National Interest*, 2nd ed. (Armonk, NY: M.E. Sharpe, 1996).

20. For example, see Kalena E. Cortes, "Are Refugees Different from Economic Immigrants? Some Empirical Evidence on the Heterogeneity of Immigrant Groups in the United States," Working Paper No. 41 (Berkeley, CA: Center for Labor Economics, September 2001).

21. Henry C. Simons, *Economic Policy for a Free Society* (Chicago: University of Chicago Press, 1948), 251.

22. Ibid.

23. Melvin W. Reder, "Chicago Economics: Permanence and Change," *Journal of Economic Literature* (March 1982): 31.

24. Milton Friedman, *Capitalism & Freedom* (Chicago: University of Chicago Press, 1962), chap. 2.

25. Milton Friedman and Rose Friedman, *Free to Choose: A Personal Statement* (San Diego: Harcourt Brace Janovich, 1990), 35–36.

26. David A. Coleman, "The Ins and Outs of British Migration Policy," *The Social Contract* (June 1994): 254–60.

27. Reder, "Chicago Economics: Permanence and Change," 31.

28 Melvin W. Reder, "The Economic Consequences of Increased Immigration," *The Review of Economics and Statistics* (August 1963): 227.

29. Ibid.

30. Ibid., 229.

31 Ibid., 230.

32. Ibid. [Emphasis is in the original.]

33. Gary S. Becker, "An Open Door for Immigrants—The Auction," *Wall Street Journal*, October 14, 1992, A-14.

34. Joseph A. Schumpeter, *History of Economic Analysis* (New York: Oxford University Press, 1954), 4.

35. "The Re-Kindled Flame," *Wall Street Journal*, July 3, 1989, 6.

36 Julian L. Simon, "The Case for Greatly Increased Immigration," *The Public Interest* (Winter 1991): 89–103. See also Julian Simon, *The Economic Consequences of Immigration* (London: Basil Blackwell, 1989).

37. Robert Reinhold, "In California, New Talk About a Taboo Subject," *New York Times*, December 3, 1991, A-20.

38. See Stephen Moore's essay, "The Economic Case for More Immigrants," in Vernon M. Briggs, Jr., and Stephen Moore, *Still an Open Door? U.S. Immigration Policy and the American Economy* (Washington, DC: American University Press, 1994), 77–148.

39. John Kenneth Galbraith, *The Nature of Mass Poverty* (Cambridge, MA: Harvard University Press, 1979), 136 ff.

40. Jagdish N. Bhagwati, "U.S. Immigration Policy: What Next?" in *Essays on Legal and Illegal Immigration*, ed. Susan Pozo (Kalamazoo, MI: W.E. Upjohn Institute for Employment Research, 1986), 117. See also Jagdish Bhagwati, "Behind the Green Card," *The New Republic*, May 14, 1990, 31–39.

Chapter 3. Citizenship and Naturalization

1. William R. Brubaker, "Citizenship and Naturalization: Policies and Politics," in *Immigration and the Politics of Citizenship in Europe and North America*, ed. W.R. Brubaker (Lanham, MD: University Press of America, 1989), chap. 5.

2. Stanley A. Renshon, "Dual Citizenship in America: An Issue of Vast Proportion and Broad Significance," *Backgrounder* (Washington, DC: Center for Immigration Studies, July 2000), 7. See also Stanley A. Renshon, *Dual Citizenship and American National Identity* (Washington, DC: Center for Immigration Studies, 2001), center paper #20.

3. Nancy H. Montwiller, *The Immigration Reform Law of 1986* (Washington, DC: The Bureau of National Affairs, 1987), 27, 59.

4. *United States Constitution*, Amendment 14, Section 1, Clause 1.

5. Office of the Governor of the State of California, "Wilson Proposes Measures to Curb Massive Illegal Immigration," *News Release*, Sacramento, California, August 9, 1993, 2.

6. For a review of the provisions of a number of these legislative proposals, see, for example, Sarah A. Adams, "The Basic Right of Citizenship: A Comparative Study,"

Backgrounder No. 7–93 (Washington, DC: Center for Immigration Studies, September 1993), 1–2.

7. Neil A. Lewis, "Bill Seeks to End Automatic Citizenship for All Born in the U.S.," *New York Times*, December 14, 1995, A-26.

8. Ibid.

9. William F. Chip, "Citizenship Isn't a Birthright," *Washington Post*, August 30, 1996, A-31.

10. *Elk* v. *Wilkens* (1884).

11. Brubaker, *Immigration and the Politics of Citizenship*, 101.

12. Ibid., 102.

13. *Miller* v. *Albright* (1998) and *Nguyen* v. *I.N.S* (2001).

14. Linda Greenhouse, "Facet of Immigration Law Is Argued," *New York Times*, November 5, 1997, A-22.

15. *United States Constitution*, Article 1, Section 8, Clause 4.

16. *Ozawa* v. *United States*, 260 U.S. 178 (1922).

17. U.S. Committee on the Judiciary, United States Senate, "History of the Immigration and Naturalization Service," *A Report*, 96th Cong., 2nd sess. (Washington, DC: Government Printing Office, 1980), 13.

18. Ibid.

19. For example, see A.T. Lane, "American Trade Unions, Mass Immigration, and the Literacy Test: 1900–1917," *Labor History* (Winter 1984): 5–25.

20. U.S. Committee on the Judiciary, *Report*, 48–52.

21. For example, see Francine Knowles, "Illinois Improve Non-citizen Access to State Licensed Jobs," *Chicago Sun-Times*, September 23, 1999, 1.

22. Kris Axtman, "A Boom in Citizenship Request," *Christian Science Monitor*, February 11, 2002, 1.

23. David North, "Why Democratic Governments Cannot Cope with Illegal Immigration," paper presented at the International Conference on Migration, sponsored by the Organization for Economic Cooperation and Development, Rome, Italy, March 13, 1991.

24. "Statement by Barbara Jordan, Chair of the U.S. Commission on Immigration Reform," issued June 17, 1995, by the U.S. Commission on Immigration Reform, Washington, DC, 6.

25. Ibid., 8.

Chapter 4. Prelude to Mass Immigration

1. Spanish explorers had been active since 1540 in the region that, centuries later, would become the Southwest of the United States. But the Spanish explorations were not originally interested in creating settlements in this region. It was over a century later, in 1610, that the first effort to establish a white settlement in the region was made by Governor and Captain-General Don Juan de Onate. It was located near what is today Santa Fe, New Mexico. Its establishment was three years after the British successfully founded a colony in Jamestown, Virginia, in 1607. Unlike the Jamestown colony that subsequently thrived, however, the original Santa Fe colony was completely destroyed in 1680 by Indian attacks. Even after being re-established in 1692, it was still an isolated settlement by the time it was incorporated into the United States in 1848.

· 2. Henry Pelling, *American Labor* (Chicago: University of Chicago Press, 1960), 1–2.

3. Leonard Dinnerstein and David Reimers, *Ethnic Americans: A History of Immigration*, 3d ed. (New York: Harper and Row, 1988), 4.

4. Stanley Lebergott, *Manpower in Economic Growth* (New York: McGraw-Hill, 1964), 510.

5. Ibid., 139.

6. Henry Bamford Parkes, *The United States of America: A History* (New York: Alfred A. Knopf, 1953), 23.

7. Ibid.

8. Lebergott, *Manpower in Economic Growth*, 8.

9. Alvin M. Josephy, *The Indian Heritage of America* (New York: Bantam Books, 1969), 322–24.

10. Parkes, *The United States of America*, 189.

11. Dee Brown, *Bury My Heart at Wounded Knee: An Indian History of the American West* (New York: Holt, Rinehart and Winston, 1970), chap. 1.

12. Stanley M. Elkins, *Slavery* (New York: Grosset and Dunlap, 1959), 49.

13. W.E.B. DuBois, *The Suppression of the African Slave Trade to the United States of America 1638–1870* (New York: Schocken Books, 1969), 152–53.

14. Lebergott, *Manpower in Economic Growth*, 20.

15. Ibid., 108–18.

16. Ibid., 102.

17. Paul Horgan, *Great River: The Rio Grande in North American History* (New York: Holt, Rinehart and Winston, 1954), vols. 1 and 2.

18. Carey McWilliams, *North from Mexico* (New York: Greenwood Press, 1968), chaps. 3 and 4.

19. Ibid., 52.

20. Ibid. See also Oscar J. Martinez, "On the Size of the Chicano Population: New Estimates, 1850–1900," *Atzlan* (Spring 1975): 43–67.

21. McWilliams, *North from Mexico*, 51.

22. Ibid., 7.

23. Ibid., 53.

24. Harry E. Cross and James A. Sandos, *Across the Border* (Berkeley, CA: Institute of Governmental Studies, 1981).

Chapter 5. Creating a Nonagricultural Labor Force: The "First Wave" of Mass Immigration

1. Stanley Lebergott, *Manpower in Economic Growth* (New York: McGraw-Hill, 1964), 101.

2. Marcus L. Hansen, *The Immigrant in American History* (Cambridge, MA: Harvard University Press, 1942), 11. [emphasis is in the original text]

3. Lebergott, *Manpower in Economic Growth*, 40.

4. *Annals of the Congress of the United States*, vol. 31, 15th Cong., 1st sess., 1818 (Washington, DC: Galen and Seaton, 1854), 1053–54.

5. Hansen, *The Immigrant in American History*, 132.

6. Ibid.

7. David Montgomery, "The Working Classes of the Pre-Industrial American City," *Labor History* (Winter 1968): 9.

8. Hansen, *The Immigrant in American History*, 60–68, 72–76.

9. Lebergott, *Manpower in Economic Growth*, 128.

10. Ibid.

11. Ibid., 37.

12. Rodman W. Paul, "The Origins of the Chinese Issue in California," *Mississippi Valley Historical Review* (September 1938): 181–96.

13. Foster Rhea Dulles, *Labor in America* (New York: Thomas Y. Crowell, 1955), 78.

14. Ibid.

15. Hugh Davis Graham and Ted Robert Gurr, *The History of Violence in America* (New York: Bantam Books, 1968), 54.

16. Ibid.

17. Dulles, *Labor in America*, 79.

18. John F. Kennedy, *A Nation of Immigrants*, rev. ed. (New York: Harper and Row, 1964), 70–71.

19. Vernon M. Briggs, Jr., *Immigration and American Unionism* (Ithaca, NY: Cornell University Press, 2001), chap. 2.

Chapter 6. Expanding the Urban Labor Force: The "Second Wave" of Mass Immigration

1. Stanley Lebergott, *Manpower in Economic Growth* (New York: McGraw-Hill, 1964), 103.

2. Marcus L. Hansen, *Atlantic Migration: 1607–1860* (Cambridge, MA: Harvard University Press, 1940), 10.

3. Lebergott, *Manpower in Economic Growth*, 28.

4. Ibid., 28–29.

5. A. Ross Eckler and Jack Zlotnick, "Immigration and the Labor Force," *Annals of the American Academy of Political and Social Sciences* (March 1949): 96–97.

6. Vernon M. Briggs, Jr., *Immigration and American Unionism* (Ithaca, NY: Cornell University Press, 2001), 36–38.

7. Peter Kwong, *Forbidden Workers: Illegal Chinese Immigrants and American Labor* (New York: New Press, 1997), 143.

8. Ibid., 45.

9. For elaboration, see Briggs, *Immigration and American Unionism*, 38–40.

10. Kwong, *Forbidden Workers*, 42–43.

11. Max Thalen, "The Chinese Exclusion Act," *The Social Contract* (Winter 1997–98): 113.

12. Briggs, *Immigration and American Unionism*, 42.

13. Lebergott, *Manpower in Economic Growth*, 163.

14. Timothy H. Hatton and Jeffrey G. Williamson, "The Impact of Immigration on American Labor Markets Prior to the Quotas," Working Paper No. 5185 (Cambridge, MA: National Bureau of Economic Research, 1995), 30.

Chapter 7. Rapid Industrialization Expands the Demand for Labor: The "Third Wave" of Mass Immigration

1. Robert D. Patton, *The American Economy* (Chicago: Scott Foresman, 1953), 238.

2. Harry A. Millis and Royal E. Montgomery, *Labor's Progress and Some Basic Labor Problems* (New York: McGraw-Hill, 1938), 239.

3. Ibid., 244.

4. For example, see the descriptions of urban living conditions in Jacob Riis, *How the Other Half Lives* (New York: Hill and Wang, 1957). [reprint of the 1890 edition]

5. William T. Moye, "The End of the 12 Hour Day in the Steel Industry," *Monthly Labor Review* (September 1977): 22–27.

6. Upton Sinclair, *The Jungle* (New York: Viking Press, 1950). [reprint of the 1906 edition]

7. Peter Roberts, *The New Immigration* (New York: Macmillan, 1913), 363.

8. U.S. Immigration Commission, *Abstracts of the Reports of the U.S. Immigration Commission* (Washington, DC: Government Printing Office, 1911), vol. 1, 58–59.

9. Roberts, *The New Immigration*, 363–64.

10. U.S. Immigration Commission, *Abstracts of the Reports of the U.S. Immigration Commission*, 60.

11. Paul H. Clyde, *The Far East: A History of the Impact of the West on Eastern Asia* (Englewood, NJ: Prentice Hall, 1958), 492–96.

12. U.S. Immigration Commission, *Abstracts of the Reports of the U.S. Immigration Commission*, 660–76.

13. Ibid., 658.

14. Ibid., 663.

15. Ibid. See also Roberts, *The New Immigration*, 364.

16. Stanley Lebergott, *Manpower in Economic Growth* (New York: McGraw-Hill, 1964), 28.

17. U.S. Immigration Commission, *Abstracts of the Reports of the U.S. Immigration Commission*, 297–313.

18. Ibid., 151.

19. Lebergott, *Manpower in Economic Growth*, 162. See also Timothy J. Hatton and Jeffrey G. Williamson, "The Impact of Immigration on American Labor Markets Prior to the Quotas," Working Paper Series, Working Paper No. 5185 (Cambridge, MA: National Bureau of Economic Research, 1995).

20. Vernon M. Briggs, Jr., *Immigration and American Unionism* (Ithaca, NY: Cornell University Press, 2001), 72–80.

21. *Henderson v. Mayor of the City of New York*, 92 U.S. 259 (1876).

22. *Ekiu v. United States*, 142 U.S. 651 (1892).

23. U.S. Congress, Senate Committee on the Judiciary, *History of the Immigration and Naturalization Service* (Washington, DC: Government Printing Office, 1980), 13.

24. Samuel Gompers, *Seventy Years of Life and Labor* (New York: E.P. Dutton, 1925), vol. 2, 154.

25. Ibid., 157.

26. Philip Taft, *Organized Labor in American History* (New York: Harper and Row, 1964), 306.

27. Gompers, *Seventy Years of Life and Labor*, vol. 2, 159.

28. Thomas A. Bailey, *Theodore Roosevelt and the Japanese-American Crisis* (Palo Alto, CA: Stanford University Press, 1934), chap. 2.

29. The law allowed the president to deny persons with foreign passports entry to the United States if he feels their presence is detrimental to labor conditions in the country. It does not say that it is directed at Japanese workers seeking to move from Hawaii to the mainland, but it was understood to mean precisely that and that is how the administration applied it.

30. A.T. Lane, "American Trade Unions, Mass Immigration, and the Literacy Test, 1990–1917," *Labor History* (Winter 1984): 5–25.

31. Oscar Handlin, *Race and Nationality in American Life* (Garden City, NY: Doubleday, 1957), 80–84.

32. Hatton and Williamson, "The Impact of Immigration on American Labor Markets Prior to the Quotas," 30. See also Lebergott, *Manpower in Economic Growth*, 162, for similar conclusions.

33. Millis and Montgomery, *Labor's Progress and Some Basic Labor Problems*, 31.

34. Taft, *Organized Labor in American History*, 308.

35. Desmond King, *Making Americans: Immigration, Race and the Origins of Diverse Democracy* (Cambridge, MA: Harvard University Press, 2000), chap. 2.

36. David Brody, *Labor in Crisis: The Steel Strike of 1919* (Philadelphia: J.B. Lippincott, 1965), 135–45, 157–59.

37. Briggs, *Immigration and American Unionism*, chap. 5.

38. See quotations contained in Daryl Scott, "Immigrant Indigestion: A. Philip Randolph, Radical and Restrictionist," *Backgrounder* (Washington, DC: Center for Immigration Studies, 1999), 3.

39. W.S. Bernard, "America's Immigration Policy: Its Evolution and Sociology," *International Migration* 2, no. 4 (1965): 235.

40. *Ozawa* v. *United States*, 260 U.S. 178.

41. Roberts, *The New Immigration*, 61.

42. Oscar Handlin, *The Uprooted: The Epic Story of the Great Migrations That Made the American People* (New York: Grosset and Dunlap, 1951), 5.

43. Booker T. Washington, "The Atlanta Exposition Address," in *Three Negro Classics* (New York: Avon Books, 1965), 147.

44. Ibid., 148.

Chapter 8. Reprieve: The Cessation of Mass Immigration

1. Kingsley Davis and Clarence Senior, "Immigration from the Western Hemisphere," *Annals of the American Academy of Political and Social Science* (March 1949): 70–81.

2. Ibid., 77–79.

3. Ibid., 75.

4. Harry E. Cross and James A. Sandos, *Across the Border: Rural Development in Mexico and Recent Migration to the United States* (Berkeley, CA: Institute of Governmental Studies, 1981), 10.

5. Carey McWilliams, *North from Mexico* (New York: Greenwood Press, 1986), 175.

6. Arthur F. Corwin and Lawrence A. Cardoso, "Vamos al Norte: Causes of Mass Mexican Migration to the United States," *Immigrants—and Immigrants: Perspectives On Mexican Labor Migration to the United States*, ed. Arthur F. Corwin (Westport, CT: Greenwood Press, 1978), 46.

7. Cross and Sandos, *Across the Border: Rural Development in Mexico and Recent Migration to the United States*, 10.

8. U.S. Congress, Senate Committee on the Judiciary, "History of the Immigration and Naturalization Service," *Report*, 96th Cong., 2nd Sess. (Washington, DC: Government Printing Office, 1980), 13.

9. Ibid., 36 ff.

10. Arthur S. Link, *American Epoch* (New York: Alfred A. Knopf, 1956), 297.

11. Robert D. Patton, *The American Economy* (Chicago: Scott Foresman, 1953), 292–94.

12. Stanley Lebergott, *Manpower in Economic Growth* (New York: McGraw-Hill, 1964), 163.

13. Link, *American Epoch*, 302.

14. Walter Buckingham, *Automation: Its Impact on Business and People* (New York: Mentor Books, 1961), 18.

15. Felicity Barringer, "Percentage of Blacks in South Rose in 1980s," *New York Times*, January 10, 1990, A-21; and "Blacks on Move to South," *Syracuse Post-Standard*, January 10, 1990, A-1.

16. Abraham Hoffman, "Mexican Repatriation During the Great Depression: A Reappraisal," *Immigrants—and Immigrants: Perspectives On Mexican Labor Migration to the United States*, ed. Arthur Corwin, (Westport, CT: Greenwood Press), chap. 8; and Rudolfo Acuna, *Occupied America* (San Francisco: Canfield Press, 1972), 190–93.

17. See David Shannon, *The Great Depression* (Englewood Cliffs, NJ: Prentice Hall, 1960) and Irving Bernstein, "Unemployment in the Great Depression," *The Social Welfare Forum* (New York: Columbia University Press, 1959), 39–48.

18. Collis Stocking, "Adjusting Immigration Requirement to Manpower Requirements," *Annals of the American Academy of Political Science and Social Science* (March 1949): 113.

19. Maurice Davie and Samuel Kolnig, "Adjustment of Refugees to American Life," *Annals of the American Academy of Political Science and Social Science* (March 1949): 159–65.

20. Ibid., 160.

21. Ibid.

22. For example, see George J. Borjas, "Immigrants in the U.S. Labor Market: 1940–80," *American Economic Review* (May 1991): 287–91.

23. Eli Ginzberg, *Manpower Agenda for America* (New York: McGraw-Hill, 1968), 12.

24. Joseph G. Rayback, *A History of American Labor* (New York: Free Press, 1966), 375.

25. Garth L. Mangum, *The Emergence of Manpower Policy* (New York: Holt, Rinehart, and Winston, 1969).

26. Ray Marshall, *The Negro and Organized Labor* (New York: John Wiley and Sons, 1965), 211.

27. Philip Taft, *Organized Labor in American History* (New York: Harper and Row, 1964), 545.

28. Patton, *The American Economy*, 330.

29. *Message to Congress from the President of the United States*, May 20, 1940, The White House, 1. [*Note:* The president misidentifies the agency as the "Bureau of Immigration and Naturalization" in this message; it was called the Immigration and Naturalization Service by this time.]

30. *White House News Release*, May 22, 1940, 2.

31. 54 *Stat.* 230.

32. *Message to Congress from the President of the United States*, 1.

33. *Public Papers and Addresses of Franklin D. Roosevelt, 1940* (New York: Macmillan, 1941), 229.

34. *Message to Congress from the President of the United States*, 1. Draft copy of the official message contained in the Franklin D. Roosevelt Library, Hyde Park, New York.

35. Letter from Attorney General Robert H. Jackson to the President, February 9, 1940. [Letter on file at the Franklin D. Roosevelt Library, Hyde Park, New York]; and "Memorandum For the President," January 9, 1944, from James Rowe, Jr., asking for clarification of the reasons for the shift for the purpose of historical explanation for the *Public Papers* volume cited in footnote 33 [Memo on file in the Franklin D. Roosevelt Presidential Library, Hyde Park, New York].

36. Frances Perkins, *The Roosevelt I Knew* (New York: Viking Press, 1946), 360–61.

37. Ibid., 361. [*Note:* The Federal Security Agency of which she refers had been created to administer domestic programs pertaining to the health and welfare of the citizenry. It was later to achieve Cabinet status as the Department of Health, Education and Welfare during the Eisenhower Administration.]

38. Ernesto Galarza, *Merchants of Labor: The Mexican Bracero Story* (Charlotte, NC: McNally and Loftin, 1964); and Philip L. Martin, *Promises to Keep: Collective Bargaining in California Agriculture* (Ames: Iowa State University Press, 1996), 66–67.

39. George C. Kiser and Martha W. Kiser, *Mexican Workers in the United States: Historical and Political Perspectives* (Albuquerque: University of New Mexico Press, 1979).

40. Vernon M. Briggs, Jr., *Immigration Policy and the American Labor Force* (Baltimore: Johns Hopkins University Press, 1984), 98–102.

41. Galarza, *Merchants of Labor*, chaps. 12, 13, 15, 16, and 17.

42. U.S. Congress, Senate Committee on the Judiciary, *A Report on Temporary Worker Programs: Background and Issues* (Washington, DC: Government Printing Office, 1980), 47–51; and President's Commission on Migratory Labor, *Migratory Labor in American Agriculture: Report* (Washington, DC: Government Printing Office, 1951).

43. Vernon M. Briggs, Jr., *Immigration and American Unionism* (Ithaca, NY: Cornell University Press, 2001), 122.

44. For details, see Briggs, *Immigration Policy and the American Labor Force*, 97–98, 102–103.

45. President's Commission on Migratory Labor, *Migratory Labor in American Agriculture: Report*, 58.

46. See U.S. Senate, Special Committee on Unemployment Problems, *Report*, 86th Cong., 2nd sess. (Washington, DC: Government Printing Office, 1960).

47. U.S. Congress, Senate Committee on the Judiciary, 81st Cong., 2nd sess., *The Immigration and Naturalization System of the United States* (Washington, DC: Government Printing Office, 1950).

48. Ibid., 455.

49. Robert Divine, *American Immigration Policy 1924–1952* (New Haven, CT: Yale University Press, 1957), 190.

50. U.S. Congress, *House Document 520*, 82nd Cong., 2nd sess., June 25, 1952, 5.

51. Ibid., 8.

52. U.S. President's Commission on Immigration and Naturalization, *Whom We Shall Welcome* (Washington, DC: Government Printing Office, 1953), 263.

53. Ibid., 52.

54. U.S. Congress, Senate Committee on the Judiciary, 92nd Cong., 2nd sess., *Review of U.S. Refugee Resettlement Programs and Policies* (Washington, DC: Government Printing Office, 1980), 8.

55. Julia V. Taft, David S. North, and David A. Ford, *Refugee Resettlement in the U.S.: Time for a New Focus* (Washington, DC: New TransCounty Foundation, 1979), 56.

56. Robert L. Bach, "The New Cuban Immigrants: Their Background and Prospects," *Monthly Labor Review* (October 1980): 39–46.

57. For example, see Borjas, *Immigrants in the U.S. Labor Market: 1940–1980*; and George J. Borjas, *Friends of Strangers: The Impact of Immigrants on the U.S. Economy* (New York: Basic Books, 1990), chaps. 6 and 7.

Chapter 9. The Redesign of Immigration Policy: Replacing Social Goals with Political Goals

1. Thorstein Veblen, *The Theory of the Leisure Class* (New York: Mentor Books, 1959), 133. [reprint of 1899 edition]

2. U.S. Congress, Senate Committee on the Judiciary, 96th Cong., 1st sess., *U.S. Immigration Law and Policy, 1952–1979* (Washington, DC: Government Printing Office, 1979), 5–6.

3. David S. North and Allen Le Bel, *Manpower and Immigration Policies in the United States* (Washington, DC: National Commission for Manpower Policy, 1978), 32–33.

4. "Statement by Secretary of State Dean Rusk before the Subcommittee on Immigration of the U.S. Senate Committee on the Judiciary," as reprinted in the *Department of State Bulletin*, "Department Urges Congress to Revise Immigration Laws," August 24, 1965, 276.

5. U.S. Congress, House of Representatives, Committee on the Judiciary, 104th Cong., 1st sess., *Immigration and Nationality Act*, 10th ed. (Washington, DC: Government Printing Office, 1989), 589.

6. For an historical review, see the National Advisory Commission on Civil Disorders, *Report of the National Advisory Commission on Civil Disorders* (New York: Bantam Books, 1968), chap. 1.

7. Ibid., 203.

8. John F. Kennedy, *A Nation of Immigrants*, rev. ed., with an Introduction by Robert F. Kennedy (New York: Harper and Row, 1964), 102.

9. Ibid., 103.

10. Ibid., 80.

11. Ibid.

12. "Should the Gates be Opened Wider," *Business Week*, October 17, 1964, 114.

13. "Statement of Secretary of State Dean Rusk," *Department of State Bulletin*, 276.

14. Ira Mehlman, "John F. Kennedy and Immigration Reform," *The Social Contract* (Summer 1991): 205.

15. U.S. Congress, Senate Committee on the Judiciary, *U.S. Immigration Law and Policy: 1952–1979*, 234–42.

16. Technically, the Immigration Act of 1965 provided that the Western Hemisphere ceiling would take effect on July 1, 1968, unless other legislation was enacted prior to that date to change it. A special commission—the Select Commission on Western Hemisphere Immigration—was appointed to study the issue, but it was unable

to agree upon a firm recommendation to Congress. As a result, the ceiling went into effect on the specified date.

17. U.S. Congress, U.S. House of Representatives Select Committee on Population, 95th Cong., 2nd sess., *Legal and Illegal Immigration to the United States* (Washington, DC: Government Printing Office, 1978), 10.

18. For example, see "Japanese-American Citizens League to Senator Thomas H. Kuchel," in U.S. Congress, Senate, *Congressional Record*, 89th Cong., 1st sess., September 17, 1965 (Washington, DC: Government Printing Office, 1965), 24, 503.

19. "Testimony of Robert F. Kennedy, U.S. Attorney General," U.S. Congress, House of Representatives before Subcommittee No. 1 of the Committee on the Judiciary, *Hearing*, 88th Cong., 2nd sess. (Washington, DC: Government Printing Office, 1964), 418.

20. U.S. Congress, House of Representatives, *Congressional Record*, 89th Cong., 1st sess., August 25, 1965 (Washington, DC: Government Printing Office, 1965), 21, 758.

21. Elizabeth J. Harper, *Immigration Laws of the United States* (Indianapolis: Bobbs-Merrill, 1975), 38.

22. U.S. Congress, Senate, *Congressional Record* (September 17, 1965), 24, 225.

23. "Statement of Senator Edward Kennedy," *Hearings on S. 500*, before the Subcommittee on Immigration and Nationality of the U.S. Senate Committee on the Judiciary, 89th Cong., 1st sess., February 10, 1965 (Washington, DC: Government Printing Office, 1965), 1–3.

24. David S. North and Marion F. Houstoun, *The Characteristics and Role of Illegal Aliens in the U.S. Labor Market: An Exploratory Study* (Washington, DC: Linton and Company, 1976), 8.

Chapter 10. Unexpected Consequences: The Revival of Mass Immigration

1. Robert L. Bach, "The New Cuban Immigrants: Their Background and Prospects," *Monthly Labor Review* (October 1980): 44.

2. Because only those refugees who were admitted to the United States under the preference system were automatically eligible to become immigrants after a residency period, special legislation was required to grant immigrant status to all persons who were admitted under the parole authority. The parole authority had originally been intended to apply only to individuals. With the extension of this authority to massive numbers of refugees, however, individual admission requirements would have caused lengthy waiting periods during which the person involved would have been in limbo while waiting for a visa slot to open. During such an interval, he or she could not have worked and would not have been eligible for most assistance services. Hence, special legislation was separately enacted for the members of those groups that received parole admissions. These enactments permitted these refugees to become permanent resident aliens outside the normal immigration channels.

3. *Silva* v. *Levi*, No. 76, C4268 (N.D., Ill. Apr. 1, 1978).

4. Robert Sherrill, "Can Miami Save Itself?" *New York Times*, July 19, 1987, 18 ff.

5. Julia V. Taft, David S. North, and David A. Ford, *Refugee Resettlement in the U.S.: Time for a New Focus* (Washington, DC: New Trans Century Foundations, 1979), 103.

6. U.S. Congress, Senate Committee on the Judiciary, 96th Cong., 2nd Sess., *Review of U.S. Refugee Resettlement Programs and Policies* (Washington, DC: Government Printing Office, 1980), 14.

7. Ibid.

8. U.S. Congress, Senate Committee on the Judiciary, 96th Cong., 1st Sess., *U.S. Immigration Law Policy, 1952–1979* (Washington, DC: Government Printing Office, 1979), 79.

9. U.S. Department of State, Office of the U.S. Coordinator for Refugee Affairs, "Proposed Refugee Admissions and Allocations for Fiscal Year 1983" (Washington, DC, 1983), 14.

10. U.S. Congress, Senate Committee on the Judiciary, *U.S. Refugee Resettlement Programs*, 38.

11. The Refugee Act of 1980 specified that all refugees who were admitted to the United States would be allowed to adjust their status to that of permanent resident aliens after one year. This change cut in half the two-year waiting period that had been imposed for the various ad hoc refugee admission programs enacted since the 1950s.

12. For example, see Roy Beck, "The Ordeal of Immigration in Wausau," *The Atlantic Monthly*, April 1994, 84–97.

13. U.S. Congress, Senate Committee on the Judiciary, 96th Cong., 2nd Sess., *Caribbean Refugee Crisis: Cubans and Haitians* (Washington, DC: Government Printing Office, 1980), 47. The quotation is from the prepared statement submitted to the committee by Ambassador-at-Large Victor H. Palmieri on May 12, 1980.

14. Felix Masud-Piloto, *With Open Arms: Cuban Migration to the United States* (Totowa, NJ: Rowman and Littlefield, 1988).

15. U.S. Congress, Senate Committee on the Judiciary, *Caribbean Refugee Crisis*, 30.

16. Sherrill, "Can Miami Save Itself?" p. 20.

17. "Carter and the Cuban Influx," *Newsweek*, May 26, 1980, 23.

18. "Eighteen Nations Move to Assist Exodus," *New York Times*, May 10, 1980, A-11.

19. Senate Committee on the Judiciary, *Caribbean Refugee Crisis*, 42.

20. Ibid.

21. For greater detail, see Vernon M. Briggs, Jr., *Immigration Policy and the American Labor Force* (Baltimore: Johns Hopkins University Press, 1984), 210–16.

22. *Jean v. Nelson*, No. 84–5240 (1985), 105 *Supreme Court Reporter*, 2992.

23. Anthony DePalma, "For Haitians, Voyage to Land of Inequality," *New York Times*, July 16, 1991, A-1, A-7.

24. Ibid., A-7.

25. "Communique," New York City, December 14, 1984. A Xerox copy of the agreement signed by representatives of Cuba and the United States on immigration matters.

26. Clifford Krauss, "U.S. Taking Steps to Bar New Wave of Cuban Emigres," *New York Times*, August 4, 1991, A-18.

27. Barbara Crossette, "Issue of Haitians Raises Debate on Asylum Policy," *New York Times*, December 2, 1991, A-11.

28. Barbara Crossette, "Forced Return of Haitians Fleeing by Boat to U.S. Is Halted by Judge," *New York Times*, November 20, 1991, A-1, A-11.

29. Howard W. French, "U.S. Begins Forcible Return of Haitians Who Fled Coup," *New York Times*, November 19, 1991, A-1, A-18.

30. Crossette, "Issue of Haitians Raises Debate," A-11.

31. Ronald Smothers, "Ban on Sending Haitians Home is Upset," *New York Times*, December 18, 1991, A-3.

32. *Sale* v. *Haitian Centers Council, Inc.* (1992), 113B *Supreme Court Reporter*, 3028.

33. Linda Richardson, "New York's Haitians Share the Fear," *New York Times*, February 3, 1992, A-6.

34. Barbara Crossette, "U.N. Official Rebukes U.S. on Haitians," *New York Times*, May 28, 1992, A-3.

35. John Kifner, "U.S. Begins Ship Processing of Haitians Seeking Asylum," *New York Times*, June 17, 1994, A-3.

36. Douglas Sehl, "U.S. Halts Hundreds of Cubans at Sea in Abrupt Policy Shift," *New York Times*, August 20, 1994, A-10.

37. Ibid.

38. "Cubans, Stay Home, Many Floridians Say," *New York Times*, August 21,1994, 29 and Miroya Navarro, "In Crisis over Cuba, Moderates and Castro Supporters Cry Out to Be Heard," *New York Times*, August 31, 1994, A-11.

39. Douglas Sehl, "Hardening its Stance, U.S. Expands Guantanamo Camp," *New York Times*, August 25, 1994, A-18.

40. Larry Rohter, "Only Broad Talks with U.S. Will End Exodus, Cuba Says," *New York Times*, August 25, 1994, A-1, A-19.

41. Steven Greenhouse, "U.S. and Cuba Talk at U.N. on Solving the Refugee Crisis," *New York Times*, September 2, 1994, A-12.

42. Paul Lewis, "Cuba Vows to End Exodus in Return for a Rise in Visas," *New York Times*, September 10, 1994, 1, 4.

43. Larry Nackerud, Alyson Springer, Christopher Larrison, and Alicia Issac, "The End of the Cuban Contradiction in the U.S. Refugee Policy," *International Migration Review* (Spring 1999): 176–92.

44. Steven Greenhouse, "U.S. Will Return Refugees to Cuba in Policy Switch," *New York Times*, May 3, 1995, A-1, A-14.

45. Ibid.

46. Ibid.

47. Sue Anne Pressley, "Faster Boats Carry Cubans, Haitians to Florida," *Washington Post*, December 31, 1998, A-2; and David Gonzales, "Boat Found as 30 Cubans Are Missing," *New York Times*, November 21, 2001, A-14.

48. Charles Maechling, Jr., "Reagan's Anti-Human Rights Policy," *New York Times*, September 4, 1983, E-15. [In this article, the quoted material that is cited is from an internal memo from Under Secretary of State Richard Kennedy to Secretary of State Alexander M. Haig, Jr.]

49. Ibid.

50. Larry Rohter, "Central American Plight Is People in Abundance," *New York Times*, September 9, 1987, A-1.

51. "Immigration Rules Are Eased for Nicaraguan Exiles in U.S.," *New York Times*, July 9, 1987, A-8.

52. *I.N.S.* v. *Cardoza-Fonseca* (1987), 107 *Supreme Court Reporter*, 1207.

53. Robert Pear, "Reagan Rejects Salvadorean Plea on Illegal Aliens," *New York Times*, May 5, 1987, A-1, A-12.

54. For a discussion of this movement, see Ignatius Bau, *This Ground is Holy: Church Asylum and the Central American Refugees* (Mahwah, NJ: Paulist Press, 1985);

Ann Critenden, *Sanctuary: A Story of American Conscience and the Law in Collision* (New York: Weidenfeld and Nelson, 1988); and David Simcox, "Refugees, Asylum, and Sanctuary: National Passion vs. National Interest," in *U.S. Immigration in the 1980s* (Boulder, CO: Westview Press, 1988), 52–58.

55. For example, see Wayne King, "Activists Vow to Continue Aiding People from Central America," *New York Times*, January 16, 1985, A-1, A-10; and Peter Applebome, "In Sanctuary Movement, Unabated Strength but Shifting Aims," *New York Times*, October 27, 1987, A-10; and "Sanctuary Leaders Say Aid to Aliens Goes On," *New York Times*, May 7, 1989, A-35.

56. Jeffrey Schmalz, "Nicaraguan Influx Tests Miami's Hospitality," *New York Times*, November 20, 1988, A-1, A-36.

57. Jeffrey Schmalz, "Dreams and Despair Collide as Miami Searches for Itself," *New York Times*, January 23, 1989, A-1, B-8; Jeffrey Schmalz, "Miami's New Ethnic Conflict: Haitians vs. American Blacks," *New York Times*, February 19, 1989, A-1, A-38; Jeffrey Weiss, "Racial Violence Subsides in Miami," *Dallas Morning News*, January 19, 1989, A-1, A-6; "Miami Riots Spread to Other City Areas," *Dallas Morning News*, January 18, 1989, A-1, A-16. See also Sherrill, "Can Miami Save Itself?" 18ff.

58. Roberto Suro, "U.S. to Detain Refugees in Tents Beginning Today," *New York Times*, February 2, 1989, A-1, 21.

59. *American Baptist Churches, et al.* v. *Thornburgh, et al.*, Civ. No. C85–3255 RFP (December 19, 1990), Stipulated District of California. See also Katherine Bishop, "U.S. Settles Suit on Ousting Aliens," *New York Times*, December 20, 1990, B-18.

60. Susan Contin, "From Refugees to Immigrants: The Legalization Strategies of Salvadoran Immigrants and Activists," *International Migration Review* (Winter 1988): 901–25.

61. U.S. Department of State, *World Refugee Report: 1988* (Washington, DC: U.S. Department of State Publications, 1987), 55.

62. "Israel Asks U.S. Not to Admit Jews as Refugees," *New York Times*, February 23, 1987, A-23.

63. Michael R. Gordon, "Shultz Holds Off on Soviet Emigres," *New York Times*, July 22, 1988, Y-5.

64. Celestine Bohlen, "Europeans Confer on Emigre Limits," *New York Times*, January 27, 1991, A-9.

65. Robert Pear, "Soviet Armenians Let in Improperly, U.S. Officials Say," *New York Times*, May 29, 1988, A-17.

66. "Matter of Chang"; see *Interpreter Releases* (July 10, 1989): 751–54.

67. "Chinese Couple Qualifies for Refugee Status," *New York Times*, May 13, 1990, A-28.

68. Paul Bedard, "Chinese Women Who Evaded Abortions to be Deported," *Washington Times National Weekly Edition*, May 1–7, 1995, 15.

69. Robert Pear, "Bush Rejects Bill on China Students," *New York Times*, December 1, 1989, A-9. See also Thomas Friedman, "Bush Is Set Back on House Override of Veto on China," *New York Times*, January 25, 1990, A-1, A-6.

70. For example, see "U.S. Seizes Yacht Carrying 85 Aliens," *New York Times*, A-18.

71. For detailed discussion, see Peter Kwong, *Forbidden Workers: Illegal Chinese Immigrants and American Labor* (New York: New Press, 1997), chap. 2.

72. William Branigin, "Thailand Extradites Key Suspect in Ill-Fated Alien Smuggling Ring," *Washington Post*, October 7, 1997, A-1. See also Ashley Dunn, "Golden Venture Passengers Opting for China," *New York Times*, April 28, 1995, A-1, B-2.

73. Kwong, *Forbidden Workers*, 7.
74. Ibid.
75. Tim Golden, "Mexico, in Switch, Decides to Accept Stranded Chinese," *New York Times*, July 15, 1993, A-1, A-18.
76. Ibid., A-18.
77. Evelyn Nieves, "Chinese Immigrants Kept Padlocked in Warehouse," *New York Times*, May 23, 1993, B-5. See also Kwong, *Forbidden Workers*, chap. 1.
78. Donatella Lorch, "A Flood of Illegal Aliens Enter the U.S. via Kennedy," *New York Times*, March 18, 1992, B-12.
79. Tim Weiner, "Pleas for Asylum Inundate System for Immigration," *New York Times*, April 25, 1993, A-1.
80. Robert Pear, "U.S. Issues Asylum Rules Praised as Fairer to Aliens," *New York Times*, July 19, 1990, A-16.
81. "Proposed Rule: Rules and Procedure for Adjudication of Applications for Asylum or Withholding of Deportation for Employment Authorization," *Congressional Quarterly Washington Alert*, March 31, 1994, 3 [printed material].
82. Ibid.
83. "INS Finalizes Asylum Reform Regulations," *Interpreter Releases*, December 5, 1994, 1577–82.
84. Sandra Peddie and Eden Laiken, "Wake-Up Call on Immigration Gaps in Anti-Terror Border Policies," *Newsday*, October 14, 2001, 1.
85. U.S. Department of Labor, "Unlawful Immigration," *Employment and Training Report of the President: 1978* (Washington, DC: Government Printing Office, 1978), 111–12.
86. Ellis W. Hawley, "The Politics of the Mexican Labor Issue, 1950–1965," in *Mexican Workers in the United States*, ed. George C. Kiser and Martha Woody Kiser (Albuquerque: University of New Mexico Press, 1979), 101. See also Juan Ramon Garcia, *Operation Wetback: The Mass Deportation of Mexican Undocumented Workers in 1954* (Westport, CT: Greenwood Press, 1980).
87. For a more detailed discussion of the problems with illegal immigration data, see Briggs, *Immigration Policy and the American Labor Force*, 131–37. See also National Research Council, *Immigration Statistics: A Story of Neglect* (Washington, DC: National Academy Press, 1985).
88. Joe Constanzo, Cynthia Dain, Calibert Irazi, Daniel Goodfriend, and Roberto Ramirez, "Evaluating Components of International Migration: The Residual Foreign Born," Working Paper Series No. 61 (Washington, DC: U.S. Bureau of the Census, December, 2001), 2.
89. Mark J. Miller and Demetrios Papademetriou, "Immigration Reform: The United States and Western Europe Compared," in *The Unavoidable Issue: U.S. Immigration Policy in the 1980s*, ed. Demetrios Papademetriou and Mark Miller (Philadelphia: Institute for the Study of Human Issues, 1983), chap. 10.
90. U.S. Congress, *U.S. Immigration Law and Policy: 1952–1979*, 75.
91. Select Commission on Immigration and Refugee Policy, *U.S. Immigration Policy and the National Interest* (Washington, DC: Government Printing Office, 1981).
92. Nicholas Laham, *Ronald Reagan and the Politics of Immigration Reform* (Westport, CT: Praeger, 2000).
93. For elaboration on both of these issues, see Vernon M. Briggs, Jr., "The 'Albatross' of Immigration Reform: Temporary Worker Policy in the United States," *International Migration Review* (Winter 1986): 995–1019; and Vernon M. Briggs, Jr.,

"Employer Sanctions and the Question of Discrimination," *International Migration Review* (Winter 1990): 803–15.

94. Robert Pear, "Schumer Offers Plan for Importing Farm Workers," *New York Times*, June 10, 1986, 19.

95. "House Committee Clears Immigration Reform Bill," *Daily Labor Report*, No. 124 (Washington, DC: Bureau of National Affairs, 1986), A-3.

96. Robert Pear, "House Panel is Setting Terms for Debate on Aliens," *New York Times*, June 26, 1986, 31.

97. U.S. Immigration and Naturalization Service, "Provisional Legalization Application Statistics," December 1, 1991, 1.

98. Michael Isikoff, "INS Policy on Families is Reversed," *Washington Post*, February 3, 1990, A-1, A-4.

99. Briggs, *Immigration Policy and the American Labor Force*, chap. 4.

100. Robert Suro, "False Migrant Claims: Fraud on a Huge Scale," *New York Times*, November 12, 1989, A-1.

101. Gary D. Thompson and Philip L. Martin, "Immigration Reform and the Agricultural Labor Force," *Labor Law Journal* (August 1991): 532.

102. U.S. Commission on Immigration Reform, *U.S. Immigration Policy: Restoring Credibility* (Washington, DC: Author, 1994), 2 of Executive Summary.

103. Ibid., 22.

104. Ibid.

105. Michael J. Piore, *Birds of Passage: Migrant Labor and Industrial Societies* (Cambridge: University of Cambridge Press, 1979), 149–54.

106. Select Commission on Immigration and Refugee Policy, *U.S. Immigration Policy and the National Interest*, 3. [emphasis is supplied]

107. Ibid., 8.

108. John Higham, "The Purpose of Legal Immigration in the 1990s and Beyond," *The Social Contract* (Winter 1990–91): 64.

109. Ibid.

110. Congressional Research Service, "Immigration: Numerical Limits and the Preference System," *Issue Brief*, March 28, 1988, CRS-3. The report was prepared by Joyce Vialet of the CRS staff.

111. U.S. Congress, Senate, *Congressional Record*, 101st Cong., 2nd sess., September 24, 1990 (Washington, DC: Government Printing Office, 1990), S13,628.

112. Robert Pear, "Lawmakers Agree on Immigration Rise," *New York Times*, October 21, 1991, A-26.

113. Vernon M. Briggs, Jr., "The Immigration Act of 1990: Retreat from Reform," *Population and Environment* (Fall 1991): 89–93.

114. Briggs, *Immigration Policy and the American Labor Force*, 231–36.

115. *Karnuth v. Albro*, 279 U.S. 231 (1929).

116. David S. North, *Soothing the Establishment: The Impact of Foreign-Born Scientists and Engineers on America* (Lanham, MD: University Press of America, 1995), 112–14.

117. Steven Camarota, "Borders and Terrorism," *The Social Contract* (Winter 2002): 89–99.

118. For example, see Peter T. Kilborn, "U.S. Workers Say Japanese Keep Them Out of Top Jobs," *New York Times*, June 3, 1991, A-1, B-6.

119. "U.S. Workers Tell House Subcommittee of Discrimination by Japanese-Owned Firms," *Daily Labor Report*, August 9, 1991, A-11, A-12.

120. U.S. General Accounting Office, *Health Care: Information on Foreign Nurses Working Under Temporary Work Visas* (Washington, DC: Author, 1989), 7.

121. Ibid., 8.

122. Norman Matloff, "High-Tech Trojan Horse: H-1B Visas and the Computer Industry," *Backgrounder* (Washington, DC: Center for Immigration Studies, September 1999). See also North, *Soothing the Establishment*, 114–16, 132.

123. Quoted in Mike McGraw, "Boon or Boondoggle: Visa Programs Hurt U.S. Workers, Foster Abuse," *The Kansas City Star*, July 16, 1995, A-14.

Chapter 11. Oversight: The Economic and Social Transformation of the U.S. Labor Market

1. Daniel Bell, "The Nature of Modernity," in Leon Barit, *The Age of Automation* (New York: Mentor Books, 1964), x–xi.

2. Jay M. Berman, "Industry Output and Employment," *Monthly Labor Review* (November 2001): 39–55.

3. W.W. Rostow, *The Stages of Economic Growth*, 2d ed. (London: Cambridge University Press, 1971), chap. 6. See also "Tracking Changes in Consumer Spending Habits," *Monthly Labor Review* (September 1999): 38–39.

4. Berman, "Industry Output and Employment," 40.

5. Richard M. Cyert and David C. Mowery, eds., *Technology and Employment* (Washington, DC: National Academy Press, 1987), chap. 4; and Edward A. Feigenbaum and Pamela McCorduck, *The Fifth Generation* (Reading, MA: Addison-Wesley, 1983), chaps. 2 and 3.

6. Norbert Wiener, *The Human Use of Human Beings: Cybernetics and Society* (New York: Avon Books, 1967), 220. [reprint version of original, published in 1950 by Houghton Mifflin]

7. Ibid., 209.

8. Bill Bryson, *The Mother Tongue: English and How It Got That Way* (New York: Morrow and Company, 1990), 78.

9. William E. Brock, U.S. Secretary of Labor, "Address to the National Press Club," Washington, DC, March 5, 1987, 8.

10. Cyert and Mowery, *Technology and Employment*, chap. 5.

11. Vernon M. Briggs, Jr., *Immigration and American Unionism* (Ithaca, NY: Cornell University Press, 2001).

12. John Bishop and Shani Carter, "How Accurate are Recent BLS Occupational Projections?" *Monthly Labor Review* (October 1991): 37–43.

13. Robert B. Reich, U.S. Secretary of Labor, "The Unfinished Agenda," Speech to the Council on Excellence in Government, Washington, DC, January 9, 1997, as reproduced in the *Daily Labor Report* on January 10, 1997, E-14, 15.

14. Ibid., E-15.

15. Daniel E. Hecker, "Occupational Employment Projections to 2010," *Monthly Labor Review* (November 2001): 57.

16. Philip L. Rones, "An Analysis of Regional Employment Growth, 1973–85," *Monthly Labor Review* (July 1986): 3–13; and William Deming, "A Decade of Economic Change and Population Shifts in U.S. Regions," *Monthly Labor Review* (November 1996): 3–14.

17. *Economic Report of the President: 2002* (Washington, DC: Government Printing Office, 2002), Table B-103, 438.

18. Ray Marshall, "Labor Market Implications of Internationalization," in *The Internationalization of the U.S. Economy: Its Labor Market Policy Implications*, ed. Vernon M. Briggs, Jr. (Salt Lake City: Olympus, 1986), 7–27.

19. Jay Mazur, "Labor's New Internationalism," *Foreign Affairs* (January-February 2000): 79–90.

20. Steven Camarota, "Immigration: Trade by Other Means?" *Immigration Review* (Spring 1998): 9–10.

21. Howard D. Samuel, "Social Goals and International Trade: A New Dimension," in *The Internationalization of the U.S. Economy*, ed. Vernon M. Briggs, Jr. (Salt Lake City: Olympus, 1986), 27–37.

22. Peter Cappelli, "Forces Driving the Restructuring of Employment"; and Harry C. Katz, "Downsizing and Employment Security," *Looking Ahead*, a publication of the National Planning Association vol. XVI, no. 2–3 (1994): 5–11 and 15–19, respectively.

23. See Lester Thurow, *Head to Head: The Coming Economic Battle Among Japan, Europe and America* (New York: William Morrow, 1992).

24. Howard N. Fullerton, Jr., and Mitra Toosi, "Labor Force Projections to 2010: Steady Growth and Changing Composition," *Monthly Labor Review* (November 2001): 21–38.

25. Howard V. Hayghe, "Family Members in the Work Force," *Monthly Labor Review* (March 1990): 14–19.

26. U.S. Census Bureau, *Profile of the Foreign-Born Population of the United States: 2000* Report #P23–206, (Washington, DC: U.S. Department of Commerce, December 2001), 19.

27. William Julius Wilson, *The Truly Disadvantaged: The Inner City, the Underclass, and Public Policy* (Chicago: University of Chicago Press, 1987). See also Louis Uchitelle, "America's Army of Non-Workers," *New York Times*, September 27, 1987, F-1, F-6.

28. U.S. Census Bureau, *Profile of the Foreign-Born . . . 2000*, 17.

29. Ibid.

30. Raymond M. Frost, *Challenge: The Magazine of Economic Affairs* (November-December 1991): 64.

31. Ibid.

32. William Frey, "Black Migration to the South Reaches Record Highs in 1990s," *Population Today* (February 1998), 1–3.

33. Barbara Vobejda, "25% of Black Women May Never Marry," *Washington Post*, November 11, 1991, A-1, A-12.

34. Alan Greenspan, "Remarks Before the Economic Club of New York" in New York on January 13, 2000 (Washington, DC: Federal Reserve Board, 2001); available at www.federalreserve.gov/boarddocs/speeches/2000200001132.htm.

35. Hudson Institute, *Workforce 2000: Work and Workers for the Twenty-First Century* (Indianapolis, IN: Hudson Institute, 1987).

36. Commission on Workforce Quality and Labor Market Efficiency, *Investing in People* (Washington, DC: U.S. Department of Labor, 1989), 1.

37. Ibid., 3. See also Jonathan Kozol, *Illiterate America* (Garden City, NY: Anchor Press, 1985).

38. "U.S. Study Says Work Force is Suffering from Shortages," *New York Times*, September 2, 1989, A-9.

39. Commission on the Skills of the American Workforce, *America's Choice: High Skills or Low Wages* (Rochester, NY: National Center on Education and the Economy, 1990).

40. Gisela Bolte, "Will Americans Work for $5 a Day?" *Time*, July 12, 1990, 12.

41. "Commission Calls for New Level of Literacy to Meet Job Needs of Information Economy," *Daily Labor Report*, June 28, 2000, A-7. [The title of the report prepared for the U.S. Department of Labor is *A Nation of Opportunity: Building America's 21st Century Workforce.*]

42. Ibid., A-8.

43. Robert B. Reich, U.S. Secretary of Labor, "The Revolt of the Anxious Class," Speech to the Democratic Leadership Conference, Washington, DC, November 22, 1994, 3.

44. Ibid., 5.

45. See Daniel H. Weinberg, "A Brief Look at Postwar U.S. Income Inequality," *Current Population Report*, *P60–191* (Washington, DC: U.S. Bureau of the Census, 1996), 1.

46. Council of Economic Advisers, *Economic Report of the President: 1999* (Washington, DC: Government Printing Office, 1999), 41–42. See also Daniel Weinberg, "Measuring 50 Years of Economic Change" (Washington, DC: U.S. Census Bureau, September 29, 1998), 3.

47. U.S. Census Bureau, *Profile of the Foreign-Born . . . 2000*, 36.

48. Ibid., 37.

Chapter 12. The National Interest: Synchronization of Immigration Policy with Economic Circumstances

1. U.S. Census Bureau, *Profile of the Foreign-Born Population in the United States: 2000*, P23–206 (Washington, DC: Government Printing Office, 2001), 8–9, 38.

2. Ibid., 36.

3. Barry R. Chiswick (ed.), *Immigration, Language and Ethnicity: Canada and the United States* (Washington, DC: American Enterprise Institute, 1992), 15; George J. Borjas, *Friends or Strangers: The Impact of Immigrants on the U.S. Economy* (New York: Basic Books, 1990), 18–22, and George J. Borjas, "The Economics of Immigration," *The Journal of Economic Literature* (December 1994): 1667–1717.

4. U.S. Department of Justice, *The Triennial Comprehensive Report on Immigration* (Washington, DC: U.S. Department of Justice, 2002), 59.

5. Ibid., 73.

6. Ibid.

7. Ibid.

8. Ibid.

9. National Research Council, *The New Americans: Economic, Demographic, and Fiscal Effects of Immigration* (Washington, DC: National Academy Press, 1997), 185–90.

10. Ibid., 181–85.

11. Ibid., 181.

12. Ibid.

13. Ibid., 235–36.

14. Ibid., 236.

15. See David North and Marion F. Houstoun, *The Characteristics and Role of Illegal Aliens in the U.S. Labor Market: An Exploratory Study* (Washington, DC: Linton, 1976), 104, and Maurice D. Van Arsdol, Jr., Joan Moore, David Heer, and

Susan P. Haynie, *Non-Apprehended and Apprehended Residents in the Los Angeles Labor Market* (Washington, DC: Government Printing Office, 1979), 69.

16. Martha Tienda et al., *The Demography of Legalization: Insights from Administrative Records of Legalized Aliens*, Report to the U.S. Department of Health and Human Services (Chicago: Population Research Center Discussion Paper Series, October 1991), Table 8, and discussion on pp. 34–36. See also U.S. Immigration and Naturalization Service, Statistics Division, *Provisional Legalization Application Statistics*, December 1, 1991, 2.

17. For example, see "Proposed Refugee Admissions for Fiscal year 1995," *Report to the Congress* (Washington, DC: Coordinator for Refugee Affairs, 1994), 360. See also Kalena E. Cortes, "Are Refugees Different from Economic Immigrants? Some Empirical Evidence on the Heterogeneity of Immigrant Groups in the United States," Working Paper No. 41 (Berkeley, CA: Center for Labor Economics, September 2001).

18. U.S. Bureau of the Census. *Poverty in the United States: 2001*, P60–219 (Washington, DC: U.S. Department of Commerce, 2002), 6.

19. Ibid., 48. See also George J. Borjas and Lynette Hilton, "Immigration and the Welfare State: Immigrant Participation in Means-Tested Entitlement Programs," *Quarterly Journal of Economics* (May 1996): 575–76.

20. U.S. General Accounting Office, *Immigrant Education*, Statement of Linda Morra, Director of Education and Employment Issues, Health Education and Human Services Division to the U.S. Senate Committee on Labor and Human Resources, April 14, 1994, GAO/T-HEHS-94–1946, 2.

21. Ibid.

22. Francisco L. Rivera-Batiz, "Immigrants and Schools: The Case of the Big Apple," *Forum for Applied Research and Public Policy* (Fall 1995): 84–89.

23. For example, see David Firestone, "Crowded Schools in Queens Find Class Space in Unusual Places," *New York Times*, June 8, 1994, A-1.

24. E. Fiske, "Racial Shifts Challenge U.S. Schools," *New York Times*, June 23, 1988, A-16.

25. U.S. Census Bureau, *Profile of the Foreign Born: 2000*, 25.

26. Ibid., 14.

27. Ibid., 16.

28. Ibid., 17.

29. Ray Marshall, "Immigration in the Golden State: The Tarnished Dream," in *U.S. Immigration in the 1980s: Reappraisal and Reform*, ed. David E. Simcox (Boulder, CO: Westview Press, 1988), 195.

30. Robert Walker, Mark Ellis, and Richard Barff, "Linked Migration Systems: Immigration and Internal Labor Flows in the United States," *Economic Geography* (July 1992): 234–48.

31. Mary Kritz and June Marie Nogle, "Nativity Concentration and Internal Migration Among the Foreign Born," *Demography* (August 1994): 1–16.

32. Quoted in Peter Passell, "A Job-Wage Conundrum," *New York Times*, September 6, 1994, D-1. See also Richard Freeman and Lawrence F. Katz, "Industrial Wage and Employment Determination in an Open Economy," in *Immigration, Trade and the Labor Market*, ed. John M. Abowd and Richard B. Freeman (Chicago: University of Chicago Press, 1991), 241–46.

33. William H. Frey, "Immigration and Internal Migration Flight: A California Case Study," *Population and Environment* (March 1995): 353–75. See also William

A. Frey, "Black Migration to the South Reaches Highs in 1990s," *Population Today* (February 1998): 1–3.

34. Richard Mines and Jeffery Avina, "Immigrants and Labor Standards: The Case of California Janitors," in *U.S. Mexico Relations: Labor Market Interdependence*, ed. Jorge A. Bustamante et al. (Stanford, CA: Stanford University Press, 1992), 429–88.

35. Council of Economic Advisers, *Economic Report of the President: 1994* (Washington, DC: Government Printing Office, 1994), 120.

36. Michael Fix, ed., *The Paper Curtain* (Washington, DC: Urban Institute Press, 1991), 304.

37. Congressional Research Service, "Memorandum: S. 358, the Immigration Act of 1990, as Approved by Congress," November 9, 1990, 1.

38. Robert Pear, "Lawmakers Agree on Immigration Rise," *New York Times*, October 21, 1990, A-26.

39. Seth Mydans, "For Skilled Foreigners, Lower Hurdles to U.S.," *New York Times*, November 5, 1990, A-12.

40. Technically, the word "Ireland" does not appear in the Immigration Act of 1990. The language says that 40 percent of the available visas for fiscal years 1992 to 1994 shall go to the country that "received the greatest number of visas" under an ad hoc diversity program that provided 5,000 nonpreference visas for two years under IRCA (see discussion in chap. 10). That country happened to be Ireland.

41. Seth Mydans, "For Winners in Visa Lottery, Round 2," *New York Times*, November 29, 1991, A-22.

42. Stephen H. Legomsky, "Diversity and the Immigration Act of 1990," *In Defense of the Alien* (Staten Island, NY: Center for Migration Studies, 1995), vol. XVII, 63–66.

43. "'Mac Attack,' Labor and INS Unhappy with Foreign Students Work Program," *Immigration Review*, no. 20 (Winter 1995): 10–11.

44. Alejandro Portes and Ruben G. Rumbaut, *Immigrant America: A Portrait* (Berkeley: University of California Press, 1990), chap. 2.

45. Philip Martin, "Network Recruitment and Labor Displacement," *U.S. Immigration Policy in the 1980s*, ed. David E. Simcox (Boulder, CO: Westview Press, 1988), 67–91. See also Donatella Lorch, "Ethnic Niches Creating Jobs that Fuel Immigrant Growth," *New York Times*, January 12, 1992, A-1, A-20.

46. Elizabeth Bogen, *Immigration in New York* (New York: Praeger, 1987), 91.

47. Ibid.

48. Jonathan Kaufman, "Help Unwanted: Immigrant Businesses Often Refuse to Hire Blacks in Inner City," *Wall Street Journal*, June 6, 1995, 1.

49. Ibid.

50. Ibid.

51. Ibid.

52. Martin, "Network Recruitment and Labor Displacement." See also Richard Mines and Philip Martin, "Immigrant Workers and the California Citrus Industry," *Industrial Relations* (Spring 1984): 139–49.

53. Portes and Rumbaut, *Immigrant America*, chap. 2.

54. Seth Mydans, "40,000 Aliens to Win Legal Status in Lottery," *New York Times*, September 25, 1991, A-1, A-19.

55. Ibid., A-19.

56. Seth Mydans, "Foreign Millionaires in No Rush to Apply for Visas, U.S. Finds," *New York Times*, December 22, 1991, A-18.

57. U.S. Commission on Immigration Reform, *U.S. Immigration Policy: Restoring Credibility* (Washington, DC: Author, 1994), 2 of Executive Summary.

58. Ibid., 2, 3.

59. Ibid., 3.

60. Ibid., 22.

61. U.S. Commission on Immigration Reform, *Legal Immigration: Setting Priorities* (Washington, DC: Author, 1995).

62. "Eliminating SSI for Immigrants," *Migration News*, April 1, 1994, 2.

63. U.S. Commission on Immigration Reform, "Statement of Professor Barbara Jordan, Chairman of the U.S. Commission on Immigration Reform," *News Release*, Washington, DC, June 8, 1995, 3.

64. Thomas Friedman, "Clinton Seeks More Power to Stem Illegal Immigration," *New York Times*, July 28, 1993, A-13.

65. "Wilson Sues U.S. to Recoup Immigrants Health Costs," *San Jose Mercury News*, May 31, 1994, 1; Office of the Governor of Florida, *The Unfair Burden: Immigration's Impact on Florida*, Tallahassee, Florida, March 13, 1994; New York State Senate, Committee on Cities, *Our Teeming Shore: A Legislative Report on The Impact of U.S. Immigration Policy on New York State*, Albany, New York, January 1994; Debra Beachy, "Study Estimates Immigrants Cost Texas $4.68 Billion in 1992," *Houston Chronicle*, March 3, 1994, A-1; and "Arizona Sues for Costs of Aliens," *Washington Times*, May 3, 1994, 1.

66. Philip Martin, "Proposition 187 in California," *International Migration Review* (Spring 1995): 255–63.

67. *League of United Latin American Citizens* v. *Wilson*, Case No. CV94–7569, November 20, 1995.

68. *Plyler* v. *Doe*, 458 U.S. 1131 (1982).

69. "Reno Calls for Immigration Reform," *Rocky Mountain News*, June 21, 1993, A-21.

70. Dane Lesher and Dan Morain, "Governor Takes an Unusual Step to Resolve Constitutionality of Controversial Immigration Measure," *Los Angeles Times*, April 16, 1999, 1.

71. Ibid.

72. Antonio Olivo, "Some Foes of Prop. 187 Now Reach Compromise," *Los Angeles Times*, May 11, 1999, 1.

73. Patrick J. McDonnell, "Davis Won't Appeal Prop.187 Ruling, Ending Court Battles Litigation," *Los Angeles Times*, July 29, 1999, 1.

74. Stephen Holmes, "House Panel Keeps Intact Bill to Restrict Immigration," *New York Times*, October 12, 1995, A-20.

75. Robert Pear, "Change in Policy for Immigration is Urged by Panel," *New York Times*, June 5, 1995, B-7.

76. "Simpson Proposes Legal Immigration Bill Requiring Surcharge for Foreign Workers," *Daily Labor Report*, November 7, 1995, A-1.

77. Ibid.

78. "Business Interests Denounce Proposal to Cut Employer-Sponsored Immigration," *Daily Labor Report*, November 14, 1995, A-3.

79. Howard Kurtz, *Spin Cycle: Inside the Clinton Propaganda Machine* (New York: Free Press, 1998), 116.

80. Ibid.

81. Austin Fragomen, "The Illegal Immigration Reform and Immigrant Responsibility Act of 1996," *International Migration Review* (June 1997): 438–60.

82. James G. Gimpel and James R. Edwards, "The Silent Majority," *Journal of Commerce* (June 23, 1998): 8A.

83. Vernon M. Briggs, Jr., *Immigration and American Unionism* (Ithaca, NY: Cornell University Press, 2001), 164–69.

84. "Meissner Announces New INS Strategy to Combat Smuggling of Illegal Workers," *Daily Labor Report*, no. 61, March 31, 1999, A-9.

85. Vernon M. Briggs, Jr., "Employer Sanctions and the Question of Discrimination: The GAO Report in Perspective," *International Migration Review* (Winter 1990): 804–15.

86. "Ex-Panel Member Blasts INS Decision to De-Emphasize Worksite Enforcement," *Daily Labor Report*, no. 127, July 2, 1999, A-3.

87. Federal Reserve Board, "Technology and the Economy," Remarks by Chairman Alan Greenspan before the Economic Club of New York, January 13, 2000, 1–10.

88. Norman Matloff, "High Tech Trojan Horse: H-1B Visas and the Computer Industry," *Backgrounder* (Washington, DC: Center for Immigration Studies, September 1999).

89. National Research Council, *Building a Workforce for the Information Economy*, www.itworkforce.org (October 24, 2002).

90. "Congress: H-1Bs," *Migration News* (November 2000): 2.

91. U.S. Department of Labor, Office of the Inspector General, *Semi-Annual Report to the Congress, April 1, 2000–September 30, 2002* (Washington, DC: Author, 2000).

92. Kenneth Bredemeier, "Work Visas Swell Area's Tech Corps," *Washington Post*, December 1, 2000, E-1.

93. Ibid.

94. "Fox Visits Bush," *Migration News* (October 2001): 4–5.

95. "Guest Workers, Legalization," *Migration News* (September 2001): 2–3.

96. Ibid., 2.

97. "Guest Workers, Legalization," *Migration News* (August 2001): 2.

98. Arthur C. Helton, "U.S. Immigration Policy," *New York Times*, August 5, 2001, A-12.

99. Rosemary Jenks, "The USA Patriot Act of 2001," *Backgrounder* (Washington, DC: Center for Immigration Studies, December 2001), 1.

100. Steven A. Camarota, *The Open Door: How Militant Islamic Terrorists Entered and Remained in the United States, 1993–2001* (Washington, DC: Center for Immigration Studies, 2002), 16.

101. "9–11: One Year Later," *Migration News* (October 2002): 1.

102. David Firestone, "Senate Vote 90–9, to Set Up a Homeland Department Geared to Fight Terrorism," *New York Times*, November 20, 2002, A-1, A-14.

103. Steven A. Camarota, "Immigrants in the United States—2002: A Snapshot of America's Foreign-Born Population," *Backgrounder* (Washington, DC: Center for Immigration Studies, November 2002), 1–2.

104. See Vernon M. Briggs, Jr., "International Migration and Labour Mobility: The Receiving Countries," in *The Economics of Labour Migration*, ed. Julien van der Broeck (Cheltenham, UK: Edward Elgar, 1996), 115–58.

105. Commission on Workforce Quality and Labor Market Efficiency, *Investing in People: A Strategy to Address America's Workforce Crisis* (Washington, DC: U.S. Department of Labor, 1989), 32.

106. Ibid.

107. John Higham, "The Purpose of Legal Immigration in the 1990s and Beyond," *Social Contract* (Winter 1990–91): 64.

108. For example, see "ILGWU Expands Campaign Against Sweatshops," *AFL-CIO News*, May 14, 1990, 7; Constance Hays, "Immigrants Strain Chinatown's Resources," *New York Times*, May 30, 1990, B-1, B-4; Peter T. Kilborn, "Tougher Enforcing of Child Labor Laws is Vowed," *New York Times*, February 8, 1990, A-22; Peter T. Kilborn, "Widespread Child Labor Violations," *New York Times*, March 16, 1990, A-10; Lisa Belkin, "Abuses Rise Among Hispanic Garment Workers," *New York Times*, November 28, 1990, A-16; Donatella Lorch, "Immigrants From China Pay Dearly to be Slaves," *New York Times*, January 3, 1991, B-1; Alan Finder, "Despite Tough Laws, Sweatshops Flourish," *New York Times*, February 6, 1995, A-1, B-4; James Sterngold, "Crime Rings Tied to Sweatshops," *New York Times*, August 2, 1995, A-1, A-16; Chaya Piotrkowski and Joanne Carriba, "Child Labor and Exploitation" in *Young Workers: Varieties of Experiences*, ed. Julian Barling and Kevin Kelloway (Washington, DC: American Psychological Association, 1999), 129–58; and Ko-Lin Chinm, "Safe Home or Hell House? Experiences of Newly Arrived Undocumented Chinese," in *Human Smuggling: Chinese Migrant Trafficking and the Challenge to America's Immigrant Tradition*, ed. Paul J. Smith (Washington, DC: The Center for Strategic and International Studies, 1997), 160–65.

Index

About the Author

Vernon M. Briggs, Jr., is professor of Labor Economics at the New York State School of Labor and Industrial Relations at Cornell University. He received his B.S. degree from the University of Maryland and his M.A. and Ph.D. degrees from Michigan State University. Before coming to Cornell in 1978, he was a member of the economics faculty of the University of Texas at Austin.

Professor Briggs specializes in the area of human resource economics and public policy. In addition to numerous articles on immigration policy, he has written or co-written the following books pertaining to the subject: *Chicanos and Rural Poverty; The Chicano Worker; Immigration Policy and the American Labor Force; The Internationalization of the U.S. Economy: Its Labor Market Implications; Immigration and the U.S. Labor Market: Public Policy Gone Awry; Still an Open Door? Immigration Policy and the American Economy;* and *Immigration and American Unionism.*

He was a member of the National Council on Employment Policy (1977–87) and chairman of the council (1985–87). He has served on the board of directors of the Corporation for Public and Private Ventures (1978–84) and of the Center for Immigration Studies (1987–present). He has also served on the editorial boards of *The Journal of Human Resources* (1971–81), *The Industrial and Labor Relations Review* (1981–94), *The Texas Business Review* (1982–83), *The Journal of Economic Issues* (1980–85), and *People and Place* (1997–present).